JOHN WILLIS

SCREEN WORLD

1982

Volume 33

CROWN PUBLISHERS, INC.
ONE PARK AVENUE
NEW YORK, NEW YORK 10016

Library of Congress Catalog Card No. 50-3023
ISBN: 0-517-547406

TO

JAMES CAGNEY

whose unique talents have
endeared him to millions of fans.
Unquestionably, he has fulfilled, and continues to
fulfill, his ambition "to give the audience
something to take away with them."

KATHARINE HEPBURN, HENRY FONDA, JANE FONDA
in "On Golden Pond" © Universal Studios
1981 ACADEMY AWARDS FOR BEST ACTRESS (KATHARINE HEPBURN)
AND BEST ACTOR (HENRY FONDA)

4

CONTENTS

EDITOR: JOHN WILLIS

Assistant Editor: Stanley Reeves

Staff: Joe Baltake, Marco Boyajian, Mark Cohen, Frances Crampon, J. C. Crampon, Mark Gladstone, Maltier Hagan, Miles Kreuger, Van Williams

Acknowledgments: This volume would not be possible without the cooperation of Harry Abranson, Gary Adelman, Tom Allen, Fern Arenstein, Fred Baker, Dianne Ball, Nina Baron, Max Bercutt, Jim Bertgen, Mitch Block, Joseph Brenner, Susan Brockman, Ken Burns, Berry Cahn, John Calhoun, Fabiano Canosa, Philip Castanza, Jerry Clark, Sandy Cobe, Maxi Cohen, Dian Collins, Lynne Dahlgren, Alberta D'Angelo, Marieanne D'Antonio, June Davenport, Francene Davidoff, Nicholas Demetroules, Cindy DePaula, Robert Dorfman, Steve Fagan, Suzanne Fedak, Ray Fisher, Tim Fisher, Pam Fivack, Dom Francella, Dore Freeman, Marvin Friedlander, Renee Furst, Kathryn Galan, Charles Gardner, Raoul Gatchalian, Bernie Glaser, James Gluckenhaus, Joseph Green, Jerry Gross, Valerie Gunderson, Earl Hadleberg, Allison Hanau, Richard Hassanein, Meg Higgins, Victoria Hill, Andy Holtzman, Salah Jamal, Barbara Javiz, Steve Johnson, Chuck Jones, Steven Jones, Elenore Kane, Jack Kerness, Sam Kitt, Don Krim, Peter Krutzer, Lloyd Leipzig, Wynn Lowenthal, Arlene Ludwig, Marian Luntz, William Lustig, Howard Mahler, Leonard Maltin, Harold Marenstein, Louis Marino, Priscilla McDonald, Peter Meyers, Tim Meyers, John Miller, Terrance Mitchell, Patrick Montgomery, Ron Mutz, Bill O'Connell, Carolyn Olman, David Owen, Frank Pergallia, Maria Peters, Jim Pike, Ruth Pologee, Pam Pritzker, Sylvana Radman, Yvonne Rainer, Mike Rappaport, Jerry Rapport, Yvonne Ramond, Robert Richter, Bruce Ricker, Frank Rodriguez, Reid Rosefelt, Madeleine Rudin, Suzanne Salter, Les Schecter, Richard Schwarz, Barbara Schwei, Art Schweitzer, Mike Scrimenti, Eve Segal, Jacqueline Sigmund, John Skauras, Gail Skilia, Fran Speelman, Alicia Springer, John Springer, Laurence Steinfeld, Marilyn Stewart, Patricia Story, Stuart Strutin, Ken Stutz, Jesse Sutherland, Cynthia Swartz, Dan Talbot, Chris Teseo, Bill Thompson, Jerry Ticman, Arthur Tolchin, Bruce Trinz, Ellen Trost, Mark Van Alstyn, Don Velde, John West, Bob Winestein, Christopher Wood, Jim Wynorski, Stuart Zakim, Mindy Zepp, Michael Zuker.

1. Burt Reynolds

2. Clint Eastwood

3. Dudley Moore

4. Dolly Parton

5. Jane Fonda

6. Harrison Ford

7. Alan Alda

8. Bo Derek

9. Goldie Hawn

10. Bill Murray

11. Cheech & Chong

12. Brooke Shields

13. Richard Pryor

14. John Belushi

15. Christopher Reeve

16. Sally Field

TOP 25 BOX OFFICE STARS OF 1981

(Tabulated by Quigley Publications)

17. Meryl Streep

18. Sissy Spacek

19. Robert Redford

20. Roger Moore

1981 RELEASES

January 1 through December 31, 1981

21. Marsha Mason

22. Chuck Norris

23. Gene Wilder

24. Steve Martin

25. Lily Tomlin

Jill Clayburgh

Barbra Streisand

Woody Allen

THE INCREDIBLE SHRINKING WOMAN

(UNIVERSAL) Producer, Hank Moonjean; Director, Joel Schumacher; Executive Producer-Screenplay, Jane Wagner; Photography, Bruce Logan; Editors, Jeff Gourson, Anthony Redman; Design, Raymond A. Brandt; Music, Suzanne Ciani; Costumes, Roberta Weiner; Set, Jennifer Politox; Assistant Director, Katy Emde; In Technicolor; 88 minutes; Rated PG; January release.

CAST

Pat Kramer/Judith Beasley	Lily Tomlin
Vance Kramer	Charles Grodin
Dan Beame	Ned Beatty
Dr. Eugene Nortz	Henry Gibson
Dr. Ruth Ruth	Elizabeth Wilson
Rob	Mark Blankfield
Concepcion	Maria Smith
Sandra Dyson	Pamela Bellwood
Tom Keller	John Glover
Logan Carver	Nicholas Hormann
Lyle Parks	James McMullan
Beth Kramer	Shelby Balik
Jeff Kramer	Justin Dana
Sidney	Richard A. Baker

Right: Ned Beatty, Charles Grodin
Top: Henry Gibson, Elizabeth Wilson
© Universal Studios

Lily Tomlin

Lily Tomlin
(also above)

WINDWALKER

(PACIFIC INTERNATIONAL ENTERPRISES) Producers, Arthur R. Dubs, Thomas E. Ballard; Director, Kieth Merrill; Screenplay, Ray Goldrup; Based on novel by Blaine M. Yorgason; Narrator, Nick Ramus; Design, Thomas Pratt; Editors, Stephen L. Johnson, Janice Hampton, Peter L. McCrea; Music, Merrill Jenson; Photography, Reed Smoot; In CIF Color; 108 minutes; Rated PG; January release.

CAST

Windwalker	Trevor Howard
Smiling Wolf/Twin Brother	Nick Ramus
Windwalker as young man	James Remar
Tashina	Serene Hedin
Dancing Moon	Dusty Iron Wing McCrea
Little Feather	Silvana Gallardo
Crow Scout	Billy Drago
Crow Eyes	Rudy Diaz
Crow Hair	Harold Goss-Coyote
Wounded Crow	Roy J. Cohoe
Spotted Deer	Emerson John
Horse That Follows	Jason Stevens
Happy Wind	Roberta Deherrera
Renegade Crow	Curtis Powers
Crooked Leg	Ivan Naranjo
Tashina's Father	Chief Tug Smith
Tashina's Mother	Fredelia Smith

and Dominique Gallegos (Tashina at 5), Marvin Takes Horse (Young Crow Eyes), Wamni-Omni-Ska-Romideau (Windwalker at 5), Jason Tahbo (Twin at 5), Benjamin Huber (Smiling Wolf at 2), David Huber (Twin Brother at 2)

Top: Silvana Gallardo, Dusty Iron Wing McCrea
Right: Billy Drago Center: Nick Ramus (C)
© Windwalker Productions

Nick Ramus

FORT APACHE, THE BRONX

(20th CENTURY-FOX/TIME-LIFE FILMS) Executive Producer, David Susskind; Producers, Martin Richards, Tom Fiorello; Director, Daniel Petrie; Screenplay, Heywood Gould; Suggested by the experiences of Thomas Mulhearn and Pete Tessitore; Co-Producers, Mary Lea Johnson, Gill Champion; Photography, John Alcott; Designer, Ben Edwards; Editor, Rita Roland; Music, Jonathan Tunick; Assistant Directors, Alex Hapsas, Joe Ray; Art Director, Christopher Nowak; Costumes, John Boxer; In Deluxe Color; 120 minutes; Rated R; February release

CAST

Murphy	Paul Newman
Connolly	Edward Asner
Corelli	Ken Wahl
Morgan	Danny Aiello
Isabella	Rachel Ticotin
Charlotte	Pam Grier
Theresa	Kathleen Beller
Jumper/Detective	Tito Goya
Hernando	Miguel Pinero
Jose	Jaime Tirelli
Track Star	Lance William Guecia
Pimp	Ronnie Clanton
Dacey	Clifford David
Dugan	Sully Boyar
Heffernan	Michael Higgins
Pantuzzi	Rik Colitti
Applebaum	Irving Metzman
Clendennon	Frank Adu
Finley	John Aquino
Lincoln	Norman Matlock
Donahue	John Ring
Moran	Tony DiBenedetto

and Terence Brady, Randy Jurgenson, Marvin Cohen (Cops at bar), Paul Gleason, Reinaldo Medina (Detectives), Darryl Edwards (Black Rookie), Donald Petrie (White Rookie), Thomas A. Carlin (Man with flat tire), Frederick Allen (Corelli's Brother), Dominic Chianese (Corelli's Father), Mike Cichette (Wild-Eyed Man), Apu Guecia (Stabbed Boy), Kim Delgado, Reyno, Dadi Pinero, Cleavant Derricks (Suspects), Dolores Hernandez (Pregnant Girl), Santos Morales (Girl's Father), Ruth Last (Girl's Mother), Jose Rabelo (Girl's Uncle), Gilbert Lewis (Mob Leader), Lisa Loomer, Sandi Franklin (Hookers), Eric Mourino, Jessica Costello (Boy and Girl on roof), Gloria Irizarry (Drug Dealer), Manuel Santiago (Intern), Joaquin LaHabana (Transvestite), Fred Strothers (Hospital Buyer), Sylvia "Kuumba" Williams (Bartender), Patricia Dratel (Hostage), Thomas Fiorello (Fence)

Left: Edward Asner
Top: Paul Newman
© Time-Life Productions

Paul Newman, Ken Wahl

Rachel Ticotin, Paul Newman

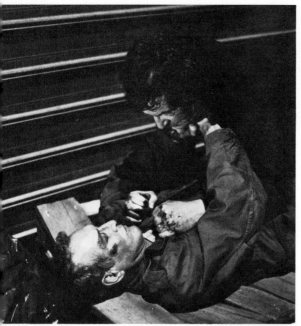
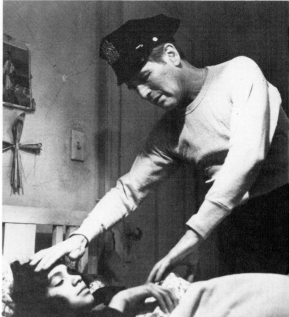

Edward Asner, Ken Wahl, Paul Newman
Top: (L) Paul Newman, Danny Aiello (R) Dolores Hernandez, Paul Newman

EYEWITNESS

(20th CENTURY-FOX) Producer-Director, Peter Yates; Screenplay, Steve Tesich; Associate Producer, Kenneth Utt; Photography, Matthew F. Leonetti; Designer, Philip Rosenberg; Music, Stanley Silverman; Editor, Cynthia Scheider; Assistant Directors, Thomas John Kane, Joseph Reidy; Costumes, Hillary Rosenfeld; In Technicolor; 114 minutes; Rated R; February release.

CAST

Daryll Deever	William Hurt
Tony Sokolow	Sigourney Weaver
Joseph	Christopher Plummer
Aldo	James Woods
Mrs. Sokolow	Irene Worth
Mr. Deever	Kenneth McMillan
Linda	Pamela Reed
Mr. Sokolow	Albert Paulsen
Israeli Woman	Sharon Goldman
Lt. Jacobs	Steven Hill
Lt. Black	Morgan Freeman
Mrs. Deever	Alice Drummond
Mr. Long	Chao-Li Chi
His Son	Keone Young
Vietnamese	Dennis Sakamoto, Henry Yuk
Shlomo	Mikhail Bogin
Cantor	Moshe Geffen
Man at concert	Jo Davidson
Sports Announcer	Bill Mazer
Anchorman	John Roland
TV Producer	James Ray Weeks

and Milton Zane, Richard Murphy, Dow McKeever, Jhoe Breedlove, Kimmy Wong, Alex Rosa, Mark Burns, Iris Whitney

William Hurt
Top: William Hurt, Sigourney Weaver

Sigourney Weaver, William Hurt Above: (L) Albert Paulsen, Sigourney Weaver, Irene Worth
(R) Sigourney Weaver, Christopher Plummer Top: (L) William Hurt, James Woods (R) Pamela Reed, William Hurt

CHARLIE CHAN AND THE CURSE OF THE DRAGON QUEEN

(AMERICAN CINEMA) Producer, Jerry Sherlock; Director, Clive Donner; Executive Producers, Michael Leone, Alan Belkin; Screenplay, Stan Burns, David Axelrod; Story, Jerry Sherlock; Photography, Paul Lohmann; Editors, Walt Hannemann, Phil Tucker; Design, Joel Schiller; Costumes, Jocelyn Rickards; Music, Patrick Williams, Assistant Directors, Richard Luke Rothschild, Rafael Elortegui, Pamela Eilerson; In Technicolor; 97 minutes; Rated PG; February release.

CAST

Charlie Chan	Peter Ustinov
Mrs. Lupowitz	Lee Grant
Dragon Queen	Angie Dickinson
Lee Chan, Jr.	Richard Hatch
Police Chief	Brian Keith
Gillespie	Roddy McDowall
Mrs. Dangers	Rachel Roberts
Cordelia Farrington III	Michelle Pfeiffer
Masten	Paul Ryan
Stefan	Johnny Sekka
Hawaiian Chief of Police	Bennett Ohta
Lee Chan, Sr.	David Hirokane
Brenda Lupowitz	Karlene Crockett
Bernard Lupowitz	Michael Fairman
Haynes	James Ray
Dr. Yu Sing	Momo Yashima
Maysie Ling	Alison Hong

and Kael Blackwood, Jerry Loo, Laurence Cohen, Robin Hoff, Kathie Kei, James Bacon, Frank Michael, John Hugh, George Chiang, David Chow, Dewi Yee, Joe Bellan, Garrick Huey, Duane Tucker, Don Parker, Kenneth Snell, Nicholas Gunn, Don Murray, Kai Wong, Miya, Gerald Okamura, Lonny Carbajal, Peter Michas, Vic Hunsberger, Larry Duran, Kay Kimler, Jim Winburn, Molly Roden, Pavla Ustinov, Trevor Hook, Paul Sanderson

Left: Michelle Pfeiffer, Lee Grant, Richard Hatch, Peter Ustinov, Roddy McDowall, Rachel Roberts, Johnny Sekka Above: Ustinov, Pfeiffer, Hatch
Top: Peter Ustinov, Richard Hatch
© American Communications Industries

Angie Dickinson

Paul Ryan, Brian Keith

AMERICAN POP

(COLUMBIA) Executive Producer, Richard St. Johns; Producers, Martin Ransohoff, Ralph Bakshi; Director, Ralph Bakshi; Screenplay, Ronni Kern; Associate Producer, Lynne Betner; Music, Lee Holdridge; Editor, David Ramirez; Assistant Director, John Sparey; In Dolby Stereo and color; 97 minutes; Rated R; February release.

An animated feature using the voices of Ron Thompson (Tony/Pete), Marya Small (Frankie), Jerry Holland (Louie), Lisa Jane Persky (Bella), Jeffrey Lippa (Zalmie), Roz Kelly (Eva Tanguay), Frank DeKova (Crisco), Richard Singer (Benny), Elsa Raven (Hannele), Ben Frommer (Palumbo), Amy Levitt (Nancy), Leonard Stone (Leo), Eric Taslitz (Little Pete), Gene Borkan (Izzy), Richard Moll (Poet), Beatrice Colen (Prostitute), Vincent Schiavelli, Hilary Beane, Lynda Wiesmeier, Philip Simms, Marcello Krakoff, Ken Johnson, Barney Pell, Robert Strom, Gene Woodbury, Marc Levine, Ty Grimes, Peter Glindeman, Auburn Burrell, A'Leshaia Brevard, Elya Baskin, M. B. West, Joey Camen, Bert Autore, Tony Autore, Johnny Brogna, Dawn Agrella, Cari Anne Warder, Don Carlson, Vance Colvig, Robert Beecher, Tony Fasce, Frank Ciaravino, Gene Krischer, David Allen Young, Lee James Jude, Timothy J. Leitch, Frederick C. Milner, Philo J. Cramer, Chester Haze, Chuck Mitchell, Bill Schneider

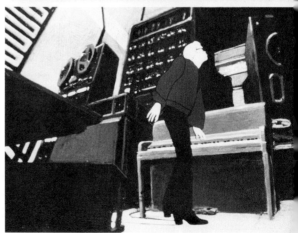

Little Pete Above: Frankie and Tony
Top: Benny © Columbia Pictures

CUTTER'S WAY

(UNITED ARTISTS CLASSICS) formerly "Cutter and Bone"; Producer, Paul R. Gurian; Director, Ivan Passer; Screenplay, Jeffrey Alan Fiskin; Based on novel "Cutter and Bone" by Newton Thornburg; Music, Jack Nitzsche; Photography, Jordan Cronenweth; Assistant Directors, Larry Franco, Jeffrey Chernov; In Technicolor; 109 minutes; Rated R; March release.

CAST

Richard Bone	Jeff Bridges
Alex Cutter	John Heard
Maureen Cutter ("Mo")	Lisa Eichhorn
Valerie Duran	Ann Dusenberry
J. J. Cord	Stephen Elliott
George Swanson	Arthur Rosenberg
Woman in hotel	Nina Van Pallandt
Mrs. Cord	Patricia Donahue
Susie Swanson	Geraldine Baron
Toyota Woman	Katherine Pass
Toyota Man	Frank McCarthy
Toyota Cop	George Planco
Security Guard	Jay Fletcher
Mortician	George Dickerson
Concession Owner	Jack Murdock
Blacks	Essex Smith, Rod Gist, Leonard Lightfoot
Young Girl	Julia Duffy
Young Man	Randy Shephard
Working Stiff	Roy Hollis
Garbage Man	Billy Drago
Garbage Truck Driver	Caesar Cordova
Police Captain	Jon Terry
Detectives	William Pelt, Ron Marcroft

Right Center: Jeff Bridges, Lisa Eichhorn
Top: Jeff Bridges, John Heard
© United Artists

John Heard, Lisa Eichhorn

John Heard, Jeff Bridges,
Arthur Rosenberg, Geraldine Baron

16

BACK ROADS

(WARNER BROS.) Producer, Ronald Shedlo; Director, Martin Ritt; Screenplay, Gary Devore; Photography, John A. Alonzo; Designer, Walter Scott Herndon; Editor, Sidney Levin; Music, Henry Mancini; Associate Producer, Golda David; Assistant Directors, Ron Wright, Ira Shuman; In DeLuxe Color and Panavision; A CBS Theatrical Films Presentation; 94 minutes; Rated R; March release.

CAST

Amy Post	Sally Field
Elmore Pratt	Tommy Lee Jones
Mason	David Keith
Angel	Miriam Colon
Tazio	Michael Gazzo
Spivey	Dan Shor
Arthur	M. Emmet Walsh
Rickey's Mom	Barbara Babcock
Waitress	Nell Carter
Enrique	Alex Colon
Red	Lee de Broux
Gosler	Ralph Seymour
Father	Royce Applegate
Ezra	Bruce M. Fischer
Gilly	John Dennis Johnston
Pete	Don "Red" Barry
Boy Thief	Billy Jacoby
Pinball Wizard	Eric Laneuville
Bleitz	Brian Frishman
Liz	Diane Sommerfield
Grover	Henry Slate

and Matthew Campion (Stromberg), Tony Ganios (Bartini), Lee McLaughlin (Deputy), Arthur Pugh (Taper), Gerry Okuneff (Oren), Louie Nicholas (Burt), Cherie Brantley (Ellen), Jim Bailey (Billy), Fred Baldwin (Gordy), Billy Holliday (Isaac), Barbara Thompson (Flo), Buddy Thompson (Peter), Phil Gordon (Caleb), Mike Barton (Cop), Richard Charles Boyle (Ernest), Sherrie Whitman (Maralyn), Lupita Corego (Cory), Bob E. Hannah (Vernon), David Powledge (Announcer), Eliott Keener (Willis), David Pellette (Referee), David Dahlgren (Mel), John Jackson (Merle), John Wilmot (Ed), Jack Shadix (Orville), Leonardo J. Noriega (Bartender), Joe Ford (Max), Woody Watson (Larry), Duke Alexander (Charlie)

Top: Tommy Lee Jones, Sally Field
(also right center) © Warner Bros.

Sally Field, Tommy Lee Jones

THIF

(UNITED ARTISTS) Producers, Jerry Bruckheimer, Ronnie Caan; Direction, Story and Screenplay, Michael Mann; Based on "The Home Invaders" by Frank Hohimer; Photography, Donald Thorin; Art Director, Mary Dodson; Editor, Dov Hoenig; Designer, Mel Bourne; Music, Tangerine Dream; Associate Producer, Richard Brams; Assistant Directors, Peter Bogart, Scott Maitland, Richard N. Graves; In Dolby Stereo and Technicolor; 126 minutes; Rated R; March release.

CAST

Frank	James Caan
Jessie	Tuesday Weld
Okla	Willie Nelson
Barry	James Belushi
Leo	Robert Prosky
Attaglia	Tom Signorelli
Carl	Dennis Farina
Nick	Nick Nickeas
Mitch	W. R. (Bill) Brown
Guido	Norm Tobin
Urizzi	John Santucci
Boreksco	Gavin MacFadyen
Ancell	Chuck Adamson
Martello	Sam Cirone
Bukowski	Spero Anast
D. Simpson	Walter Scott
Large Detective in suit	Sam T. Louis
Joseph	William LaValley
Paula	Lora Staley
Joe Gags	Hal Frank

and Del Close, Bruce Young, John Kapelos (Mechanics), Mike Genovese (Green Mill Bartender), Joan Lazzerini (Attaglia's Receptionist), Beverly Somerman (Secretary), Enrica R. Cannataro (Plating Salesman), Donna J. Fenton, Mary Louise Wade (Waitresses), William L. Peterson (Katz & Jammer Bartender), Nancy Santucci (Hojo Waitress), Nathan Davis (Grossman), Thomas O. Erhart, Jr. (Judge), Fredric Stone (Garner), Robert J. Kuper (Bailiff), Joene Hanhardt (Recorder), Marge Kolitsky (Mrs. Knowles), J. J. Saunders (Doctor), Susan McCormick (Nurse), Karen Bercovici (Ruthie), Michael Paul Chan (Waiter), Tom Howard, Richard Karie (Salesmen), Patti Ross (Marie), Margot Charlior (Rosa), Oscar DiLorenzo (Customer at Green Mill)

Robert Prosky, Tom Signorelli, James Caan
Above: Gavin MacFadyen, John Santucci

Top: Tuesday Weld, James Caan Below: Willie Nelson, Caan Right: James Caan
© United Artists

THE FINAL CONFLICT

(20th CENTURY FOX) Executive Producer, Richard Donner; Producer, Harvey Bernhard; Director, Graham Baker; Screenplay, Andrew Birkin; Based on characters created by David Seltzer; Music, Jerry Goldsmith; Associate Producer, Mace Neufeld; Photography, Robert Paynter, Phil Meheux; Associate Producer, Andrew Birkin; Designer, Herbert Westbrook; Editor, Alan Strachan; Art Director, Martin Atkinson; Assistant Directors, Dusty Symonds, Chris Newman, Kieron Phipps; In Deluxe Color, Dolby Stereo and Panavision; 108 minutes; Rated R; March release.

CAST

Damien	Sam Neill
DeCarlo	Rossano Brazzi
Dean	Don Gordon
Kate Reynolds	Lisa Harrow
Peter	Barnaby Holm
President	Mason Adams
American Ambassador	Robert Arden
Brother Matteus	Tommy Duggan
Barbara	Leueen Willoughby
Brother Paulo	Louis Mahoney
Brother Benito	Marc Boyle
Brother Simeon	Richard Oldfield
Brother Martin	Milos Kirek
Brother Antonio	Tony Vogel
Carol	Arwen Holm
Manservant	Hugh Moxey
Diplomats	William Fox, John Baskcomb
Dr. Philmore	Norman Bird
Press Officer	Marc Smith
Astronomer	Arnold Diamond
Astronomer's Technician	Eric Richard
Vicar	Richard Williams
Stigwell	Stephen Turner
Workman	Al Matthews
Orators	Larry Martyn, Frank Coda, Harry Littlewood

**Left Center: Sam Neill, Barnaby Holm
Top: Holm, Rossano Brazzi, Lisa Harrow
© 20th Century-Fox**

Sam Neill, Lisa Harrow, Barnaby Holm

Rossano Brazzi

ALL NIGHT LONG

(UNIVERSAL) Producers, Leonard Goldberg, Jerry Weintraub; Director, Jean-Claude Tramont; Screenplay, W. D. Richter; Photography, Philip Lathrop; Designer, Peter Jamison; Editor, Marion Rothman; Associate Producers, Terence A. Donnelly, Fran Roy; Music, Ira Newborn, Richard Hazard; Assistant Directors, Terence A. Donnelly, Armando M. Huerta; In Technicolor; 88 minutes; Rated R; March release.

CAST

George Dupler	Gene Hackman
Cheryl Gibbons	Barbra Streisand
Helen Dupler	Diane Ladd
Freddie Dupler	Dennis Quaid
Bobby Gibbons	Kevin Dobson
Richard H. Copleston	William Daniels
Grandmother Gibbons	Ann Doran
Grandfather Gibbons	Jim Nolan
Joan Gibbons	Judy Kerr
Jennifer Gibbons	Marlyn Gates
Ultra-Sav Doctor	Raleigh Bond
French Teacher	Annie Girardot
Nurse	Mitzi Hoag
Nevins	Charles Siebert
Hutchinson	James Ingersoll
Shuster's Secretary	Tandy Cronyn
Barney	Len Lawson
Ultra-Sav Day Manager	Terry Kiser
Emily	Vernee Watson
Russell Munk	Chris Mulkey
Leon	Steven Peterman
Pharmacist	Richard Stahl
Holdup Woman	Faith Minton
Jacob Horowitz	Jessie Lawrence Ferguson
Shoplifter	Nicholas Mele

and Joe Jacobs (Violinist), Demetre Phillips (Carpenter), Lomax Study (Security Guard), Bonnie Bartlett (Patricia), Eunice Christopher (Eunice), Virginia Kiser (Virginia), Irene Tedrow (Landlady), Peggy Pope (Waitress), Marilyn Tokuda (Michele), Hamilton Camp (Buggoms), Gary Allen (Desk Clerk), Charles White-Eagle (Gibson Lone Wolf), Adrienne Leonetti (Diva), Holly Addy (Pianist), Paul Valentine (Customer), Bob Mitchell (Boys Choir Leader)

Left: William Daniels, Diane Ladd, Dennis Quaid, Gene Hackman Top: Gene Hackman, Barbra Streisand
© Universal Studios

Gene Hackman, Vernee Watson, Steven Peterman, Chris Mulkey

Diane Ladd, Kevin Dobson

THE POSTMAN ALWAYS RINGS TWICE

(PARAMOUNT) Executive Producer, Andrew Braunsberg; Producers, Charles Mulvehill, Bob Rafelson; Director, Bob Rafelson; Screenplay, David Mamet; Based on novel by James M. Cain; Photography, Sven Nykvist; Designer, George Jenkins; Editor, Graeme Clifford; Music, Michael Small; Associate Producer, Michael Barlow; Costumes, Dorothy Jeakins; Assistant Directors, William Scott, Nick Marck; In Metrocolor; A Northstar International Picture; 125 minutes; Rated R; March release.

CAST

Frank Chambers	Jack Nicholson
Cora Papadakis	Jessica Lange
Nick Papadakis	John Colicos
Salesman	Christopher Lloyd
Katz	Michael Lerner
Kennedy	John P. Ryan
Madge	Anjelica Huston
Sackett	William Traylor
Barlow	Tom Hill
Motorcycle Cop	Jon Van Ness
Mortenson	Brian Farrell
Insurance Salesman	Raleigh Bond
Man from home town	William Newman
Beeman	Albert Henderson
Scoutmaster	Ken Magee
Doctor	Eugene Peterson
Goebel	Don Calfa
Ringmaster	Louis Turenne
Gas Station Attendant	Charles B. Jenkins
Sign Men	Dick Balduzzi, John Furlong
Ticket Clerk	Sam Edwards
Grandmother	Betty Cole
Granddaughter	Joni Palmer
Shoeshine Man	Ron Flagge
Judge	James O'Connell
Bailiff	William H. McDonald
Matron	Elsa Raven

Top: Jessica Lange, Jack Nicholson Below: Michael
Lerner, Lange Right: Nicholson
© Lorimar Films

Jack Nicholson, Jessica Lange
Above: Lange, John Colicos

THE HAND

(ORION/WARNER BROS.) Producer, Edward R. Pressman; Executive Producer, Clark L. Paylow; Direction and Screenplay, Oliver Stone; Based on book "The Lizard's Tail" by Marc Brandel; Music, James Horner; Photography, King Baggot; Designer, John Michael Riva; Editor, Richard Marks; Assistant Directors, Kim Kurumada, Andy Anderson; Associate Producers, Joe O'-Har, Bert Kamerman, Leslie Paonessa; Art Director, Richard Sawyer; Designer, Virginia Randolph; Costumes, Ernest Misko; In Technicolor and Dolby Stereo; 108 minutes; Rated R; April release.

CAST

Jon Lansdale	Michael Caine
Anne Lansdale	Andrea Marcovicci
Stella Roche	Annie McEnroe
Brian Ferguson	Bruce McGill
Doctress	Viveca Lindfors
Karen Wagner	Rosemary Murphy
Lizzie Lansdale	Mara Hobel
Sheriff	Pat Corley
Bill Richman	Nicholas Hormann
Doctor	Ed Marshall
David Maddow	Charles Fleischer
Therapist	John Stinson
Hammond	Richard Altman
Sergeant	Sparky Watt
Cop	Tracey Walter
Boy in classroom	Brian Kenneth Hume
Girl in classroom	Lora Pearson
Bum	Oliver Stone
Country Bumpkins	Jack Evans, Scott Evans, Randy Evans, Patrick Evans

Michael Caine
(also top right)

Top Left: Andrea Marcovicci, Michael Caine
also below © Orion Pictures

NIGHTHAWKS

(UNIVERSAL) Producer, Martin Poll; Director, Bruce Malmuth; Screenplay, David Shaber; Story, David Shaber, Paul Sylbert; Executive Producers, Michael Wise, Franklin R. Levy; Photography, James A. Contner; Designer, Peter Larkin; Costumes, Bob DeMora, John Falabella; Editor, Christopher Holmes; Music, Keith Emerson; Assistant Directors, Robert Girolami, Joseph Reidy, Bill Cassidy; Associate Producer, Kathryn Stellmack; In Technicolor; 99 minutes; Rated R; April release.

CAST

Deke DaSilva	Sylvester Stallone
Matthew Fox	Billy Dee Williams
Irene	Lindsay Wagner
Shakka	Persis Khambatta
Peter Hartman	Nigel Davenport
Wulfgar	Rutger Hauer
Pam	Hilarie Thompson
Lt. Munafo	Joe Spinell
Commissioner	Walter Mathews
Sergeant	E. Brian Dean
Puerto Rican Proprietor	Caesar Cordova
Dr. Ghiselin	Charles Duval
Big Mike	Tony Munafo
Disco Manager	Howard Stein
Disco Hostess	Tawn Christian
Designer	Jamie Gillis
Conductor	Luke Reilly
Mrs. Ntembwe	Yvette Hawkins
Sostrom	Einar Perry Scott
Mrs. Sostrom	Erle Björnstad
French Ambassador	Jacques Roux
Nigerian Ambassador	Clebert Ford
Swedish Ambassador	Eivind Harum
Mr. Ntembwe	Obaka Adedunyo
Suzanne Marigny	Corine Lorain
Rene Marigny	Jean-Pierre Stewart

and Thomas Rosales, John Shamsul Alam, Jose Santana (Rippers), Patrick Fox (Reporter), John Cianfrone, Tim Marquart, Tony Maffatone (Muggers), Tom Degidon (Immigration Officer), Rita Tellone (Brunette), Al Gerullo, Jr., Karl Wickman (Helicopter Pilots), Brian Osborne (Orchard), Robert Pugh (Kenna), Catherine Mary Stewart (Salesgirl), Frederick Treves (Chief Police Inspector), Susan Vanner (Girl at party), Cliff Cudney, Joe Dabenigno, Steve Daskawisz, John Devaney, Paul Farentino, Edward Fox, Randy Francklan, Al Levitsky, Richard Noyce, Dar Robinson, Judee Wales, Luke Walter (A.T.A.C. Men)

Right: Rutger Hauer, Sylvester Stallone
Above: Joe Spinell, Stallone, Billy Dee Williams
Top: Rutger Hauer, Persis Khambatta
© Universal Studios

Lindsay Wagner, Sylvester Stallone

Sylvester Stallone, Rutger Hauer

CAVEMAN

(UNITED ARTISTS) Producers, Lawrence Turman, David Foster; Director, Carl Gottlieb; Screenplay, Rudy DeLuca, Carl Gottlieb; Photography, Alan Hume; Designer, Philip M. Jefferies; Editor, Gene Fowler, Jr.; Music, Lalo Schifrin; Costumes, Robert Fletcher; Art Director, Jose Rodriguez Granada; Assistant Directors, Peter Bogart, Mario Cisneros; In Technicolor; 94 minutes; Rated PG; April release.

CAST

Atouk	Ringo Starr
Lar	Dennis Quaid
Tala	Shelley Long
Gog	Jack Gilford
Ta	Cork Hubbert
Ruck	Mark King
Flok	Paco Morayta
Nook	Evan Kim
Kalta	Ed Greenberg
Bork	Carl Lumbly
Folg	Jack Scalici
Folg's Mate	Erica Carlson
Folg's Daughter	Gigi Vorgan
Folg's Younger Daughter	Sara Lopez Sierra
Folg's Son	Esteban Valdez
Folg's Younger Son	Juan Ancona Figueroa
Folg's Youngest Son	Juan Omar Ortiz
Meeka	Anais de Melo
Tonda	John Matuszak
Lana	Barbara Bach
Ock	Avery Schreiber
Grot	Miguel Angel Fuentes
Ock's Mate	Tere Alvarez
Grot's Mate	Ana de Sade
Boola	Gerardo Zepeda
Noota	Hector Moreno
Noota's Mate	Pamela Gual
Abominable Snowman	Richard Moll

Left: John Matuszak, Barbara Bach
Top: Dennis Quaid, Ringo Starr, Shelley Long
© United Artists

Ringo Starr, Barbara Bach

Jack Gilford

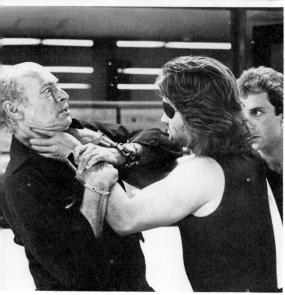

ESCAPE FROM NEW YORK

(AVCO EMBASSY) Producers, Larry Franco, Debra Hill; Director, John Carpenter; Screenplay, John Carpenter, Nick Castle; Photography, Dean Cundey; Editor, Todd Ramsay; Music, John Carpenter, Alan Howarth; Design, Joe Alves; Costumes, Stephen Loomis; Assistant Director, Larry Franco; Associate Producer, Barry Bernardi; In Metrocolor, Dolby Stereo and Panavision; 99 minutes, Rated R; April release.

CAST

Snake Plissken	Kurt Russell
Bob Hauk	Lee Van Cleef
Cabbie	Ernest Borgnine
President of the U. S.	Donald Pleasence
Duke of New York	Isaac Hayes
Girl in Chock Full O' Nuts	Season Hubley
Brain	Harry Dean Stanton
Maggie	Adrienne Barbeau
Rehme	Tom Atkins
Secretary of State	Charles Cyphers

Top: Adrienne Barbeau, Ernest Borgnine (R) Isaac Hayes, Harry Dean Stanton, Adrienne Barbeau Center: (L) Lee Van Cleef, Kurt Russell, John Strobel (R) Lee Van Cleef, Tom Atkins
© AVCO Embassy

Kurt Russell

ATLANTIC CITY

(PARAMOUNT) Producer, Denis Heroux; Director, Louis Malle; Screenplay, John Guare; Music, Michel LeGrand; Photography, Richard Ciupka; Editor, Suzanne Baron; Designer, Anne Pritchard; Associate Producers, Justine Heroux, Larry Nesis; Executive Producers, Joseph Beaubien, Gabriel Boustany; Assistant Directors, John Board, Robert McCart, Jim Chory; Costumes, Francois Barbeau; In color; Rated R; 105 minutes; April release.

CAST

Lou	Burt Lancaster
Sally	Susan Sarandon
Grace	Kate Reid
Joseph	Michel Piccoli
Chrissie	Hollis McLaren
Dave	Robert Joy
Alfie	Al Waxman
Singer	Robert Goulet
Felix	Moses Znaimer
Vinnie	Angus MacInnes
Buddy	Sean Sullivan
Waiter	Wally Shawn
Bus Driver	Harvey Atkin
Jeanne	Norma Dell'Agnese
Mr. Shapiro	Louis Del Grande
Fred	John McCurry
Mrs. Reese	Eleanor Beecroft
President of hospital	Cec Linder
Detective	Sean McCaan
Young Doctor	Vincent Glorioso
Florist	Adele Chatfield-Taylor
Poker Player	Tony Angelo
Toll Booth Operator	Sis Clark
Casino Guard	Gennaro Consalvo
Pit Boss	Lawrence McGuire
Connie Bishop	Connie Collins
Police Commissioner	John Allmond
Anchorman	John Burns
Singers in casino	Ann Burns, Marie Burns, Jean Burns

Burt Lancaster
(also top right)

Top Left: Susan Sarandon, Burt Lancaster
Below: Susan Sarandon
© Merchant Trust Co.

Susan Sarandon, Burt Lancaster Top: (L) Kate Reid, Burt Lancaster (R) Robert Joy,
Hollis McLaren, Susan Sarandon Center: (L) Michel Piccoli, Susan Sarandon
(R) Robert Joy, Burt Lancaster

CATTLE ANNIE AND LITTLE BRITCHES

(UNIVERSAL) Producers, Rupert Hitzig, Alan King; Director, Lamont Johnson; Screenplay, David Eyre, Robert Ward; Story, Robert Ward from his novel; Executive Producers, John Daly, Derek Dawson; Associate Producer, David Korda; Photography, Larry Pizer; Music, Sanh Berti, Tom Slocum; Designer, Stan Jolley; Costumes, Rita Riggs; Editor, William Haugse; Assistant Director, David Anderson; Additional Music, Richard Greene; Color by C.F.I.; 95 minutes; Rated PG; May release.

CAST

Bill Dalton	Scott Glenn
Red Buck	Redmond Gleeson
Little Dick Raidler	William Russ
George Weightman	Ken Call
Bittercreek Newcomb	John Savage
Dynamite Dick	Buck Taylor
Fireman	Roger Cudney, Jr.
Engineer	Michael Conrad
Annie	Amanda Plummer
Jenny	Diane Ladd
Bill Doolin	Burt Lancaster
Conductor	Chad Hastings
Morgan	John Quade
Mrs. Sweetman	Yvette Sweetman
Elrod	Perry Lang
Ned's Father	Tom Delaney
Ned	Matthew Taylor
Corey	John Sterlini
Tilghman	Rod Steiger
Deputy Marshall	Steven Ford
Deputy	Mike Moroff
Bank Teller	John Hock
Capps	Roger Cudney
Cop	Jerry Gatlin
Guard	Russ Hoverson

William Russ, John Savage, Amanda Plummer, Burt Lancaster, Diane Lane

Rod Steiger

Top: John Savage Right: Diane Lane
© Universal City Studios

28

THE FAN

(PARAMOUNT PICTURES) Producer, Robert Stigwood; Director, Edward Bianchi; Screenplay, Priscilla Chapman, John Hartwell; Based on novel by Bob Randall; Executive Producer, Kevin McCormick; Associate Producers, John Nicolella, Bill Oakes; Designer, Santo Loquasto; Photographer, Dick Bush; Editor, Alan Heim; Songs, Marvin Hamlisch, Tim Rice; Music, Pino Donaggio; Choreographer, Arlene Phillips; Assistant Directors, Herb Gains, Bill Eustace; Costumes, Jeffrey Kurland, Tom McKinley; Art Director, Paul Eads; In Technicolor; 95 minutes; Rated R; May release.

CAST

Sally Ross	Lauren Bacall
Jake Berman	James Garner
Belle Goldman	Maureen Stapleton
Ralph Andrews	Hector Elizondo
Douglas Breen	Michael Biehn
Emily Stolz	Anna Maria Horsford
David Branum	Kurt Johnson
Elsa	Feiga Martinez
Choreographer	Reed Jones
Douglas' Sister	Kaiulani Lee
John Vetta	Charles Blackwell
Director	Dwight Schultz
Saleswoman	Dana Delany
Young Man in bar	Terence Marinan
Heidi	Lesley Rogers
Hilda	Parker McCormick
Pop	Robert Weil
Caretaker	Ed Crowley
Assistant Choreographer	Gail Benedict
Pianist	D. David Lewis
Production Assistant	Griffin Dunne
Markham	Themi Sapountzakis
Stage Manager	Jean DeBaer
Liz Smith	Herself

and Haru Aki, Rene Ceballos, Clif DeRaita, Edyie Fleming, Linda Haberman, Sergio Lopez-Cal, Jamie Patterson, Justin Ross, Stephanie Williams, Jim Wolfe (Dancers), Thomas Saccio (Prop Man), Victoria Vanderkloot (Pen Thief), James Ogden (Drummer), Terri Duhaime (Nurse), Donna Mitchell (Hostess), Hector Osorio (Donut Vendor), Lionel Pina (Customer), Miriam Phillips (Woman on steps), Jack R. Marks, George Peters (Doormen), Esther Benson, Eric Van Valkenburg, Ann Pearl Gary, Madeline Moroff, Leo Schaff (Fans), James Bryson, J. Nesbit Clark, Tim Elliott, Paul Hummel, Jacob Laufer (Stagehands)

Right: Michael Biehn
(also top)
© **Paramount Pictures**

Lauren Bacall

Lauren Bacall, Michael Biehn

29

BUSTIN' LOOSE

(UNIVERSAL) Executive Producer, William Greaves; Producers, Richard Pryor, Michael S. Glick; Director, Oz Scott; Screenplay, Roger L. Simon; Adaptation, Lonne Elder III; Story, Richard Pryor; Photography, Dennis Dalzell; Art Directors, Charles R. Davis, John Corso; Editor, David Holden; Music, Mark Davis; Original Music composed and sung by Roberta Flack; Costumes, Bill Whitten, Stephen Loomis; Assistant Directors, Clifford C. Coleman, Maximiliano Bing, Hope Goodwin, John Syrjamaki; In Technicolor; 94 minutes; Rated R; May release.

CAST

Joe Braxton	Richard Pryor
Vivian Perry	Cicely Tyson
Martin	Alphonso Alexander
Samantha	Kia Cooper
Ernesto	Edwin DeLeon
Harold	Jimmy Hughes
Anthony	Edwin Kinter
Linda	Tami Luchow
Julio	Angel Ramirez
Annie	Janet Wong
Donald	Robert Christian
Dr. Wilson T. Renfrew	George Coe
Judge Antonio Runzuli	Bill Quinn
Klan Leader	Roy Jenson
Alfred Schuyler	Fred Carney
Gladys Schuyler	Peggy McCay

and Luke Andreas (Loader), Earl Billings (Man at parole office), Mathew Clark (Dwayne), Nick Dimitri (Frank Munjak), Les Engel (Wino), Michael A. Esler (Cop), Paul Gardner (Anchorman), Ben Gerard (Man), Gary Goetzman (Store Manager), Joe Jacobs (Watchman), Paul Mooney (Marvin), Lee Noblitt (Farmer), Inez Pedroza (Herself), Morgan Roberts (Uncle Humphrey), Vern Taylor, Rick Sawaya (Patrolmen), Gloria Jewel Waggener (Aunt Beedee), Shila Turna (Girl in card game), Jonelle White (Sales Clerk), Jewell Williams (Thiss Thomas), Sunny Woods (Linette)

Left: Richard Pryor, Nick Dimitri
Top: Richard Pryor
© **Universal City Studios**

Richard Pryor

Richard Pryor, Cicely Tyson

Cicely Tyson takes her class to Washington
Above: Richard Pryor, and Top with Mathew
Clark, Nick Dimitri

Richard Pryor, and above and top
with Cicely Tyson

KING OF THE MOUNTAIN

(**UNIVERSAL**) Producer, Jack Frost Sanders; Executive Producer, William Tennant; Director, Noel Nosseck; Screenplay, H. R. Christian; Inspired by David Barry's New West magazine article "Thunder Road"; Photography, Donald Peterman; Designer, James H. Spencer; Associate Producer, Jeffrey Benjamin; Music, Michael Melvion; Editor, William Steinkamp; Costumes, Susan Becker; Assistant Directors, Robert P. Cohen, Herb Adelman, Peter Bergquist; In Technicolor; Presented by PolyGram Pictures; 90 minutes; Rated PG; May release.

CAST

Steve	Harry Hamlin
Buddy	Joseph Bottoms
Tina	Deborah Van Valkenburgh
Roger	Richard Cox
Cal	Dennis Hopper
Rick	Dan Haggerty
Barry Tanner	Seymour Cassel
Billy T	Jon Sloan
Policeman	Steve Jones
Elaine	Ashley Cox
Jamie Winter	Lillian Muller
Neighbor	Cassandra Peterson
Fast Joe Otis	Buddy Joe Hooker
Keyboard Player	Ron Trice
Fatburger	Curt Ayers
Dean	Larry Beezer
Big Tom	Bill Forsythe
Suds	Joey Camen
Davey	Douglas Dirkson

and Jay May (Guitar Player), Susan McDonald (Buddy's Girl), Amy Gibson (Roger's Girl), Gary Hudson (Gang Leader), Dennis Hull, Vincent Guastaferro, Anthony DeLongis (Gang Members), Preston Sparks (Parking Lot Attendant), Tara Fellner (Iris), Howard Alk (Party Guest), Tony Lettieri, Sonny LaRocca (Friends), Steve Davison (Van Man), R. P. Cohen (Cashier), Owen Orr (Bartender), Lisa Friedman (Spandex Girl), Hamilton McRae (Guest), Chuck Tamburro (Cop Driver), Hank Bill Hooker (Cop), Ted Markland (Limo Driver), Jay Meyer (Agent), Tony Berg, Jeff Eyrich, Art Woods, Ronald Raison (Themselves), John Dukakis (Duke), Kathy McCullen (Duke's Girl), Juliette Marshall (Big Tom's Girl), Russell Forte (Joel), Steve Halladay, Debbie Dirkson

Top Right: Harry Hamlin, Richard Cox, Joseph Bottoms
Below: Hamlin, Dan Haggerty, Dennis Hopper
© Universal City Studios

Deborah Van Valkenburgh

Harry Hamlin, Deborah Van Valkenburgh

DEATH HUNT

(20th CENTURY-FOX) Executive Producers, Albert S. Ruddy, Raymond Chow; Producer, Murray Shostak; Director, Peter Hunt; Screenplay, Michael Grais, Mark Victor; Photography, James Devis; Designer, Ted Haworth; Editors, Allan Jacobs, John F. Burnett; Associate Producer, Robert Baylis; Music, Jerrold Immel; Assistant Directors, Frank Ernst, David MacLeod; Designer, Tom Doherty; Costumes, Olga Dimitrov; In Panavision and Technicolor; 96 minutes; Rated R; May release.

CAST

Johnson	Charles Bronson
Millen	Lee Marvin
Alvin	Andrew Stevens
Sundog	Carl Weathers
Hazel	Ed Lauter
Pilot	Scott Hylands
Vanessa	Angie Dickinson
Luce	Henry Beckman
Ned Warren	William Sanderson
Hawkins	Jon Cedar
Hurley	James O'Connell
Lewis	Len Lesser
Beeler	Dick Davalos
Clarence	Maury Chaykin
Deak de Clearque	August Schellenberg
Trappers	Dennis Wallace, James McIntire, Rayford Barnes
Charlie Rat	Maurice Kowaleski
News Reporter	Sean McCann
W. W. Douglass	Steve O. Z. Finkel
Jimmy Tom	Denis Lacroix
Indian Woman	Tantoo Martin
Buffalo Woman	Amy Marie George

Top: Lee Marvin, Carl Weathers, Andrew Stevens
Below: Marvin, August Schellenberg Top Right:
Angie Dickinson, Marvin © North Shore Investments

Charles Bronson, and above
with Ed Lauter

33

THE FOUR SEASONS

(UNIVERSAL) Producer, Martin Bregman; Direction and Screenplay, Alan Alda; Photography, Victor J. Kemper; Designer, Jack Collis; Editor, Michael Economou; Executive Producer, Louis A. Stroller; Associate Producer, Michael Economou; Costumes, Jane Greenwood; Assistant Directors, Yudi Bennett, Joan Feinstein; Music, Antonio Vivaldi; In Technicolor; 107 minutes; Rated PG; May release.

CAST

Jack Burroughs	Alan Alda
Kate Burroughs	Carol Burnett
Nick Callan	Len Cariou
Anne Callan	Sandy Dennis
Claudia Zimmer	Rita Moreno
Danny Zimmer	Jack Weston
Ginny Newley	Bess Armstrong
Beth	Elizabeth Alda
Lisa	Beatrice Alda
Room Clerk	Robert Hitt
Waitress	Kristi McCarthy
Doctor	David Stackpole

Left: Alan Alda © Universal City Studios

Carol Burnett, Beatrice Alda, Jack Weston, Alan Alda, Rita Moreno, Bess Armstrong, Len Cariou

Jack Weston, Alan Alda, Carol Burnett, Bess Armstrong, Rita Moreno, Len Cariou
Top: Rita Moreno, Sandy Dennis, Carol Burnett

OUTLAND

(LADD CO./WARNER BROS.) Producer, Richard A. Roth; Executive Producer, Stanley O'Toole; Direction and Screenplay, Peter Hyams; Music, Jerry Goldsmith; Editor, Stuart Baird; Designer, Philip Harrison; Photography, Stephen Goldblatt; Assistant Directors, David Tringham, Bob Wright; Art Director, Malcolm Middleton; Costumes, John Mollo; Associate Producer, Charles Orme; Choreographer, Anthony Van Laast; In Panavision, Dolby Stereo and Technicolor; 109 minutes; Rated R; May release.

CAST

O'Niel	Sean Connery
Sheppard	Peter Boyle
Lazarus	Frances Sternhagen
Montone	James B. Sikking
Carol	Kika Markham
Ballard	Clarke Peters
Sagan	Steven Berkoff
Tarlow	John Ratzenberger
Paul O'Niel	Nicholas Barnes
Lowell	Manning Redwood
Mrs. Spector	Pat Starr
Nelson	Hal Galili
Hughes	Angus MacInnes
Walters	Stuart Milligan
Cane	Eugene Lipinski
Slater	Norman Chancer
Fanning	Ron Travis
Morton	Anni Domingo

and Bill Bailey (Hill), Chris Williams (Caldwell), Marc Boyle (Spota), Richard Hammat (Yario), James Berwick (Rudd), Gary Olsen (Worker), Isabelle Lucas (Nurse), Sharon Duce (Prostitute), P. H. Moriarty (Man #1), Angelique Rockas (Maintenance Woman), Judith Alderson, Rayner Bourton (Prostitutes in Leisure Club), Doug Robinson (Man #2), Dancers in Leisure Club: Julia Depyer, Nina Francoise, Brendon Hughes, Philip Johnston, Norri Morgan

Top: Sean Connery, Peter Hyams Below: Frances Sternhagen, Connery Right: Connery, and top with Kika Markham © Ladd Company

36

Peter Boyle

THE NIGHT THE LIGHTS WENT OUT IN GEORGIA

(AVCO EMBASSY) Producers, Elliot Geisinger, Howard Kuperman, Ronald Saland, Howard Smith; Executive Producers, William Blake, Carol Blake; Director, Ronald F. Maxwell; Music, David Shire; Designer, Gene Rudolf; Costumes, Joseph G. Aulisi; Editor, Anne Goursaud; Photography, Bill Butler, Fred Batka; Story and Screenplay, Bob Bonney; Based on song by Bobby Russell; Assistant Directors, Ray Marsh, Debra Michaelson; Associate Producers, Marcel Broekman, Chaim Sprei; In color by C.F.I.; 120 minutes; June release.

CAST

Amanda Child	Kristy McNichol
Travis Child	Dennis Quaid
Conrad	Mark Hamill
Melody	Sunny Johnson
Seth	Don Stroud
Andy	Arlen Dean Snyder
Wimbish	Barry Corbin
Boogie Woogie	Lulu McNichol
Luther	Royce Clark
Woman on bus	Marilyn Hickey
L. C.	Jerry Rushing
Odie	Jerry Campbell
Boys	Maxwell Morrow, Bill Bribble, Lonnie Smith
Verna	Elaine Falone
Wanda	Terry Browning
B. G.	Barrie Geisinger
Nellie	Ellen Saland
Hawkins	J. Don Ferguson
Woman with Hawkins	S. Victoria Marlowe
Texan	William Phillips

and Fred Covington (Man in jail), Ralph Pace (Judge), Nikola Colton (Court Officer), Cindy Partlow (Mavis), Peter Bridgemen (Cook), Wanda Strange (Woman), Bobby Leroux (Elmer), Harry Wilcox (Norman), Rita Teeter (Fat Woman), Robert Harrison, Jr. (Dishwasher), Lisa Riblet (Luther's Daughter), Lit Connah, Elsie Sligh (Elderly Women), Roger Teeter (Clerk), Charles Franzen (Bus Driver), Terry Beaver (Sheriff), Luther McLaughlin (Clerk), Anne Haney (Waitress), Joan Riordan (Barmaid), Ron Maxwell (Policeman)

**Right: Kristy McNichol, Dennis Quaid, Mark Hamill
Top: Sunny Johnson, Don Stroud, Dennis Quaid
© AVCO Embassy**

Mark Hamill, Kristy McNichol, Dennis Quaid

Kristy McNichol

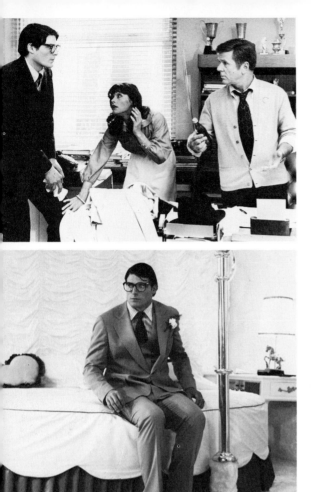

SUPERMAN II

(WARNER BROS.) Executive Producer, Ilya Salkind; Producer, Pierre Spengler; Director, Richard Lester; Screenplay, Mario Puzo, David Newman, Leslie Newman; Story, Mario Puzo; Music, Ken Thorne; Photography, Geoffrey Unsworth, Bob Paynter; Design, John Barry, Peter Murton; Editor, John Victor-Smith; Special Effects, Colin Chilvers; Costumes, Yvonne Blake, Susan Yelland; Art Director, Maurice Fowler; In Panavision, Technicolor, and Dolby Stereo; 127 minutes; Rated PG; June release.

CAST

Lex Luthor	Gene Hackman
Superman/Clark Kent	Christopher Reeve
Otis	Ned Beatty
Perry White	Jackie Cooper
Ursa	Sarah Douglas
Lois Lane	Margot Kidder
Non	Jack O'Halloran
Eve Teschmacher	Valerie Perrine
Lara	Susannah York
Sheriff	Clifton James
President	E. G. Marshall
Jimmy Olsen	Marc McClure
General Zod	Terence Stamp

and Leueen Willoughby (Leueen), Robin Pappas (Alice), Roger Kemp (Spokesman), Roger Brierley, Anthony Milner, Richard Griffiths (Terrorists), Melissa Wiltsie (Nun), Alain DeHay (Gendarme), Marc Boyle (C.R.S. Man), Alan Stuart (Cab Driver), John Ratzenberger, Shane Rimmer (Controllers), John Morton (Nate), Jim Dowdell (Boris), Angus McInnes (Warden), Antony Sher (Bellboy), Elva May Hoover (Mother), Hadley Kay (Jason), Todd Woodcroft (Father), John Hollis (Krypton Elder), Gordon Rollings (Fisherman), Peter Whitman (Deputy), Bill Bailey (J. J.), Dinny Powell (Boog), Hal Galili (Man at bar), Marcus D'Amico (Willie), Jackie Cooper (Dino), Richard Parmentier (Reporter), Don Fellows (General), Michael J. Shannon (President's Aide), Tony Sibbald (Presidential Imposter), Tommy Duggan (Diner Owner), Pamela Mandell (Waitress), Pepper Martin (Rocky), Eugene Lipinski (Newsvendor), Cleon Spencer, Carl Parris (Kids)

Left: Christopher Reeve, and top with Margot Kidder, Jackie Cooper © DC Comics

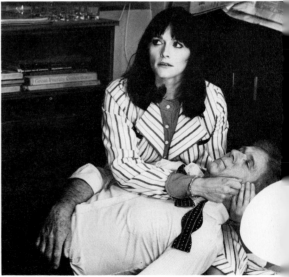

Margot Kidder, Jackie Cooper

Valerie Perrine, Gene Hackman Above: Margot
Kidder, Sarah Douglas, Terence Stamp
Top: Christopher Reeve

Christopher Reeve, and top with Margot
Kidder Above: Terence Stamp

Burt Reynolds, Dom DeLuise Above: Mel
Tillis, Terry Bradshaw

THE CANNONBALL RUN

(20th CENTURY-FOX) Producer, Albert S. Ruddy; Director, Hal Needham; Screenplay, Brock Yates; Executive Producer, Raymond Chow; Photography, Michael Butler; Art Director, Carol Wenger; Editors, Donn Cambern, William D. Gordean; Associate Producer, David Shamroy Hamburger; Assistant Directors, Bill Coker, Frank Bueno; Special Effects, Cliff Wenger, Sr.; In Panaflex and Technicolor; 95 minutes; Rated PG; June release.

CAST

J. J. McClure	Burt Reynolds
Seymour	Roger Moore
Pamela	Farrah Fawcett
Victor	Dom DeLuise
Jamie Blake	Dean Martin
Fenderbaum	Sammy Davis, Jr.
Doctor	Jack Elam
Marcie	Adrienne Barbeau
Terry	Terry Bradshaw
Subaru Drivers	Jackie Chan, Michael Hui
Brad	Bert Convy
Sheik	Jamie Farr
Chief Biker	Peter Fonda
A. F. Foyt	George Furth
Sheik's Sister	Bianca Jagger
Mom Goldfarb	Molly Picon
The Greek	Jimmy "The Greek" Snyder
Mel	Mel Tillis
Mad Dog	Rick Aviles
Shakey Finch	Warren Berlinger

and Tara Buckman (Jill), John Fiedler (Clerk), Norman Grabowski (Petoski), Joe Klecko (Racing Driver), Grayce Spence (Chairperson), Bob Tessier (Biker), Alfie Wise (Batman), Johnny Yune (TV Talk Show Host), Ben Rogers (Penn. Patrolman), Jim Lewis (Mo. Patrolman), Fred Smith, Bob Stenner, Ken Squier (Calif. Patrolmen), Roy Tatum (Conn. Patrolman), Dudley Remus, Hal Carter (N.J. Patrolmen), Brock Yates (Organizer), Kathleen M. Shea (Starting Girl), Nancy Austin (Phone Booth Lady), Vickie Reigle (Car Hop), Samir Kamoun (Bedouin), John Megna (Arthur), Linda McClure (Dour Lady), Laura Lizer Sommers (Lady in distress), Richard Losee (TransAm Driver), Richie Burns Wright (Farmboy), Seymour's Girls: Lois Areno, Simone Burton, Finele Carpenter, Susan McDonald, Janet Woytak

Top: Roger Moore, Molly Picon
Left: Farrah Fawcett, Burt Reynolds
© Eurasia Investments Ltd.

Standing: Bert Convy, Warren Berlinger, Michael Hui, Jackie Chan, Jack Elam, Dom DeLuise, Farrah Fawcett, Burt Reynolds, Dean Martin, Sammy Davis, Jr., Roger Moore, Simone Burton, Bob Tessier Front: Tara Buckman, Adrienne Barbeau, Rick Aviles, Peter Fonda, Alfie Wise

FOR YOUR EYES ONLY

(UNITED ARTISTS) Producer, Albert R. Broccoli; Director, John Glen; Screenplay, Richard Maibaum, Michael G. Wilson; Executive Producer, Michael G. Wilson; Music, Bill Conti; Design, Peter Lamont; Associate Producer, Tom Pevsner; Title Song sung by Sheena Easton; Lyrics, Michael Leeson; Photography, Alan Hume; Editor, John Grover; Assistant Director, Anthony Waye; Art Director, John Fenner; Costumes, Elizabeth Waller; In Technicolor, Panavision, and Dolby Stereo; 148 minutes; Rated PG; June release.

CAST

James Bond	Roger Moore
Melina	Carole Bouquet
Columbo	Topol
Bibi	Lynn-Holly Johnson
Kristatos	Julian Glover
Lisl	Cassandra Harris
Brink	Jill Bennett
Locque	Michael Gothard
Kriegler	John Wyman
Havelock	Jack Hedley
Moneypenny	Lois Maxwell
Q	Desmond Llewelyn
Denis	John Wells
Prime Minister	Janet Brown
Minister of Defense	Geoffrey Keen
General Gogol	Walter Gotell
Tanner	James Villiers
Ferrara	John Moreno
Claus	Charles Dance
Karageorge	Paul Angelis
Iona Havelock	Toby Robins
Apostis	Jack Klaff

and Alkis Kritikos (Santos), Stag Theodore (Nikos), Stefan Kalipha (Gonzales), Graham Crowden (First Sea Lord), Noel Johnson (Vice Admiral), William Hoyland (McGregor), Paul Brooke (Bunky), Eva Rueber-Staier (Rublevich), Fred Bryant (Vicar), Robbin Young (Girl in flower shop), Graham Hawkes (Mantis Man), Max Vesterhalt (Girl at casino), Lalla Dean (Girl at pool), and Bond Beauties: Evelyn Drogue, Laoura Hadzivageli, Koko, Chai Lee, Kim Mills, Tula, Vanya, Viva, Lizzie Warville, Alison Worth

Left: Carole Bouquet, Roger Moore
Top: Roger Moore
© Danjaq, S. A.

Roger Moore, Carole Bouquet

Julian Glover

Carole Bouquet, Roger Moore, Julian Glover Above: Roger Moore, Julian Glover; Jill Bennett, Lynn-Holly Johnson, Topol Top: Johnson, Moore; Topol, Bouquet, Paul Angelis

RAIDERS OF THE LOST ARK

(PARAMOUNT) Producer, Frank Marshall; Director, Steven Spielberg; Screenplay, Lawrence Kasdan; Story, George Lucas, Philip Kaufman; Executive Producers, George Lucas, Howard Kazanjian; Music, John Williams; Editor, Michael Kahn; Associate Producer, Robert Watts; Photography, Douglas Slocombe; Designer, Norman Reynolds; Costumes, Deborah Nadolman; Assistant Directors, David Tomblin, Roy Button, Patrick Cadell; Art Director, Leslie Dilley; In Metrocolor, Panavision, Dolby Stereo; 115 minutes; Rated PG; June release.

CAST

Indy	Harrison Ford
Marion	Karen Allen
Belloq	Paul Freeman
Toht	Ronald Lacey
Sallah	John Rhys-Davies
Brody	Denholm Elliott
Dietrich	Wolf Kahler
Gobler	Anthony Higgins
Satipo	Alfred Molina
Barranca	Vic Tablian
Col. Musgrove	Don Fellows
Major Eaton	William Hootkins
Bureaucrat	Bill Reimbold
Jock	Fred Sorenson
Australian Climber	Patrick Durkin
Second Nazi	Matthew Scurfield
Ratty Nepalese	Malcom Weaver
Mean Mongolian	Sonny Caldinez
Mohan	Anthony Chinn
Giant Sherpa	Pat Roach
Otto	Christopher Frederick
Imam	Tutte Lemkow
Omar	Ishaq Bux
Abu	Kiran Shah
Fayah	Souad Messaoudi
Monkey Man	Vic Tablian

and Terry Richards (Swordsman), Steve Hanson (German Agent), Pat Roach (1st Mechanic), Frank Marshall (Pilot), Martin Kreidt (Young Soldier), George Harris (Katanga), Eddie Tagoe (Messenger Pirate), John Rees (Sergeant), Tony Vogel (Tall Captain), Ted Grossman (Peruvian Porter), Jack Dearlove (Stand-In)

Left: Harrison Ford
© **Lucasfilm Ltd.**

1981 ACADEMY AWARDS FOR BEST EDITING, BEST SOUND, BEST VISUAL EFFECTS, BEST ART AND SET DIRECTION, BEST SOUND EFFECTS EDITING

Harrison Ford, Karen Allen

John Rhys-Davies, Harrison Ford

Harrison Ford (also top), and above
with Paul Freeman

Harrison Ford, Karen Allen

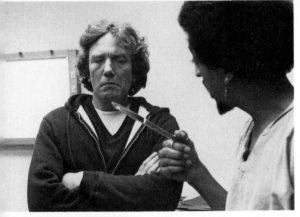

WOLFEN

(ORION/WARNER BROS.) Executive Producer, Alan King; Producer, Rupert Hitzig; Director, Michael Wadleigh; Story and Screenplay, David Eyre, Michael Wadleigh; Based on novel by Whitley Strieber; Music, James Horner; Special Effects, Robert Blalack; Photography, Gerry Fisher, Fred Abeles; Designer, Paul Sylbert; Assistant Directors, Steve Barnett, Alex Hapsas, Steven Felder, Hall Hitzig; Editors, Chris Lebenzon, Dennis Dolan, Martin Bram, Marshall M. Borden; Art Director, David Chapman; Costumes, John Boxer; In Technicolor, Panavision, and Dolby Stereo; 115 minutes; Rated R; July release.

CAST

Dewey Wilson	Albert Finney
Rebecca Neff	Diane Venora
Eddie Holt	Edward James Olmos
Whittington	Gregory Hines
Ferguson	Tom Noonan
Warren	Dick O'Neill
Old Indian	Dehl Berti
Ross	Peter Michael Goetz
Mayor	Sam Gray
Commissioner	Ralph Bell
Christopher Vanderveer	Max M. Brown
Pauline Vanderveer	Anne Marie Photamo
Cicely Rensselaer	Sarah Felder
Morgue Attendant	Reginald Vel Johnson
Baldy	James Tolkan
Sayad Alve	John McCurry
Janitor	Chris Manor
Lawyer	Donald Symington
Interrogation Operator	Jeffery Ware
Fouchek	E. Brian Dean
Harrison	Jeffery Thompson
Roundenbush	Victor Arnold
Scola	Frank Adonis
Policeman	Richard Minchenberg

Detectives .... Raymond Serra, Thomas Ryan and Tony Latham, David Connell, Jery Hewitt, Ray Brocksmith, Michael Wadleigh, Joaquin Rainbow, John Ferraro, Rino Thunder, Glenn Benoit, Eddy Navas, Ricky Hawkeye, Pete Dyer, Paul Skyhorse, Gordon Eagle, Javier First-Day-of-Light, George Stonefish, Julie Evening Lilly, Jane Lind, Annie Gagen, Cullen Johnson, Robert Moberly, Tony Stratta, Max Goff, Robert L. King, Caitlin O'Heaney, William Sheridan

Diane Venora, Albert Finney
Above: Finney, Gregory Hines

Top: Gregory Hines Left: Albert Finney,
Diane Venora © Orion Pictures

THE FOX AND THE HOUND

(BUENA VISTA) Executive Producer, Ron Miller; Co-Producers, Wolfgang Reitherman, Art Stevens; Direction, Art Stevens, Ted Berman, Richard Rich; Story, Larry Clemmons, Ted Berman, Peter Young, Steve Hulett, David Michener, Burny Mattinson, Earl Kress, Vance Gerry; Based on book by Daniel P. Mannix; Music, Buddy Baker; Songs, Richard O. Johnston and Stan Fidel, Jim Stafford, Richard Rich and Jeffrey Patch; Supervising Animators, Randy Cartwright, Cliff Nordberg, Frank Thomas, Glen Keane, Ron Clements, Ollie Johnston; Art Director, Don Griffith; Editors, James Melton, Jim Koford; Assistant Directors, Don Hahn, Mark A. Hester, Terry L. Noss; A Walt Disney Production in Technicolor; 83 minutes; Rated G; July

CAST
The voices of:
Mickey Rooney as Tod
Pearl Bailey as Big Mama
Kurt Russell as Copper
Jack Albertson as Amos Slade
Sandy Duncan as Vixey
Jeanette Nolan as Widow Tweed
Pat Buttram as Chief
John Fiedler as Porcupine
John McIntire as Badger
Dick Bakalyan as Dinky
Paul Winchell as Boomer
Keith Mitchell as Young Tod
Corey Feldman as Young Copper
Squeeks the Caterpillar

Copper and Tod Above: Amos Slade, Widow Tweed; Dinky, Boomer, Big Mama
Top: Hound and Fox © Walt Disney Productions

47

TARZAN, THE APE MAN

(MGM/UNITED ARTISTS) Producer, Bo Derek; Directed and Photographed by John Derek; Screenplay, Tom Rowe, Gary Goddard; Based on characters created by Edgar Rice Burroughs; Art Director, Alan Roderick-Jones; Editor, James B. Ling; Music, Perry Botkin; Assistant Directors, Jack Oliver, Michael Lally, Warner Warnasiri; Costumes, Patricia Edwards; A Svengali Production in color; 112 minutes; Rated R; July release.

CAST

Jane	Bo Derek
Parker	Richard Harris
Holt	John Phillip Law
Tarzan	Miles O'Keefe
Africa	Akushula Selayah
Ivory King	Steven Strong
Riano	Maxime Philoe
Feathers	Leonard Bailey
Club Members	Wilfrid Hyde-White, Laurie Mains, Harold Ayer
Orangutan	C. J.

Left: Miles O'Keefe, Bo Derek
© MGM Film Co.

Richard Harris, Bo Derek, John Phillip Law

Miles O'Keefe, Bo Derek

ENDLESS LOVE

(UNIVERSAL) Producer, Dyson Lovell; Director, Franco Zeffirelli; Screenplay, Judith Rascoe; Based on novel by Scott Spencer; Executive Producer, Keith Barish; Photography, David Watkin; Designer, Ed Wittstein; Editor, Michael J. Sheridan; Costumes, Kristi Zea; Music, Jonathan Tunick; Title Song, Lionel Richie; Performed by Diana Ross and Lionel Richie; Assistant Directors, Bob Girolami, Henry Bronchstein; Art Director, Ed Pisoni; Original soundtrack album by Mercury Records; Presented by Polygram Pictures; In color; 115 minutes; Rated R; July release.

CAST

Jade	Brooke Shields
David	Martin Hewitt
Anne	Shirley Knight
Hugh	Don Murray
Arthur	Richard Kiley
Rose	Beatrice Straight
Keith	Jimmy Spader
Sammy	Ian Ziering
Dr. Miller	Robert Moore
Ingrid	Penelope Milford
Mrs. Switzer	Jan Miner
Mr. Switzer	Salem Ludwig
Judge	Leon B. Stevens
Sonia	Vida Wright
Leonard	Jeff Marcus
Bob Clark	Patrick Taylor
Susan	Jamie Bernstein
Billy	Tom Cruise
Stuart	Jeffrey B. Versalle
Patty	Jami Gertz
Girlfriend	Maria Todd
Teacher in museum	Douglas Alan-Mann
Weaver	Steve Calicchio
Gene	Robert Kahn
Jeremy	Jeremy Bar-Illan
Gabe	Scott Cushman
Walter	David Willis

and Barry Pruitt, Amy Whitman, Kenneth Cory, Teri Shields, Sylvia Short, Ethelmae Mason, Anna Berger, Joan Glasco, Mark Hopson Arnold, Kathy Bernard, Philip Lenkowsky, Arthur Epstein, Leonard H. Pass, Lawrence Sellars, Ron Perkins, Gilbert Stafford, Marvin Foster, Millidge Mosley, Walt Gorney, Willie Wenger, Robert Altman, Ruth Last, George Kyle, Lee Kimball, Martin Pinckney, Duffy Piccini

Brooke Shields

Top: Brooke Shields, Shirley Knight

**Brooke Shields, and top
with Martin Hewitt**

Martin Hewitt

VICTORY

(LORIMAR/PARAMOUNT) Producer, Freddie Fields; Director, John Huston; Screenplay, Evan Jones, Yabo Yablonsky; Story, Yabo Yablonsky, Djordje Milicevic, Jeff Maguire; Photography, Gerry Fisher; Design, J. Dennis Washington; Editor, Roberto Silvi; Associate Producer, Annie Fargue; Executive Producer, Gordon McLendon; Music, Bill Conti; Soccer Plays, Pele; Costumes, Tom Bronson; Assistant Director, Elie Cohn; A Co-Production of the Victory Company and Tom Stern in association with Andy Vajna and Mario Kassar; In Metrocolor, Panavision and Dolby Stereo; 117 minutes; Rated PG; July release.

CAST

The Players: Sylvester Stallone (Robert Hatch), Michael Caine (John Colby), Pele (Luis Fernandez), Bobby Moore (Terry Brady), Osvaldo Ardiles (Carlos Rey), Paul Van Himst (Michel Fileu), Kazimierz Deyna (Paul Wolchek), Hallvar Thorensen (Gunnar Hilsson), Mike Summerbee (Sid Harmor), Co Prins (Pieter Van Beck), Russell Osman (Doug Clure), John Wark (Arthur Hayes), Soren Linsted (Erik Borge), Kevin O'Calloghan (Tony Lewis), The Germans: Max Von Sydow (Major Karl Von Steiner), Gary Waldhorn (Coach Mueller), George Mikell (Kommandant), Laurie Sivell (Goalie), Arthur Brauss (Lutz), Robin Turner (Player), Michael Wolf (Lang), Jurgen Andersen (Propaganda Civilian), David Shawyer (Strauss), Werner Roth (Team Captain Baumann), The French: Amidou (Andre), Benoit Ferreux (Jean Paul), Jean Francois Stevenin (Claude), Jack Lenoir (Georges), Folton Gera (Viktor), Carole Laure (Renee), The English: Tim Pigott-Smith (Rose), Julian Curry (Shurlock), Clive Merrison (The Forger), Maurice Roeves (Pyrie), Michael Cochrane (Farrell), Jack Kendrick (Williams), Daniel Massey (Col. Waldron), Commentators: Anton Diffring (Chief Commentator), Gunter Wolbert (German), Capacci Eolo (Italian), Michel Drhey (French)

Right: Sylvester Stallone (standing center) and international soccer stars in film
Top: Sylvester Stallone, Pele
© Lorimar Productions

Max von Sydow, Michael Caine

Sylvester Stallone, Carole Laure

BLOW OUT

(FILMWAYS) Producer, George Litto; Direction and Screenplay, Brian DePalma; Executive Producer/Production Manager, Fred Caruso; Photography, Vilmos Zsigmond; Assistant Director, Joe Napolitano; Editor, Paul Hirsch; Designer, Paul Sylbert; Sets, Jeannine Oppewall; Costumes, Vicki Sanchez; Music, Pino Donaggio; In Panavision, Dolby Stereo and color; 147 minutes; Rated R; July release.

CAST

Jack	John Travolta
Sally	Nancy Allen
Burke	John Lithgow
Manny Karp	Dennis Franz
Sam	Peter Boyden
Frank Donohue	Curt May
Jim	Ernest McClure
Anchor Man #1	Dave Roberts
Jack Manners	Maurice Copeland
Joan (Anchor Woman)	Claire Carter
Detective	John Aquino
McRyan	John Hoffmeister
Officer Nelson	Patrick McNamara
Lawrence Henry	Terrence Currier
Policeman	Tom McCarthy
Campus Guard	Dean Bennett

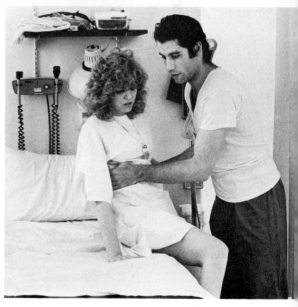

Top: John Travolta Right: Dennis Franz, Nancy Allen
Below: John Lithgow, Allen; Travolta, Allen
© Filmways Pictures

Nancy Allen, John Travolta

53

S.O.B.

(LORIMAR/PARAMOUNT) Producers, Blake Edwards, Tony Adams; Direction and Screenplay, Blake Edwards; Photography, Harry Stradling; Designer, Roger Maus; Editor, Ralph E. Winters; Music, Henry Mancini; Executive Producer, Michael B. Wolf; Associate Producer, Gerald T. Nutting; Art Director, William Craig Smith; Costumes, Theadora Van Runkle; Choreographer, Paddy Stone; Assistant Directors, L. Andrew Stone, Emmitt-Leon O'Neill; In Panavision and Metrocolor; 121 minutes; Rated R; July release.

CAST

Sally Miles	Julie Andrews
Tim Culley	William Holden
Mavis	Marisa Berenson
Dick Benson	Larry Hagman
Herb Maskowitz	Robert Loggia
Gary Murdock	Stuart Margolin
Felix Farmer	Richard Mulligan
Dr. Irving Finegarten	Robert Preston
Willard	Craig Stevens
Polly Reed	Loretta Swit
David Blackman	Robert Vaughn
Ben Coogan	Robert Webber
Eva Brown	Shelley Winters
Lila	Jennifer Edwards
Capitol Studios Vice-President	John Pleshette
Guard	Ken Swofford
Chinese Chef	Benson Fong
Guru	Larry Storch
Mortician	Byron Kane
Jogger	Stiffe Tanney
Babs	Rosanna Arquette
Capitol Studios Vice-President	John Lawlor
Lab Manager	Hamilton Camp
Gardener	Bert Rosario
Sam Marshall	David Young
Mortician's Wife	Virginia Gregg
Tommy Taylor	Katherine MacMurray
Barker	Paddy Stone
Clive Lytell	Gene Nelson

and Joe Penny, Stephen Johnson, Pat Colbert, Erica Yohn, Charles Lampkin, Kevin Justrich, Kimberly Woodward, Scott Arthur Allen, Corbin Bernsen, Joseph Benti, Rebecca Edwards, Neil Flanagan, Todd Howland, Jill Jaress, Alexandra Johnson, Len Lawson, Shelby Leverington, Gisele Lindley, Dominick Mazzie, Fay McKenzie, Bill McLaughlin, Tony Miller, Dave Morick, Charles Parks, Charles Rowe, James Purcell, Gay Rowan, Borah Silver, Ken Smolka, Henry Sutton, Noel Toy, Howard Vann, Sharri Zak

Top Left: Julie Andrews Below: Julie Andrews, Robert Webber, Richard Mulligan, William Holden
© **Lorimar Productions**

Jennifer Edwards, Robert Preston

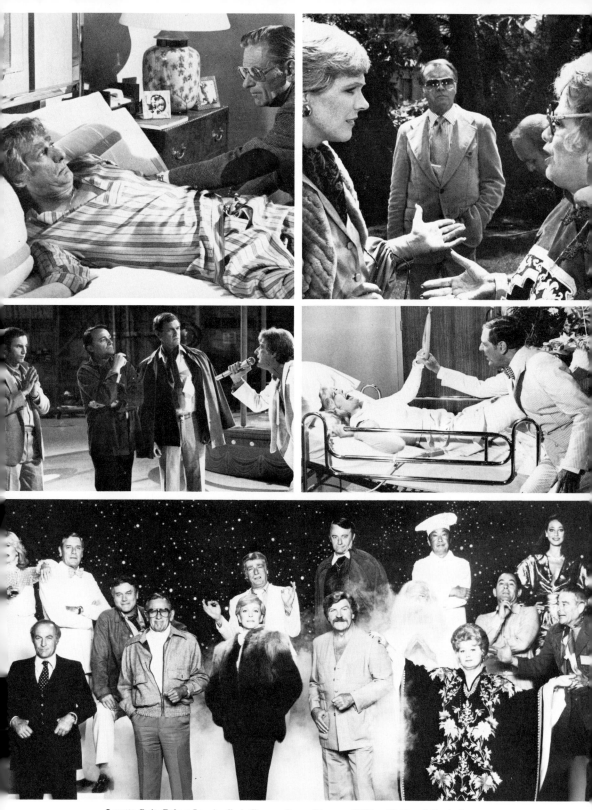

Loretta Swit, Robert Loggia, Craig Stevens, Larry Hagman, William Holden, Julie Andrews,
Richard Mulligan, Robert Preston, Robert Vaughn, Larry Storch, Benson Fong, Shelley
Winters, Stuart Margolin, Marisa Berenson, Robert Webber Top: Mulligan, Holden; Andrews, Winters;
Below: John Pleshette, Vaughn, Hagman, Mulligan; Swit, Stevens

55

ARTHUR

(ORION/WARNER BROS.) Executive Producer, Charles H. Joffe; Producer, Robert Greenhut; Direction and Screenplay, Steve Gordon; Music, Burt Bacharach; Lyrics, Carole Bayer Sager; Photography, Fred Schuler; Editor, Susan E. Morse; Designer, Stephen Hendrickson; Costumes, Jane Greenwood; Assistant Directors, Robert Greenhut, Thomas Reilly; In Technicolor; 117 minutes; July release.

CAST

Arthur Bach	Dudley Moore
Linda Marolla	Liza Minnelli
Hobson	John Gielgud
Martha Bach	Geraldine Fitzgerald
Susan Johnson	Jill Eikenberry
Burt Johnson	Stephen Elliott
Bitterman	Ted Ross
Ralph Marolla	Barney Martin
Stanford Bach	Thomas Barbour
Gloria	Anne DeSalvo
Hooker	Marjorie Barnes
Oak Room Maitre D'	Dillon Evans
Uncle Peter	Maurice Copeland
Aunt Pearl	Justine Johnston
Oak Room Waiter	Paul Vincent
Secretary	Mary Alan Hokanson
Executive	Paul Gleason
Saleslady	Phyllis Somerville
Security Guard	Irving Metzman
Kids in street	Joe Doolan, John Doolan, Melissa Ballan
Mrs. Nesbitt	Florence Tarlow
Plant Store Owner	Lou Jacobi
Prize Man	Gordon Press
Harriet	Marcella Lowry
Johnson Butler	Jerome Collamore
Waiter	Mark Fleischman
Perry's Wife	Helen Hanft
Perry	John Bentley
Racetrack Owner	Raymond Serra
Preston	Peter Evans
Party Guest	Dominic Guastaferro
Orderly	Phil Oxnam
Bill	Richard Hamilton
Bartender	George Riddle
Man in coffee shop	Lawrence Tierney
Lady in coffee shop	Bobo Lewis
Wedding Guests	B. Constance Barry, Kurt Schlesinger

Top: Dudley Moore
© Orion Pictures

Liza Minnelli

1981 ACADEMY AWARD FOR BEST SUPPORTING ACTOR (JOHN GIELGUD), BEST SONG (BEST THAT YOU CAN DO)

John Gielgud Top: Dudley Moore, Liza Minnelli

THEY ALL LAUGHED

(20th CENTURY-FOX) Producers, George Morfogen, Blaine Novak; Executive Producer, Mike Moder; Associate Producer, Russell Schwartz; Direction and Screenplay, Peter Bogdanovich; Photography, Robby Muller; Music, Douglas Dilge; Editor, Scott Vickrey; Art Director, Kert Lundell; Assistant Directors, Robert Girolami, Henry Bronchtein; A Copa de Oro Picture; A Time-Life Films Production in Movielab Color; 115 minutes; Rated PG; August release.

CAST

Angela Niotes	Audrey Hepburn
John Russo	Ben Gazzara
Charles Rutledge	John Ritter
Christy Miller	Colleen Camp
Sam (Deborah Wilson)	Patti Hansen
Dolores Martin	Dorothy Stratten
Leon Leondopolous	George Morfogen
Arthur Brodsky	Blaine Novak
Jose	Sean Ferrer
Amy Lester	Linda MacEwen
Michael Niotes	Glenn Scarpelli
Stavros Niotes	Vassily Lambrinos
Stefania Russo	Antonia Bogdanovich
Georgina Russo	Alexandra Bogdanovich
Barbara Jo	Sheila Stodden
Tulips	Lisa Dunsheath
Sylvia	Joyce Hyser
Rita	Elizabeth Pena
Martin	Riccardo Bertoni
Laura	Shawn Casey

and Earl Poole Ball, Jo-El Sonnier, Eric Kaz, Ken Kosek, Larry Campbell, Lincoln Schleifer, John Sholle, Brigitte Catapano, Parris Bruckner, Vivien Landau, Lillian Silverstone, Steve Cole, Steven Fromewick, Tzi Ma, William Craft, William DeNino, Kelly Donnally, Linda Ray, Andrea Weber, Spike Spigener, Nick Micskey, Robert Hawes, Michael McGifford, Vittorio Tiburz, Alex MacArthur, George Cardini, Robert Skilling, Kennely Noble, Anthony Paige, Violetta Landek, Brandy Roven, Joan Lauren, Debora Lass, Noel King, Don Marino, John Murray, Sharon Spits, Marty Greene, Harry Matson, Brett Smrz, Brian Smrz, Alex Stevens, Victoria Van Der Kloot

Colleen Camp, Blaine Novak, John Ritter Top: Ben Gazzara, Audrey Hepburn
© Time-Life Productions

CHU CHU AND THE PHILLY FLASH

(20th CENTURY-FOX) Executive Producer, Melvin Simon; Producer, Jay Weston; Director, David Lowell Rich; Screenplay, Barbara Dana; Story, Henry Barrow; Music, Pete Rugolo; Photography, Victor J. Kemper; Design, Daniel Lomino; Editor, Argyle Nelson; Costumes, Ron Talsky; Associate Producer, Tony Wade; Assistant Directors, Mike Salamunovich, Bradley Gross; Choreography, Don Crichton; In DeLuxe Color; 100 minutes; Rated PG; August release.

CAST

Flash	Alan Arkin
Emily	Carol Burnett
Commander	Jack Warden
Johnson	Danny Aiello
Charlie	Adam Arkin
Morgan	Danny Glover
Vince	Sid Haig
B. J.	Vincent Schiavelli
Consuelo	Ruth Buzzi
Vittorio	Vito Scotti
Landlord	Lou Jacobi
Betty	Barbara Dana
Harry	Scott Beach
Clem	Geoff Hoyle
Butts	Morgan Upton
Car Woman	Neile McQueen
Puppeteer	Tony Arkin
Poet	Francine Lembi
Wally	Dabbs Greer
Snyder	John Steadman
Mr. Sitro	Jerry Anderson
Bum	Arnold Johnson
Russian	Ray Reinhardt
Cat Men	Sammy Warren, Steven Hirsch
Ticket Lady	Jennifer Ann Lee
Frankie	Michael Grodenchik
Little Girl	Valerie Caplan
Little Boy	Matthew Hautau
Passerby	Matthew Arkin
Hot Dog Men	Jim Haynie, Eugene G. Choy, Ralph Chesse
Mimes	Jeanne Lauren, Carl Arena, Daniel Forrest

Right Center: Jack Warden, Ruth Buzzi
Above: Adam Arkin, Carol Burnett, Alan Arkin
Top: Vito Scotti, Carol Burnett, Alan Arkin
© Simon Film Productions

Carol Burnett, Alan Arkin

Carol Burnett, Barbara Dana

FIRST MONDAY IN OCTOBER

(PARAMOUNT) Producers, Paul Heller, Martha Scott; Director, Ronald Neame; Screenplay, Jerome Lawrence, Robert E. Lee from their play of same title; Photography, Fred J. Koenekamp; Music, Ian Fraser; Design, Philip M. Jefferies; Editor, Peter E. Berger; Assistant Directors, Thomas Lofaro, Chris Soldo; Associate Producer, Charles Matthau; Art Director, John V. Cartwright; In Panavision, Metrocolor; 95 minutes; Rated R; August release.

CAST

Dan Snow	Walter Matthau
Ruth Loomis	Jill Clayburgh
Chief Justice Crawford	Barnard Hughes
Christine Snow	Jan Sterling
Mason Woods	James Stephens
Bill Russell	Joshua Bryant
Justice Harold Webb	Wiley Harker
Justice Waldo Thompson	F. J. O'Neil
Justice Josiah Clewes	Charles Lampkin
Justice Benjamin Halperin	Lew Palter
Justice Richard Carey	Richard McMurray
Justice Ambrose Quincy	Herb Vigran
Committee Chairman	Edmund Stoiber
Nebraska Attorney	Noble Willingham
Hostile Senator	Richard McKenzie
Storekeeper	Ann Doran
Norman	Dallas Alinder
Ms. Radabaugh	Olive Dunbar
Southern Senator	Hugh Gillin
Court Marshall	James E. Brodhead
Custodians	Arthur Adams, Sig Frohlich
Plaintiff's Attorney	Nick Angotti
Waitress	Jeanne Joe
Robinson	Christopher Tenney
Photographer	Richard Balin
TV Commentator	Martin Agronsky

and Bob Sherman, Ray Colbert (Senators), Carol Coggin (Attorney), Kenneth DuMain (Guard), Stanley Lawrence (Court Guard), Dick Winslow (Barber), Joe Terry, Sandy Chapin (Clerks), Dudley Knight (Assistant Manager), Edwin M. Adams (Clergyman), Ronnie Thomas (Firing Party Commander), Jeff Scheulen (Ambulance Attendant), Jordan Charney (Doctor), Mary Munday (Head Nurse), Bebe Drake-Massey (Nurse), Richard de Angeles (News Producer), Jim Vanko (Chief Ranger), Dale House (Pilot), William G. Clark, Wendy E. Taylor (Cab Drivers)

Jill Clayburgh, Barnard Hughes Top Left: Jill Clayburgh, and below with Walter Matthau, James Stephens (R) © Paramount Pictures

**Walter Matthau, Barnard Hughes Above: Matthau,
Jill Clayburgh Top: Ann Doran, Matthau**

**Walter Matthau, Jill Clayburgh (also top)
Above: Clayburgh, Joshua Bryant**

BODY HEAT

(LADD/WARNER BROS.) Producer, Fred T. Gallo; Direction and Screenplay, Lawrence Kasdan; Music, John Barry; Photography, Richard H. Kline; Design, Bill Kenney; Editor, Carol Littleton; Associate Producer, Robert Grand; Assistant Directors, Michael Grillo, Jeffrey Chernov; Costumes, Renie Conley; Choreographer, Tad Tadlock; In Technicolor; 113 minutes; Rated R; August release.

CAST

Ned Racine	William Hurt
Matty Walker	Kathleen Turner
Edmund Walker	Richard Crenna
Peter Lowenstein	Ted Danson
Oscar Grace	J. A. Preston
Teddy Lewis	Mickey Rourke
Mary Ann	Kim Zimmer
Stella	Jane Hallaren
Roz Kraft	Lanna Saunders
Miles Hardin	Michael Ryan
Heather Kraft	Carola McGuinness
Judge Costanza	Larry Marko
Beverly	Deborah Lucchessi
Angela	Lynn Hallowell
Michael Glenn	Thom J. Sharp
Mrs. Singer	Ruth Thom
Glenda	Diane Lewis
Prison Trustee	Robert Traynor
Nurse	Meg Kasdan
Betty, the housekeeper	Ruth P. Strahan
Hostess at Tulios	Filomena Triscari
Man on the beach	Bruce A. Lee
Cuban Trio .. Ramiro Velasco, Tomas Choy, Servio T. Moreno

Richard Crenna Top: William Hurt, Kathleen Turner
© The Ladd Co.

Kathleen Turner, William Hurt (also top right)
Top Left: J. A. Preston, William Hurt, Ted Danson

PRINCE OF THE CITY

(ORION/WARNER BROS.) Producer, Burtt Harris; Director, Sidney Lumet; Executive Producer, Jay Presson Allen; Screenplay, Jay Presson Allen, Sidney Lumet; Based on book by Robert Daley; Photography, Andrzej Bartkowiak; Designer, Tony Walton; Costumes, Anna Hill Johnstone; Editor, John J. Fitzstephens; Music, Paul Chihara; Associate Producer, Ray Hartwick; Assistant Directors, Alan Hopkins, Robert E. Warren; Art Director, Edward Pisoni; In color; 167 minutes; Rated R; August release.

CAST

Daniel Ciello	Treat Williams
Gus Levy	Jerry Orbach
Joe Marinaro	Richard Foronjy
Bill Mayo	Don Billett
Dom Bando	Kenny Marino
Gino Mascone	Carmine Caridi
Raf Alvarez	Tony Page
Rick Cappalino	Norman Parker
Brooks Paige	Paul Roebling
Santimassino	Bob Balaban
D. P. Polito	James Tolkan
Mario Vincente	Steve Inwood
Carla Ciello	Lindsay Crouse
Ronnie Ciello	Matthew Laurance
Socks Ciello	Tony Turco
Nick Napoli	Ron Maccone
Dave DeBennedeto	Ron Karabatsos
Carl Alagretti	Tony DiBenedetto
Rocky Gazzo	Tony Munafo
The King	Robert Christian
Sam Heinsdorff	Lee Richardson
Tug Barnes	Lane Smith
Marcel Sardino	Cosmo Allegretti
Mr. Kanter	Bobby Alto
Michael Blomberg	Michael Beckett

and Burton Collins (Young Virginia Guard), Henry Ferrantino (Older Guard), Carmine Foresta (Ernie), Conard Fowkes (Elroy), Peter Friedman (D.A. Goldman), Peter Michael Goetz (Attorney DeLuth), Lance Henricksen (D. A. Burano), Eddie Jones (Ned), Don Leslie (D. A. Amato), Dana Lorge (Ann), Harry Madsen (Bubba), E. D. Miller (Sgt. Edelman), Cynthia Nixon (Jeannie), Lionel Pina (Sancho), Jose Santana (Jose)

Don Billett, Jerry Orbach, Richard Foronjy, Treat Williams (also top left)
© Orion Pictures

Treat Williams, Lindsay Crouse Top: (L) Williams, also (R) with Richard Foronjy
Center: Williams, Norman Parker, Paul Roebling; Williams, Jerry Orbach

Beverly D'Angelo, Beau Bridges
Above: Frances Lee McCain, William Devane

HONKY TONK FREEWAY

(UNIVERSAL/ASSOCIATED FILM DISTRIBUTION) Producers, Don Boyd, Howard W. Koch, Jr.; Director, John Schlesinger; Screenplay, Edward Clinton; Photography, John Bailey; Editor, Jim Clark; Art Director, Edwin O'Donovan; Costumes, Ann Roth; Music, George Martin, Elmer Bernstein; Assistant Director, Benjy Rosenberg; In Technicolor; 107 minutes; Rated R; August release.

CAST

Duane Hansen	Beau Bridges
Sherm	Hume Cronyn
Carmen Shelby	Beverly D'Angelo
Mayor Calo	William Devane
Eugene	George Dzundza
Ericka	Teri Garr
Osvaldo	Joe Grifasi
Snapper	Howard Hesseman
T. J. Tupus	Paul Jabara
Sister Mary Clarise	Geraldine Page
Carol	Jessica Tandy
Claire Calo	Frances Lee McCain
Sister Mary Magdalen	Deborah Rush
Betty Boo Radley	Alice Beardsley

Top: William Devane (L) George Dzundza, Joe
Grifasi © Universal City Studios

CONTINENTAL DIVIDE

(UNIVERSAL) Producer, Bob Larson; Director, Michael Apted; Screenplay, Lawrence Kasdan; Executive Producers, Steven Spielberg, Bernie Brillstein; Music, Michael Small; Associate Producers, Zelda Barron, Jack Rosenthal; Assistant Director, Kim Kurumada; Theme Song ("Never Say Goodbye"), Michael Small, Carol Bayer Sager; Sung by Helen Reddy; Costumes, Moss Mabry; In Technicolor; 103 minutes; Rated PG; September release.

CAST

Souchak	John Belushi
Nell	Blair Brown
Howard	Allen Goorwitz
Sylvia	Carlin Glynn
Possum	Tony Ganios
Yablonowitz	Val Avery
Deke	Liam Russell
Fiddle	Everett Smith
Train Conductor	Bill Henderson
Hellinger	Bruce Jarchow
Jimmy	Eddie Schwartz
Mr. Feeney	Harold Holmes
Mrs. Feeney	Elizabeth Young

Right: Blair Brown, John Belushi
Below: Brown, Tony Ganios
© Universal City Studios

John Belushi, Blair Brown
Above: Allen Goorwitz, Belushi

John Belushi

ONLY WHEN I LAUGH

(COLUMBIA) Producers, Roger M. Rothstein, Neil Simon; Director, Glenn Jordan; Screenplay, Neil Simon; Based on his play "The Gingerbread Lady"; Photography, David M. Walsh; Design, Albert Brenner; Music, David Shire; Editor, John Wright; Costumes, Ann Roth; Assistant Directors, Bill Beasley, Jim Van Wyck; Art Director, Jim Van Wyck; In Metrocolor; 120 minutes; Rated R; September release.

CAST

Georgia	Marsha Mason
Polly	Kristy McNichol
Jimmy	James Coco
Toby	Joan Hackett
David	David Dukes
Actor (Lou)	John Bennett Perry
Man	Guy Boyd
Dr. Komack	Ed Moore
Tom	Byron Webster
Mr. Tarloff	Peter Coffield
Adam Kasabian	Mark Schubb
Receptionist	Ellen LaGamba
Nurse Garcia	Venida Evans
Heidi	Nancy Nagler
Jason	Dan Monahan
Paul	Michael Ross
Kyle	Tom Ormeny
Waiter	Ken Weisbrath
Director (George)	Henry Olek
Doreen	Jane Atkins
Don	Kevin Bacon
Gary	Ron Levine
Denise Summers	Rebecca Stanley
Bartender	Nick LaPadula
Super	Phillip Lindsay
Super's Wife	Birdie Hale
Father	Wayne Framson
Manuel	Jon Vargas

© Columbia Pictures

Kristy McNichol, Marsha Mason
Top: Marsha Mason

Joan Hackett

James Coco, Marsha Mason
Top: Kristy McNichol, Marsha Mason

RAGGEDY MAN

(UNIVERSAL) Producers, Burt Weissbourd, William D. Wittliff; Director, Jack Fisk; Screenplay, William D. Wittliff; Photography, Ralf Bode; Art Director, John Lloyd; Editor, Edward Warschilka; Music, Jerry Goldsmith; Associate Producer, Terry Nelson; Costumes, Joe I. Tompkins; Assistant Director, Peter Gries; Original Sound Track on MGM Records and Tapes; In Technicolor; 94 minutes; Rated PG; September release.

CAST

Nita	Sissy Spacek
Teddy	Eric Roberts
Bailey	Sam Shepard
Calvin	William Sanderson
Arnold	Tracey Walter
Rigby	R. G. Armstrong
Harry	Henry Thomas
Henry	Carey Hollis, Jr.
Mr. Calloway	Ed Geldart
Sheriff	Bill Thurman
Jean Lester	Suzi McLaughlin
Crescencio the Barkeeper	Lupe Juarez
Miss Pud	Jessie Lee Fulton
Miss Beulah	LuBelle Camp
Ticket Taker	James N. Harrell
Old Man	Lee Wackerhagen
Deputy	Dave Davis
Pilots	Archie Donahue, Marvin Gardner

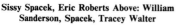

Sissy Spacek, Eric Roberts Above: William
Sanderson, Spacek, Tracey Walter

Top: Sam Shepard Below: Carey Hollis, Jr.,
Henry Thomas, Sissy Spacek, Eric Roberts
© Universal City Studios

70

SO FINE

(WARNER BROS.) Producer, Mike Lobell; Direction and Screenplay, Andrew Bergman; Music, Ennio Morricone; Photography, James A. Contner; Associate Producers, Ray Hartwick, Mike Haley; Editor, Alan Heim; Design, Santo Loquasto; Assistant Directors, Mike Haley, Gaetano Lisi, Ellen Rauch; Art Director, Paul Eads; Costumes, Rose Trimarco, Bill Christians; Chorographer, Grover Dale; In Technicolor; 91 minutes; Rated R; September release.

CAST

Bobby	Ryan O'Neal
Jack	Jack Warden
Lira	Mariangela Melato
Eddie	Richard Kiel
Chairman Lincoln	Fred Gwynne
Sam Schlotzman	Mike Kellin
Professor McCarthy	David Rounds
Professor Yarnell	Joel Stedman
Sylvia	Angela Pietro Pinto
Jay Augustine	Michael Lombard
Vicki	Jessica James
Sir Alec	Bruce Millholland
Dave	Merwin Goldsmith
Accountant	Irving Metzman
Waitress in House of Pancakes	Lois DeBanzie
Rick	Rick Lieberman
Mr. Eddie's Associates	Anthony Siricco, Jr., Michael LaGuardia
Wise Guy in disco	Chip Zien
Gas Station Attendant	Bill Luhrs
Lino	Dick Boccelli
Manicurist	Lydia Laurens

and Margaret Hall (Saleslady), Sally Jane Heit (Shopper), Henry Lawrence (Security Guard), James Hong, Danny Kwan (Orientals), Paul Price (Man in towel), Tyra Farrell (Receptionist), Joseph Montabo, Jose Machado (Shipping Clerks), Sophie Schwab (Sophie), Jerome Binder (Sy), Hy Mencher (Hy), Maria Tai, Beda Elliot (Seamstresses), Joseph Ilardi (Gus), John Bentley (Elevator Starter), Herb Schlein (Delivery Boy), Alma Cuervo (Prof. Adler), John Stockwell (Jim), Beverly May (Mrs. Lincoln), P. K. Fields (Coed in office), Webster Whinery, Kathie Flusk (Couple in Volkswagon), Randy Jones, Christopher Loomis (Campus Cops), Hyla Marrow, Gail Lawrence (Nuns), Martha Gaylord (Texas Buyer), Bernie McInerny (St. Paul Buyer), Alan Leach, Pamela Lewis (Buyers), Jim Jansen (Conductor), Pierre Epstein (Prompter), Tony Aylward, Todd Isaacson (Stage Managers), Adam Stolarsky (Enzo), Judith Cohen (Renata)

Right: Mariangela Melato, Ryan O'Neal, Richard Kiel **Top:** Mariangela Melato, Ryan O'Neal © Warner Bros.

Jack Warden, Fred Gwynne Mariangela Melato, Ryan O'Neal

Rick Lieberman, Merwin Goldsmith, Ryan O'Neal

MOMMIE DEAREST

(PARAMOUNT) Producer, Frank Yablans; Director, Frank Perry; Screenplay, Frank Yablans, Frank Perry, Tracy Hotchner, Robert Getchell; Based on book by Christina Crawford; Executive Producers, David Koontz, Terence O'Neill; Photography, Paul Lohmann; Design, Bill Malley; Editor, Peter E. Berger; Music, Henry Mancini; Associate Producer, Neil A. Machlis; Costumes, Irene Sharaff; Assistant Directors, Michael Daves, Alan B. Curtiss, Robert J. Doherty; Art Director, Harold Michelson; In Metrocolor; 129 minutes; Rated PG; September release.

CAST

Joan Crawford	Faye Dunaway
Christina Crawford (Adult)	Diana Scarwid
Greg Savitt	Steve Forrest
L. B. Mayer	Howard Da Silva
Christina as a child	Mara Hobel
Carol Ann	Rutanya Alda
Al Steele	Harry Goz
Ted Gelber	Michael Edwards
Barbara Bennett	Jocelyn Brando
Mrs. Chadwick	Priscilla Pointer
Captain	Joe Abdullah
Jimmy (Photographer)	Gary Allen
Connie	Selma Archerd
Woman Guest	Adrian Aron
Christopher Crawford (Adult)	Xander Berkeley
Bruce, Actor in soap	Matthew Campion
Mother Superior	Carolyn Coates
Interviewer	Jerry Douglas
Mother Superior (Orphanage)	Margaret Fairchild
Ginny	Ellen Feldman
Master of Ceremonies	James Kirkwood
Beth Simpson	Virginia Kiser

and Phillip R. Allen, Michael D. Gainsborough, Matthew Faison (Executives), Robert Harper (David), Cathy Lind Hayes (Nurse), Victoria James (Photographer), Dawn Jeffory (Vera), S. John Launer (Chairman of Board), Russ Marin (Funeral Director), Nicholas Mele (Assistant Director), Belita Moreno (Belinda Rosenberg), Warren Munson (Lawyer), Alice Nunn (Helga), Norman Palmer (Male Guest), David F. Price (Tony), Jeremy Scott Reinbolt (Christopher Crawford at 5), Michael Talbott (Driver), Arthur Taxier (Decorator), Joseph Warren (Mr. Dodd), Erica Wexler (Susan)

Left: Steve Forrest, Faye Dunaway Above: Dunaway,
Howard Da Silva Top: Faye Dunaway
© Paramount Pictures

Mara Hobel, Jeremy Scott Reinbolt,
Faye Dunaway

Mara Hobel, Faye Dunaway

Faye Dunaway, and above with Harry Goz
Top with Diana Scarwid

Faye Dunaway Above: Xander Berkeley, Diana
Scarwid (also top)

TRUE CONFESSIONS

(UNITED ARTISTS) Producers, Irwin Winkler, Robert Chartoff; Director, Ulu Grosbard; Screenplay, John Gregory Dunne, Joan Didion; Based on novel by John Gregory Dunne; Music, Georges Delerue; Photography, Owen Roisman; Design, Stephen S. Grimes; Editor, Lynzee Klingman; Costumes, Joe I. Tompkins; Associate Producer, James D. Brubaker; Assistant Directors, Tom Mack, Bill Elvin, Duncan S. Henderson; Art Director, W. Stewart Campbell; Choreographer, Alfonse L. Palermo; In Technicolor; 108 minutes; Rated R; September release.

CAST

Des Spellacy	Robert DeNiro
Tom Spellacy	Robert Duvall
Jack Amsterdam	Charles Durning
Dan T. Campion	Ed Flanders
Seamus Fargo	Burgess Meredith
Brenda Samuels	Rose Gregorio
Cardinal Danaher	Cyril Cusack
Frank Crotty	Kenneth McMillan
Howard Terkel	Dan Hedeya
Mrs. Fazenda	Gwen Van Dam
Mr. Fazenda	Tom Hill
Mrs. Spellacy	Jeanette Nolan
Eduardo Duarte	Jorge Cervera, Jr.
Bride	Susan Myers
Whore	Louisa Moritz
Lorna Keane	Darwyn Carson
Sonny McDonough	Pat Corley
Reporter #2	Matthew Faison
Ambulance Driver	Richard Foronjy
Deputy Coroner	Joe Medalis
Coroner Wong	James Hong
Detectives	Ron Ryan, Louis Basile, Paul Valentine
Older Nun	Louise Fitch
Nun #2	Margery Nelson
Brenda's Trick	Fredric Cook

and Kirk Brennan (Acolyte), Fred Dennis (Man), Shelly Batt (Girl), Mary Munday (Nun), Colin Hamilton (Headwaiter), Amanda Cleveland (Lois), Pierrino Mascarino (Suspect), Michael Callahan (Sub-Deacon), Harry Pavelis (Cardinal's Attendant), Luisa Leschin (Towel Girl), Bob Arthur, Bill Furnell (Newscasters), Sig Frohlich (Waiter), Steve Arvin (Radio Announcer), Steve Powers (Photographer), Joseph H. Choi (Pathologist), Sharon Miller (Movie Star), Kevin Breslin (Boy), Jeff Howard (Priest #2), Harry Duncan (Priest at banquet)

Left: Robert DeNiro, Jeanette Nolan, Robert Duvall Above: Duvall, DeNiro Top: DeNiro
© United Artists

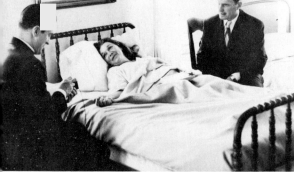

Robert Duvall, Kenneth McMillan

Burgess Meredith, Robert DeNiro, Cyril Cusack

Robert DeNiro, Burgess Meredith Above:
DeNiro, Robert Duvall Top: Charles
Durning

Robert Duvall, Robert DeNiro Above:
Charles Durning Top: DeNiro

RICH AND FAMOUS

(MGM/UNITED ARTISTS) Producer, William Allyn; Director, George Cukor; Screenplay, Gerald Ayres; Based on play "Old Acquaintance" by John Van Druten; Photography, Don Peterman; Design, Jan Scott; Art Director, Fred Harpman; Editor, John F. Burnett; Music, Georges Delerue; Costumes, Theoni V. Aldredge; Assistant Directors, James Quinn, Tom Seidman; Art Director, James A. Taylor; In Metrocolor; 117 minutes; Rated R; October release.

CAST

Liz Hamilton	Jacqueline Bisset
Merry Noel Blake	Candice Bergen
Doug Blake	David Selby
Chris Adams	Hart Bochner
Jules Levi	Steven Hill
Debby at 18	Meg Ryan
The Boy Jim	Matt Lattanzi
Ginger Trinidad	Daniel Faraldo
Debby at 8	Nicole Eggert
Martin Fornam	Joe Maross
Judy Heller	Kres Mersky
Martha Antilles	Cloyce Morrow
Voice (UCLA)	Cheryl Robinson
Desk Clerk	Allan Warnick
Max's Wife	Ann Risley
Max's Son	Damion Sheller
Max's Daughter	Haley Fox
Professor Fields	Fay Kanin
Stewardess	Tara Simpson
Waiter	Herb Graham
Clerk in Cartier	Charlotte Moore
Waldorf Doorman	William Schilling
Limo Driver	John Perkins
Waiter in hallway	Herb Bress
Photographer	Alan Berliner

Top: Jacqueline Bisset, Candice Bergen
Below: Hart Bochner, Bisset
© MGM Film Co.

Candice Bergen, Jacqueline Bisset (also above)
Top: Bergen, David Selby

LOOKER

(LADD CO./WARNER BROS.) Producer, Howard Jeffrey; Direction and Screenplay, Michael Crichton; Photography, Paul Lohmann; Design, Dean Edward Mitzner; Editor, Carl Kress; Music, Barry DeVorzon; Associate Producer, John Lugar; Assistant Directors, Scott Easton, John Kretchmer; Art Director, Jack G. Taylor, Jr.; Costumes, Betsy Cox; In Technicolor, Panavision and Dolby Stereo; 94 minutes; Rated PG; October release.

CAST

Dr. Larry Roberts	Albert Finney
John Reston	James Coburn
Cindy	Susan Dey
Jennifer Long	Leigh Taylor-Young
Lt. Masters	Dorian Harewood
Moustache Man	Tim Rossovich
Dr. Jim Belfield	Darryl Hickman
Tina	Kathryn Witt
Lisa	Terri Welles
Senator Harrison	Michael Gainsborough
Candy	Ashley Cox
Ellen	Donna Benz
Jan	Catherine Parks
Commercial Director	Terry Kiser
Cindy's Mother	Georgann Johnson
Cindy's Father	Richard Venture
Masters' Assistant	Anthony Charnota
Scanning Room Technician	Terrence McNally
Guard	David Adams
Policemen	John Sanderford, Scott Mulhern
Suzy	Jeana Tomasino
Commercial Producer	Barry Jenner

and Arthur Taxier, Richard Milholland, Darrel Maury, Paul Jasmin, Eloise Hardt, Melissa Prophet, Lila Christianson, Lorna Christianson, Gary Combs, Kelly Black, Jerry Douglas, Randi Brooks, Jesse Logan, Joe Medalis, Estelle Omens, Steve Strong, Tawny Moyer, Dick Christie, Katherine DeHetre, Allison Balson, Adam Starr.

Right: Albert Finney, Michael Crichton
Top: Finney, Dorian Harewood
© The Ladd Co.

Leigh Taylor-Young, Albert Finney

James Coburn

MY DINNER WITH ANDRE

(NEW YORKER) Producers, George W. George, Beverly Karp; Associate Producers, Keith W. Rouse, David Franke; Director, Louis Malle; Screenplay, Wallace Shawn, Andre Gregory; Photography, Jeri Sopanen; Assistant Director, Norman Berns; Design, David Mitchell; Editor, Suzanne Baron; Music, Allen Shawn; Costumes, Jeffrey Ullman; Art Director, Stephen McCabe; In color; 110 minutes; Not rated; October release.

CAST

Wally	Wallace Shawn
Andre	Andre Gregory
Waiter	Jean Lenauer
Bartender	Roy Butler

Top: Andre Gregory
Below: Jean Lenauer

Roy Butler
Top: Wallace Shawn

Wallace Shawn, Andre Gregory (also top)

CHANEL SOLITAIRE

(UNITED FILM DISTRIBUTION) Producer, Larry Spangler; Executive Producer, Eric Rochat; Director, George Kaczender; Photography, Ricardo Aronovich; Costumes, Rosine Delamare; In color; 120 minutes; Rated R; October release.

CAST

Gabrielle Chanel	Marie-France Pisier
Boy Capel	Timothy Dalton
Etienne De Balsan	Rutger Hauer
Emilienne D'Alencon	Karen Black
Adrienne	Brigitte Fossey
Coco Chanel as a child	Liela Frechet

**Right: Timothy Dalton, Marie-France Pisier
Below: Rutger Hauer, Karen Black Left Center:
Timothy Dalton, Marie-France Pisier**

Marie-France Pisier

...... ALL THE MARBLES

(MGM/UNITED ARTISTS) Producer, William Aldrich; Director, Robert Aldrich; Screenplay, Mel Frohman; Photography, Joseph Biroc; Design, Carl Anderson; Editors, Irving C. Rosenblum, Richard Lane; Music, Frank De Vol; Art Director, Beala Neel; Costumes, Bob Mackie; Associate Producers, Walter Blake, Eddie Saeta; Assistant Directors, Tom McCrory, Chuck Myers, Robert Shue, Paul Moen; Choreographer, Kathryn Doby; In Metrocolor; 112 minutes; Rated R; October release.

CAST

Harry	Peter Falk
Iris	Vicki Frederick
Molly	Laurene Landon
Eddie Cisco	Burt Young
Diane	Tracy Reed
June	Ursaline Bryant-King
Solly	Claudette Nevins
Reno Referee	Richard Jaeckel
Big John Stanley	John Hancock
Jerome	Lenny Montana
Merle LeFevre	Charlie Dell
Chick Hearn	Himself
Obese Promoter	Cliff Emmich
Clyde Yamashito	Clyde Kusatu
Joe Greene	Himself
Akron Wrestlers	Marlene Petrilli, Karen McKay
Akron Doctor	Jon Terry
Geisha Doctor	Alvin Hammer
Louise	Angela Aames
Myron	Stanley Brock
Big Mama	Faith Minton

and Susan Mechsner, Leslie Henderson, Taemi Hagiwara, Ayumi Hori, Irma Eugenia Aguilar, Martha Louisa Coello, Gustavo Torres, Paul Greenwood, Adolfo Plascencia, William J. Kulzer, Don Brodie, Lennie Bremen, Gloria Hayes, Perry Cook, Charles Anderson, Randy McClane, Ray Homesley, Steve White, Cosmo Sardo, Ernie Fuentes, Johnnie Decker, Nicholas Shields, Dan Magiera, Susan Barnes, Gary McLarty, Joseph Margo, Ivan Ditmars

Right: Richard Jaeckel, Peter Falk, Tracy Reed, Laurene Landon, Vicki Frederick Top: Frederick, Falk, Landon © MGM Film Co.

Laurene Landon, Peter Falk, Vicki Frederick, Richard Jaeckel, Ursaline Bryant-King, John Hancock, Tracy Reed

ON GOLDEN POND

(UNIVERSAL) Producer, Bruce Gilbert; Director, Mark Rydell; Screenplay, Ernest Thompson from his play of the same title; Photography, Billy Williams; Design, Stephen Grimes; Editor, Robert L. Wolfe; Music, Dave Grusin; Costumes, Dorothy Jeakins; Assistant Directors, Gary Daigler, Venita Ozols; In color; 110 minutes; Rated PG; November release.

CAST

Ethel Thayer	Katharine Hepburn
Norman Thayer, Jr.	Henry Fonda
Chelsea Thayer Wayne	Jane Fonda
Billy Ray	Doug McKeon
Bill Ray	Dabney Coleman
Charlie Martin	William Lanteau
Sumner Todd	Chris Rydell

Top: Jane Fonda, Henry Fonda, Katharine Hepburn
© Universal City Studios

Doug McKeon, Henry Fonda

1981 ACADEMY AWARDS FOR BEST ACTOR (HENRY FONDA), BEST ACTRESS (KATHARINE HEPBURN), BEST ADAPTED SCREENPLAY

Dabney Coleman, Jane Fonda, Katharine
Hepburn, Henry Fonda Above: Hepburn, Fonda
Top: Fonda, Coleman

Henry Fonda, Katharine Hepburn
(also at top) Above: Hepburn

GHOST STORY

(UNIVERSAL) Producer, Burt Weissbourd; Director, John Irvin; Screenplay, Lawrence D. Cohen; Based on novel by Peter Straub; Photography, Jack Cardiff; Editor, Tom Rolf; Co-Producer, Douglas Green; Art Director, Norman Newberry; Assistant Directors, Dan Kolsrud, Phil Bowles; Music, Philippe Sarde; In Technicolor; 110 minutes; Rated R; November release.

CAST

Ricky Hawthorne	Fred Astaire
John Jaffrey	Melvyn Douglas
Edward Wanderley	Douglas Fairbanks, Jr.
Sears James	John Houseman
Don/David	Craig Wasson
Alma/Eva	Alice Krige
Milly	Jacqueline Brookes
Stella	Patricia Neal
Gregory Bate	Miguel Fernandes
Fenny Bate	Lance Holcomb
Young Jaffrey	Mark Chamberlin
Young Hawthorne	Tim Choate
Young Wanderley	Kurt Johnson
Young James	Ken Olin
Sheriff	Brad Sullivan

Left: Fred Astaire
© Universal City Studios

Kurt Johnson, Ken Olin, Tim Choate, Mark Chamberlin

Douglas Fairbanks, Jr., John Houseman, Fred Astaire, Melvyn Douglas
Top: Alice Krige, Craig Wasson

TICKET TO HEAVEN

(UNITED ARTISTS CLASSICS) Executive Producer, Ronald I. Cohen; Producer, Vivienne Leebosh; Co-Producer, Alan Simmonds; Director, R. L. Thomas; Screenplay, R. L. Thomas, Anne Cameron; Based on book "Moonwebs" by Josh Freed; Music, Micky Erbe, Maribeth Solomon; Photography, Richard Leiterman; Editor, Ron Wisman; Assistant Directors, Bill Corcoran, Bruce Moriarty, David Storey; Design, Susan Longmire; Art Director, Jill Scott; Costumes, Lynda Kemp; In color; 107 minutes; Rated PG; November release.

CAST

David	Nick Mancuso
Larry	Saul Rubinek
Ingrid	Meg Foster
Ruthie	Kim Cattrall
Linc Strunk	R. H. Thomson
Lisa	Jennifer Dale
Eric	Guy Boyd
Sarah	Dixie Seatle
Morley	Paul Soles
Mr. Stone	Harvey Atkin
Patrick	Robert Joy
Karl	Stephen Markle
Greg	Timothy Webber
Dr. Dryer	Patrick Brymer
Esther	Marcia Diamond
Danny	Michael Zelnicker
Bonnie	Denise Naples
Paul	Angelo Rizacos
Buffy	Cindy Girling
Sandy	Gina Dick
Simon	Christopher Britton

and Margot Dionne, Claire Pimpare, Lynne Kolber, Lyn Harvey, Josh Freed (Sharing Group), Candace O'Conner (Ginny), Michael Wincott (Gerry), Doris Petrie (Mrs. Foster), David Main (Business Man), Les Rubie (Short Order Cook), Sandra Gies (Airport Bookseller), Susan Hannon (Nanny at mansion), Marie Lynn Hammond (Singer at mansion), Paul Booth, Charlie Gray, Brian Leonard, Ron Nigrini, Craig Stephens, Grant Slater (Musicians)

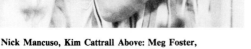
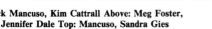

Nick Mancuso, Kim Cattrall Above: Meg Foster,
Jennifer Dale Top: Mancuso, Sandra Gies

Top: Saul Rubinek, Kim Cattrall
Below: Meg Foster, Nick Mancuso, Robert Joy
© United Artists

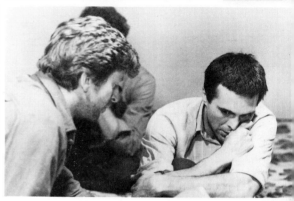

Nick Mancuso, Robert Joy
Top: Mancuso, Stephen Markle

Nick Mancuso, and above with R. H.
Thomson, and top with Saul Rubinek

ABSENCE OF MALICE

(COLUMBIA) Producer-Director, Sydney Pollack; Screenplay, Kurt Luedtke; Executive Producer, Ronald L. Schwary; Photography, Owen Roizman; Music, Dave Grusin; Editor, Sheldon Kahn; Costumes, Bernie Pollack; Assistant Directors, David McGiffert, Rafael Elortegui; A Mirage Enterprises Production in color; 116 minutes; Rated PG; November release.

CAST

Gallagher	Paul Newman
Megan	Sally Field
Rosen	Bob Balaban
Teresa	Melinda Dillon
Malderone	Luther Adler
Waddell	Barry Primus
McAdam	Josef Sommer
Davidek	John Harkins
Quinn	Don Hood
Wells	Wilford Brimley
Eddie Frost	Arnie Ross
Nickie	Anna Marie Napoles
Sarah Wylie	Shelley Spurlock
Hoods	Shawn McAllister, Joe Petrullo
Walker	Rooney Kerwin
John	Oswaldo Calvo
Donna	Clardy Malugen
Secretary	Sharon Anderson
Raggedy Lady	Jody Wilson
Nun	Ilse Earl
Rodriguez	Alfredo Alvarez Colderon
Meersma	Pat Sullivan
Priest	Bill Hindman

and John Archie, Timothy Hawkins, Ricardo Marquez (FBI Agents), Diane Zolten, Kathy Suergiu, Jeff Gillen (Reporters), Ted Bartsch (Beverage Manager), Sugar Ray Mann (Copy Boy), Richard O'Feldman (Driver), Chuck Lupo (Dock Boy), John DiSanti (Longshoreman), Laurie V. Logan (McAdam's Assistant), Patricia Matzdorff (Susan), Gary Van Auken (Marshall), Jack McDermott, Mark Harris, Bobbie-Ellyne Kosstrin, Lynn Parraga, Lee Sandman, Barry Hober (News Staff)

Left: Sally Field, Paul Newman
Top: Paul Newman
© Columbia Pictures

Sally Field

Josef Sommer, Sally Field

Paul Newman Above: Sally Field,
Melinda Dillon Top: Field

Sally Field, Paul Newman
(also at top)

PENNIES FROM HEAVEN

(M-G-M) Producers, Herbert Ross, Nora Kaye; Director, Herbert Ross; Screenplay and Original Material, Dennis Potter; Photography, Gordon Willis; Executive Producer, Richard McCallum; Associate Producer, Ken Adam; Editor, Richard Marks; Choreography, Danny Daniels; Art Directors, Fred Tuch, Bernie Cutler; Costumes, Bob Mackie; Music, Marvin Hamlisch, Billy May; Assistant Directors, L. Andrew Stone, Emmitt-Leon O'Neil, Hal Bell; Original Soundtrack Album on Warner Bros. Records; In Metrocolor; 108 minutes; Rated R; December release.

CAST

Arthur	Steve Martin
Eileen	Bernadette Peters
Tom	Christopher Walken
Joan	Jessica Harper
Accordion Man	Vernel Bagneris
Mr. Warner	John McMartin
Detective	John Karlen
Banker	Jay Garner
Al	Robert Fitch
Ed	Tommy Rall
Blind Girl	Eliska Krupka
Bartender	Frank McCarthy
Mr. Barrett	Raleigh Bond
Prostitute	Gloria LeRoy
Old Whore	Nancy Parsons
Tarts	Toni Kaye, Shirley Kirkes
Elevator Operator	Jack Fletcher
Boy	Hunter Watkins
Motorcycle Police	Arell Blanton, George Wilbur
Young Policeman	M. C. Gainey
Newsboy	Mark Campbell
Schoolboy	Mark Martinez
Countermen	Duke Stroud, Joe Medalis
Father Everson	Will Hare

and Richard Blum, William Frankfather, James Mendenhall, Jim Boeke, Robert Lee Jarvis, Luke Andreas, Joshua Cadman, Paul Valentine, Bill Richards, John Craig, Alton Ruff, Karla Bush, Robin Hoff, Linda Montana, Dorothy Cronin, Twink Caplan, Lillian D'Honau, Barbara Nordella, Dean Taliaferro, Wayne Storm, Gene Ross, Edward Heim, Dave Adams, Greg Finley, Paul Michael, Joe Ross, Conrad Palmisano, Richard E. Butler, Ronald G. Oliney.

Left: Bernadette Peters, Christopher Walken
Top: Bernadette Peters
© MGM Film Co.

Jessica Harper, Steve Martin

Steve Martin, Bernadette Peters

Bernadette Peters Above: Tommy Rall, Steve Martin,
Robert Fitch Top: Vernel Bagneris

Steve Martin, Bernadette Peters Above
and Top: Christopher Walken

TAPS

(20th CENTURY-FOX) Producers, Stanley R. Jaffe, Howard B. Jaffe; Director, Harold Becker; Screenplay, Darryl Ponicsan, Robert Mark Kamen; From novel "Father Sky" by Devery Freeman; Adaptation, James Lineberger; Photography, Owen Roizman; Art Directors, Stan Jolley, Alfred Sweeney; Editor, Maury Winetrobe; Music, Maurice Jarre; Assistant Directors, Tom Mack, Bill Elvin, Michael Looney; In Dolby Stereo and DeLuxe Color; 122 minutes; Rated PG; December release.

CAST

General Harlan Bache	George C. Scott
Brian Moreland	Timothy Hutton
Colonel Kerby	Ronny Cox
Alex Dwyer	Sean Penn
David Shawn	Tom Cruise
Charlie Auden	Brendan Ward
Edward West	Evan Handler
Derek Mellott	John P. Navin, Jr.
Bug	Billy Van Zandt
J. C. Pierce	Giancarlo Esposito
Billy Harris	Donald Kimmel
John Cooper	Tim Wahrer
Hulk	Tim Riley
Shovel	Jeff Rochlin
Rusty	Rusty Jacobs
Mst. Sgt. Kevin Moreland	Wayne Tippett
Dean Ferris	Jess Osuna
Lt. Hanson	Earl Hindman
Sheriff	James Handy
Marshal	Steven Ryan
Deputy	Michael Longfield
Interviewer	Jay Gregory
Woman Announcer	Karen Braga
Stewart	Ralph Drischell
Secretary	Jane Cecil
Male Clerk	Thomas Medearis
Mrs. Malloy	Amelia Romano
Lori Cable	Sheila Marra

and Gary McCleery, Arnie Mazer, L. Michael Craig, Chris Hagan, John Taylor, Eugene Krumenacker, David McGinley, John Faucher, Declan Weir, Ryan Helm, Lou Milione, John McBrearty, Frank Chambers, John Newmuis, Paul Lyons, Tom Hutchinson (Cadets), Tom Klunis, Brenda Currin, Elizabeth Perry, Jeanne Fisher, Robena Rogers, Jim Arnett (Parents)

Top: Timothy Hutton (L), George C. Scott (R)
© 20th Century-Fox

Timothy Hutton, George C. Scott, Tim Wahrer
Above: George C. Scott

Brendan Ward, Timothy Hutton, John Navin
Above: Sean Penn, Hutton Top: Tom Cruise,
Hutton, Penn

Timothy Hutton, and above with Penn, Ward,
Handler, Esposito, Riley

RAGTIME

(PARAMOUNT) Producer, Dino De Laurentiis; Director, Milos Forman; Screenplay, Michael Weller; Based on novel by E. L. Doctorow; Music, Randy Newman; Executive Producers, Michael Hausman, Bernard Williams; Associate Producer, Fredric M. Sidewater; Photography, Miroslav Ondricek; Design, John Graysmark; Editors, Anne V. Coates, Antony Gibbs, Stanley Warnow; Costumes, Anna Hill Johnstone; Choreographer, Twyla Tharp; Art Directors, Patrizia von Brandenstein, Anthony Reading; Song "One More Hour" sung by Jennifer Warnes; Music and Lyrics, Randy Newman; In Todd-AO and Technicolor; 155 minutes; Rated PG; December release.

CAST

Police Commissioner Waldo	James Cagney
Younger Brother	Brad Dourif
Booker T. Washington	Moses Gunn
Evelyn Nesbit	Elizabeth McGovern
Willie Conklin	Kenneth McMillan
Delmas	Pat O'Brien
Evelyn's Dance Teacher	Donald O'Connor
Father	James Olson
Tateh	Mandy Patinkin
Coalhouse Walker, Jr.	Howard E. Rollins
Mother	Mary Steenburgen
Sarah	Debbie Allen
Houdini	Jeff DeMunn
Harry K. Thaw	Robert Joy
Stanford White	Norman Mailer

and Bruce Boa (Jerome), Hoolihan Burke (Brigit), Norman Chancer (Agent), Edwin Cooper (Grandfather), Jeff Daniels (O'-Donnell), Fran Drescher (Mameh), Frankie Faison, Hal Galili, Alan Gifford, Richard Griffiths, Samuel L. Jackson, Michael Jeter, Calvin Levels, Bessie Love, Christopher Malcolm, Herman Meckler, Billy J. Mitchell, Jenny Nichols, Max Nichols, Zack Norman, Eloise O'Brien, Don Plumley, Ted Ross, Dorsey Wright, Robert Arden, Robert Boyd, Thomas A. Carlin, John Clarkson, Brian E. Dean, Harry Ditson, Robert Dorning, Geoffrey Greenhill, Ray Hassett, Robert Hitt, Rodney James, George Harris, George J. Manos, Val Pringle, Ron Weyand

Left: Robert Joy Top:
Jenny Nichols, Mandy Patinkin
© Dino DeLaurentiis Corp.

Elizabeth McGovern, Donald O'Connor

Howard E. Rollins

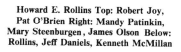

Howard E. Rollins Top: Robert Joy,
Pat O'Brien Right: Mandy Patinkin,
Mary Steenburgen, James Olson Below:
Rollins, Jeff Daniels, Kenneth McMillan

Brad Dourif

James Cagney Above: Howard E. Rollins,
Debbie Allen

SHARKEY'S MACHINE

(ORION/WARNER BROS.) Producer, Hank Moonjean; Director, Burt Reynolds; Screenplay, Gerald Di Pego; Based on novel by William Diehl; Photography, William A. Fraker; Design, Walter Scott Herndon; Editor, William Gordean; Associate Producer, Edward Teets; Costumes, Norman Salling; Assistant Directors, Benjy Rosenberg, Jim Van Wyck, Don Wilkerson, Paul Moen; Choreographer, Anthony Ferro; A Deliverance Productions Film in Technicolor and Dolby Stereo; 122 minutes; Rated R; December release.

CAST

Sharkey	Burt Reynolds
Victor	Vittorio Gassman
Papa	Brian Keith
Friscoe	Charles Durning
Hotchkins	Earl Holliman
Arch	Bernie Casey
Billy Score	Henry Silva
Nosh	Richard Libertini
Smiley	Darryl Hickman
Dominoe	Rachel Ward
Joe Tipps	Joseph Mascolo
Mabel	Carol Locatell
Highball Mary	Hari Rhodes
Barrett	John Fiedler
Twigs	James O'Connell
Man with Siakwan	Val Avery
Siakwan	Suzee Pai
Tiffany	Aarika Wells
Kitten	Tony King
Percy	William Diehl

and Dan Inosanto (Chin 1), Weaver Levy (Chin 2), May Keller Pearce (May), Sheryl Kilby (Lisa), James Lewis, Scott Newell (Police), Glynn Ruben (Pregnant Woman), Bennie Moore (Bus Driver), Alveda King Beale, Gayle Davis Atiim Kweli (Rus Riders), Brenda Bynum (Aging Hooker), Gus Mann (Flasher), Elaine Falone, Wanda Strange, Barbara Stokes (Hookers), John Greenwell (Rachel), John Arthur (Pusher), Terrayne Crawford, Mary Beth Busbee, J. Don Ferguson, Monica Kaufman, Dave Michaels, Wes Sarginson, Forrest Sawyer, Colonel Beach, Danny Nelson, Lamar Jackson, Sue Cockrell, Lisa Hall, Pam Newman, April Reed, Susan Williamson, Diana Szlosberg

Top: Burt Reynolds
© Orion Pictures

Rachel Ward
Top: Burt Reynolds

Burt Reynolds, Vittorio Gassman
Top: (L) Bernie Casey, Burt Reynolds (R) Rachel Ward, Burt Reynolds

FOUR FRIENDS

(FILMWAYS PICTURES) Producers, Arthur Penn, Gene Lasko; Director, Arthur Penn; Screenplay, Steven Tesich; Executive Producers, Michael Tolan, Julia Miles; Associate Producer, Steve Kesten; Photography, Ghislain Cloquet; Editors, Barry Malkin, Marc Laub; Assistant Director, Cheryl Downey; Choreographer, Julie Arenal; Music, Elizabeth Swados; Design, David Chapman; Costumes, Patricia Norris; A Florin Production; A Cinema 77/Geria Film in Technicolor; 115 minutes; Rated R; December release.

CAST

Danilo Prozor	Craig Wasson
Georgia Miles	Jodi Thelen
Tom Donaldson	Jim Metzler
David Levine	Michael Huddleston
Louie Carnahan	Reed Birney
Adrienne Carnaham	Julia Murray
Gergley	David Graf
Rudy	Zaid Farid
Mr. Prozor	Miklos Simon
Mrs. Prozor	Elizabeth Lawrence
Mrs. Zoldos	Beatrice Fredman
Mr. Carnahan	James Leo Herlihy
Mrs. Carnahan	Lois Smith

Craig Wasson, Jodi Thelen, Michael Huddleston, Jim Metzler Center: (R) Jodi Thelen, Reed Birney (L) Wasson, Elizabeth Lawrence, Miklos Simon Top: Thelen, Wasson

Elizabeth Lawrence, Miklos Simon, Craig Wasson Above: (L) Michael Huddleston
(C) Wasson, Jodi Thelen (R) Reed Birney Top: Huddleston, Wasson, Jim
Metzler, Jodi Thelen

ROLLOVER

(ORION/WARNER BROS.) Producer, Bruce Gilbert; Director, Alan J. Pakula; Screenplay, David Shaber; Story, David Shaber, Howard Kohn, David Weir; Photography, Giuseppe Rotunno; Design, George Jenkins; Editor, Evan Lottman; Music, Michael Small; Costumes, Ann Roth; Associate Producer, Wendi Lazar; Assistant Directors, Alex Hapsas, Joe Ray; An IPC Films production in Technicolor; 118 minutes; Rated R; December release.

CAST

Lee Winters	Jane Fonda
Hub Smith	Kris Kristofferson
Maxwell Emery	Hume Cronyn
Roy Lefcourt	Josef Sommer
Sal Naftari	Bob Gunton
Mr. Fewster	Macon McCalman
Gil Hovey	Ron Frazier
Betsy Okamoto	Jodi Long
Warner Ackerman	Crocker Nevin
Mr. Lipscomb	Marvin Chatinover
Mr. Whitelaw	Ira B. Wheeler
Khalid	Paul Hecht
Hishan	Norman Snow
Lee Winter's Maid	Nelly Hoyos
Mrs. Emery	Lansdale Chatfield
Mrs. Fewster	Sally Sockwell
Fewster's Older Daughter	Martha Plimpton
Fewster's Younger Daughter	Gaby Glatzer
Dodds	Howard Erskine
Winterchem Limo Driver	Michael Fiorillo
Newscaster	Marilyn Berger
Mystery Man	Alex Wipf
Older Arab Father	Ahmed Yacoubi
Faculty Member	Charlie Laiken
Sam, Nightwatchman	Stanley Simmonds

and E. Brian Dean (Nightwatchman), James Sutton (Vice-President), Joel Stedman (Asst. Vice-Pres.), Garrison Lane (Winters), Nina Reeves (Secretary), Michael Prince, Carolyn Larsen, Ron Vaad, Rebecca Brooks, Richard Barbour, Danny Redmon, Eric Bethancourt, Steve Bullard, Neela Eriksen, Lawrence Sellars, Ernie Garrett, Art Hansen, Ira Lewis, Sharon Casey, Bernie Rachelle, Keith Eager, Dave Ellsworth, Bill Anagnos, Art Lambert, Jerry Hewitt, Mark Sutton, Debbie Watkins

Jane Fonda, Kris Kristofferson

Top: (L) Kris Kristofferson (R) Hume Cronyn
© Orion Pictures

Jane Fonda, Kris Kristofferson (also above)

WHOSE LIFE IS IT ANYWAY?

(M-G-M) Producer, Lawrence P. Bachmann; Director, John Badham; Executive Producers, Martin C. Schute, Ray Cooney; Screenplay, Brian Clark, Reginald Rose; Based on play of same title by Brian Clark; Design, Gene Callahan; Photography, Mario Tosi; Music, Arthur B. Rubinstein; Editor, Frank Morriss; Assistant Directors, Katy Emde, J. A. Ingraffia, Lawrence Mirisch; Costumes, Marianna Elliott; Choreographer, Marge Champion; Art Director, Sydney Z. Litwack; In Panavision and Metrocolor; 119 minutes; Rated R; December release.

CAST

Ken Harrison	Richard Dreyfuss
Dr. Michael Emerson	John Cassavetes
Dr. Clare Scott	Christine Lahti
Carter Hill	Bob Balaban
Judge Wyler	Kenneth McMillan
Mary Jo	Kaki Hunter
Orderly John	Thomas Carter
Nurse Rodriguez	Alba Oms
Pat	Janet Eilber
Mrs. Boyle	Kathryn Grody
Dr. Jacobs	George Wyner
Dr. Barr	Mel Stewart
Mr. Eden	Ward Costello
Day Nurse	Alston Ahern
ICU Nurse	Betty Cole
Emergency Room Doctor	Lyman Ward
Stella, Student Nurse	Juli Andelman
Lissa	Abigail Hepner
Third Year Student	Alan Stock
First Year Intern	Jeffrey Combs
Hoffman	Steven Bourne
Physiotherapist	John Garber
Anesthesiologist	Katie Guymon
Guard	J. J. Johnston
Intern	Michael Steve Jones
Court Clerk	Fred Slyter
Orthopedic Surgeon	Tony Simotes
Old Man	Robert Telford
Technician	Roberta Jean Williams
Nurses	Francine Henderson, Lissa Layng, Dorothy Meyer, Karla Pitti, Beth Renner

Richard Dreyfuss, and above with Janet Eilber

Richard Dreyfuss, Thomas Carter, John Cassavetes

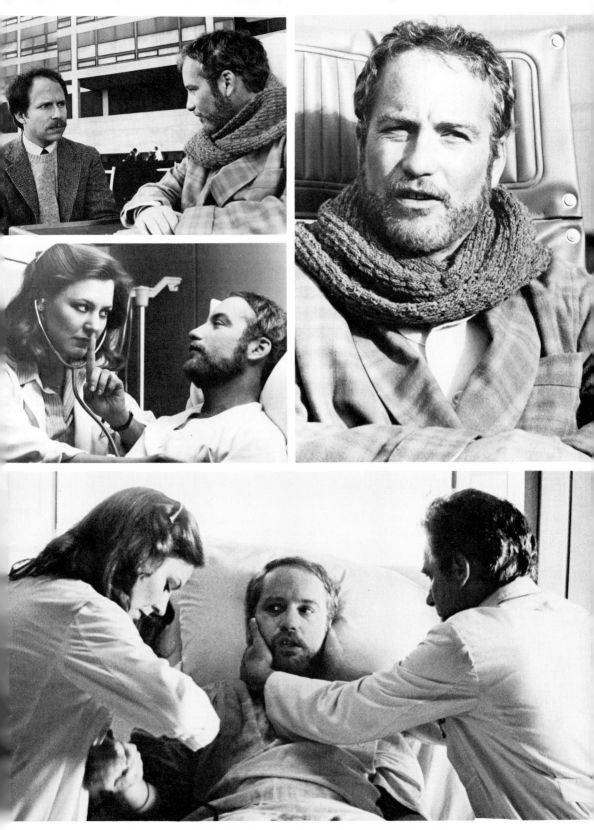

Christine Lahti, Richard Dreyfuss, John Cassavetes Top: (L) Bob Balaban, Richard
Dreyfuss Below: Christine Lahti, Richard Dreyfuss (R) Richard Dreyfuss

REDS

(PARAMOUNT) Producer-Director, Warren Beatty; Screenplay, Warren Beatty, Trevor Griffiths; Editors, Dede Allen, Craig McKay; Executive Producers, Simon Relph, Dede Allen; Photography, Vittorio Storaro; Design, Richard Sylbert; Costumes, Shirley Russell; Associate Producer, David L. MacLeod; Original Music, Stephen Sondheim; Additional Music, Dave Grusin; Assistant Director, Simon Relph; Art Director, Simon Holland; In Technicolor; 200 minutes; Rated PG; December release.

CAST

John Reed	Warren Beatty
Louise Bryant	Diane Keaton
Max Eastman	Edward Herrmann
Grigory Zinoviev	Jerzy Kosinski
Eugene O'Neill	Jack Nicholson
Louis Fraina	Paul Sorvino
Emma Goldman	Maureen Stapleton
Paul Trullinger	Nicolas Coster
Speaker-Liberal Club	M. Emmet Walsh
Mr. Partlow	Ian Wolfe
Mrs. Partlow	Bessie Love
Carl Walters	MacIntyre Dixon
Helen Walters	Pat Starr
Mrs. Reed	Eleanor D. Wilson
Floyd Dell	Max Wright
Horace Whigham	George Plimpton
Maurice Becker	Harry Ditson
Ida Rauh	Leigh Curran
Crystal Eastman	Kathryn Grody
Marjorie Jones	Brenda Currin
Jane Heap	Nancy Duiguid
Barney	Norman Chancer
Big Bill Haywood	Dolph Sweet
Police Chief	Ramon Bieri
Pinkerton Guard	Jack O'Leary
Pete Van Wherry	Gene Hackman
Dr. Lorber	Gerald Hiken
Julius Gerber	William Daniels
Allan Benson	Dave King
Joe Volski	Joseph Buloff

and Stefan Gryff (Gomberg), Denis Pekarev (Interpreter), Roger Sloman (Lenin), Stuart Richman (Trotsky), Oleg Kerensky (Kerensky), Nikko Seppala (Young Bolshevik), John J. Hooker (Senator Overman), Shane Rimmer (MacAlpine), Jerry Hardin (Harry), Jack Kehoe (Eddie), Christopher Malcolm, Tony Sibbald (CLP Members), R. G. Armstrong (Agent), Josef Sommer (Official), Jan Triska (Radek), Ake Lindman (Escort), Pertti Weckstrom (Finnish Doctor), Nina Macarova (Russian Nurse), Jose DeFillippo (Russian Doctor), Andreas LaCasa (Boy), Witnesses: Roger Baldwin, Henry Miller, Adela Rogers St. Johns, Dora Russell, Scott Nearing, Tess Davis, Heaton Vorse, Hamilton Fish, Isaac Don Levine, Rebecca West, Will Durant, Will Weinstone, Oleg Kerensky, Emmanuel Herbert, Arne Swabeck, Adele Nathan, George Seldes, Kenneth Chamberlain, Blanch Hays Fagen, Galina Von Meck, Art Shields, Andrew Dasburg, Hugo Gellert, Dorothy Frooks, George Jessel, Jacob Bailin, John Ballato, Lucita Williams, Bernadine Szold-Fritz, Jessica Smith, Harry Carlisle, Arthur Mayer

Left Center: Maureen Stapleton, Warren Beatty
Above: Jack Nicholson, Diane Keaton
Top: Warren Beatty
© Barclay's Mercantile Industrial Finance Ltd.

1981 ACADEMY AWARDS FOR BEST DIRECTOR, BEST SUPPORTING ACTRESS (MAUREEN STAPLETON), BEST CINEMATOGRAPHY

Diane Keaton

Warren Beatty (R) above Jack Nicholson
Top: Jerzy Kosinski, Edward Herrmann
Below: Gene Hackman, Paul Sorvino

Diane Keaton, Warren Beatty
(also above)

BUDDY BUDDY

(M-G-M/UNITED ARTISTS) Producer, Jay Weston; Director, Billy Wilder; Executive Producer, Alain Bernheim; Screenplay, Billy Wilder, I. A. L. Diamond; Based on play and story by Francis Veber; Photography, Harry Stradling, Jr.; Editor, Argyle Nelson; Music, Lalo Schifrin; Design, Daniel A. Lomino; Associate Producer, Charles Matthau; Assistant Director, Gary Daigler; In Technicolor and Panavision; 96 minutes; Rated R; December release.

CAST

Victor Clooney	Jack Lemmon
Trabucco	Walter Matthau
Celia Clooney	Paula Prentiss
Dr. Zuckerbrot	Klaus Kinski
Captain Hubris	Dana Elcar
Eddie the Bellhop	Miles Chapin
Assistant Manager	Michael Ensign
Receptionist	Joan Shawlee
Rudy Disco Gambola	Fil Formicola
Kowalski	C. J. Hunt
Mexican Maid	Bette Raya
Hippy Husband	Ronnie Sperling
Pregnant Wife	Suzie Galler

Left: Jack Lemmon, Klaus Kinski
Top: Jack Lemmon, Walter Matthau
© Metro-Goldwyn-Mayer Film Co.

Paula Prentiss, Jack Lemmon

Jack Lemmon, Walter Matthau
Above: Matthau, Miles Chapin

Robert Hegyes, Dirk Benedict
in "Underground Aces"
© American International Pictures

John Saxon in "Blood Beach"
© Jerry Gross Organization

UNDERGROUND ACES (Filmways) Producer, Jay Weston; Executive Producer, Samuel Z. Arkoff; Director, Robert Butler; Screenplay, Jim Carabatsos, Lenore Wright, Andrew Peter Marin; Associate Producer, Joe Cavalier; Assistant Director, Gene Law; Art Director, Dan Lomino; Photography, Tom Del Ruth; Editor, Argyle Nelson; Music, Pete Rugolo; Title Song composed and performed by The Commodores; In Movielab Color; 95 minutes; Rated PG; January release. CAST: Dirk Benedict (Huff), Melanie Griffith (Lucy), Robert Hegyes (Tico), Jerry Orbach (Penlitter), Frank Gorshin (Kruger), Rick Podell (Joe), Randy Brooks (Ollie), T.K. Carter (DeeJay), Joshua Daniel (Wally), Sid Haig (Faoud), Fawne Harriman (Mitzi), Audrey Landers (Anne), Mimi Maynard (Madelyn), Kario Salem (Sheik), Ralph Seymour (Zig), Michael Winslow (Nate)

INDEPENDENCE DAY (Unifilm) Producers, Bobby Roth, Neil Rapp; Direction and Screenplay, Bobby Roth; Associate Producer, Beth Sullivan; Editor, John Carnochan; Photography, Elliot Davis; Assistant Director, David Osrerhout; Art Director, Jeffrey White; Music, Mauro Bruno; In color; 87 minutes; Not rated; January release. CAST: Mel Rosier (Fred), Gammy Burdett (Delores), Michelle Davison (Helen), Henry Gayle Sanders (Charles), Charles Branklyn (Maurice), Nikki Sanz (Kathleen), Fred Parker, Jr. (Glenn), Cal Williams (Felix), Robert Rosen (Rosen), Thomas Carter (Carter), Jack Carone (Jack), George Travis (Travis), Kamalo Deen (Kamalo), Martha Charles (Caroline), Tammy Mitchell (Young Delores), Ray Cherry (Young Fred), Herb Schmidt (Foreman)

THE DAY AFTER TRINITY: J. ROBERT OPPENHEIMER AND THE ATOMIC BOMB (Jon Else) Producer-Director, Jon Else; Written by David Peoples, Janet Peoples, Jon Else; Editors, David Peoples, Ralph Wikke; Narrator, Paul Frees; Associate Producers, Courtney Flavin, Martha Olson, Kathryn Witte; Photography, Tom McDonough, David Espar, Stephen Lighthill, Jon Else; Music, Martin Bresnick; In color; Not rated; 88 minutes; January release. A documentary feature about J. Robert Oppenheimer and the people who build nuclear weapons

BLOOD BEACH (Jerry Gross) Producer, Steven Nalevansky; Executive Producer, Sidney Beckerman; Director, Jeffrey Bloom; Art Director, William Sandell; Editor, Gary Griffen; Associate Producer, Neil Canton; Music, Gil Melle; Screen play, Jeffrey Bloom; Story, Jeffrey Bloom, Steven Nalevansky; Photography, Steve Poster; Assistant Directors, Elie Cohn, Andrew Ackerman; In MetroColor; Rated R; 92 minutes; January release. CAST: David Huffman (Harry), Mariana Hill (Catherine), John Saxon (Pearson), Otis Young (Piantadosi), Stefan Gierasch (Dimitrios), Burt Young (Royko), Darrell Fetty (Hoagy), Lynne Marta (Jo), Eleanor Zee (Mrs. Selden), Lena Pousette (Marie), Pamela McMyler (Mrs. Hench), Harriet Medin (Ruth), Mickey Fox (Moose), Laura Burkett, Marleta Giles, Jacqueline Randall, Charles Rowe Rook, John Joseph Thomas, Julie Dolan, Sandra Friebel, Christopher Franklin, Bobby Bass, Read Morgan, Mary Jo Catlett, Robert Newirth, James Ogg, Judy Walker, Norton Buffalo, Yancy E. Burns III, Michael Lewis, Laurin Rinder

FEAR NO EVIL (Avco Embassy) Producers, Frank LaLoggia, Charles M. LaLoggia; Direction and Screenplay, Frank LaLoggia; Photography, Fred Goodich; Editor, Edna Ruth Paul; Music, Frank LaLoggia, David Spear; In color; 99 minutes; Rated R; Janaury release. CAST: Stefan Arngrim (Andrew), Elizabeth Hoffman (Mikhail/Margaret), Kathleen Rowe McAllen (Gabrielle/Hulie), Frank Birney (Father Daly), Daniel Eden (Tony), Jack Holland (Rafael/Father Damon), Barry Cooper (Mr. Williams), Alice Sachs (Mrs. Williams), Paul Haber (Mark), Roslyn Gugino (Marie), Richard Jay Silverthorn (Lucifer)

FISH HAWK (Avco Embassy) Producer, Jon Slan; Director, Donal Shebib; Screenplay, Blanche Hanalis; Based on novel by Mitchell Jayne; Photography, Rene Verzier; Editor, Ron Wisman; Music, Samuel Matlofsky; In color; 95 minutes; Rated G; January release. CAST: Will Sampson (Fish Hawk), Charlie Fields (Corby), Geoffrey Bowes (Towsack), Mary Pirie (Sarah), Don Francks (Deut), Chris Wiggins (Marcus), Kay Hawtrey (Mary), Mavor Moore (Joke)

Jerry Orbach, Frank Gorshin
in "Underground Aces"
© American International Pictures

Mariana Hill in "Blood Beach"
© Jerry Gross Organization

Donna Stillwell, Jamie Gillis
in "Night of the Zombies"
© NMD Film Distributing Co.

Fernando Rey, Charles Bronson
in "Caboblanco"

THE PRESIDENT'S WOMEN (Krona) Producer, Cael Gurevich; Directed and Edited by John Avildsen; Screenplay, David Odel, Jack Richardson, Don Greenberg; Photography, Ralph Bode; Music, Stan Vincent, Gary William Friedman; In color; 76 minutes; Rated R; January release. CAST: Zero Mostel (President/Godfather), Estelle Parsons (First Lady/Barmaid), Pat Paulsen (Norman), Paul Dooley (Salesman), Jerry Orbach (Lorsey), George S. Irving (Roberto/Reverend), Irwin Corey (Professor), Michele Clark Lawrence (Announcer), Laurie Heineman (Trixie), Joe Palmieri (Alfredo), Andrew Duncan (Hurdlemeyer)

LET THERE BE LIGHT directed by John Huston; Written by John Huston and Charles Kaufman; Produced by the Army Signal Corps; 60 minutes; Not rated; January release. A documentary about the treatment of psychoneurotic combat veterans at Mason General Hospital on Long Island toward the end of World War II

NIGHT OF THE ZOMBIES (NMD) formerly "Gamma 693"; Producer, Lorin E. Price; Direction and Screenplay, Joel M. Reed; Editor, Samuel Pollard; Costumes, Eaves; In color by TVC; 85 minutes; Rated R; January release. CAST: Jamie Gillis (Nick), Ryan Hilliard (Dr. Proud), Ron Armstrong (Capt. Fleck), Shoshana Ascher (Prostitute), Dick Carballo (Man in bar), Richard DeFaut (Sgt.), Alphonse DeNoble (CIA Agent), Samantha Grey (Susan), Juni Kulis (GRO Officer), Lorin E. Price (Priest), Noel M. Reed (Neo-Nazi), Ranate Schlessinger (Madam), Kuno Sponholtz (Doorman), John Barilla, Michael Casconi, Gordon C. Dixon, Bob Laconi, Charlene Matus, Lee Moore, Glen A. Pence, Donald K. Wallace, Bill Williams, Carl Woerner, Kai Wulff

EARTHBOUND (Taft International) Executive Producer, Charles E. Sellier, Jr; Produced and Written by Michael Fisher; Director, James Conway; In Technicolor; 94 minutes; Rated PG; January release. CAST: Burl Ives (Ned), Christopher Connelly (Zef), Meredith MacRae (Lara), Joseph Campanella (Conrad), Marc Gilpin (Dalem), Elissa Leeds (Teva), Todd Porter (Tommy), John Schuck (Sheriff), Stuart Pankin (Deputy), Joey Forman (Madden), Peter Isacksen (Willy), Doodles Weaver (Sterling), John Hansen (1st Rider), Tiger Thompson (Butch), Daryl Bingham (Pudge), Michael Witt (Snodgrass), April Gilpin (Bridgette), H.E.D. Redford (General), Michael Ruud (Coach), Mindy Dow (Rosie)

CABOBLANCO (Avco Embassy) Producers, Lance Hool, Paul A. Joseph; Director, J. Lee Thompson; Executive Producer, Martin V. Smith; Screenplay, Mort Fine, Milton Gelman; Editor, Michael F. Anderson; Photography, Alex Phillips, Jr.; Music, Jerry Goldsmith; Associate Producer, Alan Hool; In Panavision, Dolby Stereo and color; 87 minutes; Rated R; January release. CAST: Charles Bronson (Giff), Jason Robards (Gunter), Dominique Sanda (Marie-Claire), Fernando Rey (Teredo), Simon MacCorkindale (Lewis), Camilla Sparv (Hira), Denny Miller (Horst), Gilbert Roland (Dr. Ramirez)

THE GLOVE (Pro International) Producer, Julian Roffman; Executive Producer, William B. Silberkleit; Director, Ross Hagen; Screenplay, Hubert Smith, Julian Roffman; Photography, Gary Graver; Editor, Bob Fitzgerald; Music, Robert O. Ragland; A Tommy J. Production in Metrocolor; 90 minutes; Rated R; January release. CAST: John Saxon (Sam), Roosevelt Grier (Victor), Joanna Cassidy (Sheila), Joan Blondell (Mrs. Fitzgerald), Jack Carter (Walter), Keenan Wynn (Bill), Aldo Ray (Guard), Michael Pataki (Harry), Misty Bruce (Lisa), Howard Honig (Kruger)

NEW YEAR'S EVIL (Cannon) Producers, Menahem Golan, Yoram Globus; Director, Emmett Alston; Executive Producer, Billy Fines; Screenplay, Leonard Neubauer; Music, Laurin Rinder, W. Michael Lewis; In color; 90 minutes; Rated R; January release. CAST: Roz Kelly, Kip Niven, Chris Wallace, Grant Cramer, Louisa Moritz, Jed Mills

EMERSON, LAKE & PALMER IN CONCERT (Prestige) Producers, Bud Murphy, Andy DiMartino; Director, Ron Kantor; Executive Producer, Peter Bennet; Co-Producer, Michael Huemmer; Photography, Pierre Peladeau, Rene Daiole, Daniel Fournier; In color; 91 minutes; Rated G; January release. CAST: Keith Emerson, Greg Lake, Carl Palmer and a 65-piece orchestra

SWEET DIRTY TONY (Marvin) formerly "Cuba Crossing"; A Key West Production; Producer Peter J. Barton; Direction and Screenplay, Chuck Workman; In color; 90 minutes; January release. CAST: Stuart Whitman (Capt. Tony Terracino), Robert Vaughn (Hudd), Raymond St. Jacques (Bell), Caren Kaye (Tracy), Woody Strode (Titi), Sybil Danning (Veronica), Mary Lou Gassen (Maria), Albert Salmi (Delgato), Michael Gazzo (Rosselini), Monty Rock III (Bar Gay)

KAHUNA! (Oakwood) Executive Producer, Lloyd Berman; Director, Frank Sillman; From novel by Allan Silliphant; Photography, Chris Condon; Music, Rich Gibbs; In Stereovision 4D and color; Rated R; January release. CAST: Debbie Jones, Luana King, Pat Waid, Maria Cortez, Danielle Roe, Julie Rohde, Sandy Johnson, Steven Atlas

CLOSE SHAVE (Tobann International) Producers, Robert Hendrickson, Tobyann Hendrickson; Director, Robert Hendrickson; Screenplay, Ronald Collier, Robert Hendrickson; Associate Producer, Richard A. Rosenthal; Music, Steve Rucker, Tony Coppola; In color; Rated R; January release, CAST: Scott Gaba, Toni Benson, Harry Levinthal, Corey Reagan Hendrickson

Ned Anderson, Meredith MacRae, Burl Ives
in "Earthbound"

Orson Welles in "The Man Who Saw
Tomorrow" © Warner Bros.

Lesley-Anne Down, Frank Langella
in "Sphinx" © Orion Pictures

I SPIT ON YOUR GRAVE (Jerry Gross) carried in Volume 30 as "Day of the Woman."

THE MAN WHO SAW TOMORROW (Warner Bros.) Executive Producer, David L. Wolper; Producers, Robert Guenette, Lee Kramer, Paul Drane; Director, Robert Guenette; Screenplay, Mr. Guenette; Music, William Loose, Jack Tillar; Associate Producers, Alan Goland, Peter Wood; Editors, Peter Wood, Scott McLennan; Art Director, Mike Minor; Costumes, Pat Tonnema, Clair Griffin; In Technicolor; 88 minutes; Rated PG; January release. CAST: Orson Welles (Narrator), Philip L. Clarke (Voice of Nostradamus), Bob Ruggiero, Roy Edmonds, Ray Chubb (French Soldiers), Ray Laska (Warlord), Richard Butler (Nostradamus as older man), Jason Nesmith (Nostradamus as a child), Howard Ackerman (Nostradamus as a young man), Brass Adams (Grandfather), Terry Clotiaux (Nostradamus' father), David Burke (Friar), Bob Bigelow (Dinner Host), Marji Martin (Maid), Thor Nielsen (Cook), Ross Evans (President), Paul Valentine (Secretary of State), Harry Bugin, Emile Hamaty, Dante Rochetti, Howard David, Charles Castilla

THE DECLINE OF WESTERN CIVILIZATION (Nu-Image) Producer-Director, Penelope Spheeris; Executive Producers, Jeffrey Prettyman, Gordon Brown; Editors, Charles Mullin, Peter Wiehl, David Colburn; Photography, Steve Conant, Bill Muerer, Penelope Spheeris; In color; 100 minutes; Not rated; February release. A documentary with footage of concerts by the punk groups Fear, Black Flag, Germs, X, Alice Bag Band, the Circle Jerks and Catholic Discipline

SPHINX (Warner Bros./Orion) Executive Producer-Director, Franklin J. Schaffner; Producer, Stanley O'Toole; Screenplay, John Byrum; From novel by Robin Cook; Music, Michael J. Lewis; Lyrics, Wendy Waldman; Photography, Ernest Day; Designer, Terence Marsh; Art

Director, Gil Parrondo; Costumes, Judy Moorcroft; Editors, Robert E. Swink, Michael F. Anderson; Assistant Director, Jose Lopez Rodero; In Technicolor, Panavision and Dolby Stereo; 119 minutes; Rated PG; February release. CAST: Lesley-Anne Down (Erica), Frank Langella (Ahmed), Maurice Ronet (Yvon), John Gielgud (Abdu), Vic Tablian (Khalifa), Martin Benson (Muhammed), John Rhys-Davies (Stephanos), Nadim Sawalha (Gamal), Tutte Lemkow (Tewfik), Saeed Jaffrey (Selim), Eileen Way (Aida), William Hootkins (Don), Mark Kingston (Carter), James Cossins (Lord Carnarvon), Victoria Tennant (Lady Carnarvon), and Cengiz Saner, Kevork Malikyan, Ismat Rafat, Yashar Adem, Ahmed Abdel Wareth, Ahmed Hegazi, Abdullah Mahmoud, Mohamed Metwalli, Seif Allah Mokhtar, Behrouz Vossoughi, Abdel Reheim El Zorkani, Abdel Salem Mohamed

THE BUSHIDO BLADE (Trident) Producer, Arthur Rankin, Jr; Director, Tom Kotani; Screenplay, William Overgard; Associate Producers, Benni Korzen, Masaki Iizuka; Music, Maury Laws; In color; Rated R; February release. CAST: Richard Boone, Sonny Chiba, Frank Converse, Laura Gemser, James Earl Jones, Mako, Timothy Murphy, Michael Starr, Tetsuro Tamba, Toshiro Mifune

THE FUNHOUSE (Universal) Producers, Derek Power, Steven Bernhardt; Executive Producers, Mace Neufeld, Mark Lester; Director, Tobe Hooper; Screenplay, Larry Block; Photography, Andrew Laszlo; Designer, Morton Rabinowitz; Editor, Jack Hofstra; Music, John Beal; Associate Producer, Brad Neufeld; Assistant Directors, Norman Cohen, Adrienne Bourbeau; Art Director, Jose Duarte; In Technicolor, Panavision and Dolby Stereo; 96 minutes; Rated R; March release. CAST: Elizabeth Berridge (Amy), Shawn Carson (Joey), Jeanne Austin (Mrs. Harper), Jack McDermott (Harper), Cooper Huckabee (Buzz), Largo Woodruff (Liz), Miles Chapin (Richie), David Carson (Geek), Sonia Zomina (Bag Lady), Ralph Marino (Truck Driver), Kevin Conway (Barker), Herb Robins (Carnival Manager), Mona Agar (Stripper), Wayne Doba (Monster), William Finley (Marco), Susie Malnik (Carmella), Sylvia Miles (Mme. Zena), Sid Raymond (M.C.), Larry Ross (Heckler), Frank Grimes (Voyeur), Frank Schuller (Poker Player), Peter Conrad (Midget), Mildred Hughes (Tall Lady), Glen Lawrence, Mike Montalvo (Spectators), Shawn McAllister, Sandy Mielke (Garbage Collectors)

Sylvia Miles, Elizabeth Berridge
in "The Funhouse"
© Universal City Studios

Cooper Huckabee, Elizabeth Berridge
in "The Funhouse" © Universal

109

"The Wobblies"

Elliott Gould, Julie Budd
in "The Devil and Max Devlin"
© Walt Disney Productions

THE DOZENS (First Run Features/Calliope Film Resources) Produced, Directed and Edited by Christine Dall, Randall Conrad; Screenplay, Marian Taylor, Christine Dall, Randall Conrad; Photography, Joe Vitagliano; Associate Producer, Annie Jurgielewicz; Assistant Directors, Jacqueline Shearer, Michael Nozik; 78 minutes; Not rated; March release. CAST: Debra Margolies (Sally), Edward Mason (Sonny), Marian Taylor (Russel), Jessica Hergert (Jessie), Ethel Michelson (Mother), Genevieve Reale (Debbie), Sumru Tekin (Nivia), Catherine DeLeon (Gypsy), Michelle Green (Michelle), Brenda A. Woolley (Cathy), Sharon Brown (Star), Brenda Joyce Wynn (Tour Guide), Debra Kinlaw (Betsy), Jack Sheridan (Parole Officer), Helene Back (Cottage Officer), Mary Jane Williams (Mrs. Bridewell), Dick McGoldrick, Daniel Welch (Police), Jack Borden (Factory Owen), Jackie Brooks, Lanie Zera, George J. Finn, Aida Suris, William J. Sahlein

THE WOBBLIES (First-Run Features) Producers-Directors-Editors, Stewart Bird, Deborah Shaffer; Narrator, Roger Baldwin; Photography, Sandi Sissel, Judy Irola, Peter Gessner, Bonnie Friedman; 90 minutes; Not rated; March release. A documentary about the Industrial Workers of the World (IWW) from its founding in 1905 until its demise during World War I.

EYES OF A STRANGER (Warner Bros) Producer, Ronald Zerra; Director, Ken Wiederhorn; Screenplay, Mark Jackson, Eric L. Bloom; Music, Richard Einhorn; Editor, Rick Shaine; Photography, Mini Rojas; Art Director, Jessica Sack; Associate Producer, Roslyn M. Meyer; Assistant Directors, Robert H. Eastman, Bill Murphy; 85 minutes; In color; Rated R; March release. CAST: Lauren Tewes (Jane), Jennifer Jason Leigh (Tracy), John DiSanti (Stanley), Peter DuPre (David), Gwen Lewis (Debbie), Kitty Lunn (Annette), Timothy Hawkins (Jeff), Ted Richert (Roger), Toni Crabtree (Mona), Bob Small (Dr. Bob), Stella Rivera (Dancer), Dan Fitzgerald (Bartender), Jose Bahamande (Jimmy), Luke Halpin (Tape Editor), Rhonda Flynn (Woman in car), Tony Federico (Man in car), Alan Lee (Photographer), Amy Krug (Young Jane), Tabbetha Tracey (Young Tracy), Sarah Hutcheson (Friend), Jillian Lindig (Mother), George DeVries (Father), Melvin Pape (Doctor), Robert Goodman (Crewman), Pat Warren (Su-

san), Kathy Suergiu (Karen), Madeline Curtis (Nurse), Richard Allen (News Director), Herb Goldstein, Sonia Zomina (Elderly Couple), Michael de Silva (Technical Director)

THE DEVIL AND MAX DEVLIN (Buena Vista) Executive Producer, Ron Miller; Producer, Jerome Courtland; Director, Steven Hilliard Stern; Screenplay, Mary Rodgers; Story, Mary Rodgers, Jimmy Sangster; Photography, Howard Schwartz; Music, Buddy Baker; Songs, Marvin Hamlisch, Carole Bayer Sager; Art Directors, John B. Mansbridge, Leon R. Harris; Editor, Raymond A. de Leuw; Assistant Directors, Irby Smith, Christopher D. Miller, Stephen M. McEveety; Costumes, Bill Thomas; A Walt Disney production in Technicolor; 96 minutes; Rated PG; March release. CAST: Elliott Gould (Max), Bill Cosby (Barney), Susan Anspach (Penny), Adam Rich (Toby), Julie Budd (Stella), Sonny Shroyer (Big Billy), David Knell (Nerve), Charles Shamata (Jerry), Deborah Baltzell (Heidi), Ronnie Schell (Greg), Jeannie Wilson (Laverne), Stanley Brock (Counterman), Ted Zeigler (Billings), Vic Dunlop (Brian), Reggie Nalder (Chairman), Lillian Muller (Veronica), Julie Parrish (Sheila), Sally K. Marr (Mrs. Gormley), Madelyn Cates (Mrs. Trent), Stu Gilliam (Orderly), Denise DuBarry (Secretary), Ruth Manning (Mrs. Davis)

MODERN ROMANCE (Columbia) Producers, Andrew Scheinman, Martin Shafer; Director, Albert Brooks; Screenplay, Albert Brooks, Monica Johnson; Photography, Eric Saarinen; Designer, Edward Richardson; Music, Lance Rubin; Editor, David Finfer; Assistant Directors, Steven H. Perry, Michael Looney; In Metrocolor; 102 minutes; Rated R; March release. CAST: Albert Brooks (Robert), Kathryn Harrold (Mary), Tyann Means (Waitress), Bruno Kirby (Jay), Jane Hallaren (Ellen), Karen Chandler (Neighbor), Dennis Kort (Health Food Salesman), Bob Einstein (Sporting Goods Salesman), Virginia Feingold (Bank Receptionist), Thelma Leeds (Mother), Candy Castillo (Drugstore Manager), James L. Brooks (David), George Kennedy (Himself/Zeron), Rick Beckner (Zeon), Jerry Belson (Jerry), Harvey Skolnik (Harvey), Ed Weinberger (Ed), Meadowlark Lemon (Himself), Albert Henderson (Head Mixer), Cliff Einstein (Music Mixer), Gene Garvin (Sound Effects Mixer), Hugh Warden (Bank Dick), Kelly Ann Nakano (Hostess), Joe Bratcher (Jim), George Sasaki, Victor Toyota, Roger Ito (Japanese Businessmen)

Albert Brooks in "Modern Romance"
© Columbia Pictures

Kathryn Harrold, Albert Brooks
in "Modern Romance" © Columbia Pictures

Chris Parker
in "Permanent Vacation"

Dr. Helen Caldicott
in "8 Minutes to Midnight"

PERMANENT VACATION (Cinesthesia) Produced, Directed, Edited and Written by Jim Jarmusch; Photography, James A. Lebovitz, Thomas DiCillo; Assistant Director, Sara Driver; Music, Jim Jarmusch, John Lurie; In Duart Color; 80 minutes; Not rated; March release. CAST: Chris Parker (Allie), Leila Gastil (Leila), John Lurie (Sax Player), Richard Boes (War Vet), Sara Driver (Nurse), Charlie Spademan (Patient), Jane Fire (Nurse), Ruth Bolton (Mother), Evelyn Smith (Patient), Maria Duval (Latin Girl), Lisa Rosen (Popcorn Girl), Frankie Faison (Man in lobby), Suzanne Fletcher (Girl in car), Felice Rosser (Woman by mailbox), Eric Mitchell (Car Fence), Chris Hameon (French Traveller)

HARRY'S WAR (Taft International) Executive Producer, David B. Johnston; Producers, Jack N. Reddish, Kieth Merrill; Direction and Screenplay, Kieth Merrill; Design, Douglas G. Johnson; Editors, B. Lovitt, Peter L. McCrea; Music, Merrill B. Jenson; Photography, Reed Smoot; In DeLuxe Color; 98 minutes; Rated G; March release. CAST: Edward Herrmann (Harry), Geraldine Page (Beverly), Karen Grassle (Kathy), David Ogden Stiers (Ernie), Salome Jens (Wilda), Elisha Cook (Sgt. Billy), James Ray (Commissioner), Douglas Dirkson (Draper), Jerrold Ziman (Attorney), Jim McKrell (Newsman), Noble Willingham (Maj. Andrews), Prentiss Rowe (Sheriff), Vernon Weddle (Ponde), Max Lewis (Judge), Alan Cherry, Bruce Robinson, Rex Cutter (Agents), Kamee Aliessa (Shawn), Kieri Valee (Shelly), Scott Wilkinson, Robert Daugherty (Mailmen), David Mason Daniels (Aide), Spencer McMullin (Hammel), Jean Stringham (Receptionist), Leslie Perry (Relief Girl), Oscar Rowland (Wino), Marc Raymond (rodney), David Sterago (Reporter), Terry Afton Lee (Soldier), Charles Chagnon (Indigent), Dolly Big Soldier (Indian Mother), Paul Anderson (Banker), Larry Roupe (Supervisor), Jack Reddish (Confused Man), Leola Green (Duchess), Star Roman (Hooker), Mickey Wodrich (Elderly Lady), Jay Bernard (Lumberman)

THE LAND OF NO RETURN (International Picture Show) Producer-Director, Kent Bateman; Screenplay, Kent Bateman, Frank Ray Perilli; Photography, Joao Fernandes; Editor, Dick Alweis; Music, Ralph Geddes; In DeLuxe Color; 84 minutes; Rated PG; March release. CAST: Mel Torme (Zak O'Brien), William Shatner (Curt Benell), Donald Moffat (Air Traffic Controller)

THE PRESIDENT MUST DIE (Jensen Farley) Producer, Charles E. Sellier, Jr.; Director, James L. Conway; Written by Mr. Conway and Cliff Osmond; Music, Don Perry; Photography, Paul Hipp; Design, Paul Staheli; Assistant Director, Leon Dudevoir; Editor, Trevor Jolly; Wardrobe, Julie Staheli; Art Director, Chip Radaelli; In color; 106 minutes; Rated PG; March release. A documentary on the assassination of John F. Kennedy

RUCKUS (New World) formerly "The Loner"; Producer, Paul Maslansky; Direction and Screenplay, Max Kleven; Songs, Willie Nelson, Hank Cochran; Executive Producer, Ric Lacivita; In color; Rated PG; March release. CAST: Dirk Benedict, Linda Blair, Richard Farnsworth, Matt Clark, Jon Van Ness, Ben Johnson, Taylor Lacher

EIGHT MINUTES TO MIDNIGHT: A PORTRAIT OF DR. HELEN CALDICOTT (Caldicott Project) Producer-Director, Mary Benjamin; Co-Director and Photographer, Boyd Estus; Associate Producer and Editor, Susanne Simpson; In color; 60 minutes; Not rated; March release. A documentary portrait of pediatrician, author, and nuclear activist, Dr. Helen Caldicott

AMY (Buena Vista) Executive Producer, William Robert Yates; Producer, Jerome Courtland; Director, Vincent McEveety; Screenplay, Noreen Stone; Photography, Leonard J. South; Music, Robert F. Brunner; Art Directors, John B. Mansbridge, Mark W. Mansbridge; Editor, Gregg McLaughlin; Assistant Directors, Howard Grace, James Turley, Lynda Leigh Karjola; A Walt Disney Production in Technicolor; 100 minutes; Rated G; April release. CAST: Jenny Agutter (Amy), Barry Newman (Dr. Ben Corcoran), Kathleen Nolan (Helen), Chris Robinson (Elliot), Lou Fant (Lyle), Margaret O'Brien (Hazel), Nanette Fabray (Malvina), Lance LeGault (Edgar Wamback), Lucille Benson (Rose), Jonathan Daly (Clyde), Lonny Chapman (Virgil), Brian Frishman (Melvin), Jane Daly (Molly), Dawn Jeffory (Caroline), Frances Bay (Mrs. Lindey), Peggy McCay (Mrs. Grimes), Len Wayland (Grimes), Virginia Vincent (Edna), Norman Burton (Caruthers), Otto Rechenberg (Henry), David Hollander (Just George), Bumper (Wesley), Alban Branton (Eugene), Ronnie Scribner (Walter)

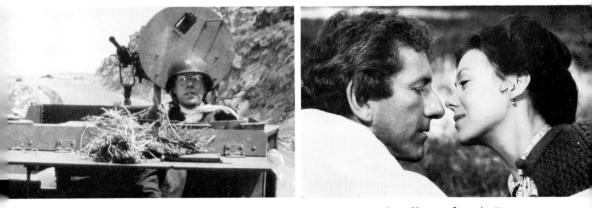

Edward Herrmann
in "Harry's War"

Barry Newman, Jenny Agutter
in "Amy" © Walt Disney Productions

111

Tony Danza, Danny DeVito
in "Going Ape!" © Barclays
Mercantile Industrial Finance Ltd.

Jerry Lewis, Susan Oliver, Roger C.
Carmel in "Hardly Working"
© Hardly Working Ltd.

GOING APE! (Paramount) Producer, Robert L Rosen; Executive Producer, John Daly; Direction and Screenplay, Jeremy Joe Kronsberg; Photography, Frank V. Phillips; Art Director, Robert Kinoshita; Editor, John W. Wheeler; Music, Elmer Bernstein; Costumes, Robert Harris, Jr.; Assistant Director, Albert Shapiro; In Movielab Color; 89 minutes; Rated PG; April release. CAST: Tony Danza (Foster), Jessica Walter (Fiona), Stacey Nelkin (Cynthia), Danny DeVito (Lazlo), Art Metrano (Joey), Frank Sivero (Bad Habit), Rick Hurst (Brandon), Howard Mann (Jules), Joseph Maher (Gridley), Leon Askin (Zabrowski), Jacquelyn Hyde (Zelda), Ted White, Bob Terhune, Jay Durkus (Goons), Angus Duncan (Farley), Ellen Gerstein, Poppy Lagos, Marji Marvin, Donna Ponterotto, D.J. Sullivan (Sisters), Hamilton Mitchell (Marcin), Ruth Gillette (Marianne), Henry Charles (Ringmaster), Gene LeBell (Faraday), Merie Earle (Binocular Lady). Luke Andreas (Carter)

DELUSION (New Line) Producers, Alan Beattie, Peter Shanaberg; Director, Alan Beattie; Screenplay, Jack Viertel; Executive Producer, John Cofrin; Not rated; March release. CAST: Patricia Pearcy, David Hayward, John Dukakis, Joseph Cotten

SCARED TO DEATH (Lone Star) Direction and Screenplay, William Malone; Photography, Patrick Prince; In color; 96 minutes; Rated R; March release. CAST: John Stinson, Diana Davidson, Jonathan David Moses, Toni Jannotta, Kermit Eller

THE WIZARD OF WAUKESHA (First Run Features) Producer-Director, Catherine Orentreich; Co-Directed and Edited by Susan Brockman; Photography, Mark Obenhaus, Don Lenzer, Ed Gray; In color; 60 minutes; Not rated; April release. A documentary about Les Paul, jazz and pop guitarist.

THE PRIVATE EYES (New World Pictures) Producers, Lang Elliott, Wanda Dell; Director, Lang Elliott; Screenplay, Tim Conway, John Myhers; Photography, Jacques Haitkin; Art Director, Vincent Peranio; Editor, Patrick M. Crawford; Music, Peter Matz; Costumes, Christine Goulding; Assistant Director, Doug Wise; In DeLuxe Color; 94 minutes; Rated PG; April release. CAST: Tim Conway (Dr. Tart), Don Knotts (Inspector Winship), Trisha Noble (Phyllis), Bernard Fox (Justin), Grace Zabriskie (Nanny), John Fujioka (Uwatsum), Stan Ross

(Tibet), Irwin Keyes (Jock), Suzy Mandel (Hilda), Fred Stuthman (Lord Morley), Mary Nel Santacroce (Lady Morley), Robert V. Barron (Gas Station Attendant), Patrick Cranshaw (Roy)

HARDLY WORKING (20th Century-Fox) Producers, James J. McNamara, Igo Kantor; Director, Jerry Lewis; Screenplay, Michael Janover, Jerry Lewis; Story, Michael Janover; Associate Producers, Jeffrey Berlatsky, Leslie Maylath; Music, Morton Stevens; Editor, Michael Luciano; Photography, James Pergola; Assistant Directors, Hal Bell, Adrienne Bourbeau, Alice West; Art Director, Don Ivey; In color; 91 minutes; Rated PG; April release. CAST: Jerry Lewis (Bo), Susan Oliver (Claire), Roger C. Carmel (Robert), Deanna Lund (Millie) , Harold J. Stone (Frank), Steve Franken (Steve), Buddy Lester (Claude), Leonard Stone (Ted), Jerry Lester (Slats), Billy Barty (Sammy), Alex Henteloff (Balling), Britt Leach (Gas Station Manager), Peggy Mondo (Woman in restaurant), Amy Krug (Michele), Stephen Baccus (Peter), Tommy Zibelli II (Bobby), Buffy Dee (C.B.), Lou Marsh, Tony Adams, Bob May (Clowns), Angela Bomford (Curio Lady), Jack McDermott (Banker), Cary Hoffman (Waiter), Rick O'Feldman (Chuck), Jack Wakefield (Disco Manager), Woody Woodbury, Charles Pitts, Ed Blessington (Policemen), Jordana Wester (Lady in house), John Disanti, Bobby Kosser (Newsmen), Erica Huddy (Newswoman), John Rice, Greg Rice (Midget Clowns)

KNIGHTRIDERS (United Film Distribution Co.) Executive Producer, Salah M. Hassanein; Producer, Richard P. Rubinstein; Direction and Screenplay, George A. Romero; Photography, Michael Gornick; Associate Producer, David E. Vogel; Music, Donald Rubinstein; Editors, George A. Romero, Pasquale Buba; Designer, Cletus Anderson; Assistant Directors, Pasquale Buba, Clayton Hill, John Roddick; In Technicolor; 145 minutes; Rated R; April release. CAST: Ed Harris (Billy), Gary Lahti (Alan); Tom Savini (Morgan), Amy Ingersoll (Linet), Patricia Tallman (Julie), Christine Forrest (Angie), Warner Shook (Pippin), Brother Blue (Merlin), Cynthia Adler (Rocky), John Amplas (Whiteface), Don Berry (Bagman), Amanda Davies (Sheila), Martin Ferrero (Bontempi), Ken Foree (Little John), Ken Hixon (Steve), John Hostetter (Tuck), Harold Wayne Jones (Bors), Randy Kovitz (Punch), Michael Moran (Cook), Scott Reiniger (Marhalt), Maureen Sadusk (Judy), Albert Amerson (Indian), Ronald Carrier (Hector), Tom Dileo (Corncook), David Early (Bleoboris), John Harrison (Pellinore)

Tim Conway, Don Knotts
in "The Private Eyes"
© New World Pictures

Ed Harris, Amy Ingersoll
in "Knightriders"
© United Film Distribution Co.

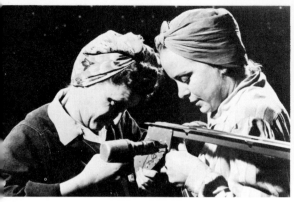

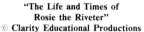

"The Life and Times of
Rosie the Riveter"
© Clarity Educational Productions

Isabelle Huppert, Kris Kristofferson
in "Heaven's Gate" © United Artists

THE LIFE AND TIMES OF ROSIE THE RIVETER (First Run Features) Producer-Director, Connie Field; Associate Producers, Ellen Geiger, Lorraine Kahn, Jane Scantlebury, Bonnie Bellow; Editors, Lucy Massie Phenix, Connie Field; Associate Director, Lorraine Kahn; Photography, Cathy Zheutlin, Bonnie Friedman, Robert Handley, Emiko Omori; In color; 65 minutes; Not rated; April release. A documentary about women workers during World War II with Wanita Allen, Gladys Belcher, Lyn Childs, Lola Weixel, Margaret Wright

HEAVEN'S GATE (United Artists) Re-edited; Producer, Joann Carelli; Direction and Screenplay, Michael Cimino; Photography, Vilmos Zsigmond; Editors, Tom Rolf, William Reynolds, Lisa Fruchtman, Gerald Greenberg; Art Director, Tambi Larsen; Music, David Mansfield; Costumes, Allen Highfill; Art Directors, Spencer Deverill, Maurice Fowler; Choreographer, Eleanor Fazan; 150 minutes; In Panavision, Technicolor, and Dolby Stereo; Rated R; April release. CAST: Kris Kristofferson (Averill), Christopher Walken (Champion), John Hurt (Irvine), Sam Waterston (Canton), Brad Dourif (Eggleston), Isabelle Huppert (Ella), Joseph Cotten (Rev. Doctor), Jeff Bridges (Bridges), Ronnie Hawkins (Wolcott), Paul Koslo (Mayor), Geoffrey Lewis (Trapper), Richard Masur (Cully), Roseanne Vela (Beautiful Girl), Mary C. Wright (Nell), Nicholas Woodeson (Small Man), Stefan Shcherby (Large Man), Waldemar Kalinowski (Photographer), Terry O'Quinn (Capt. Minardi), John Conley (Morrison), Margaret Benczak (Mrs. Eggleston), Tom Noonan (Jake), James Knobeloch (Kopestonsky), Erika Petersen (Mrs. Kopestonsky), Robin Bartlett (Mrs. Lezak)

HARD COUNTRY (Associated Film Distribution) Executive Producer, Martin Starger; Producers, David Greene, Mack Bing; Co-Producer, John Nartmann; Director, David Greene; Screenplay, Michael Kane; Story, Michael Kane, Michael Martin Murphey; Music, Jimmie Haskell; Presented by Lord Grade; Photography, Dennis Dalzell; Designer, Edward Richardson; Editor, John A. Martinelli; Assistant Directors, Jan R. Lloyd, Judith Vogelsang; Designer, Mark L. Fabus; Costumes, Dianne Anthony; In color; 104 minutes; Rated PG; April release. CAST: Jan-Michael Vincent (Kyle), Kim Basinger (Jodie), Michael Parks (Royce), Gailard Sartain (Johnny), Tanya Tucker (Caro-

line), Sierra Pecheur (Mama Palmer), John Chappell (Daddy Palmer), Daryl Hannah (Loretta), Lewis Van Bergen (Ransom), Ted Neeley (Wesley), Curtis Credel (Dale), Scotch Byerley (Aaron), Richard Lineback (Larry), Elise Caitlin, Danone Camden, Holly Haber (Cowgirls), Richard Moll (Top Gun), Ron Spivey (Shitkicker), Cisse Cameron (Royce's wife), Jack Rader (Foreman), Laura Madison (Tracy), Delana Michaels (Telephone Operator), Terri Foster Brooks (Waitress), David Haney, (Bartender), Garrie Kelly (Interviewer), A'Leisha Brevard (Snoopy Lady), Jay Kerr (Deputy), Cheryl Carter, Henry G. Sanders (Customers), Tina Menard (Maid), Jane Abbott (Woman at airport), Delores Aguirre (Security Guard), Stephen C. Bradbury (Airport Clerk), West Buchanan (Airport Agent), Kirby Buchanan, Mitch Carter (Police at airport)

SUBWAY RIDERS (Hep Pictures) Producers, Johanna Heer, Amos Poe; Direction and Screenplay, Amos Poe; Photography, Johanna Heer; Music, Robert Fripp, Ivan Kral, John Lurie and The Lounge Lizards; In color; 120 minutes; Not rated; April release. CAST: Robbie Coltrane, Charlene Kaleina, John Lurie, Cookie Mueller, Amos Poe, Susan Tyrrell, Robert Fripp, Ivan Kral

THE KIRLIAN WITNESS (Sarno) Producer-Director, Jonathan Sarno; Screenplay, Mr. Sarno, Lamar Sanders; Story, Mr. Sarno; Photography, Joao Fernandes; Editors, Len Dell'Amico, Edward Salier; Music, Harry Mandredini; In Technicolor; Rated PG; 91 minutes; April release. CAST: Nancy Snyder (Rilla), Ted Laplat (Dusty), Joel Colodner (Robert), Nancy Boykin (Laurie), Lawrence Tierney (Detective), Maia Danziger (Claire)

HOT DALLAS NIGHTS (Miracle Films) Producers, Julian Orynski, Vivian O'Dell; Director, Tony Kendrick; Screenplay, Robert Oakwood, Tony Kendrick; Photography, D. B. Cooper; Music, Leonard Conjurski; Editor, James Armin; Executive Producer, Lester Krevetz; In color; 83 minutes; Not rated; April release. CAST: Alexander Kingsford (Duke), R. J. Reynolds (R. J.), Raven Turner (Pat), Tara Flynn (Mary Ellen), Turk Lyon (Robbie), Hillary Summers (Lyndie), Slim Grady (Rock), Greer Shapiro (Miss Millie)

Jan-Michael Vincent, Kim Basinger
in "Hard Country" © AFD

Susan Tyrrell
in "Subway Riders"

Lee Majors
in "The Last Chase"

Barbara Harris, Robert Blake
in "Second-Hand Hearts"
© Lorimar Productions

THE LAST CHASE (Crown International) Producer-Director, Martyn Burke; Co-Producer, Fran Rosati; Executive Producer, Gene Slott; Screenplay, C. R. O'Christopher, Taylor Sutherland, Martyn Burke; Photography, Paul Van Der Linden; Editor, Steve Weslake; Art Director, Roy Forge Smith; In color; 101 minutes; Rated PG; April release. CAST: Lee Majors (Frank), Burgess Meredith (Capt. Williams), Chris Makepeace (Ring), Alexandra Stewart (Eudora), George Touliatos (Hawkins), Ben Gordon (Morely), Diane D'Aquila (Santana)

DEAD AND BURIED (AVCO Embassy) Executive Producer, Richard R. St. Johns; Producers, Ronald Shusett, Robert Fentress; Director, Gary A. Sherman; Screenplay, Ronald Shusett, Dan O'Bannon; Based on story by Jeff Millar, Alex Stern; Associate Producer, Michael I. Rachmil; Music, Joe Renzetti; Photography, Steve Poster; Editor, Alan Balsam; Art Directors, Bill Sandell, Joe Aubel; Assistant Directors, Brian E. Frankish, Andy Ackerman, Scott Ira Thaler; Designer, James E. Tocci; Costumes, Bill Jobe; In Technicolor; 93 minutes; Rated R; May release. CAST: James Farentino (Dan), Melody Anderson (Janet), Jack Albertson (Dobbs), Dennis Redfield (Ron), Nancy Locke Hauser (Linda), Lisa Blount (Girl on beach), Robert Englund (Harry), Bill Quinn (Ernie), Michael Currie (Herman), Christopher Allport (George/Freddie), Joe Medalis (Doctor), Macon McCalman (Ben). Lisa Marie (Hitchhiker), Estelle Omens (Betty), Barry Corbin (Phil), Linda Turley (Waitress), Ed Bakey (Fisherman), Glenn Morshower (Jimmy), Robert Boler (Haskell), Michael Pataki (Sam), Jill Fosse (Nurse), Mark Courtney/Michael Courtney (Jamie), Renee McDonell (Girl #1), Dottie Catching (Lady Car Passenger), Colby Smith (Female Stranger), Judy Ashton (Joyce), Bill Couch, Bill Couch, Jr., Charles Couch, Tony Cecere, Angelo DeMeo

SAVAGE HARVEST (20th Century-Fox) Producers, Ralph Helfer, Sandy Howard; Director, Robert Collins; Screenplay, Robert Blees, Robert Collins; Based on story by Ralph Helfer, Ken Noyle; Associate Producer, Frank Hildebrand; Music, Robert Folk; Photography, Ronnie Taylor; Designer, Brian Eatwell; Editors, Patrick Kennedy, Scott Wallace; Executive Producers, Derek Gibson, Joe Harris; Co-Producer, Lamar Card; Art Director, Alan Roderick-Jones; Assistant Director, Brian Frankish; Costumes, Ellis Cohen; In DeLuxe Color; 86 minutes; Rated PG; May release. CAST: Tom Skerritt (Casey), Michelle Phillips (Maggie), Shawn Stevens (Jon), Anne-Marie Martin (Wendy), Derek

Partridge (Derek), Arthur Malet (Dr. MacGruder), Tana Helfer (Kristie), Vincent Isaac (Jurogi), Eva Kiritta (Halima), Rene LeVant (Alayo), Bill Okwirry (Yumadi), Abdullah Sunado (Katinga), Levit Tereria (Asian), Philip Chege (Customs Officer), Greg Odhambo (Wireless Operator)

SECOND-HAND HEARTS (Lorimar/Paramount) formerly "Hamster of Happiness"; Producer, James William Guercio; Director, Hal Ashby; Screenplay, Charles Eastman; Photography, Haskell Wexler; Music, Willis Alan Ramsey; Assistant Directors, David Hamburger, Toby Lovallo; Art Director, Richard Carter; In MovieLab Color; 102 minutes; Rated PG; May release. CAST: Robert Blake (Loyal), Barbara Harris (Dinette), Collin Boone (Human), Amber Rose Gold (Iota), Jessica Stansbury, Erica Stansbury (Sandra Dee), Bert Remsen (Voyd), Sondra Blake (Ermy), Shirley Stoler (Maxy), Woodrow Chambliss (Deaf Attendant), Gwen Van Dam (Waitress), Joe Wilson (Snake Rustler), Louis Williams (Carwash Employer), James Steven Beverly (Alton), Spencer Quinn (Swollen Boy), Antonio Abeyta (Chicano Youth), Carol Cox (Diesel Driver), Beege Barkette (Waitress), Sherry Lowell (Cook), David Welch (Cop), Elisa Martinez (Chicano Mother), Ron Spivey (God-Fearing Customer), Kenneth Osman (M.C.), Patsy Wilcox (Cashier), Larry Bettis (Macon Billy), Billie Joe Marlin (Billie Jo)

FRIDAY THE 13TH PART 2 (Paramount) Producer-Director, Steve Miner; Screenplay, Ron Kurz; Based on characters created by Victor Miller; Co-Producer, Dennis Murphy; Editor, Susan E. Cunningham; Associate Producer, Frank Mancuso, Jr.; Executive Producers, Tom Gruenberg, Lisa Barsamian; Music, Harry Manfredini; Designer, Virginia Field; Photography, Peter Stein; Assistant Directors, Charles Layton, Richard Feury; Costumes, Ellen Lutter; In DeLuxe Color; 87 minutes; Rated R; May release. CAST: Amy Steel (Ginny), John Furey (Paul), Adrienne King (Alice), Kirsten Baker (Terry), Stu Charno (Ted), Warrington Gillette (Jason), Walt Gorney (Crazy Ralph), Marta Kober (Sandra), Tom McBride (Mark), Bill Randolph (Jeff), Lauren-Marie Taylor (Vickie), Russell Todd (Scott), Betsy Palmer (Mrs. Voorhees), Cliff Cudney (Max), Jack Marks (Cop), Steve Daskawisz (Jason Stunt Double), Jerry Wallace (Prowler), David Brand, China Chen, Carolyn Loudon, Jaime Perry, Tom Shea, Jill Voight (Counselors)

Melody Anderson, James Farentino
in "Dead & Buried"

John Furey, Amy Steel
in "Friday the 13th Part 2"
© Georgetown Productions

114

Robert Hays, Art Carney in "Take This Job and Shove It"

Charles Ludlam, Michael Burg in "Impostors"

TAKE THIS JOB AND SHOVE IT (AVCO Embassy) Executive Producers, William J. Immerman, J. David Marks; Producer, Greg Blackwell; Director, Gus Trikonis; Photography, James Devis; Associate Producers, Al Kasha, Paul Baratta; Screenplay, Barry Schneider; Story, Jeffrey Bernini, Barry Schneider; Based on song by David Allan Coe; Music, Billy Sherrill; Editor, Richard Belding; Assistant Directors, Frank Glenn, James M. Freitag; Art Director, Jim Dultz; A Cinema Group presentation in color; 106 minutes; Rated PG; May release. CAST: Robert Hays (Frank), Art Carney (Charlie), Barbara Hershey (J.M.), David Keith (Harry), Tim Thomerson (Ray), Martin Mull (Dick), Eddie Albert (Ellison), Penelope Milford (Lenore), David Allan Coe (Mooney), Lacy J. Dalton (Mrs. Mooney), Charlie Rich (Hooker), George Lindsay (Semi-Truck Driver), Johnny Paycheck (Man with hamburgers), Len Lesser (Roach), Royal Dano (Beeber), Virgil Frye (Cleach), Bruce Fischer (Jimmy), Mike Genovese (Marvin), Suzanne Kent (Charmaine), Robert Swan (Virgil), James Karen (Loomis), Wally Engelhardt (Doomar), Sharon Ernster (Doreen), Joan Prather (Madelene), Fran Ryan (Mrs. Hinkle), Carole Mallory (B-Jo), Brenda King (Secretary), David Selburg (Harvard Type), Stephan B. Meyers (Harry, Jr.), Mary Pat Hennagir (Patricia Ann), Mare O'Brien (Mary), Brad Alan Waller (Dugan), James Whittle (Installer)

HEARTWORN HIGHWAYS (First Run Features) Direction and Photography, James Szalapski; Producer; Graham Leader; Editor, Phillip Schopper; In color; 92 minutes; Rated R; May release. A documentary about the new American music, referred to as "new", "progressive," or "outlaw country" with Guy Clark, Larry Jon Wilson, Townes Van Zandt, Charlie Daniels, Barefoot Jerry, Rodney Crowell, Steve Young, Gamble Rogers, Seymour Washington, Big Mac McGowan, and David Allan Coe.

BEYOND THE REEF (Universal) Producer, Raffaella DeLaurentiis; Director, Frank C. Clark; Screenplay, Louis LaRusso II, Jim Carabatsos; Based on novel "Tikoyo and His Shark" by Clement Richer; Music, Francis Lai; Photography, Sam Martin; Underwater Sequences, Ramon Bravo; Editor, Ian Crafford; Designer, A Nui Ben Teriitehau; Assistant Directors, Jan Kowalski, John Soldatis; Choreographer, Coco Ellacott; In Technicolor; 91 minutes; May release. CAST: Dayton Ka'ne (Tikoyo), Maren Jensen (Diana), Kathleen Swan (Milly), Keahi Farden (Jeff), Oliverio Maciel Diaz (Manidu), George Tapare (Hawaiian), David Nakuna (Mischima), Robert Atamu (Maku), Bob Spiegel (Turpin),

Maui Temaui (Milly's Boyfriend), Teriitehu Star (Grandfather), Joseph Ka'ne (Tikoyo as a child), Titaua Castel (Diana as a child), Andre Garnier (Jeff as a child)

IMPOSTORS (First Run Features) Produced, Directed and Written by Mark Rappaport; Photography, Fred Murphy; Associate Producers, Joanne Mallas, Steve Miller; Editors, Mark Rappaport, Meri Weingarten; In color; 110 minutes; Not rated; May release. CAST: Peter Evans (Peter), Ellen McElduff (Tina), Charles Ludlam (Chuckie), Michael Burg (Mikey), Lina Todd (Gina), Randy Danson (Stephanie), Kevin Wade, Shelley Desai, John Brockmeyer, Betty James

A CELTIC TRILOGY (First Run Features) Producer-Director-Editor, Kathleen Dowdey; Photography, Peter O'Neill; A Cecropia production in color; 96 minutes; Not rated; May release. A documentary based on writings from Celtic mythology, literature and history narrated by Siobhan McKenna

MS. 45 (Navaron) Director, Abel Ferrara; Screenplay, Nicholas St. John; Photography, James Momel; Editor, Christopher Andrews; Music, Joe Delis; In color; 90 minutes; Rated R; May release. CAST: Zoe Tamerlia (Thana), Steve Singer (Photographer), Jack Thibeau (Man in bar), Peter Yellen (2nd Rapist), Darlene Stuto (Laurie), Editta Sherman (Landlady), Albert Sinkys (Boss), Jimmy Laine (1st Rapist), Bogey (Phil)

INCHON (One Way Productions) Producer, Mitsuharu Ishii; Director, Terence Young; Screenplay, Robin Moore, Laird Koenig; Story, Robin Moore, Paul Savage; Photography, Bruce Surtees; Music, Jerry Goldsmith; Special Adviser, Sun Myung Moon; In color; 140 minutes; Not rated; May release. CAST: Laurence Olivier (Gen. MacArthur), Jacqueline Bisset (Barbara Hallsworth), Ben Gazzara (Maj. Hallsworth), Toshiro Mifune (Saito-San), Richard Roundtree (Sgt. Henderson), David Janssen (Feld), Nam Goon Won (Park), Gabriele Ferzetti (Turkish Brigadier), Rex Reed (Longfellow), Sabine Sun (Marguerite), Dorothy James (Mrs. MacArthur), Karen Kahn (Lim), Lydia Lei (Mila), James Callahan (Gen. Almond), Anthony Dawson (Gen. Collins), Peter Burton (Adm. Sherman), John Pochna (Lt. Haig), William Dupree (Turkish Sgt.), Grace Chan (Ah Cheu), Dwang Nam Yang (Pres. Rhee), Mickey Knox (Adm. Doyle)

Maren Jensen in "Beyond the Reef"
© **Dino Laurentiis Corp.**

Siobhan McKenna in "A Celtic Trilogy"

Priscilla and Elvis Presley
in "This Is Elvis" © Warner Bros.

Cleavon Little, James Brolin, Chick Vennera,
Bruce Davison in "High Risk"
© Viacom International

THIS IS ELVIS (Warner Bros.) Executive Producer, David L. Wolper; Produced, Directed and Written by Malcolm Leo, Andrew Solt; Music, Walter Scharf; Editor, Bud Friedgen; Associate Producer, Bonnie Peterson; Co-Editor, Glenn Farr; Photography, Gil Hubbs; Assistant Director, Bob Stein; In Technicolor and Dolby Stereo; 101 minutes; Rated PG; May release. CAST: David Scott (Elvis at 18), Paul Boensch III (Elvis at 10), Johnny Harra (Elvis at 42), Lawrence Koller (Vernon Presley), Rhonda Lyn (Priscilla Presley), Debbie Edge (Gladys Presley), Larry Raspberry (Dewey Phillips), Furry Lewis (Bluesman), Liz Robinson (Minnie Mae Presley), Dana MacKay (Elvis at 35), Knox Phillips (Sam Phillips), Cheryl Needham (Linda Thompson), Andrea Cyrill (Ginger Alden), Jerry Phillips (Bill Black) Emory Smith (Scotty Moore), Narration: Ral Donner (Elvis), Joe Esposito (Himself). Linda Thompson (Herself), Lisha Sweetnam (Priscilla), Virginia Kiser (Gladys), Michael Tomack (Vernon Presley)

HIGH RISK (American Cinema) Executive Producer, John Daly; Producers, Joe Raffill, Gerald Green; Direction and Screenplay, Steward Raffill; Art Director, Ron Foreman; Editor, Tom Walls, Jr; Photography, Alex Phillips, Jr.; Designer, Augustin Ituarte; In color; 97 minutes; Rated R; May release. CAST: James Brolin (Stone), Lindsay Wagner (Olivia), Anthony Quinn (Mariano), Cleavon Little (Rockney), Bruce Davison (Dan), Chick Vennera (Tony), James Coburn (Serrano), Ernest Borgnine (Clint), David Young (Bradley), Richard Young (Mike), Stephanie Faulkner (Charlene), Udana Power (Gail), Fernando Palavicini (Manuel), Douglas Sandoval (Julio), Sergio Calderon (Hueso), Eduard Noriega (General), Mario Valdez (His Assistant), Roberto Sosa (Boy), Alvaro Carcano, Paco Morayta (Gays in jail), Tony Rubio (Bearded Man), Sammy Ortiz (Conductor), Polo Salazar Flores (Waiter), Eduardo Paxon (Mark), Samantha Borzaui (Liz), Leonard Smith (Mike), Luz Maria Pena (Voluptuous Lady), Rudolfo de Alexandre (Skinny Man), Xochitl del Rosario (Fat Whore), Gerardo Cepeda (Policeman), Daniel Garcia (Roberto), Rene Barrera (Guard), Angel Aragon, Carlos Romano, Rebecca Johnson (Pool Players), Ana de Sade (Nude), Evelyn Klippian (Bikini Girl)

GETTING OVER (Continental) Producers, John R. Daniels; Cassius V. Weathersby, Jr.; Direction and Screenplay, Bernie Rollins; Story by Daniels and Rollins; Photography, and Editing, Stephen B. Kim; Music, Johnny Rodgers; Art Director, Hayward Perkins, Laurence Lochard; Assistant Director, Jefferson Richard; Associate Producers, Joseph A. Hubbard, Jr., Alonzo K. Daniels; In CFI Color; 108 minutes; Rated PG; May release. CAST: John R. Daniels (Mike), Gwen Brisco (Gwen), Bernice Givens (Bernice), Mary Hopkins (Mary), Sheila Dean (Sheila), Renee Gentry (Renee), Sandra Sully (Sandy), Paulette Gibson (Paulette), Donniece Jackson (Penny), George Pelster (Lou), John F. Goff (Arnold), Sheldon Lee (Sol), Andrew "Buzz" Cooper, Dap Sugar Willie, Floyd "Wildcat" Chatman, Arthur Adams, Don Edmonds, Aurelia Sweeney, Mabel King, Bryan O'Dell, David Hubbard, Michael Hiat, Peggy Foster

SEPARATE WAYS (Crown International) Executive Producer, Marlene Schmidt; Producer-Director, Howard Avedis; Screenplay, Leah Appel; Story, Leah Appel, Howard Avedis, Marlene Schmidt; Music, John Cacavas; Associate Producer, Bill Kawata; In DeLuxe Color; 92 minutes; Rated R; May release. CAST: Karen Black (Valentine), Tony LoBianco (Ken), Arlene Golonka (Annie), David Naughton (Jerry), Jack Carter (Barney), Sharon Farrell (Karen), William Windom (Huey), Robert Fuller (Woody), Walter Brooke (Lawrence), Jordan Charney (Harry), Sybil Danning (Mary), Angus Duncan (Allen), Bob Hastings (Jack), Noah Hathaway (Jason), Katherine Justice (Sheila), Josh Taylor (Jim), Cissy Wellman (Darlene), Howard Avedis (Director), Marc Bentley (Allen, Jr.), Pamela Bryant (Waitress), Doris Dowling (Rebecca)

GRADUATION DAY (IFI/Scope III) Producers, David Baughn, Herb Freed; Director, Herb Freed; Screenplay, Anne Marisse, Herb Freed; Photography, Daniel Yarussi; Editor, Martin Jay Sadoff; In color; 85 minutes; Rated R; May release. CAST: Christopher George (Coach), Patch MacKenzie (Anne), E. Danny Murphy (Kevin), E.J. Peaker (Blondie), Michael Pataki

GLEN OR GLENDA (Paramount) Producer, George G. Weiss; Direction and Screenplay, Edward D. Wood, Jr; Photography, William C. Thompson; Editor, Bud Schelling; In black and white; Formerly "I Led Two Lives"; 67 minutes; Rated PG; May release. CAST: Bela Lugosi (Scientist), Lyle Talbot (Policeman), Daniel Davis (Glen/Glenda), Dolores Fuller (Barbara), Tommy Haynes (Alan/Ann), Timothy Farrell (Psychiatrist), Charles Crofts, Conrad Brooks

Anthony Quinn in "High Risk"
© Viacom International

Tony LoBianco, Karen Black
in "Separate Ways"

Klinton Spilsbury, Michael Horse
in "The Legend of the Lone Ranger"
© Universal City Studios

James Ryan in "Kill and Kill
Again" © FVI

THE LEGEND OF THE LONE RANGER (Universal/Associated Film Distribution) Executive Producer, Martin Starger; Producer, Walter Coblenz; Director, William A. Fraker; Screenplay, Ivan Goff, Ben Roberts, Michael Kane, William Roberts; Adaptation, Jerry Derloshon; Photography, Laszlo Kovacs; Designer, Albert Brenner; Editor, Thomas Stanford; Music, John Barry; Lyrics, Dean Pitchford; "Man in the Mask" Sung by Merle Haggard; Assistant Directors, Charles Okun, Joseph A. Ingraffia; Associate Producer, Dick Gallegly; Art Director, David M. Haber; Costumes, Noel Taylor; Photography, Bobby Byrne; In Panavision and Technicolor; 98 minutes; Rated PG; May release. CAST: Klinton Spilsbury (Lone Ranger), Michael Horse (Tonto), Christopher Lloyd (Cavendish), Matt Clark (Sheriff), Juanin Clay (Amy), Jason Robards (Pres. Grant), John Bennett Perry (Dan Reid), David Hayward (Collins), John Hart (Lucas), Richard Farnsworth (Wild Bill Hickok), Lincoln Tate (Gen. Custer), Ted Flicker (Buffalo Bill Cody), Marc Gilpin (Young John Reid), Patrick Montoya (Young Tonto), David Bennett (Gen. Rodriguez), Rick Traeger (German), James Bowman (Gambler), Kit Wong (Chinese), Daniel Nunez (Agent), R. L. Tolbert (Stagecoach Driver), Clay Boss (Shotgun), Jose Rey Toledo, Max Cisneros (Chiefs), Ted White (Reid), Chere Bryson (Mrs. Reid), James Lee Crite (Waiter), Min Burke (Stephenson), Jeff Ramsey (Alcott), Bennie Dobbins (Lopez), Henry Wills (Little), Greg Walker (Rankin), Mike Adams (Palmer), Ben Bates (Post), Bill Hart (Carner), Larry Randles (Stacy), Robert Hoy (Perlmutter), Ted Gehring (Stillwell), Buck Taylor (Gattlin), Tom R. Diaz (Eastman), Chuck Hayward (Wald), Tom Laughlin (Neeley), Terry Leonard (Valentine), Steve Meador (Russell), Joe Finnegan (Westlake), Roy Bonner (Richardson), John M. Smith (Whitloff)

KILL AND KILL AGAIN (Film Ventures International) Executive Producer, Edward L. Montoro; Producer, Igo Kantor; Director, Ivan Hall; Screenplay, John Crowther; Photography, Tai Krige; Editors, Peter Thornton, Robert Leighton; Assistant Director, Chris Gilliam; Costumes, Sherry Cliffe; In color by DeLuxe; An APC picture in Panavision; 100 minutes; Rated PG; May release. CAST: James Ryan (Steve), Anneline Kriel (Kandy), Ken Gampu (Gorilla), Norman Robinson (Gypsy Billy), Stan Schmidt (Fly), Bill Flynn (Hotdog), Michael Mayer (Marduk), Marloe Scott-Wilson (Minerva), John Ramsbottom (Dr. Kane), Eddie Dorie (Optimus), Mervyn John (President)

UNCLE SCAM (New World Pictures of Philadelphia) Produced and Directed by Tom Pileggi, Michael Levanios, Jr.; Associate Producers, Joseph Pileggi, Michael Levanios III; Screenplay, Tom Pilong, Michael Levanios, Jr., Tom Pileggi, Joe Ryan; Photography, John Burke; Editor, Michael Levanios, Jr.; Music, Michael Levanios III; In color; 105 minutes; Not rated; May release. CAST: Tom McCarthy (Tom), Maxine Greene (Ginger), John Russell (Art), James E. Myers (Steve), Sharon Victoria (Linda), David Cassling (Herbie), Matt Myers, Pat Cooper, Joan Rivers, Alan Jay, Shari Thomas, Diane Moore, Pat Canuso, Elaine Filoon, Marvin Stafford, Joe Pileggi

THE NESTING (Feature Films) Producer-Director, Armand Weston; Executive Producers, Sam Lake, Robert Sumner; Screenplay, Daria Price, Armand Weston; Photography, Joao Fernandes; Editor, Jack Foster; Music, Jack Malken, Kim Scholes; Assistant Director, Fred Berner; Associate Producer, Don Walters; In color; 104 minutes; Rated R; May release. CAST: Robin Groves (Lauren), Christopher Loomis (Mark), Michael David Lally (Daniel), John Carradine (Col. LeBrun), Gloria Grahame (Florinda), Bill Rowley (Frank), David Tabor (Abner), Patrick Farelley (Dr. Webb)

THE BURNING (Filmways) carried in SCREEN WORLD Volume 31 as "Don't Go in the House."

THE HAUNTING OF M (Nu-Image) Produced, Directed, and Written by Anna Thomas; Photography, Gregory Nava; Editors, Michael Bockman, Trevor Black, Anna Thomas; Associate Producers, Gregory Nava, Robert Yerkington; Music, Leos Janacek, Gustav Mahler, Frederick Chopin, Colin Wyllie; In color; 100 minutes; Rated R; May release. CAST: Sheelagh Gilbey (Marianna), Nini Pitt (Halina), Evie Garratt (Daria), Alan Hay (Karol), Jo Scott Matthews (Aunt Teresa), Isolde Cazelet (Yola), William Bryan (Marian), Peter Austin (Stefan), Peter Stenson (Doctor), Varvara Pepper (Irka), Ernest Bale (Stahu), Jenny Greenaway (Gypsy), Gwen Williams (Cousin Julia), Ruby Melvin (Cousin Maria), William Payne (Priest), Stephen Hartford (Fisherman), Ina Menzies (Housekeeper), Jock MacPherson (Fire-eater), and performers from the Austin Brothers Circus

Anneline Kriel, James Ryan
in "Kill and Kill Again" © FVI

William Bryan, Sheelagh Gilbey
in "The Haunting of M"

Tab Hunter, Divine in "Polyester"
© New Line Cinema

Henry Tomaszewski, Laura Harrington
in "The Dark End of the Street"

POLYESTER (New Line Cinema) Produced, Directed and Written by John Waters; Executive Producer, Robert Shaye; Associate Producer, Sara Risher; Photography, David Insley; Costumes, Van Smith; Designer, Vincent Peranio; Line Producer, Robert Maier; Editor, Charles Roggero; Music, Chris Stein, Michael Kamen; Lyrics, Deborah Harry; In color and Odorama; 86 minutes; Rated R; May release. CAST: Divine (Francine), Tab Hunter (Todd), Edith Massey (Cuddles), Mink Stole (Sandra), David Samson (Elmer), Joni Ruth White (LaRue), Mary Garlington (Lulu), Ken King (Dexter), Hans Kramm (Chauffeur), Stiv Bators (Bo-Bo), George Stover, Steve Yeager (Press)

THE DARK END OF THE STREET (First Run Features) Executive Producer, Rikk Larsen; Producer, Dian K. Miller; Direction and Screenplay, Jan Egleson; Music, Marion Gillon, Tyrone Johnson; Photography, D'Arcy Marsh; Editor, Jerry Bloedow; Assistant Director, Steve Seidel; Associate Producer, Jeannie Sullivan; In color; 89 minutes; Not rated; June release. CAST: Laura Harrington (Donna), Henry Tomaszewski (Billy), Michelle Green (Marlene), Lance Henriksen (Jimmy), Pamela Payton-Wright (Mary Ann), Terence Grey (Ethan), Al Eaton (Brian), Gustave Johnson (Reynolds). George Martin (Salvucci), Flash Wiley (Mr. Thomas), Bennie Wiley (Mrs. Thomas)

STRIPES (Columbia) Producers, Ivan Reitman, Dan Goldberg; Director, Ivan Reitman; Screenplay, Len Blum, Dan Goldberg, Harold Ramis; Photography, Bill Butler; Designer, James Spencer; Editors, Eva Ruggiero, Michael Luciano, Harry Keller; Music, Elmer Bernstein; Costumes, Richard Bruno; Assistant Directors, Richard Learman, James M. Freitag, Donald J. Newman; Associate Producer, Joe Medjuck; Choreographers, Ronn Forella, Arthur Goldweit; In color; 105 minutes; Rated R; June release. CAST: Bill Murray (John), Harold Ramis (Russell), Warren Oates (Sgt. Hulka), P.J. Soles (Stella), Sean Young (Louise), John Larroquette (Capt. Stillman), John Voldstad (Aide), John Diehl (Cruiser), Lance LeGault (Col. Glass), Roberta Leighton (Anita), Conrad Dunn (Psycho), Judge Reinhold (Elmo), Antone Pagan (Hector), Glenn-Michael Jones (Leon), Bill Lucking (Recruiter), Fran Ryan (Dowager), Joseph P. Flaherty, Nick Toth (Guards), Dave Thomas (M.C.), Robert Klein (Cheerleader), Robert J. Wilke (Gen. Barnicke), Lois Areno (Stilman's Girlfriend), Samuel Briggs (Corporal), Joseph X. Flaherty (Sgt. Crocker), Hershel B. Harlson (Shoeshine Man), Timothy Busfield (Soldier with Mortar), Solomon Schmidt (Store Owner), Craig Schaefer (Soldier outside motor pool), Arkady Rakhman (Immigrant), Pamela Bowman (Cruiser's Girl)

STUDENT BODIES (Paramount) Executive Producers, Jerry Belson, Harvey Miller; Producer, Allen Smithee; Direction and Screenplay, Mickey Rose; Associate Producer, Melvin Shapiro; Designer, Donald Nunley; Photography, Robert Ebinger; Editor, Kathryn Ruth Hope; Music, Gene Hobson; Costumes, Kristin Nelson; A Universal Southwest Cinema production in association with Allen Smithee Classic Films; In color; 86 minutes; Rated R; June release. CAST: Kristin Riter (Toby), Matthew Goldsby (Hardy), Richard Brando (The Breather), Joe Flood (Dumpkin), Joe Talarowski (Principal), Mimi Weddell (Miss Mumsley), Carl Jacobs (Dr. Sigmund), Peggy Cooper (Ms. Van Dyke), Janice E. O'Malley (Nurse Krud), Kevin Mannis (Scott), Sara Eckhardt (Patti), Brian Batytis (Wheels), Cullen G. Chambers (Charles), Joan Browning Jacobs (Mrs. Hummers), Angela Bressler (Julie), Kay Ogden (Ms. LeClair), Douglas Cotner (Mr. Hummers), Charles L. Trotter (Announcer), Jonathan Walling (Al), Keith Singleton (Charlie), Dario O. Jones (Mawamba), Thomas D. Cannon II (Ralph), Oscar James (Coach), Robyn Flanery (Joan), Tammie M. Tignor (Dagmar), Anita Taylor (Bertha), John M. Armstrong (Joe), Brenda Maduzia (Punker), Dorothy Rich (Mrs. Peters), Anne Bell (Teacher), Kathryn Reve Doster (Sue), Janice Elaine Berridge (Student).

CHEECH & CHONG'S NICE DREAMS (Columbia) Producer, Howard Brown; Director, Thomas Chong; Screenplay, Thomas Chong, Richard Cheech Marin; Photography, Charles Correll; Designer, James Newport; Editor, Scott Conrad; Associate Producer, Shelby Fiddis; Assistant Directors, Robert P. Cohen, Alice West; Costumes, Sharon Day; Music, Harry Betts, Ruban Guevara, Cheech & Chong, Gaye Delorme; In color; Rated R; 110 minutes; June release. CAST: Thomas Chong, Cheech Marin, Dr. Timothy Leary (Themselves), Evelyn Guerrero (Donna), Stacy Keach (Sarge), Robert 'Big Buck' Maffei (Goon), Rikki Marin (Blonde in car), Sally K. Marr (Nut #5), Louis Guss (Herb), Danny Kwan (Lab Technician), Michael Lansing (Nut #15), Sab Shimono (Bus Boy), Paul Zegler (Herb, Jr.), Roderick E. Daniels (Janitor), Jeff Pomerantz (CHP#2), Paul Reubens (Howie), Tim Rossovich (Noodles), Roosevelt Smith (Cop).

Harold Ramis, Warren Oates, Bill Murray
in "Stripes" © Columbia Pictures

Cheech and Chong in "Nice Dreams"
© Columbia Pictures

Mary-Margaret Humes, Mel Brooks, Gregory
Hines, Paul Mazursky in "History of
the World" © Brooksfilms Ltd.

"Texas Lightning"

HISTORY OF THE WORLD, PART I (20th Century-Fox) Produced, Directed and Written by Mel Brooks; Associate Producers, Stuart Cornfeld, Alan Johnson; Photography, Woody Omens; Designer, Harold Michelson; Special Effects, Albert J. Whitlock; Editor, John C. Howard; Music, John Morris; "The Inquisition" song by Mel Brooks, Ronny Graham; Choreography, Alan Johnson; Costumes, Patricia Norris; Art Director, Norman Newberry; Assistant Directors, Jerry Ziesmer, Mitchell Bock; Editor, Danford B. Greene; In DeLuxe Color, Panavision; 93 minutes; Rated R; June release. CAST: Orson Welles (Narrator), Mel Brooks (Moses, Comicus, Torquemada, Jacques, King Louis XVI), Dom DeLuise (Nero), Madeline Kahn (Empress Nympho), Harvey Korman (Count Monet), Cloris Leachman (Mme. DeFarge), Ron Carey (Swiftus), Gregory Hines (Josephus), Pamela Stephenson (Mlle. Rimbaud), Andreas Voutsinas (Bearnaise), Shecky Greene (Marcus Vindictus), Sid Caesar (Chief Caveman), Howard Morris (Court Spokesman), Rudy DeLuca (Capt. Mucus), Mary-Margaret Humes (Miriam), Bea Arthur (Clerk), Charlie Callas (Soothsayer), Dena Dietrich (Competence), Paul Mazursky (Roman Officer), Ron Clark, Jack Riley (Stoned Soldiers), Art Metrano (Leonardo DaVinci), Diane Day (Caladonia), Henny Youngman (Chemist), Hunter Von Leer (Lt. Bob), Fritz Feld (Maitre d'), Hugh Hefner (Entrepreneur), Pat McCormick (Plumbing Salesman), Sid Gould (Barber), Jim Steck (Gladiator), Ronny Graham (Oedipus), John Myhers (Senate Leader), Lee Delano (Wagon Driver), Robert B. Goldberg, Alan U. Schwartz, Jay Burton (Senators), Robert Zappy, Ira Miller, Milt Freedman (Roman Citizens), Johnny Silver (Small Liar), Charles Thomas Murphy (Auctioneer), Rod Haase (Officer), Eileen Saki (Slave), John Hurt (Jesus), Jackie Mason, Ronny Graham (Jews), Phil Leeds (Chief Monk), Jack Carter (Rat Vendor), Jan Murray (Nothing Vendor), Spike Milligan (M. Rimbaud), John Hillerman (Rich Man), Sidney Lassick (Applecore Vendor), Jonathan Cecil (Poppinjay), Andrew Sachs (Gerard), Fiona Richmond (Queen), Nigel Hawthorne (Official), Bella Emberg (Baguette), Geoffrey Larder (Footman), George Lane Cooper (Executioner), Stephanie Marrian (Lady Marie), Royce Mills (Duke D'Honnefleur), Mike Cottrell (Tartuffe), Gerald Stadden (LeFevre), John Gavin (Marche), Rusty Goff (LeMuff)

TUCK EVERLASTING (Coe Films) Producer, Howard Kling; Director, Frederick King Keller; Screenplay, Stratton Rawson, Fred A. Keller, Frederick King Keller, Jim Bisco; Based on novel by Natalie Babbitt; Art Director, Michael Bucur; Music, Malcolm Daiglish, Grey Larson; In color; 114 minutes; Not rated; June release. CAST: Fred A. Keller, James McGuire, Paul Flessa, Margaret Chamberlain, Sonia Raimi, Bruce D'Aurio, Frank O'Hara, Barbara Harmon

SEARCH AND DESTROY (Film Ventures International) Producer, James Margellis; Director, William Fruet; Screenplay, Don Enright; Music by FM; A Jack Barry and Dan Enright presentation; An R. Ben Efraim production in color; 93 minutes; Rated PG; June release. CAST: Perry King (Kip), Don Stroud (Buddy), Tisa Farrow (Kate), Park Jong Soo (Assassin), George Kennedy (Fusqua), Tony Sheer (Frank)

TEXAS LIGHTNING (Film Ventures International) Producer, Jim Sotos; Direction and Screenplay, Gary Graver; In color; 93 minutes; Rated R; June release. CAST: Cameron Mitchell, Channing Mitchell, Maureen McCormick, Peter Jason, Danone Camden, J.L. Clark

FINAL EXAM (Bedford Entertainment Group) Producers, John L. Chambliss, Myron Meisel; Executive Producers, John L. Chambliss, Lon J. Kerr, Michael Mahern; Direction and Screenplay, Jimmy Huston; Photography, Darrell Cathcart; Editor, John O'Connor; Music, Gary Scott; Assistant Director, Charles Reynolds; Associate Producers, Todd Durham, Carol Bahoric; In DeLuxe Color; 90 minutes; Rated R; June release. CAST: Cecile Bagdadi (Courtney), Joel S. Rice (Radish), Ralph Brown (Wildman), Deanna Robbins (Lisa), Sherry Willis-Burch (Janet), John Fallon (Mark), Terry W. Farren (Pledge), Timothy L. Raynor (Killer), Sam Kilman (Sheriff), Don Hepner (Dr. Reynolds), Jerry Rusing (Coach)

BEATLEMANIA (American Cinema) Producers, Edie and Ely Landau, Steven Leber, David Krebs; Director, Joseph Manduke; Conceived and Designed by Bob Gill, Robert Rabinowitz; Photography, King Baggot; Music, The Beatles; In Dolby Stereo and color; 86 minutes; Rated PG: July release. CAST: Mitch Weissman, Ralph Castelli, David Leon, Tom Teeley as The Beatles

"Student Bodies"
© Paramount Pictures

"Beatlemania"

Richard Norton (R)
in "Force 5"

Victoria Abril, Tony Anthony
in "Comin' at Ya!"
© Filmways Pictures

FORCE: FIVE (American Cinema) Producer, Fred Weintraub; Direction and Screenplay, Robert Clouse; Based on screenplay by Emil Farkas, George Goldsmith; Assistant Directors, Ed Milkovich, Steven McEvetty; Photography, Gill Hubbs; Editor, Bob Bring; Art Director, Richard Lawrence; Designer, Joel David Lawrence; In color; 95 minutes; Rated R; July release. CAST: Joe Lewis (Jim), Master Bong Soo Han (Rev. Rhee), Pam Huntington (Laurie), Sonny Barnes (Lockjaw), Benny Urquidez (Billy), Richard Norton (Ezekiel), Ron Hayden (Willard), Bob Schott (Carl), Michael Prince (Stark), Amanda Wyss (Cindy), Matthew Tobin (Becker), Peter MacLean (Sen. Forester), Dennis Mancini (John), Patricia Alice Albrecht (Cathy), Edith Fields (Sarah), Mel Novak (Assassin), Tom Vilard (Disciple), Dolores Cantu (Nina), Loren Janes (Hank)

COMIN' AT YA! (Filmways) Producer, Tony Anthony; Director, Ferdinando Baldi; Executive Producers, Gene Quintano, Brud Talbot; Associate Producer, Marshall Lupo; Co-Producer, Stan Torchia; Screenplay, Lloyd Battista, Wolf Lowenthal, Gene Quintano; Story, Tony Petitto; Music, Carlo Savina; Art Director-Costumes, Luciano Spadoni; Special Effects, Fredy Unger; Editor, Franco Fraticelli; Photography, Fernando Arribas; In Dimensionscope, Technicolor, and Dolby Stereo; 91 minutes; Rated R; July release. CAST: Tony Anthony (H. H. Hart), Gene Quintano (Pike), Victoria Abril (Abilene), Ricardo Palacios (Polk), Lewis Gordon (Old Man)

UNDER THE RAINBOW (Orion/Warner Bros.) Executive Producer, Edward H. Cohen; Producer, Fred Bauer; Director, Steve Rash; Screenplay, Pat McCormick, Harry Hurwitz, Martin Smith, Pat Bradley, Fred Bauer; Story, Fred Bauer, Pat Bradley; Music, Joe Renzetti; Costumes, Mike Butler; Associate Producer, Frances Avrut-Bauer; Editor, David Blewitt; Design, Peter Wooley; Photographer, Frank Stanley; Assistant Directors, Robert J. Smawley, Maggie Rash, James S. Simons; In DeLuxe Color; 98 minutes; Rated PG; July release. CAST: Chevy Chase (Bruce), Carrie Fisher (Annie), Eve Arden (Duchess), Joseph Maher (Duke), Robert Donner (Assassin), Billy Barty (Otto), Mako (Nakamuri), Cork Hubbert (Rollo), Pat McCormick (Tiny), Adam Arkin (Henry), Richard Stahl (Lester), Freeman King (Otis), Peter Isacksen (Homer), Jack Kruschen (Louie), Bennett Ohta (Akido), Gary Friedkin (Wedgie), Michael Lee Gogin (Fitzgerald), Pam Vance (Lana), Louisa Moritz (Operator), Anthony Gordon (Inspector), John Pyle (Steward), Bill Lytle (Clerk), Ted Lehmann (Hitler), Patty Ma-

loney (Rosie), Zelda Rubinstein (Iris), Bobby Porter (Ventriloquist), Charlie Messenger (Hitler's Aide), Robert Murvin (Lefty), David Haney (Dispatcher), Leonard Barr (Pops), Geraldine Papel (Waitress)

ZORRO, THE GAY BLADE (20th Century-Fox) Producers, George Hamilton, C. O. Erickson; Director, Peter Medak; Screenplay, Hal Dresner; Based on character created by Johnston M. McCulley; Story, Hal Dresner, Greg Alt, Don Moriarty, Bob Randall; Photography, John A. Alonzo; Design, Herman A. Blumenthal; Editor, Pembroke J. Herring; Costumes, Gloria Gresham; Music, Ian Fraser; Art Director, Adrian Gorton; Choreographer, Alex Romero; Associate Producers, Don Moriarty, Greg Alt; Assistant Directors, Daniel J. McCauley, Joseph Paul Moore, Steve McEveety; In DeLuxe Color; 96 minutes; Rated PG; July release. CAST: George Hamilton (Don Diego Vega/Bunny Wigglesworth), Lauren Hutton (Charlotte), Brenda Vaccaro (Florinda), Ron Leibman (Esteban), Donovan Scott (Paco), James Booth (Velasquez), Helen Burns (Consuela), Clive Revill (Garcia), Carolyn Seymour (Dolores), Eduardo Noriega (Don Francisco), Jorge Russek (Don Fernando), Eduardo Alcaraz (Don Jose), Carlos Bravo (Luis), Roberto Dumont (Ferraro), Jorge Bolio (Pablito), Dick Balduzzi (Old Man), Ana Elisa Perez Bolanos (Granddaughter), Francisco Mauri (Guard), Julian Colman (Martinez), Francisco Morayta (Ramirez), Pilar Pellicer (Francisco's Wife), Owen Lee (Sgt.), Gustavo Ganem (Barman), Armando Duarte (Soldier), Norm Blankenship (Whipping Master), Frank Welker (Narrator)

ON ANY SUNDAY II (International Film Marketing/Arista) Producers, Roger Riddell, Don Shoemaker; Directors, Ed Forsyth, Don Shoemaker; Executive Producers, David M. Walden, James L. Cavanaugh; Photography, Henning Schellerup, Tom Harvey, H. Allan Seymour II; Editors, Ed Forsyth, Patrick Crawford; Music, Allan Alper; Narrator, Larry Huffman; In CFI Color; 90 minutes; Rated PG; July release. A documentary on motorcycle racing.

HOLLYWOOD HIGH PART II (Lone Star) Producers, Colleen Meeker, Cotton Whittingham; Directors, Caruth C. Byrd, Lee Thornberg; Screenplay, Whittingham, Byrd, Meeker, Thornberg; Photography, Gary Gravers; Music and Songs, Doug Goodman; Editor, Warren Chadwick; In color; Rated R; July release. CAST: April May, Donna Lynn, Camille Warner, Brad Cowgill, Drew Davis, Bruce Dobos, Con Covert, Alisa Ann Hull, Angela Field, Anne Morris

Carrie Fisher, Chevy Chase in "There's Always Room under the Rainbow"
© Orion Pictures

Brenda Vaccaro, George Hamilton in "Zorro, the Gay Blade"
© Simon Film Productions

Maureen Stapleton, Gary Coleman
in "On the Right Track"
© Zephyr Productions

"Heavy Metal"

ON THE RIGHT TRACK (20th Century-Fox) Producer, Ronald Jacobs; Director, Lee Philips; Written and Co-Produced by Tina Pine, Avery Buddy, Richard Moses; Executive Producers, Harry Evans Sloan, Lawrence L. Kuppin; Photography, Jack Richards; Music, Arthur B. Rubinstein; Editor, Bill Butler; Assistant Directors, Penelope Foster, C. Tad Devlin; Art Director, William Fosser; A TLP Production in association with Zephyr Productions; In C.F.I. color; 98 minutes; Rated PG; July release. CAST: Gary Coleman (Lester), Maureen Stapleton (Mary/Bag Lady), Norman Fell (Mayor), Michael Lembeck (Frank), Lisa Eilbacher (Jill), Bill Russell (Robert), Herb Edelman (Sam), David Selburg (Felix), C. Thomas Cunliffe (Shoeshine Concessioner), Belinda Bremner (Lady with suitcase), Nathan Davis (Mario), Mike Bacarella (Sean), Jack Wasserman (Vito), Fern Persons (Flower Lady), Arthur Smith (Gerald), Mike Genovese (Louis), Harry Gorsuch (Harry), George Brengel (Bookstore Man), Corin Rogers (Mark), Page Hannah (Sally), I. W. Klein (IRS Man), Muriel Bach (Beauty Salon Boss), Ronda Pierson, Linda Golla, Brenda Lively (Salon Girls), John Mohrlein (Thief), Sally Benoit (Interview), Thom Brandolino (Crewman), Jerry McKay (Pantyhose Peddler), Mario Tanzi (Racetrack Window Man), Rick LeFevour (Mugger), Edna Moreno (Old Lady), Bert Weineberg (Monkey Man), James Hogan, Jr. (Minister), Debbie Hall (Bride), Jamie Gertz (Big Girl), Steve Marmer (Customer with cold), Gil Cantanzaro, Sr. (Cab Driver), Gil Cantanzaro, Jr. (Truck Driver), Chelcie Ross, Felix Shuman (Customers), James Andelin, Al Nuti (Transit Cops), Mark Hutter, T. W. Miller (Policemen)

NOBODY'S PERFEKT (Columbia) Producer, Mort Engelberg; Director, Peter Bonerz; Screenplay, Tony Kenrick; Based on his novel "Two for the Price of One"; Executive Producer, Ted Swanson; Photography, James Pergola; Art Director, Don K. Ivey; Music, David McHugh; Editor, Neil Travis; Assistant Directors, David Whorf, Stephen Lofaro, Ricou Browning; In Metrocolor; 96 minutes; Rated PG; August release. CAST: Gabe Kaplan (Dibley), Alex Karras (Swaboda), Robert Klein (Walter), Susan Clark (Carol), Paul Stewart (Dr. Segal), Alex Rocco (Boss), Arthur Rosenberg (Mayor), Bobby Ramsen (New Yorker), John DiSanti (Knuckles), Ric Applewhite (Louie), Will Knickerbocker (Mechanic), Peter Bonerz (Randall Kendall), Harold Bergman (Captain), Roz Simmons (Mrs. Freeman), Alden McKay (Freeman), Omkar Spencer (Young Wife), Keshav Haeseler (Young Husband), Al Kiggins

(Col. Brogan), Ray Forchion (Army Officer), Luke Halpin (Deckhand), Julio Mechoso, Jose Fong, Jorge Gil (Gangmembers), John Archie, Lee Krug (Mayor's Aides), Jeff Gillen, Dan Rambo, Lillian Zuckerman, Clarence Thomas, Henry LeClair, Sean Brennan, Laurie Stark

HEAVY METAL (Columbia) Producer, Ivan Reitman; Director, Gerald Potterton; Screenplay, Dan Goldberg, Len Blum; Based on original art and stories by Richard Corben, Angus McKie, Dan O'Banon, Thomas Warkentin, Berni Wrightson; Music, Elmer Bernstein; Songs, Black Sabbath, Blue Oyster Cult, Cheap Trick, Devo, Donald Fagen, Don Felder, Grand Funk Railroad, Sammy Hagar, Journey, Nazareth, Stevie Nicks, Riggs, Trust; Executive Producer, Leonard Mogel; Associate Producers, Michael Gross, Peter Lebensold, Lawrence Nesis; Designer, Michael Gross; In Dolby Stereo and color; 90 minutes; Rated R; August release. CAST: The voices of Roger Bumpass, Jackie Burroughs, John Candy, Joe Flaherty, Don Francks, Martin Lavut, Eugene Levy, Marilyn Lightstone, Alice Playten, Harold Ramis, Susan Roman, Richard Romanos, August Schellenberg, John Vernon, Zal Yanovsky

PRIVATE LESSONS (Jensen Farley Pictures) Exectuive Producers, Jack Barry, Dan Enright; Co-Executive Producer, Irving Oshman; Producer, R. Ben Efraim; Director, Alan Myerson; Screenplay, Dan Greenburg from his novel "Philly"; Photography, Jan deBont; Editor, Fred Chulack; Assistant Directors, Beau Marks, Russell Vreeland; In Metrocolor; 87 minutes; Rated R; August release. CAST: Sylvia Kristel (Nicole), Howard Hesseman (Lester), Eric Brown (Philly), Patrick Piccininni (Sherman), Ed Begley, Jr. (Jack), Pamela Bryant (Joyce), Meredith Baer (Miss Phipps), Ron Foster (Philly's Dad), Peter Elbling (Waiter), Dan Barrows (Green), Marian Gibson (Florence), Dan Greenburg (Hotel Owner), Judy Helden (Double)

HELL NIGHT (Aquarius) Executive Producers, Joseph Wolf, Chuck Russell; Producers, Irwin Yablans, Bruce Cohn Curtis; Director, Tom DeSimone; Screenplay, Randolph Feldman; Photography, Mac Ahlberg; Editor, Tony DiMarco; Music, Dan Wyman; Assistant Director, John Ross Bush; In Metrocolor; 101 minutes; Rated R; August release. CAST: Linda Blair (Marti), Vincent Van Patten (Seth), Peter Barton (Jeff), Kevin Brophy (Peter), Jenny Neumann (May), Suki Goodwin (Denise), Jimmy Sturtevant (Scott)

Gabe Kaplan, Robert Klein, Alex Karras
in "Nobody's Perfekt"
© Columbia Pictures

Eric Brown, Sylvia Kristel, Howard
Hesseman in "Private Lessons"

121

Chuck Norris, Mako in "An Eye for
an Eye" © AVCO Embassy Pictures

Lee Majors, Valerie Perrine
in "Agency" © Jensen Farley Pictures

AN EYE FOR AN EYE (Avco Embassy) Executive Producer, Robert Rehme; Producer, Frank Capra, Jr.; Director, Steve Carver; Screenplay, William Gray, James Bruner; Story, James Bruner; Photography, Roger Shearman; Art Director, Vance Lorenzini; Editor, Anthony Redman; Music, William Goldstein; Associate Producers, James Bruner, Milan Mrdjenovich; Assistant Directors, Yoram Ben-Ami, Louis S. Muscate, Donald P. Borchers; Designer, Sandy Veneziano; An Adams Apple Production; A South Street Film; a Wescom Productions Presentation in CIF color; Rated R; 106 minutes; August release. CAST: Chuck Norris (Sean), Christopher Lee (Morgan), Richard Roundtree (Capt. Stevens), Matt Clark (Tom), Mako (Chan), Maggie Cooper (Heather), Rosalind Chao (Linda), Toru Tanaka (Giant), Stuart Pankin (Nicky), Terry Kiser (Davie), Mel Novak (Montoya), Richard Prieto (Stark), Sam Hiona (Ambler), Dorothy Dells (Cab Driver), Dov Gottesfeld (Doctor), J. E. Freeman (Tow Truck Dude), Joe Bellan (Truck Driver), Daniel Forest (VW Driver), Joseph DeNicola (Parlor Manager), Jeff Bannister (Man on walkie-talkie), Robert Behling (Coroner), Edsel Fung (Proprietor), Harry Wong (Shop Owner), Nancy Fish, Gary T. New, Joe Lerer, Michael Christy (Reporters), Earl Nichols (Officer Ed), Don Pike (Watcher), Tim Culbertson (Policeman).

DEADLY BLESSING (United Artists/Polygram) Producers, Micheline Keller, Max Keller, Pat Herskovic; Director, Wes Craven; Screenplay, Glenn M. Benest, Matthew Barr, Wes Craven; Story, Glenn M. Benest, Matthew Barr; Executive Producer, William Gilmore; Photography, Robert Jessup; Designer, Jack Marty; Associate Producers, Glenn M. Benest, Matthew Barr; Music, James Horner; Editor, Richard Bracken; Assistant Directors, Jerram Swartz, John Eyler; Costumes, Patricia McKiernan; In Metrocolor; An Interplanetary Production; 102 minutes; Rated R; August release. CAST: Maren Jensen (Martha), Susan Buckner (Vicky), Sharon Stone (Lana), Jeff East (Schmidt), Lisa Hartman (Faith), Lois Nettleton (Louisa), Ernest Borgnine (Isaiah), Coleen Riley (Melissa), Doug Barr (Jim), Michael Berryman (Gluntz), Kevin Cooney (Sheriff), Bobby Dark (Theatre Manager), Kevin Farr (Fat Boy), Neil Fletcher (Gravedigger), Jonathon Gulla (Tom), Chester Kulas, Jr. (Leopold), Lawrence Montaigne (Matthew), Lucky Mosley (Sammy), Dan Shackelford (Medic), Annabelle Weenick (Ruth), Jenna Worthen (Mrs. Gluntz), Percy Rodrigues (Narrator)

AGENCY (Jensen Farley) Producers, Robert Lantos, Stephen J. Roth; Director, George Kaczender; Screenplay, Noel Hynd; Based on novel by Paul Gottlieb; Associate Producer, Robert Baylis; Photography, Miklos Lente; Design, Bill Brodie; Music, Lewis Furey; Editor, Kirk Jones; Costumes, Olga Dimitrov; Assistant Directors, Charles Braive, Dani Hausmann, Pedro Gandol; Art Director, Alicia Grunsky; In color; 94 minutes; Rated R; August release. CAST: Robert Mitchum (Ted), Lee Majors (Philip), Valerie Perrine (Brenda), Saul Rubinek (Sam), Alexandra Stewart (Mimi), Hayward Morse (Tony), Anthony Parr (Charlie), Michael Kirby (Peters), Gary Reineke (Jones), George Touliatos (Sgt. Eckersly), Jonathan Welsh (Det. Ross), Hugh Webster (Inmate), Franz Russell (George), Malcolm Nelthorpe (Cy), Marylin Gardner (Jill), Eric Donkin (Henry), Donald Davis (Alexander), Pierre Sevigny, Anthony Sherwood, Patti Oatman, Don Arioli, Henry Gamer, Militia Battlefield, Camille Belanger, Rollie Nincheri, Barry Simpson, Robert Parson, Jane Woods, Allen Goulem, Michael Shore, Art Grosser, Judy London, John Lefebvre, Jim Walton, Wally Martin, Celina Bacon, Rose Wilkinson, Davidson Thomson, George Zeeman, Lee Murray, Catherine Vaneri, Margo Dionne, Martin Kevin, Roberta Bolduc, Don Eagleton, Shawna Sexsmith, Wally Boland, Doug Smith, Eric Cord, Daetan Lafrance, Elizabeth Mudry, Francois Pratt

SOUTHERN COMFORT (20th Century-Fox) Producer, David Giler; Director, Walter Hill; Screenplay, Michael Kane, Walter Hill, David Giler; Executive Producer, William J. Immerman; Photography, Andrew Laszlo; Design, John Vallone; Editor, Freeman Davies; Music, Ry Cooder; Assistant Directors, Pat Kehoe, Bob Roe; A Phoenix Company and Cinema Group Venture Production in DeLuxe Color; 95 minutes; Rated R; September release. CAST: Keith Carradine (Spencer), Powers Boothe (Hardin), Fred Ward (Reece), Franklyn Seales (Simms), T. K. Carter (Cribbs), Lewis Smith (Stuckey), Les Lannom (Casper), Peter Coyote (Poole), Carlos Brown (Bowden), Brion James (Trapper), Sonny Landham, Allan Graf, Ned Dowd, Rob Ryder (Hunters), Greg Guirard, June Borel (Cajun Couple), Jeanne Louise Bulliard, Ore Borle, Jeannie Spector (Cajun Dancers), Marc Savoy, Frank Savoy, Dewey Balfa, John Stelly (Cajun Musicians)

Susan Buckner, Jeff East in "Deadly
Blessing" © United Artists Corp.

Franklyn Seales, Powers Boothe, Keith
Carradine in "Southern Comfort"
© Cinema Group Inc.

"The Unseen"

George Segal, Denzel Washington
in "Carbon Copy"

THE UNSEEN (World Northal) Executive Producer, Howard Goldfarb; Producer, Anthony B. Unger; Co-Producer, Don P. Behrns; Director, Peter Foleg; Screenplay, Michael L. Grace; Photography, Roberto Quezada; Editor, Jonathan Braun; Music, Michael J. Lewis; Assistant Director, Richard Wallace; Art Director, Dena Roth; In Metrocolor; 89 minutes; Rated R; September release. CAST: Barbara Bach (Jennifer), Sydney Lassick (Ernest), Stephen Furst (Junior), Lelia Goldoni (Virginia), Karen Lamm (Karen), Doug Barr (Tony), Lois Young (Vicki)

PATERNITY (Paramount) Producers, Lawrence Gordon, Hank Moonjean; Director, David Steinberg; Screenplay, Charlie Peters; Executive Producer, Jerry Tokofsky; Photography, Bobby Byrne; Design, Jack Collis; Editor, Donn Cambern; Costumes, Albert Wolsky; Music, David Shire; Assistant Directors, Benjy Rosenberg, Herbert S. Adelman; Art Director, Pete Smith; In Movielab Color; 94 minutes; Rated PG; September release. CAST: Burt Reynolds (Buddy), Beverly D'Angelo (Maggie), Norman Fell (Larry), Paul Dooley (Kurt), Elizabeth Ashley (Sophia), Lauren Hutton (Jenny), Juanita Moore (Celia), Peter Billingsley (Tad), Jacqueline Brookes (Aunt Ethel), Linda Gillin (Cathy), Mike Kellin (Guide), Victoria Young (Patti), Elsa Raven (Pre-Natal Nurse), Carol Locatell (Ms. Werner), Kay Armen (Claudia), Murphy Dunne (Singing Telegram Man), Toni Kalen (Diane), Kathy Bendett (Laurie), MacIntyre Dixon (Nature Walk Teacher), Alfie Wise (Cab Driver), Tony DiBenedetto (Butcher), Dick Wienad (Mario), Eugene Troobnick (Vendor), Ken Magee (Man in bar), Elaine Giftos (Woman in bar), Sydney Daniels (Receptionist), Hector Troy (Carlos), Roger Etienne (Waiter), Jason Delgado, Aaron Jessup (Jugglers), Frank Bongiorno (News Vendor), Frank Hamilton (Old Man on boat), James Harder (Doorman), Irena Ferris (Connie), Lee An Duffield (Girl with mask), Clotilde (Emily), Brad Trumbull, John Gilgreen, Jeff Lawrence (Salesmen), Robin Blake (Nurse), Paula Holland (Pretty Girl), Laura Grayson (Receptionist), Susanna Dalton (Gloria)

TATTOO (20th Century-Fox) Producers, Joseph E. Levine, Richard P. Levine; Director, Bob Brooks; Screenplay, Joyce Bunuel; Photography, Arthur Ornitz; Editor, Thom Noble; Design, Stuart Wurtzel; Associate Producer, Robert F. Colesberry; Assistant Director, Jim Bishop Riggio;

Music, Barry DeVorzon; In Technicolor; 103 minutes; Rated R; September release. CAST: Bruce Dern (Karl), Maud Adams (Maddy), Leonard Frey (Halsey), Rikke Borge (Sandra), John Getz (Buddy), Peter Iacangelo (Dubin), Alan Leach (Customer), Cynthia Nixon (Cindy), Trish Doolan (Cheryl), Anthony Mannino (George), Lex Monson (Dudley), Patricia Roe (Doris). Jane Hoffman (Teresa), Robert Burr (Ralph), John Snyder (Hawker)

CARBON COPY (Avco Embassy) Producers, Carter DeHaven, Stanley Shapiro; Director, Michael Schultz; Screenplay, Stanley Shapiro; Photography, Fred Koenekamp; Music, Bill Conti; Editor, Marion Segal; Design, Ted Howorth; Assistant Director, Skip Beaudine; In Panavision and color; 92 minutes, Rated PG: September release. CAST: George Segal (Walter Whitney), Susan St. James (Vivian Whitney), Jack Warden (Nelson), Denzel Washington (Roger), Paul Winfield (Bob), Dick Martin (Victor), Vicky Dawson (Marie-Ann), Tom Poston (Rev. Hayworth), Macon McCalman (Tubby), Parley Baer (Dr. Bristol), Vernon Weddle (Wardlow), Edward Marshall (Freddie), Ed Call (Basketball Father), Angelina Estrada (Bianca)

FOURTEEN AMERICANS (Blackwood Productions) Produced by Michael Blackwood and Nancy Rosen; 90 minutes; Not rated; September release. A documentary exploring the artistic directions of a new generation of painters, sculptors and performance artists, including Vito Acconci, Laurie Anderson, Alice Aycock, Scott Burton, Peter Campus, Chuck Close, Nancy Graves, Joseph Kosuth, Gordon Matta-Clark, Mary Miss, Elizabeth Murray, Dennis Oppenheim, Dorothea Rockburne, Joel Shapiro

THE WOMAN INSIDE (20th Century-Fox) Producer, Sidney H. Levine; Executive Producer, Thomas L. Marshall; Direction and Screenplay, Joseph Van Winkle; Photography, Ron Johnson; Editor, John Duffy; Associate Producer, George E. Mather; Music, Eddy Lawrence Manson; In CFI Color; 94 minutes: Rated R; September release. CAST: Gloria Manon (Holly/Hollis), Dane Clark (Dr. Rosner), Joan Blondell (Aunt Coll), Michael Champion (Nolan), Marlene Tracy (Dr. Paris), Michael Mancini (Marco), Luce Morgan (Maggie), Terri Haven (Agnes)

Bruce Dern, Maud Adams in "Tattoo"
© Joseph E. Levine Presents Inc.

Burt Reynolds, Beverly D'Angelo
in "Paternity" © Paramount Pictures

Pamela Bryant, Rosanne Katon, Candy Moore
in "Lunch Wagon"

Erin Moran, Sid Haig in "Galaxy
of Terror" © New World Pictures

LUNCH WAGON (Seymour Borde) Producer, Mark Borde; Executive Producer, Seymour Borde; Director, Ernest Pintoff; Screenplay, Leon Phillips, Marshall Harvey, Terrie Frankie; Photography, Fred Lemler; Editor, Edward Salier; Music, Richard Band; Assistant Director, Harry F. Hogan III; In DeLuxe Color; 88 minutes; Rated R; September release. CAST: Pamela Bryant (Marcy), Rosanne Katon (Shannon), Candy Moore (Diedra), Rick Podell (Al), Rose Marie (Mrs. Schmeckler), Chuck McCann (Turtle), Jimmie Van Patten (Biff), Nels Van Patten (Scotty), Michael Tucci (Arnie), Louisa Moritz (Sunshine), Vin Dunlop, Maurice Sneed, Michael Mislove, Biff Manard, Anthony Charnota, George Memmoli, Gary Levy, Peggy Mannix, Steve Tannen

ST. HELENS (Parnell) Producer, Michael Murphy; Associate Producers, Peter Davis, Bill Panzer; Director, Ernest Pintoff; Screenplay, Peter Bellwood, Larry Ferguson; Photography, Jacques Haitkin; Editor, George Berndt; Music, Goblin & Buckboard; In DeLuxe Color; 90 minutes: Rated PG; September release. CAST: Art Carney, David Huffman, Cassie Yates, Ron O'Neal, Bill McKinney, Albert Salmi, Tim Thomerson, Henry Darrow, Nehemiah Persoff

HUNGRY i REUNION (Cinema Ventures) Producer-Director, Thomas A. Cohen; Executive Producer-Photography, Steve Michelson; Editor, B. J. Sears; In color; 93 minutes; Rated PG; September release. CAST: Lenny Bruce, Prof. Irwin Corey, Kingston Trio, Limeliters, Mort Sahl, Ronnie Schell, Jackie Vernon, Stan Wilson, Jonathan Winters, Enrico Banducci, Maya Angelou, Don Asher, Stella Brooks, Bill Cosby, Grover Sales, Mike Stepanian, Bill Dana, Phyllis Diller, John Sebastian, Rudy Tellez, Larry Tucker

LORANG'S WAY (Extension Media Center) Producers-Directors, Judith and David MacDougall; Photography, David MacDougall; In tribal dialects with English subtitles; 70 minutes; October release; Not rated. A documentary filmed among the Turkana in northeastern Kenya.

SMOKEY BITES THE DUST (New World) Producer, Roger Corman; Director, Charles B. Griffith; Co-Producer, Gale Hurd; Screenplay, Max Apple; Based on story by Brian Williams; Photography, Gary Graver; Editor, Larry Bock; Music, Bent Myggen; In Metrocolor; 85 minutes; Rated PG; October release. CAST: Jimmy McNichol (Roscoe), Janet Julian (Peggy Sue), Walter Barnes (Sheriff), Patrick Campbell (Lester), Kari Lizer (Cindy), John Blyth Barrymore (Harold), Kedric Wolfe (Deputy), Bill Forsythe (Kenny)

GALAXY OF TERROR (New World) Formerly "Planet of Horrors"; Producer, Roger Corman; Director, Bruce Clark: Screenplay, Marc Siegler, Bruce Clark; Co-Producer, Marc Siegler; Photography, Jacques Haitkin; Editors, Robert J. Kizer, Larry Boch, Barry Zetlin; Music, Barry Schrader; In color; 80 minutes; Rated PG; October release. CAST: Edward Albert (Cabren), Erin Moran (Aluma), Ray Walston (Kore), Bernard Behrens (Ilvar), Zalman King (Baelon), Robert Englund (Ranger), Taaffe O'Connell (Dameia), Sid Haig (Quuhod), Grace Zabriskie (Capt. Trantor), Jack Blessing (Cos), Mary Ellen O'Neill (Mitre)

THE CREATURE WASN'T NICE (Creatures Features) Producer, Mark Haggard; Direction and Screenplay, Bruce Kimmel; Executive Producers, Albert Schwartz, Elyse England; Photography, Denny Lavil; Editor, David Blangsted; Design, Lee Cole; Assistant Director, Patrick Regan; Associate Producers, Alain Silver, Patrick Regan; Costumes, Katherine Dover; Music, David Spear; In Metrocolor; 88 minutes; Rated PG; October release. CAST: Cindy Williams (McHugh), Bruce Kimmel (John), Leslie Nielsen (Jameson), Gerrit Graham (Rodzinski), Patrick Macnee (Stark), Ron Kurowski (Creature)

THE WORM EATERS (New American) Producer, Ted V. Mikels; Direction and Screenplay, Herb Robins; Story, Nancy Kapner; Photography, Willis Hawkins; Editor, Soly Bina; Music, Theodore Stern; Assistant Director, John Tenorio; Design, Jack DeWolf; In Eastmancolor; 94 minutes; Not rated; October release. CAST: Herb Robins, Lindsay Armstrong Black, Joseph Sacket, Robert Garrison, Muriel Cooper, Mike Garrison, Barry Hostetler, Carla

Enrico Banducci
in "Hungry i Reunion"

Ngimare, Lorang
in "Lorang's Way"

Leon Isaac Kennedy, Muhammad Ali, Jayne
Kennedy in "Body and Soul"
© Cannon Releasing Corp.

Jamie Lee Curtis, Donald Pleasence
in "Halloween II"
© Universal City Studios

THE AFFAIRS OF ROBIN HOOD (Lima) Producers, Edward E. Paramore, John Harvey; Associate Producer, Murray Perlstein; Director, Richard Kanter; In color; 70 minutes; Rated R; October release. CAST: Ralph Jenkins, Dee Lockood, Danelle Carver

BODY AND SOUL (Cannon Group) Producers, Menahem Golan, Yoram Globus; Director, George Bowers; Editors, Sam Pollard, Skip Schoolnik; Music, Webster Lewis; Screenplay, Leon Isaac Kennedy; Photography, James Forrest; Art Director, Bob Ziembicki; Fight Choreographer, Bob Minor; Dance Choreographers, Hope Clarke, Valentino; Costumes, Celia; In color; 115 minutes; Rated R; October release. CAST: Leon Isaac Kennedy (Leon), Jayne Kennedy (Julie), Peter Lawford (Big Man), Perry Lang (Charles), Nikki Swassy (Kelly), Mike Gazzo (Frankie), Kim Hamilton (Mrs. Johnson), Muhammad Ali (Himself), Chris Wallace (Dr. Bachman), Robbie Epps (Iceman), J. B. Williamson (Assassin), Al Denavo (Mad Man Santiago), Mel Welles (Joe), Danny Wells, Johnny Brown (Sports Announcers), DeForrest Covan (Cut Man), Azizi Johari (Pussy), Roseann Katon (Melody), Al Garcia (Mad Man's Manager), Jimmy Lennon (Ring Announcer), Mike Garfield (Official), Hazel Girtman (Nurse)

NIGHT SCHOOL (Lorimar/Paramount) Executive Producers, Marc Gregory Comjean, Bernard Kebadjian; Producers, Larry Babb, Ruth Avergon; Screenplay, Ruth Avergon; Director, Kenneth Hughes; Photography, Mark Irwin; Editor, Robert Reitano; Music, Brad Fiedel; In Movielab Color; 98 minutes; Rated R; October release. CAST: Leonard Mann (Judd Austin), Rachel Ward (Eleanor), Drew Snyder (Prof. Millett), Joseph R. Sicari (Taj), Nicholas Cairis (Gus)

LIGHTNING OVER WATER (Gray City Films) Producer, Chris Sievernich; Directors, Nicholas Ray, Wim Wenders; Photography, Ed Lachman, Martin Schaefer; Editor, Peter Pryzygodda; Music, Ronee Blakley; 91 minutes; Not rated; October release. A documentary on Nicholas Ray's life with Gerry Bamman, Ronee Blakley, Pierre Cottrell, Stefan Dzapsky, Mitch Dubin, Tom Farrell, Becky Johnston, Tom Kaufman, Maryte Kayaliauskas, Pat Kirck, Ed Lachman, Martin Mueller, Craig Nelson, Nicholas Ray, Susan Ray, Timothy Ray, Martin Schaefer, Chris Sievernich, Wim Wenders

HALLOWEEN II (Universal) Producers, Debra Hill, John Carpenter; Director, Rick Rosenthal; Screenplay, John Carpenter, Debra Hill; Executive Producers, Irwin Yablans, Joseph Wolf; Photography, Dean Cundey; Design, Michael Riva; Associate Producer, Barry Bernardi; Music, John Carpenter, Alan Howarth; Editors, Mark Goldblat; Skip Schoolnik; Assistant Directors, William S. Beasley, Duncan S. Henderson; In Metrocolor, Panavision, Dolby Stereo; 92 minutes; Rated R; October release. CAST: Jamie Lee Curtis (Laurie), Donald Pleasence (San), Charles Cyphers (Leigh), Jeffrey Kramer (Graham), Lance Guest (Jimmy), Pamela Susan Shoop (Karen), Hunter Von Leer (Gary), Dick Warlock (The Shape), Leo Rossi (Budd), Gloria Gifford (Mrs. Alves), Tawny Moyer (Jill), Ana Alicia (Janet), Ford Rainey (Dr. Mixter), Cliff Emmich (Garrett), Nancy Stephens (Marion), John Zenda (Marshall), Catherine Bergstrom (Producer), Alan Haufrect (Announcer), Lucille Bensen (Mrs. Elrod), Bill Warlock (Craig), Jonathan Prince (Randy)

NIGHTMARE (21st Century Distribution) Executive Producer, David Jones; Producer, John L. Watkins; Direction and Screenplay, Romano Scavolini; Photography, Gianni Fiore; Editor, Robert T. Megginson; Music, Jack Eric Williams; In Technicolor; 97 minutes; Not rated; October release. CAST: Baird Stafford (George), Sharon Smith (Susan), C. J. Cooke (C. J.), Mik Cribben (Bob), Kathleen Ferguson (Barbara), Danny Ronan (Babysitter), John L. Watkins (Man with cigar)

TEENAGE TEASERS (Intercontinental) Producer-Director, Jack Angel; In color; 90 minutes; Rated R; October release. CAST: Dany Daniel, Nadine Perles, Daniel Fawcett

SLAUGHTERDAY (Intercontinental) Director, Peter Patzak; Screenplay, Peter Patzak, Walter Kindler, Ossi Bronner; Photography, Walter Kindler; In color; Rated R; 86 minutes; October release. CAST: Rita Tushingham, Michael Hausserman, Frederick Jaeger, William Berger, Gordon Mitchell, Vicki Wolf, Klaus Dahlen, Heinz Marecek

"Night School"
© Fiducial Resource International

Lance Guest, Jamie Lee Curtis
in "Halloween II"
© Universal City Studios

Treat Williams, Kathryn Harrold in "The
Pursuit of D. B. Cooper"
© Universal City Studios

Bugs Bunny, Daffy Duck in "The Looney
Looney Looney Bugs Bunny Movie"

BLACK AND BLUE (United Artists Classics) Producers, George Harrison, Sandy Pearlman, Steve Schenck; Director, Jay Dubin; Associate Producer, Jeanne Suggs; A Daltyn Filmworks production; In color; Not rated; October release. A concert starring Black Sabbath and Blue Oyster Cult.

THE PURSUIT OF D. B. COOPER (Universal) Producers, Daniel Wigutow, Michael Taylor; Director, Roger Spottiswoode; Screenplay, Jeffrey Alan Fiskin; Based on book "Free Fall" by J. D. Reed; Associate Producer, Ron Shelton; Executive Producers, William Tennant, Donald Kranze; Photography, Harry Stradling; Design, Preston Ames; Editors, Robbe Roberts, Allan Jacobs; "Shine" written and sung by Waylon Jennings; Music Score, James Horner; Assistant Directors, Richard Learman, Dan Attias, Louis Muscate, R. Anthony Brown; Original Soundtrack Album on Polydor Records; In Metrocolor; 100 minutes; Rated PG; November release. CAST: Robert Duvall (Gruen), Treat Williams (Meade), Kathryn Harrold (Hannah), Ed Flanders (Brigadier), Paul Gleason (Remson), R. G. Armstrong (Dempsey), Dorothy Fielding (Denise), Nicolas Coster (Avery), Cooper Huckabee (Homer), Howard K. Smith (Himself), Christopher Curry (Hippie), Ramon Chavez (El Capitan), Stacy Newton (Cowboy), Pat Ast (Horse Lady), Jack Dunlap, Brad Sergi, Michael Potter, Charles Benton, Mike Casper, James Lee, Henry Kendrick, James Wiers, Mark Jeffreys, D. G. Smilnak, David Adams, Charles Haigh, Stephen Blood, Tommy Ciulla, Karen Newhouse, Richard Brown, Michael O'Hare, Robert Sola, Tom May, Sanford Gibbons, Lynn Radcliffe, Mearl Ross, Patrick Garcia, Gregory Suke, Jessica Garcia, Leigh Webb, Jim Clouse, David Falkosky, John Herold, Bill Townsend, Christine Dolny, Michael Goodsite, Glenda Young, Dave Gilbert, Bill Whitman, Conrad Marshall

HEARTBEEPS (Universal) Producer, Michael Phillips; Director, Allan Arkush; Screenplay, John Hill; Executive Producer, Douglas Green; Associate Producer, John Hill; Photography, Charles Rosher, Jr.; Design, John W. Corso; Editor, Tina Hirsch; Music, John Williams; Assistant Directors, Don Zepfel, Dean Stephen Lyras; Costumes, Madeline Graneto, Theadora Van Runkle; Special Effects, Stan Winston, Albert Whitlock; In Technicolor and Panavision; 88 minutes; Rated PG; November release. CAST: Andy Kaufman (Val), Bernadette

Peters (Aqua), Randy Quaid (Charlie), Kenneth McMillan (Max), Melanie Mayron (Susan), Christopher Guest (Calvin), Richard B. Shull (Factory Boss), Dick Miller (Watchman), Kathleen Freeman (Helicopter Pilot), Mary Woronov (Party House Owner), Paul Bartel, Anne Wharton (Guests), Barry Diamond, Stephanie Faulkner (Firing Range Technicians), Jeffrey Kramer (Butler Robot), Irene Forrest, Karsen Lee Gould (Maid Robots), David Gene Lebell (Forklift Drive Robot)

THE LOONEY LOONEY LOONEY BUGS BUNNY MOVIE (Warner Bros.) Producer- Director, Friz Freleng; Executive Producer, Hal Geer; Screenplay, John Dunn, David Detiege, Friz Freleng; Sequence Directors, David Detiege, Phil Monroe, Gerry Chiniquy; Music, Rob Walsh, Don McGinnis, Milt Franklyn, Bill Lava, Shorty Rogers, Carl Stalling; Voice Characterizations, Mel Blanc, June Foray, Frank Nelson, Frank Welker, Stan Freberg, Ralph James; Editor, Jim Champin; Associate Producer, Jean H. MacCurdy; Design, Cornelius Cole; Animators, Warren Batcheller, Charles Downs, Marcia Fertig, Bob Matz, Manuel Perez, Virgil Ross, Lloyd Vaughan; In Technicolor; 80 minutes; Rated G; November release. CAST: Bugs Bunny, Yosemite Sam, Devil, Rocky, Mugsy, Tweety Pie, Daffy Duck, and others.

SHOCK TREATMENT (20th Century-Fox) Executive Producers, Lou Adler, Michael White; Producer, John Goldstone; Director, Jim Sharman: Music, Richard Hartley, Richard O'Brien; Book and Lyrics, Richard O'Brien; Screenplay, Richard O'Brien, Jim Sharman; Additional Ideas, Brian Thomson; Design, Brian Thomson; Costumes, Sue Blane; Photography, Mike Molloy; Editor, Richard Bedford; Choreography, Gillian Gregory; Assistant Director, Roger Simons; Art Director, Andrew Sanders; In Technicolor and Dolby Stereo; 94 minutes; Rated PG; November release. CAST: Jessica Harper (Janet Majors), Cliff DeYoung (Brad/Farley), Richard O'Brien (Cosmo), Patricia Quinn (Nation), Charles Gray (Judge Wright), Ruby Wax (Betty), Nell Campbell (Nurse), Rik Mayall (Ricky), Barry Humphries (Bert), Darlene Johnson (Emily), Manning Redwood (Harry), Wendy Raebeck (Macy), Jeremy Newson (Ralph), Chris Malcolm (Vance), Ray Charleson (Floor Manager), Eugene Lipinski (Kirk), Barry Dennen (Irwin), Imogen Claire (Wardrobe Mistress), Betsy Brantley, Perry Bedden, Rufus Collins (Neely and Her Crew)

Bernadette Peters, Andy Kaufman
in "Heartbeeps"
© Universal City Studios

Jessica Harper, Cliff DeYoung
in "Shock Treatment"
© 20th Century-Fox Film Corp.

Kevin Brando, Richard Benjamin
in "Saturday the 14th"
© Saturday the 14th Productions

Dan Haggerty in "Legend
of the Wild"

COASTER (Atlantic Film Group I) Produced, Directed and Photographed by Jon Craig Cloutier; Screenplay, Herbert H. Rosen; Music and Lyrics, Gordon Bok; Editors, Mike Ritter, Robert C. Eckhart, Mr. Cloutier; In color; Not rated: November release. A documentary about the building of the coasting schooner John F. Leavitt. Narrated by Barton Heyman

SATURDAY THE 14th (New World) Producer, Julie Corman; Co-Producer, Jeff Begun; Direction and Screenplay, Howard R. Cohen; Photography, Daniel LaCambre; Editors, Joanne D'Antonio, Kent Beyda; Assistant Directors, Nicole Scott, Jude Parker; Art Director, Arlene Alen; In color; 75 minutes; Rated PG; November release. CAST: Richard Benjamin (John), Paula Prentiss (Mary), Severn Darden (Van Helsing), Jeffrey Tambor (Waldemar), Kari Michaelsen (Debbie), Kevin Brando (Billy), Nancy Lee Andrews (Yolanda), Craig Coulter (Duane), Roberta Collins (Rhonda), Thomas Newman (Phil), Rosemary DeCamp (Aunt Lucille), Carol Androsky (Marge), Annie O'Donnell (Annette), Michael Miller (Cop), Stacy Keach, Sr. (Attorney), Paul "Mousie" Garner (Major), Patrick Campbell (Mailman), Irwin Russo (Truck Driver)

STRONG MEDICINE (Film Forum) Direction and Screenplay, Richard Foreman; Co-Producers, Mary Milton, Simon Nuchtern, Eric Franck, Jordan Bojilov; Associate Producer, Bill Milling; Photography, Babette Mangolte; Editors, Richard Foreman, Karen Stern; Music, Stanley Silverman; Art Director, Ed Vincent; 84 minutes; Not rated; November release. CAST: Kate Manheim (Rhoda), Scotty Snyder (Old Woman), Bill Raymond (Young Man), Harry Roskolenko (Old Man), Ron Vawter (Max), David Warrilow (Doctor), Ruth Maleczech (Eleanor), Jill Haworth, Buck Henry, Raul Julia, Carol Kane, Joan Jonas, Michael Kirby, Jay Leyda, Ron Vance, George Bartenieff, Eliot Caplan, Crystal Field, Carl Fredericks, Rena Gill, Yolanda Hawkins, Lillian Kiesler, Ted Kirby, Jonas Mekas, Gerald Rabkin, Jack Eric Williams

LEGEND OF THE WILD (Jensen Farley) Produced and Written by Charles E. Sellier, Jr., Brian Russell; Editor, Michael Spence; In color; 93 minutes; Rated G; November release. CAST: Dan Haggerty, Denver Pyle, Dan Shanks, Ken Curtis, Jack Kruschen, Linda Arbizu, Kristen Curry, Don Galloway, Norman Goodman, Lucky Hayes, Hank Kendrick, Daine McBain, T. Miratti, Steven Robertson

BROOKLYN BRIDGE (Florentine Films) Producer, Director, Photographer, Co-Editor, Ken Burns; Writer-Editor, Amy Stechler; Produced in association with the City of New York; Assistant Director, Buddy Squires; Additional Photography, Buddy Squires, Terry Hopkins; Animation, Jessica Spohn; Music, Jesse Carr; Titles, James Madden; In Du-Art Color; 60 minutes; Not rated; November release. Voices of Paul Roebling, Julie Harris, Kurt Vonnegut, Arthur Miller, Richard Pini, Richard Rescia, Fred Sherry, Austin Stevens

GARLIC IS AS GOOD AS 10 MOTHERS (Unifilm/Flower) Produced, Directed and Photographed in color by Les Blank; Editor, Maureen Gosling; 51 minutes; Not rated; November release. A documentary on food.

EL SALVADOR: ANOTHER VIETNAM (Icarus Films) Producers and Directors, Glenn Silber, Tete Vasconcellos; Editor, Deborah Shaffer; A Catalyst Media production in association with M.J. & E. Productions; Photography, Tom Sigel; Music, Wendy Blackstone, Bernardo Palombo; Narration written by Claudis Vianello; Narrator, Mike Farrell; In color, black and white; 53 minutes; Not rated; November release. A documentary with participants: Enrique Alvarez, John Bushnell, Terence Cardinal Cooke, Jose Napoleon Duarte, William Dyess, Ita Ford, Jose Guillermo Garcia, General Alexander Haig, Ana Guadalupe Martinez, Dan Mica, Herb Mills, Ronald Reagan, Archbishop Arturo Rivera Y Damas, William Rogers, Archbishop Oscar Arnulfo Romero, Salvador Samayoa, Gerry E. Studds, Guillermo Ungo, Murat Williams, Charles Wilson, and the people of El Salvador

Kate Manheim (L)
in "Strong Medicine"

"El Salvador: Another Vietnam"

Chevy Chase, Nell Carter, Patti
D'Arbanville in "Modern Problems"
© 20th Century-Fox Film Corp.

Mark Cardova, Darren Brown
in "Clarence and Angel"

FANTASIES (Joseph Brenner) Producer, Kevin Casselman; Written, Directed and Photographed by John Derek; Music, Jeff Silverman; Editor, Bref Weston; In color; 86 minutes; Rated R; November release. CAST: Bo Derek/Cathy Collins (Anastasia), Peter Hooten (Damir), Anne Axexiadis (Mayor), Pheacton Gheorghitais (Photographer), Nicos Paschalidis (Priest), Constantine Beladames (Godfather), Therese Bohlin (Model), Boucci Simma (Beautifuloni), Vienneula Koussefhane (Saleslady), and the people of Mykonos, Greece.

MODERN PROBLEMS (20th Century-Fox) Executive Producer, Douglas C. Kenney; Producers, Alan Greisman, Michael Shamberg; Director, Ken Shapiro; Screenplay, Ken Shapiro, Tom Sherohman, Arthur Sellers; Music, Dominic Frontiere; Photography, Edmund Koons; Design, Jack Senter: Editor, Michael Jablow; In color; 92 minutes; Rated PG; December release. CAST: Chevy Chase (Max), Patti D'Arbanville (Darcy), Mary Kay Place (Lorraine), Nell Carter (Dorita), Brian Doyle-Murray (Brian), Mitche Kreindel (Bary), Dabney Coleman (Mark), Arthur Sellers (Mobile Supervisor), Sandy Helberg (Pete), Neil Thompson, Carl Irwin (Controllers), Ron House (Vendor), Buzzy Linhart (Tile Man), Henry Corden (Dubrovnik), Christine Nazareth (Redhead), Luke Andreas (Tough Guy), Jan Speck (Brunette), Vincenzo Gagliardi (Singer), Francois Cartier (Pianist), Pat Proft (Maitre d'), Jim Hudson (Doctor), Tom Sherohman (Waiter), Frank Birney (Man in lobby), Reid Olson (Principal Dancer)

NEIGHBORS (Columbia) Producers, Richard D. Zanuck, David Brown; Director, John G. Avildsen; Executive Producers, Irving Paul Lazar, Bernie Brillstein; Screenplay, Larry Gelbart; Based on novel by Thomas Berger; Photography, Gerald Hirschfeld; Music, Bill Conti; Design, Peter Larkin; Editor, Jane Kurson; Costumes, John Boxer; Assistant Directors, Yudi Bennett, Paula Mazur, Mark McGann; In Technicolor; 95 minutes; Rated R; December release. CAST: John Belushi (Earl Keese), Kathryn Walker (Enid Keese), Cathy Moriarty (Ramona), Dan Aykroyd (Vic), Igors Gavon (Chic), Dru-Ann Chukron (His Wife), Tim Kazurinsky (Pa Greavy), Tino Insana (Perry), P.L. Brown, Henry Judd Baker (Police), Lauren-Marie Taylor (Elaine Keese), Dale Two Eagle (Thundersky), Sherman Lloyd, Bert Kittel, J. B. Friend, Bernie Friedman, Edward Kotkin, Michael Manoogian (Firemen)

CLARENCE AND ANGEL (Gardner) Produced, Written and Directed by Robert Gardner; Photography, Doug Harris; In color; 75 minutes: Not rated; December release. CAST: Darren Brown (Clarence), Mark Cardova (Angel), Cynthia McPherson (Teacher), Louise Mike (Claree's Mother), Lolita Lewis (Robert's Mother), Robert Leroy Smith, Ellwoodson Williams (Man in barbershop), Janice Jenkins (Principal), Robert Middleton (Assistant Principal)

DAWN OF THE MUMMY (Harmony Gold) Producer-Director, Frank Agrama; Executive Producer, Lewis Horwitz; Screenplay, Daria Price, Ronald Dobrin, Mr. Agrama; Photography, Sergio Rubini; Editor, Jonathon Braun; Music, Shuki Y. Levy; In Technicolor; 88 minutes; Not rated; December release. CAST: Brenda King, Barry Sattels, George Peck, John Salvo, Joan Levy, Diane Beatty

SOURDOUGH (Film Saturation) Executive Producers, George E. Lukens, Jr., Robert B. Pendleton; Director, Martin J. Spinelli; Screenplay, Lewis N. Turner, Mr. Spinelli; Story, Rod Perry; Photography, Rod Perry; Editor, George Folsey, Jr. Music, Jerrold Immel; In Eastmancolor; 94 minutes; Rated G; December release. Starring Gil Perry with narration by Gene Evans

FRONT LINE (Cinema Ventures) Produced and Directed by David Bradbury; Photography, David Perry; Editor, Stewart Young; Music, Denise Wykes, Lindsay Lee and Midnight Oil; In color; 65 minutes; Not rated; December release. A documentary on the Vietnam War, focusing on the eleven-year experiences of Australian news-cameraman in the combat zone.

AGAINST WIND AND TIDE: A CUBAN ODYSSEY (Filmmakers Library) Producers, Suzanne Bauman, Paul Neshamkin, Jim Burroughs; Director, Jim Burroughs; Photography, Jeffrey Wayman, Editors, Ms. Baumann, Mr. Neshamkin; Associate Producer, Dan Devaney; Screenplay, Jim Burroughs, David Fanning; Narrated by Jim Burroughs; Music, Mr. Burroughs; Executive Producer, David Fanning; A Seven League Production in color; Not rated; 60 minutes; May release. A documentary about Cuban immigration.

Kathryn Walker, John Belushi, Dan
Aykroyd in "Neighbors"
© Columbia Pictures Industries

"Against Wind and Tide ..."

PROMISING NEW ACTORS 1981

HART BOCHNER

BLAIR BROWN

JANET EILBER

PETER MacNICOL

MARA HOBEL

DOUG McKEON

HOWARD E. ROLLINS

CHRISTINE LAHTI

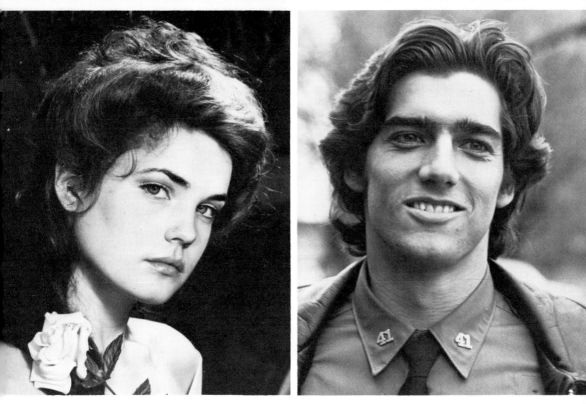

ELIZABETH McGOVERN

KEN WAHL

DENZEL WASHINGTON

RACHEL TICOTIN

131

CHARIOTS OF FIRE

(LADD CO./WARNER BROS.) Producer, David Puttnam; Director, Hugh Hudson; Screenplay, Colin Welland; Executive Producer, Dodi Fayed; Music, Vangelis Papathanassiou; Photography, David Watkin; Associate Producer, James Crawford; Editor, Terry Rawlings; Costumes, Milena Canonero; Assistant Director, Jonathan Benson; Art Director, Roger Hall; Allied Stars presents an Enigma Production in Dolby Stereo and color; 123 minutes; Rated PG; September release.

CAST

Harold Abrahams	Ben Cross
Eric Liddell	Ian Charleson
Lord Andrew Lindsay	Nigel Havers
Aubrey Montague	Nicholas Farrell
Sam Mussabini	Ian Holm
Master of Trinity	John Gielgud
Master of Caius	Lindsay Anderson
Lord Birkenhead	Nigel Davenport
Jennie Liddell	Cheryl Campbell
Sybil Gordon	Alice Krige
Charles Paddock	Dennis Christopher
Jackson Scholz	Brad Davis
Lord Cadogan	Patrick Magee
Duke of Sutherland	Peter Egan
Sandy McGrath	Struan Rodger
Prince of Wales	David Yelland
George Andre	Yves Beneyton
Henry Stallard	Daniel Gerroll
President Gilbert & Sullivan Society	Jeremy Sinden
President Cambridge Athletic Club	Gordon Hammersley
Secretary Gilbert & Sullivan Society	Andrew Hawkins
Head Porter, Caius College	Richard Griffiths
Rev. J. D. Liddell	John Young
Rob Liddell	Benny Young
Mrs. Liddell	Yvonne Gilan

and Jack Smethurst (Sleeping Car Attendant), Gerry Slevin (Col. Keddie), Peter Cellier (Savoy Head Waiter), Stephen Mallatratt (Watson), Colin Bruce (Taylor), Alan Polonsky (Paxton), Edward Wiley (Fitch), Philip O'Brien (American Coach), Ralph Lawton (Harbor Master), John Rutland (Caius Porter), Alan Dudley (Caius Manservant), Tommy Boyle (Reporter), Kim Clifford (Sybil's Maid), Wallace Campbell (Highland Provost), Pat Doyle (Jimmie), David John (Ernest Liddell), Teresa Dignan (Schoolgirl), Ruby Wax (Bunty), Michael Jeyes (Footman), David Kivlin, Eddie Hughson (Scots Boys), Rosy Clayton (Linda Wallis), Sarah Roache (Doreen Sloane), James Usher (Steve Ambrose), Leonard Mullen (Peter Jones), Dave Turner (Phil Tait), Gayle Grayson, Paul Howard, Garth Jones, Sue Sammon, Alan Lorimer, Graham Brooke, Carol Ashby, Michael Lonsdale, Paul Maho, Linda Boyland.

Top Left: Ben Cross, Nigel Havers
Below: Ian Holm, Ben Cross
© Warner Bros./Ladd Co.

1981 ACADEMY AWARDS FOR BEST PICTURE, BEST ORIGINAL SCREENPLAY, BEST SCORE, BEST COSTUME DESIGN

Nigel Havers, Nicholas Farrell, Ian Charleson, Daniel Gerroll, Ben Cross

1981 ACADEMY AWARD FOR BEST PICTUR

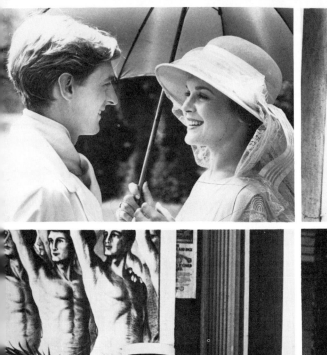

Nicholas Farrell, Nigel Havers, Daniel Gerroll,
Ben Cross Above: Ian Holm Top:
Nigel Havers, Alice Krige

Ben Cross, Alice Krige Above: Ian
Charleson Top: John Gielgud, Lindsay
Anderson

KATHARINE HEPBURN
in "On Golden Pond"

1981 ACADEMY AWARD FOR BEST ACTRESS

HENRY FONDA
in "On Golden Pond"

1981 ACADEMY AWARD FOR BEST ACTOR

JOHN GIELGUD
in "Arthur"

1981 ACADEMY AWARD FOR BEST SUPPORTING ACTOR

MAUREEN STAPLETON
in "Reds"

1981 ACADEMY AWARD FOR BEST SUPPORTING ACTRESS   137

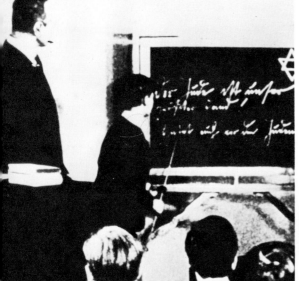

GENOCIDE

(SIMON WIESENTHAL CENTER) Producer-Director, Arnold Schwartzman; Narrated by Elizabeth Taylor and Orson Welles; Introduced by Simon Wiesenthal; Written by Martin Gilbert, Rabbi Marvin Hier; Screenplay Created by Arnold Schwartzman; Music Composed and Conducted by Elmer Bernstein; Performed by London's Royal Philharmonic Orchestra; Co-Produced by Simon Wiesenthal Center; Editors, Roy Watts, Robert Jenkis, Richard Zukaitis; "The Butterfly" designed and directed by Pat Gavin, animated by Diane Jackson, Ted Rockely; Location Cinematography, David and Peter Shillingford; Historical Consultant, Efraim Zuroff; In black and white and color, and Dolby Stereo; 90 minutes; Not rated; December release.

1981 ACADEMY AWARD FOR BEST FEATURE DOCUMENTARY

MEPHISTO

(ANALYSIS FILM RELEASING CORP.) Director, Istvan Szabo; Screenplay, Istvan Szabo, Peter Dobai; Based on novel by Klaus Mann; Photography, Lajos Koltai; Music, Zdenko Tamassy; Produced in color by Mafilm-Objectiv Studio (Budapest) in cooperation with Manfred Durniok Productions; In German with English subtitles; 144 minutes; Not rated; December release.

CAST

Hendrik Hofgen	Klaus Maria Brandauer
Barbara Bruckner	Krystyna Janda
Nicoletta Von Niebuhr	Ildiko Bansagi
Juliette Martens	Karin Boyd
The General	Rolf Hoppe
Lotte Lindenthal	Christine Harbot
Hans Miklas	Gyorgy Cserhalmi
Professor	Martin Hellberg
Cesar Von Muck	Christiane Graskoff
Otto Ulrichs	Peter Andorai
Dora Martin	Ildiko Kishonti
Oskar H. Kroge	Tamas Major

Left: Klaus Maria Brandauer
© **Analysis Film Releasing Corp.**

Karin Boyd, Klaus Maria Brandauer

Klaus Maria Brandauer, Krystyna Janda
Above: Klaus Maria Brandauer

1981 ACADEMY AWARD FOR BEST FOREIGN-LANGUAGE FILM

Ildiko Bansagi, Klaus Maria Brandauer
Top: Klaus Maria Brandauer, Krystyna Janda, Ildiko Bansagi

| Marlon Brando | Luise Rainer | Anthony Quinn | Claudette Colbert | Yul Brynner | Helen Hayes |

PREVIOUS ACADEMY AWARD WINNERS

(1) Best Picture, (2) Actor, (3) Actress, (4) Supporting Actor,
(5) Supporting Actress, (6) Director, (7) Special Award, (8)
Best Foreign Language Film

1927–28: (1) "Wings," (2) Emil Jannings in "The Way of All Flesh," (3) Janet Gaynor in "Seventh Heaven," (6) Frank Borzage for "Seventh Heaven," (7) Charles Chaplin.

1928–29: (1) "Broadway Melody," (2) Warner Baxter in "Old Arizona," (3) Mary Pickford in "Coquette," (6) Frank Lloyd for "The Divine Lady."

1929–30: (1) "All Quiet on the Western Front," (2) George Arliss in "Disraeli," (3) Norma Shearer in "The Divorcee," (6) Lewis Milestone for "All Quiet on the Western Front."

1930–31: (1) "Cimarron," (2) Lionel Barrymore in "A Free Soul," (3) Marie Dressler in "Min and Bill," (6) Norman Taurog for "Skippy."

1931–32: (1) "Grand Hotel," (2) Fredric March in "Dr. Jekyll and Mr. Hyde" tied with Wallace Beery in "The Champ," (3) Helen Hayes in "The Sin of Madelon Claudet," (6) Frank Borzage for "Bad Girl."

1932–33: (1) "Cavalcade," (2) Charles Laughton in "The Private Life of Henry VIII," (3) Katharine Hepburn in "Morning Glory," (6) Frank Lloyd for "Cavalcade."

1934: (1) "It Happened One Night," (2) Clark Gable in "It Happened One Night," (3) Claudette Colbert in "It Happened One Night," (6) Frank Capra for "It Happened One Night," (7) Shirley Temple.

1935: (1) "Mutiny on the Bounty," (2) Victor McLaglen in "The Informer," (3) Bette Davis in "Dangerous," (6) John Ford for "The Informer," (7) D. W. Griffith.

1936: (1) "The Great Ziegfeld," (2) Paul Muni in "The Story of Louis Pasteur," (3) Luise Rainer in "The Great Ziegfeld," (4) Walter Brennan in "Come and Get It," (5) Gale Sondergaard in "Anthony Adverse," (6) Frank Capra for "Mr. Deeds Goes to Town."

1937: (1) "The Life of Emile Zola," (2) Spencer Tracy in "Captains Courageous," (3) Luise Rainer in "The Good Earth," (4) Joseph Schildkraut in "The Life of Emile Zola," (5) Alice Brady in "In Old Chicago," (6) Leo McCarey for "The Awful Truth," (7) Mack Sennett, Edgar Bergen.

1938: (1) "You Can't Take It with You," (2) Spencer Tracy in "Boys' Town," (3) Bette Davis in "Jezebel," (4) Walter Brennan in "Kentucky," (5) Fay Bainter in "Jezebel," (6) Frank Capra for "You Can't Take It with You," (7) Deanna Durbin, Mickey Rooney, Harry M. Warner, Walt Disney.

1939: (1) "Gone with the Wind," (2) Robert Donat in "Goodbye, Mr. Chips," (3) Vivien Leigh in "Gone with the Wind," (4) Thomas Mitchell in "Stagecoach," (5) Hattie McDaniel in "Gone with the Wind," (6) Victor Fleming for "Gone with the Wind," (7) Douglas Fairbanks, Judy Garland.

1940: (1) "Rebecca," (2) James Stewart in "The Philadelphia Story," (3) Ginger Rogers in "Kitty Foyle," (4) Walter Brennan in "The Westerner," (5) Jane Darwell in "The Grapes of Wrath," (6) John Ford for "The Grapes of Wrath," (7) Bob Hope.

1941: (1) "How Green Was My Valley," (2) Gary Cooper in "Sergeant York," (3) Joan Fontaine in "Suspicion," (4) Donald Crisp in "How Green Was My Valley," (5) Mary Astor in "The Great Lie," (6) John Ford for "How Green Was My Valley," (7) Leopold Stokowski, Walt Disney.

1942: (1) "Mrs. Miniver," (2) James Cagney in "Yankee Doodle Dandy," (3) Greer Garson in "Mrs. Miniver," (4) Van Heflin in "Johnny Eager," (5) Teresa Wright in "Mrs. Miniver," (6) William Wyler for "Mrs. Miniver," (7) Charles Boyer, Noel Coward.

1943: (1) "Casablanca," (2) Paul Lukas in "Watch on the Rhine," (3) Jennifer Jones in "The Song of Bernadette," (4) Charles Coburn in "The More the Merrier," (5) Katina Paxinou in "For Whom the Bell Tolls," (6) Michael Curtiz for "Casablanca."

1944: (1) "Going My Way," (2) Bing Crosby in "Going My Way," (3) Ingrid Bergman in "Gaslight," (4) Barry Fitzgerald in "Going My Way," (5) Ethel Barrymore in "None but the Lonely Heart," (6) Leo McCarey for "Going My Way," (7) Margaret O'Brien, Bob Hope.

1945: (1) "The Lost Weekend," (2) Ray Milland in "The Lost Weekend," (3) Joan Crawford in "Mildred Pierce," (4) James Dunn in "A Tree Grows in Brooklyn," (5) Anne Revere in "National Velvet," (6) Billy Wilder for "The Lost Weekend," (7) Walter Wanger, Peggy Ann Garner.

1946: (1) "The Best Years of Our Lives," (2) Fredric March in "The Best Years of Our Lives," (3) Olivia de Havilland in "To Each His Own," (4) Harold Russell in "The Best Years of Our Lives," (5) Anne Baxter in "The Razor's Edge," (6) William Wyler for "The Best Years of Our Lives," (7) Laurence Olivier, Harold Russell, Ernst Lubitsch, Claude Jarman, Jr.

1947: (1) "Gentleman's Agreement," (2) Ronald Colman in "A Double Life," (3) Loretta Young in "The Farmer's Daughter," (4) Edmund Gwenn in "Miracle On 34th Street," (5) Celeste Holm in "Gentleman's Agreement," (6) Elia Kazan for "Gentleman's Agreement," (7) James Baskette, (8) "Shoe Shine."

1948: (1) "Hamlet," (2) Laurence Olivier in "Hamlet," (3) Jane Wyman in "Johnny Belinda," (4) Walter Huston in "The Treasure of the Sierra Madre," (5) Claire Trevor in "Key Largo," (6) John Huston for "The Treasure of the Sierra Madre," (7) Ivan Jandl, Sid Grauman, Adolph Zukor, Walter Wanger, (8) "Monsieur Vincent."

1949: (1) "All the King's Men," (2) Broderick Crawford in "All the King's Men," (3) Olivia de Havilland in "The Heiress." (4) Dean Jagger in "Twelve O'Clock High," (5) Mercedes McCambridge in "All the King's Men," (6) Joseph L. Mankiewicz for "A Letter to Three Wives," (7) Bobby Driscoll, Fred Astaire, Cecil B. DeMille, Jean Hersholt, (8) "The Bicycle Thief."

1950: (1) "All about Eve," (2) Jose Ferrer in "Cyrano de Bergerac," (3) Judy Holliday in "Born Yesterday," (4) George Sanders in "All about Eve," (5) Josephine Hull in "Harvey," (6) Joseph L. Mankiewicz for "All about Eve," (7) George Murphy, Louis B. Mayer, (8) "The Walls of Malapaga."

1951: (1) "An American in Paris," (2) Humphrey Bogart in "The African Queen," (3) Vivien Leigh in "A Streetcar Named Desire," (4) Karl Malden in "A Streetcar Named Desire," (5) Kim Hunter in "A Streetcar Named Desire," (6) George Stevens for "A Place in the Sun," (7) Gene Kelly, (8) "Rashomon."

1952: (1) "The Greatest Show on Earth," (2) Gary Cooper in "High Noon," (3) Shirley Booth in "Come Back, Little Sheba," (4) Anthony Quinn in "Viva Zapata," (5) Gloria Grahame in "The Bad and the Beautiful," (6) John Ford for "The Quiet Man," (7) Joseph M. Schenck, Merian C. Cooper, Harold Lloyd, Bob Hope, George Alfred Mitchell, (8) "Forbidden Games."

1953: (1) "From Here to Eternity," (2) William Holden in "Stalag 17," (3) Audrey Hepburn in "Roman Holiday," (4) Frank Sinatra in "From Here to Eternity," (5) Donna Reed in "From Here to Eternity," (6) Fred Zinnemann for "From Here to Eternity," (7) Pete Smith, Joseph Breen.

1954: (1) "On the Waterfront," (2) Marlon Brando in "On the Waterfront," (3) Grace Kelly in "The Country Girl," (4) Edmond O'Brien in "The Barefoot Contessa," (5) Eva Marie Saint in "On the Waterfront," (6) Elia Kazan for "On the Waterfront," (7) Greta Garbo, Danny Kaye, Jon Whitely, Vincent Winter, (8) "Gate of Hell."

1955: (1) "Marty," (2) Ernest Borgnine in "Marty," (3) Anna Magnani in "The Rose Tattoo," (4) Jack Lemmon in "Mister Roberts," (5) Jo Van Fleet in "East of Eden," (6) Delbert Mann for "Marty," (8) "Samurai."

1956: (1) "Around the World in 80 Days," (2) Yul Brynner in "The King and I," (3) Ingrid Bergman in "Anastasia," (4) Anthony Quinn in "Lust for Life," (5) Dorothy Malone in "Written on the Wind," (6) George Stevens for "Giant," (7) Eddie Cantor, (8) "La Strada."

1957: (1) "The Bridge on the River Kwai," (2) Alec Guinness in "The Bridge on the River Kwai," (3) Joanne Woodward in "The Three Faces of Eve," (4) Red Buttons in "Sayonara," (5) Miyoshi Umeki in "Sayonara," (6) David Lean for "The Bridge on the River Kwai," (7) Charles Brackett, B. B. Kahane, Gilbert M. (Bronco Billy) Anderson, (8) "The Nights of Cabiria."

1958: (1) "Gigi," (2) David Niven in "Separate Tables," (3) Susan Hayward in "I Want to Live," (4) Burl Ives in "The Big Country," (5) Wendy Hiller in "Separate Tables," (6) Vincente Minnelli for "Gigi," (7) Maurice Chevalier, (8) "My Uncle."

1959: (1) "Ben-Hur," (2) Charlton Heston in "Ben-Hur," (3) Simone Signoret in "Room at the Top," (4) Hugh Griffith in "Ben-Hur," (5) Shelley Winters in "The Diary of Anne Frank," (6) William Wyler for "Ben-Hur," (7) Lee de Forest, Buster Keaton, (8) "Black Orpheus."

1960: (1) "The Apartment," (2) Burt Lancaster in "Elmer Gantry," (3) Elizabeth Taylor in "Butterfield 8," (4) Peter Ustinov in "Spartacus," (5) Shirley Jones in "Elmer Gantry," (6) Billy Wilder for "The Apartment," (7) Gary Cooper, Stan Laurel, Hayley Mills, (8) "The Virgin Spring."

1961: (1) "West Side Story," (2) Maximilian Schell in "Judgment at Nuremberg," (3) Sophia Loren in "Two Women," (4) George Chakiris in "West Side Story," (5) Rita Moreno in "West Side Story," (6) Robert Wise for "West Side Story," (7) Jerome Robbins, Fred L. Metzler, (8) "Through a Glass Darkly."

1962: (1) "Lawrence of Arabia," (2) Gregory Peck in "To Kill a Mockingbird," (3) Anne Bancroft in "The Miracle Worker," (4) Ed Begley in "Sweet Bird of Youth," (5) Patty Duke in "The Miracle Worker," (6) David Lean for "Lawrence of Arabia," (8) "Sundays and Cybele."

1963: (1) "Tom Jones," (2) Sidney Poitier in "Lilies of the Field," (3) Patricia Neal in "Hud," (4) Melvyn Douglas in "Hud," (5) Margaret Rutherford in "The V.I.P's," (6) Tony Richardson for "Tom Jones," (8) "8½."

1964: (1) "My Fair Lady," (2) Rex Harrison in "My Fair Lady," (3) Julie Andrews in "Mary Poppins," (4) Peter Ustinov in "Topkapi," (5) Lila Kedrova in "Zorba the Greek," (6) George Cukor for "My Fair Lady," (7) William Tuttle, (8) "Yesterday, Today and Tomorrow."

1965: (1) "The Sound of Music," (2) Lee Marvin in "Cat Ballou," (3) Julie Christie in "Darling," (4) Martin Balsam in "A Thousand Clowns," (5) Shelley Winters in "A Patch of Blue," (6) Robert Wise for "The Sound of Music," (7) Bob Hope, (8) "The Shop on Main Street."

1966: (1) "A Man for All Seasons," (2) Paul Scofield in "A Man for All Seasons," (3) Elizabeth Taylor in "Who's Afraid of Virginia Woolf?," (4) Walter Matthau in "The Fortune Cookie," (5) Sandy Dennis in "Who's Afraid of Virginia Woolf?," (6) Fred Zinnemann for "A Man for All Seasons," (8) "A Man and A Woman."

1967: (1) "In the Heat of the Night," (2) Rod Steiger in "In the Heat of the Night," (3) Katharine Hepburn in "Guess Who's Coming to Dinner," (4) George Kennedy in "Cool Hand Luke," (5) Estelle Parsons in "Bonnie and Clyde," (6) Mike Nichols for "The Graduate," (8) "Closely Watched Trains."

1968: (1) "Oliver!," (2) Cliff Robertson in "Charly," (3) Katharine Hepburn in "The Lion in Winter" tied with Barbra Streisand in "Funny Girl," (4) Jack Albertson in "The Subject Was Roses," (5) Ruth Gordon in "Rosemary's Baby," (6) Carol Reed for "Oliver!," (7) Onna White for "Oliver!" choreography, John Chambers for "Planet of the Apes" make-up, (8) "War and Peace."

1969: (1) "Midnight Cowboy," (2) John Wayne in "True Grit," (3) Maggie Smith in "The Prime of Miss Jean Brodie," (4) Gig Young in "They Shoot Horses, Don't They?," (5) Goldie Hawn in "Cactus Flower," (6) John Schlesinger for "Midnight Cowboy," (7) Cary Grant, (8) "Z."

1970: (1) "Patton," (2) George C. Scott in "Patton," (3) Glenda Jackson in "Women in Love," (4) John Mills in "Ryan's Daughter," (5) Helen Hayes in "Airport," (6) Franklin J. Schaffner for "Patton," (7) Lillian Gish, Orson Welles, (8) "Investigation of a Citizen above Suspicion."

1971: (1) "The French Connection," (2) Gene Hackman in "The French Connection," (3) Jane Fonda in "Klute," (4) Ben Johnson in "The Last Picture Show," (5) Cloris Leachman in "The Last Picture Show," (6) William Friedkin for "The French Connection," (7) Charles Chaplin, (8) "The Garden of the Finzi-Continis."

1972: (1) "The Godfather," (2) Marlon Brando in "The Godfather," (3) Liza Minnelli in "Cabaret," (4) Joel Grey in "Cabaret," (5) Eileen Heckart in "Butterflies Are Free," (6) Bob Fosse for "Cabaret," (7) Edward G. Robinson, (8) "The Discreet Charm of the Bourgeoisie."

1973: (1) "The Sting," (2) Jack Lemmon in "Save the Tiger," (3) Glenda Jackson in "A Touch of Class," (4) John Houseman in "The Paper Chase," (5) Tatum O'Neal in "Paper Moon," (6) George Roy Hill for "The Sting," (8) "Day for Night."

1974: (1) "The Godfather Part II," (2) Art Carney in "Harry and Tonto," (3) Ellen Burstyn in "Alice Doesn't Live Here Anymore," (4) Robert DeNiro in "The Godfather Part II," (5) Ingrid Bergman in "Murder on the Orient Express," (6) Francis Ford Coppola for "The Godfather Part II," (7) Howard Hawks, Jean Renoir, (8) "Amarcord."

1975: (1) "One Flew over the Cuckoo's Nest," (2) Jack Nicholson in "One Flew over the Cuckoo's Nest," (3) Louise Fletcher in "One Flew over the Cuckoo's Nest," (4) George Burns in "The Sunshine Boys," (5) Lee Grant in "Shampoo," (6) Milos Forman for "One Flew over the Cuckoo's Nest," (7) Mary Pickford, (8) "Dersu Uzala."

1976: (1) "Rocky," (2) Peter Finch in "Network," (3) Faye Dunaway in "Network," (4) Jason Robards in "All the President's Men," (5) Beatrice Straight in "Network," (6) John G. Avildsen for "Rocky," (8) "Black and White in Color."

1977: (1) "Annie Hall," (2) Richard Dreyfuss in "The Goodbye Girl," (3) Diane Keaton in "Annie Hall," (4) Jason Robards in "Julia," (5) Vanessa Redgrave in "Julia," (6) Woody Allen for "Annie Hall," (7) Maggie Booth (film editor), (8) "Madame Rosa."

1978: (1) "The Deer Hunter," (2) Jon Voight in "Coming Home," (3) Jane Fonda in "Coming Home," (4) Christopher Walken in "The Deer Hunter" (5) Maggie Smith in "California Suite," (6) Michael Cimino for "The Deer Hunter," (7) Laurence Olivier, King Vidor, (8) "Get Out Your Handkerchiefs."

1979: (1) "Kramer vs. Kramer," (2) Dustin Hoffman in "Kramer vs. Kramer," (3) Sally Field in "Norma Rae," (4) Melvyn Douglas in "Being There," (5) Meryl Streep in "Kramer vs. Kramer," (6) Robert Benton for "Kramer vs. Kramer," (7) Robert S. Benjamin, Hal Elias, Alec Guinness, (8) "The Tin Drum."

1980: (1) "Ordinary People," (2) Robert DeNiro in "Raging Bull,"(3) Sissy Spacek in "Coal Miner's Daughter," (4) Timothy Hutton in "Ordinary People," (5) Mary Steenburgen in "Melvin and Howard," (6) Robert Redford for "Ordinary People," (7) Henry Fonda, (8) "Moscow Does Not Believe in Tears."

1981 FOREIGN FILMS

CADDIE

(ATLANTIC RELEASING CORP.) Producer, Anthony Buckley; Director, Donald Crombie; Screenplay, Joan Long; Photography, Peter James; Art Director, Owen Williams; Costumes, Judith Dorsman; Editor, Tim Wellburn; Music, Patrick Flynn; In color; Not rated; 107 minutes; January release.

CAST

Caddie	Helen Morse
Peter	Takis Emmanuel
Ted	Jack Thompson
Josie	Jacki Weaver
Leslie	Melissa Jaffer
Bill	Ron Blanchard
Sonny	Drew Forsythe
Esther	Kirrili Nolan
Maudie	Lynette Currin

Right: Helen Morse, also below with Takis Emmanuel
© Atlantic Releasing Corp.

Jack Thompson

Helen Morse

MAN OF MARBLE

(NEW YORKER) Director, Andrzej Wajda; Screenplay, Aleksander Scibor-Rylski; Photography, Edward Klosinki; Music, Andrzej Korzhnski; Editor, Halina Pugarowa; Art Director, Allan Starski; In color and black and white; 160 minutes; Not rated; In Polish with English subtitles; January release.

CAST

Agnieszka ....Krystyna Janda
Mateusz Birkut .... Jersy Radziwilowicz
Burski .... Tadeusz Lomnicki/Jacek Lomnicki
Hanka Tomczyk ....Krystyna Zachwatowicz
Witek ....Michal Tarkowski
Michalak .... Piotr Cieslak
Film Editor .... Wieslaw Wojcik
Agnieszka's Producer .... Boguslaw Sobczuk
Cameraman .... Leonard Zajaczkowski
Sound Engineer .... Jacek Domanski
Agnieszka's Father .... Zdzislaw Kozien
Museum Employee ....Irena Laskowska
Bar Owner.. Wieslaw Drzewicz
Colonel .... Kazimierz Kaczor
Secretary .... Ewa Zietek

Right: Jerzy Radziwilowicz

Krystyna Janda

NAPOLEON

(ZOETROPE) Abel Gance's 1927 masterpiece; Music, Carmine Coppola; Performed by the American Symphony Orchestra with Carmine Coppola as guest conductor; Organist, Leonard Raver; A Robert A. Harris/Images Film Archive release; Presented by Francis Ford Coppola; Not rated; 240 minutes with an intermission; January release.

CAST

Vladimir Roudenko (Napoleon as a boy), Albert Dieudonne (Napoleon Bonaparte), Gina Manes (Josephine de Beauharnais), Nicolas Koline (Tristan Fleuri), Alexandre Koubitzky (Danton), Antonin Artaud (Marat), Edmond Van Daele (Maximilien Robespierre), Harry Krimer (Rouget de Lisle), Annabella (Violine Fleuri), Serge Freddykarll (Marcellin Fleuri), Robert Vidalin (Camille Desmoulins), Maryse Damia (La Marseillaise), Louis Sance (Louis XVI), Suzanne Bianchetti (Marie Antoinette), Carvalho (Fortune-Teller), Yvette Dieudonne (Elisa Bonaparte), Eugenei Buffet (Laetitia Bonaparte), Simone Genevois (Pauline Bonaparte), Georges Lampin (Joseph Bonaparte), Sylvio Caviccia (Lucien Bonaparte), Henri Baudin (Santo-Ricci), Maurice Schutz (Pasquale Paoli), Acho Chakatouny (Pozzo Di Borgo), M. Day (Admiral Lord Samuel Hood), Leon Courtois (Gen. Carteaux), Philippe Heriat (Antonio Salicetti), Alexandre Bernard (Gen. Dugommier), Daniel Burret (Augustin Robespierre), M. Caillard (Thomas Gasparin), Pierre de Canolle (Capt. August Marmont), Pierre Danis (Col, Muiron), M. Dacheux (Gen. DuTeil), Jean Henry (Sgt. Andoche Junot), Jack Rye (Gen. O'Hara), Henry Krauss (Moustache), Marguerite Gance (Charlotte Corday), M'Viguier (Couthon), Abel Gance (Louis Saint-Just), Francine Mussey (Lucille Desmoulins), Pierre Barcheff (Gen. Lazare Hoche), Georges Cahuzac (Vicomte De Beauharnais), Jean d'Yd (La Bussiere), Boris Fastovich (L'Oeil-Vert), M. Maxudian (Paul Barras), Jean Gaudray (Jean Lambert Tallien), M. Mathillon (Gen. Sherer), Genica Missirio (Capt. Joachim Murat), M. Faviere (Joseph Fouche), Andree Standard (Therese Tallien), Suzy Vernon (Mme. Racamier), Roger Blum (Francois Talma), Janine Pen (Hortense De Beauharnais), Philippe Rolla (Gen. Andre Massena)

LES BONS DÉBARRAS
("Good Riddance")

(INTERNATIONAL FILM EXCHANGE) Director, Francis Mankiewicz; Screenplay, Rejean Ducharme; Producers, Marcia Couelle, Claude Godbout; Photography, Michel Brault; Editor, Andre Corriveau; Assistant Directors, Lise Abastado, Alain Chartrand; Art Director, Michel Proulx; Costumes, Diane Paquet; Music, Bernard Buisson; In color; 112 minutes; Not rated; In French with English subtitles; January release.

CAST

Manon	Charlotte Laurier
Michelle	Marie Tifo
Guy	Germain Houde
Mme. Viau-Vachon	Louis Marleau
Maurice	Roger Lebel
Gaetan	Gilbert Sicotte
Lucien	Serge Theriault
Fernand	Jean-Pierre Bergeron
Samaritan	Leo Ilial
Princesse	Henri
Girls in bar	Madeleine Chartrand, Louis Rinfret
Cousins	Eric Beausejour, Jean-Pierre DuPlessis, Marcella Fajardo, Marie Laurier

Right: Marie Tifo, Charlotte Laurier
Below: Marie Tifo, Gilbert Sicotte
© IFEX

Charlotte Laurier

Gilbert Sicotte, Charlotte Laurier

THE EARTHLING

(**FILMWAYS PICTURES**) Executive Producer, Stephen W. Sharmat; Producers, Elliot Schick, John Strong; Director, Peter Collinson; Screenplay, Lanny Cotler; Editor, Frank Morriss; Music, Dick DeBenedictis; "Halfway Home" by David Shire and Carol Connors; Sung by Maureen McGovern; Photography, Don McAlpine; Designer, Bob Hilditch; Assistant Director, Mark Egerton; Presented by Samuel Z. Arkoff; 98 minutes; Rated PG; February release.

CAST

Patrick Foley	William Holden
Shawn Daley	Ricky Schroder
Ross Daley	Jack Thompson
Bettina Daley	Olivia Hamnett
Molly Ann Hogan	Jane Harders
Christian Neilson	Alwyn Kurts
Meg Neilson	Pat Evison
Bobby Burns	Redmond Phillips
R. C.	Willie Fennell
Harlan	Allan Penney
Uncle	Walter Pym
McGroaty	Harry Neilson
Red	Tony Barry

Right: William Holden
© **Filmways Pictures**

Ricky Schroder, William Holden
Above: Ricky Schroder

Ricky Schroder

THE LAST METRO

(UNITED ARTISTS) Director, Francois Truffaut; Screenplay, Francois Truffaut, Suzanne Schiffman, Jean-Claude Grumberg; Photography, Nestor Almendros; Art Director, Jean-Pierre Kohut-Svelko; Assistant Director, Suzanne Schiffman; Costumes, Lisele Roos; Music, Georges Delerue; Editor, Martine Barraque; In color; French with English sub-titles; 133 minutes; Rated R; February release.

CAST

Marion Steiner	Catherine Deneuve
Bernard Granger	Gerard Depardieu
Jean-Loup Cottins	Jean Poiret
Lucas Steiner	Heinz Bennent
Arlette Guillaume	Andrea Ferreol
Germaine Fabre	Paulette Dubost
Nadine Marsac	Sabine Haudepin
Daxiat	Jean-Louis Richard
Raymond, stage manager	Maurice Risch
Merlin	Marcel Berbert
Gestapo Agent	Richard Bohringer
Christian Leglise	Jean-Pierre Klein
Jacquot (Eric)	Franck Pasquier
German Singer	Renata
Rene Bernardini	Jean-Jose Richer
Martine the Thief	Martine Simonet
Lt. Bergen	Laszlo Szabo
Yvonne, lady's maid	Henia Ziv
Rosette Goldstern	Jessica Zucman
Marc	Alain Tasma

Left: Catherine Deneuve, Heinz Bennent
© United Artists Corp.

Gerard Depardieu, Catherine Deneuve

Catherine Deneuve Above: Jean Poiret, Catherine Deneuve

SPETTERS

(SAMUEL GOLDWYN CO.) Producer, Joop Van Den Ende; Director, Paul Verhoeven; Screenplay, Gerard Soeteman; Photography, Jost Vacano; Art Director, Dick Schillemans; Costumes, Yan Tax; Editor, Ine Schenkkan; In color; 109 minutes; Rated R; February release

CAST

Eve	Toon Agterberg
Hans	Maarten Spanjer
Reen	Hans Van Tongeren
Maya	Marianne Boyer
Fientje	Renee Soutendijk
Henkhof	Jeroen Krabbe
Witkamp	Rutger Hauer

Top: Maarten Spanjer, Hans van Tongeren,
Toon Agterberg Below: Renee Soutendijk

Faith Healer, Hans van Tongeren, Marianne Boyer
Top: Rutger Hauer, Hans van Tongeren Below: Renee
Soutendijk, Maarten Spanjer

THE DOGS OF WAR

(UNITED ARTISTS) Producer, Larry DeWaay; Director, John Irvin; Screenplay, Gary DeVore, George Malko; Based on novel by Frederick Forsyth; Executive Producers, Norman Jewison, Patrick Palmer; Photography, Jack Cardiff; Design, Peter Mullins; Editor, Antony Gibbs; Assistant Directors, Candace Suerstedt-Rehmet, Michelle Marx, Lewis Gould, John Robertson; Music, Geoffrey Burgon; Costumes, Emma Porteous; Art Directors, John Siddall, Bert Davey; In Technicolor and Dolby Stereo; 122 minutes; Rated R; February release.

CAST

Shannon	Christopher Walken
Drew	Tom Berenger
North	Colin Blakely
Endean	Hugh Millais
Derek	Paul Freeman
Michel	Jean-Francois Stevenin
Jessie	JoBeth Williams
Capt. Lockhart	Robert Urquhart
Dr. Okoye	Winston Ntshona

Central America: Pedro Armendariz (Major), Harlan Cary Poe (Richard), New York: Ed O'Neill (Terry), Isabel Grandin (Evelyn), Ernest Graves (Warner), Kelvin Thomas (Black Boy), Shane Rimmer (Dr. Oaks), Father Joseph Konrad (Priest), Bruce McLane (Shop Manager), London: George W. Harris (Col. Bobi), David Schofield (Endean's Man), Terence Rigby (Hackett), Tony Mathews (Bank Vice President), John Quentin (Party Guest), Paris: Jean-Pierre Kalfon (Benny), Christopher Malcolm (Baker), Belgium: Jack Lenoir (Boucher), Andre Penvern, Lawrence Davidson (Policemen), Spain: Martin LaSalle, Mario Sanchez (Customs Officers), Africa: Maggie Scott (Gabrielle), Hugh Quarshie (Zangaron Officer), Olu Jacobs (Customs Officer), Christopher Asante (Geoffrey), Thomas Baptiste (Dexter), Eddie Tagoe (Jinja), Kenny Ireland, Jim Broadbent (Film Crew), Andre Toffel (Priest), Diana Bracho (Nun), Ilarrio Bisi Pedro (Kimba), Joanne Flanagan (Godmother) Robert Berger, William B. Cain, Russell T. Carr (Poker Players), Jose Rabelo (Hotel Clerk), Victoria Tennant, Errica Creer, Sheila Ruskin (Dinner Party Guests)

Right: Paul Freeman, Christopher Walken, Tom Berenger, Jean-Francois Stevenin Above: Christopher Walken, Colin Blakely, Maggie Scott Top: Walken, JoBeth Williams © United Artists Corp.

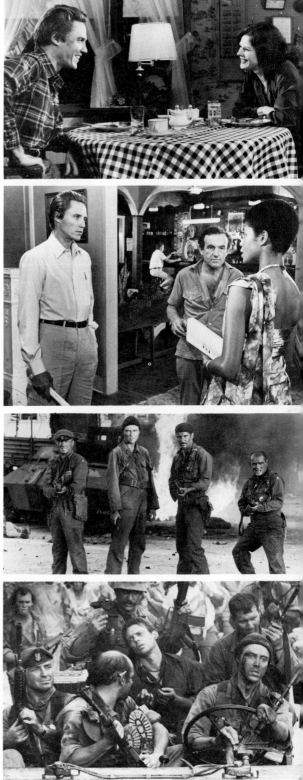

Eddie Tagoe, Tom Berenger, Jean-Francois Stevenin, Paul Freeman

Paul Freeman (L), Christopher Walken (R)

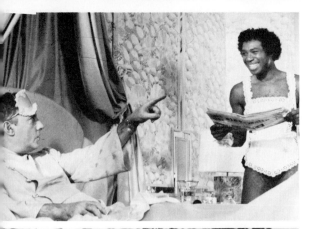

LA CAGE AUX FOLLES II

(UNITED ARTISTS) Executive Producer, Marcello Danon; Director, Edouard Molinar; Story, Francis Veber, Jean Poiret, Marcello Danon; Screenplay, Francis Veber; Music, Ennio Morricone; Photography, Armando Nannuzzi; Designer, Luigi Scaccianoce; Costumes, Ambra Danon; Editor, Robert Isnardon; Assistant Director, Rinaldo Ricci; A French-Italian Co-Production; In color; 100 minutes; Rated R; February release.

CAST

Renato Baldi	Ugo Tognazzi
Albin Mougeotte/Zaza Napoli	Michel Serrault
Barman at cabaret	Gianni Frisoni
Caramel	Mark Bodin
Jacob	Benny Luke
Walter	Gianrico Tondinelli
Waiter (Negresco)	Philippe Cronenberver
Handsome Young Man	Francis Missana
Pretty Girl	Marie-Claude Douquet
Desk Clerk (Hotel de Lys)	Ricardo Berlingeri
Killer in hotel	Piero Morgia
Broca	Marcel Bozzuffi
Simon Charrier	Michel Galabru
Milan	Giovanni Vettorazzo
Proprietor Le Roi du Bleu	Pierre Desmet
Andrew Manderstam	Tom Felleghy
Dr. Boquillon	Danilo Recanatesi
Mangin	Nello Pazzafini
Rouget	Renato Basso
Michaux	Antonio Francioni
Demis	Nazareno Natale
Hans	Stelio Candelli
Gunther	Giorgio Cerioni
Ralph	Roberto Bisacco
Terrorist Accomplice	Roberto Caporali
Signora Baldi	Paola Borboni
Luigi	Glauco Onorato

Left: Michel Serrault, Ugo Tognazzi
Top: Michel Serrault, Benny Luke
© United Artists Corp.

Michel Serrault, Ugo Tognazzi

Michel Serrault, Ugo Tognazzi

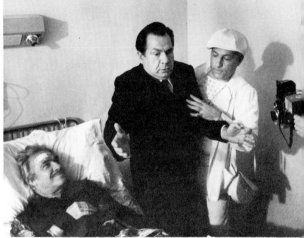

**Michel Serrault, also top with Marcel Bozzuffi
Above: Serrault, Gianrico Tondinelli**

**Michel Serrault, Ugo Tognazzi, and above
with Michel Galabru (C)**

CONFIDENCE

(NEW YORKER) Director, Istvan Szabo; Screenplay, Istvan Szabo from stroy by Szabo and Erika Szanto; Photography, Lajos Koltai; Editor, Zsuzsa Csakany; Art Director, Jozsef Romvary; In Hungarian with English subtitles; In color; 104 minutes; Not rated; March release.

CAST

Kata	Ildiko Bansagi
Janos Biro	Peter Andorai
Old Woman	Mrs. Oszkar Gombik
Old Man	Karoly Csaki
Bozsi	Ildiko Kishonti
Kata's Husband	Lajos Balazsovits
Hoffmann, German Officer	Tamas Dunai
Pali	Zoltan Bezeredi
Dr. Czako	Dr. Laszlo Littmann
Janos' Wife	Judit Halasz

Right: Ildiko Bansagi
Below (L) Bansagi, Peter Andorai
(R) Bansagi, Andorai

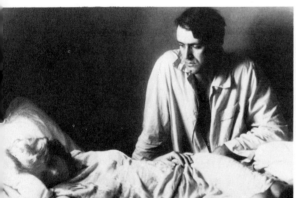

Ildiko Bansagi, Peter Andorai

Ildiko Bansagi, Peter Andorai

156

THE ROADS OF EXILE

(CORINTH) Producer, Etienne Laroche; Director, Claude Goretta; Screenplay, Georges Haldas, Claude Goretta; Photography, Philippe Rousselot; Editor, Joele Van Effenterre; Music, Arie Dzierlatka; Presented by Ruth Gardener; In French with English subtitles; 169 minutes; Not rated; In color; March release.

CAST

Jean-Jacques Rousseau	Francois Simon
Therese Levasseur	Dominique Labourier
Bernardinde St. Pierre	Roland Bertin
Richard Davenport	David Markham
David Hume	John Sharp
Le Prince de Conti	Gabriel Cattand
Madame de Warens	Corrine Coderey

Right: Francois Simon

Dominique Labourier, Francois Simon

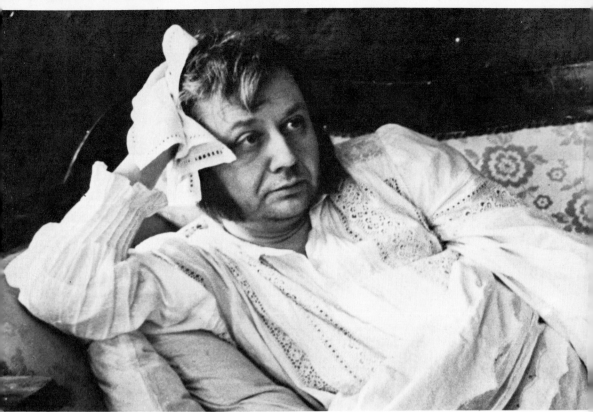

Oleg Tabakov

Elena Solovei
© **IFEX**

OBLOMOV

(INTERNATIONAL FILM EXCHANGE) Director, Nikita Mikhalkov; Screenplay, Alexander Adabashyan, Nikita Michalkov; Based on novel by Ivan Goncharov; Photography, Pavel Lebechev; Produced by Mosfilm Studio in color; 146 minutes; In Russian with English subtitles; Not rated; March release

CAST

Oblomov .... Oleg Tabakov
Olga .... Elena Solovei
Zakhar .... Andrei Popov
Stolz .... Yuri Bogatyrev

Oleg Tabakov, Elena Solovei, Yuri Bogatyrev
Top: Oleg Tabakov, Yuri Bogatyrev

VOYAGE EN DOUCE

(NEW YORKER) (also "Sentimental Journey") Executive Producer, Maurice Bernart; Director, Michel Deville; Screenplay, (French with English subtitles) Michel Deville, Francois-Regis Bastide, Camille Bourniquel, Muriel Cerf, Jean Chalon, Pierrette Grainville, Yves Navarre, Jacques Perry, Maurice Pons, Beatrice Privat, Suzanne Prou, Frederic Rey, Dominique Rolin, Isaure de Saint-Pierre; Photography, Claude LeComte; Editor, Raymonde Guyot; Music, Beethoven, Brahms, Quentin Damamme; Assistant Director; Rosalinde Damamme; Art Director, Catherine Ardouin; In color; 97 minutes; Not rated; April release.

CAST

Helene	Dominique Sanda
Lucie	Geraldine Chaplin
Denis	Jacques Zabor
Perrine (Helene at 10)	Valerie Hug
Lucas	Robin Camus
Helene at 15	Marion Gautier
Lucie at 15	Myriam Roulet
The Man in the houses	Jean Crubelier
Marie, Lucie's cousin	Cecile LeBailly
Helene's Godmother	Catherine LeDall
Bellhop	Frederic Andrei
Concert Singer	Valerie Masterson
Fruit Vendor	Jacques Pieller
Vendor's Girlfriend	Jacqueline Parent
Helene's Grandmother	Francoise Morhange
Man on the train	Christopher Malavoy
Man in the museum	Dominique Delouche
Gas Station Attendant	Helene Garcia
Man at gas station	Geo Beuf

Left: Dominique Sanda, Geraldine Chaplin
Below: (L) Sanda, Jacques Zabor (R) Sanda, Robin Camus, Chaplin

Dominique Sanda, Geraldine Chaplin

Dominique Sanda, Geraldine Chaplin

LION OF THE DESERT

(UNITED FILM DISTRIBUTION) Producer-Director, Moustapha Akkad; Screenplay, H. A. L. Craig; Music, Maurice Jarre; Associate Producer, Roy Stevens; Photography, Jack Hildyard; Assistant Producer, June Bordcosh; Designers, Mario Garbuglia, Syd Cain; Costumes, Orietta Nasallirocca, Piero Cicoletti, Hassan Ben Dardaf; Assistant Director, Miguel Gil; Art Directors, Giorgio Desideri, Maurice Cain, Bob Bell; Editor, John Shirley; A Falcon International Production in Eastmancolor, Panavision, and Dolby Stereo; 162 minutes; Rated PG; April Release.

CAST

Omar Mukhtar	Anthony Quinn
Gen. Rodolfo Graziani	Oliver Reed
Benito Mussolini	Rod Steiger
Sharif El Gariani	John Gielgud
Mabrouka	Irene Papas
Diodiece	Raf Vallone
Major Tomelli	Gastone Moschin
Bu-Matari	Takis Emmanuel
Lt. Sandrini	Stefano Patrizi
Prince Amedeo	Sky Dumont
Al-Fadeel	Robert Brown
Ali's Mother	Eleonora Stathopoulou
Salem	Andrew Keir
Col. Sarsani	Adolfo Lastretti
Barillo	Pietro Gerlini
Capt. Biagi	George Sweeney
Lobitto	Mario Feliciani
President of Court	Claudio Gora
Capture Captain	Massimiliano Baratta
Gen. Graziani's Aide	Franco Fantasia
Ismail	Rodolfo Bigotti
Ali	Ihab Werfali
Sentry	Gianfranco Barra
Infantry Corporal	Mark Colleano
Machine Gun Sergeant	Scott Fensome
Aisha	Aisha Hussein
Collaborator	Mukhtar Aswad
Field Marshall	Pietro Tordi

Top: Oliver Reed, Anthony Quinn (also R)
Right Center: John Gielgud, Rod Steiger

Irene Papas

CITY OF WOMEN

(GAUMONT/NEW YORKER) Director, Federico Fellini; Screenplay, (Italian with English subtitles) Federico Fellini, Bernardino Zapponi, Brunello Rondi; Photography, Giuseppe Rotunno; Art Director, Dante Ferretti; Editor, Ruggero Mastroianni; Costumes, Gabriella Pescucci; Music, Luis Bacalov; Assistant Directors, Maurizio Mein, Giovanna Bentivoglio; Choreography, Leonetta Bentivoglio; In Technovision and color; 138 minutes; Not rated; April release.

CAST

Snaporaz	Marcello Mastroianni
Dr. Xavier Zuberkock	Ettore Manni
Elena	Anna Prucnal
Woman on train	Bernice Stegers
Feminist on roller skates	Donatella Damiani
Other Dancing Girl	Sara Tafuri
Old Woman on motorcycle	Jole Silvani
Dr. Zuberkock's conquest	Carla Terlizzi
Enderbreith Small, with 6 husbands	Katren Gebelein
Feminist	Dominique Labourier
Housewife in skit	Alessandra Panelli
Zuberkock's Elderly Maid	Mara Ciukleva
Feminist in black	Loredana Solfizi
Fishwoman of San Leo	Gabriella Giorgelli
Blond Motorcyclists	Tatiana and Brigitte Petronio
Troubadours	Armando Parracino, Umberto Zuanelli, Pietro Fumagalli

Top: Armando Parracino, Umberto Zuanelli,
Pietro Fumagalli Below: Alessandra Panelli

Marcello Mastroianni, also top with
Carla Terlizzi Above: Anna Prucnal

Ettore Manni, Carla Terlizzi Top: Bernice
Stegers, Marcello Mastroianni

Marcello Mastroianni, Donatella Damiani
Above: Ettore Manni

LA DROLESSE

(GAUMONT/NEW YORKER) (or "The Hussy") Producers, Daniele Delorme, Yves Robert; Director, Jacques Doillon; Screenplay, (French with English subtitles) Jacques Doillon, Denis Ferraris; Photography, Philippe Rousselot; Editor, Laurent Quaglio; Art Director, Jean-Denis Robert; Assistant Director, Guy Chalaud; Costumes, Mic Cheminal; In color; 90 minutes; Not rated; April release.

CAST

Mado .... Madeleine Desdevises
Francois..Claude Hebert
and Paulette Lahaye, Juliette LeCauchoix, Fernand Decaen, Janine Huet, Odette Maestrini, Ginette Mazure, Denise Garnier, Norbert Delozier, Marie Sanson, Edouard Besnehard, Henriette Adam, Jean Bruneliere, Jacques Thieule, Christian Bouilllette, Dominique Besnehard

Right: Madeleine Desdevises

Claude Hebert, Madeleine Desdevises (also above)

Claude Hebert, and above with Madeleine Desdevises

A SECOND CHANCE

(UNITED ARTISTS CLASSICS) Produced, Directed and Written by Claude Lelouch; Photography, Jacques LeFrancois; Assistant Directors, Elie Chouraqui, Arlette Gordon; Costumes, Colette Baudot; Editor, Georges Klotz; Music, Francis Lai; Lyrics, Pierre Barouh; In color; 99 minutes; Rated PG; May release.

CAST

Catherine Berger	Catherine Deneuve
Sarah Gordon	Anouk Aimee
L'Avocat	Charles Denner
Patrick	Francis Huster
Henri Lano	Niels Arestrup
Lucienne Lano	Colette Baudot
Simon Berger	Jean-Jacques Briot
Sarah's Daughter	Manuella Papatakis
Le Banquier	Jean-Francois Remy
Claude Blame	Bernard Donnadieu
L'Agent Immobilier	Jacques Villeret
Le Bijoutier	Jean-Pierre Kalfon
Zoe	Zoe Chauveau

Right: Catherine Deneuve, Anouk Aimee
© United Artists Corp.

Anouk Aimee, Colette Baudot
Above: Catherine Deneuve, Charles Denner

Anouk Aimee, Catherine Deneuve
Above: Deneuve, Jean-Jacques Briot

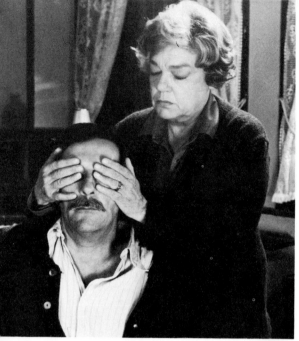

I SENT A LETTER TO MY LOVE

(ATLANTIC) Producers, Lise Fayolles; Giorgio Silvagni; Director, Moshe Mizrahi; Screenplay (French with English subtitles), Moshe Mizrahi, Gerard Brach; From novel by Bernice Rubens; Photography, Ghislain Cloquet; Editor, Francoise Bonnot; Music, Philippe Sarde; In color; 112 minutes; Rated PG; May release.

CAST
Louise .... Simone Signoret
Gilles .... Jean Rochefort
Yvette .... Delphine Seyrig

Left: Jean Rochefort, Simone Signoret
© Atlantic Releasing Corp.

Delphine Seyrig, Jean Rochefort, Simone Signoret

Jean Rochefort, Simone Signoret, Delphine Seyrig (also at top)
Above: Jean Rochefort, Simone Signoret

JUST A GIGOLO

(UNITED ARTISTS CLASSICS) Producer, Rolf Thiele; Director, David Hemmings; Screenplay, Joshua Sinclair; Photography, Charly Steinberger; Designer, Peter Rothe; Assistant Director, Eva Maria Schonecker; Choreographer, Herbert F. Schubert; Costumes, Ingrid Zore; Editors, Susan Jaeger, Fred Srp, Maxine Julius; In color; 98 minutes; A Leguan Film production; Rated R; May release.

CAST

Paul	David Bowie
Cilly	Sydne Rome
Helga	Kim Novak
Capt. Kraft	David Hemmings
Mutti	Maria Schell
Prince	Curt Jurgens
Baroness von Semering	Marlene Dietrich
Eva	Erika Pluhar
Gustav	Rudolf Schundler
Aunt Hilda	Hilde Weissner
Otto	Werner Pochath
Von Lipzig	Bela Erny
Von Muller	Friedhelm Lehmann
Lothar	Rainer Hunold
Frau Aeckerle	Evelyn Kunneke
Frau Uexkull	Karin Hardt
Frau von Putzdorf	Gudrun Genest
Greta	Ursula Heyer
Gilda	Christiane Maybach
Director	Martin Hirthe
Agent	Rene Kolldehoff

Right: Marlene Dietrich
© United Artists Corp.

Kim Novak, David Bowie

DRAGONSLAYER

(PARAMOUNT) Producer, Hal Barwood; Executive Producer, Howard W. Koch; Director, Matthew Robbins; Screenplay, Hal Barwood, Matthew Robbins; Music, Alex North; Photography, Derek Vanlint; Designer, Elliot Scott; Editor, Tony Lawson; Associate Producer, Eric Rattray; Costumes, Anthony Mendleson; Special Effects, Brian Johnson, Dennis Muren; Assistant Directors, Barry Langley, Roy Stevens, John Downes; Choreographer, Peggy Dixon; In Metrocolor, Panavision, and Dolby Stereo; 120 minutes; Rated PG; June release.

CAST

Galen	Peter MacNicol
Valerian	Caitlin Clarke
Ulrich	Ralph Richardson
Tyrian	John Hallam
Casidorus Rex	Peter Eyre
Greil	Albert Salmi
Hodge	Sydney Bromley
Princess Elspeth	Chloe Salaman
Simon	Emrys James
Horsrik	Roger Kemp
Brother Jacopus	Ian McDiarmid
Henchmen	Ken Shorter, Jason White
Victim	Yolanda Palfrey
Urlanders	Douglas Cooper, Alf Mangon, David Mount, James Payne, Chris Twinn

Right: Peter MacNicol, and below with Ralph Richardson (L), Peter Eyre (R)

Peter MacNicol, Caitlin Clarke, Emrys James

Peter MacNicol, Caitlin Clarke

THE GREAT MUPPET CAPER

(UNIVERSAL/ASSOCIATED FILM DISTRIBUTION) Producers, David Lazer, Frank Oz; Director, Jim Henson; Screenplay, Tom Patchett, Jay Tarses, Jerry Juhl, Jack Rose; Executive Producer, Martin Starger; Photography, Oswald Morris; Editor, Ralph Kemplen; Designer, Harry Lange; Choreographer, Anita Mann; Music and Lyrics, Joe Raposo; Associate Producer, Bruce Sharman; Costumes, Julie Harris; Assistant Director, Dusty Symonds; Art Directors, Charles Bishop, Terry Ackland-Snow, Leigh Malone; Muppet Costumes, Calista Hendrickson, Mary Strieff, Joanne Green, Carol Spier, Danielle Obinger; In Panavision, Technicolor, and Dolby Stereo; 95 minutes; Rated G; June release.

CAST

Jim Henson: Kermit, Rowlf, Dr. Teeth, Waldorf, Swedish Chef
Frank Oz: Miss Piggy, Fozzie Bear, Animal, Sam the Eagle
Dave Goelz: The Great Gonzo, Beauregard, Zoot, Dr. Bunsen Honeydew
Jerry Nelson: Floyd, Pops, Lew Zealand
Richard Hunt: Scooter, Statler, Sweetums, Janice, Beaker
Charles Grodin as Nicky Holiday
Diana Rigg as Lady Holiday
Guest Stars: John Cleese, Robert Morley, Peter Ustinov, Jack Warden
Steve Whitmore: Rizzo the Rat, Lips
Carroll Spinney: Oscar the Grouch
and Erica Creer (Marla), Kate Howard (Carla), Della Finch (Darla), Michael Robbins (Guard), Joan Sanderson (Dorcas), Peter Hughes (Maitre D'), Peggy Aitchison (Prison Guard), Tommy Godfrey (Bus Conductor), Katia Borg, Valli Kemp, Michele Ivan-Zadeh, Chai Lee (Models), Louise Gold, Kathryn Muller, Boy Payne, Brian Muehl, Mike Quinn, Robert Barnett, Hugh Spight, Brian Henson

Peter Ustinov, Miss Piggy
Above: Jack Warden, Fozzie Bear

170

Top: Robert Morley with Gonzo, Kermit,
Fozzie Below: Charles Grodin, Diana Rigg with
Miss Piggy, Fozzie, Gonzo, Kermit

Miss Piggy, also top, and above
with Kermit the Frog

Fozzie, Miss Piggy,
Above: Miss Piggy, Charles Grodin
Top: Miss Piggy

COUP DE SIROCCO

(NEW LINE CINEMA) Executive Producer, Jean-Claude Fleury; Director, Alexandre Arcady; Screenplay, Jan and Daniel Saint-Hamont, Alexandre Arcady; From novel by Daniel Saint-Hamont; Music, Serge Franklin; Photography, Jean-Francois Robin; In color; 100 minutes; Not rated; June release.

CAST

Albert Narboni	Roger Hanin
Marguerite Narboni	Marthe Villalonga
Lucien Bonheur	Michel Auclair
Real Estate Agent	Jacques Duby
General Bauvergne	Maurice Chevit
Paulo Narboni	Patrick Bruel
Georgio Labrouche	Philippe Sfez
Uncle Jacob	Lucien Layani
Salesgirl	Nathalie Guerin
Ruppert	Gerard Jugnot
Servant Girl	Marie-Anne Chazel
Supermarket Manager	Robert Lombard
Doctor	Pierre Vilescale
Porter	Mohamed Zineth

Right: Patrick Bruel, Marthe Villalonga, Mohamed Zineth, Roger Hanin Center Left: Roger Hanin, Marthe Villalonga, Patrick Bruel © New Line Cinema Corp.

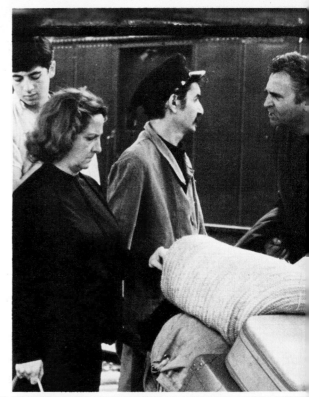

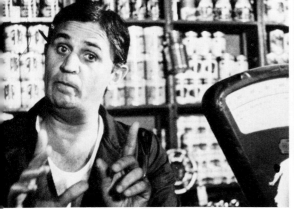

Roger Hanin

Nathalie Guerin

THE SEA WOLVES

(PARAMOUNT/LORIMAR) Executive Producer, Chris Chrisafis; Producer, Euan Lloyd; Director, Andrew V. McLaglen; Screenplay, Reginald Rose; Based on "Boarding Party" by James Leasor; Music, Roy Budd; Co-Producer, Jorge L. Araneta; Associate Producer, Harold Buck; Photography, Tony Imi; Design, Syd Cain; Editor, John Glen; Assistant Director, Bert Batt; Art Director, Maurice Cain; Costumes, Elsa Fennell; In color, Panavision, Dolby Stereo; 120 minutes; Rated PG; June release.

CAST

Colonel Lewis Pugh	Gregory Peck
Capt. Gavin Stewart	Roger Moore
Colonel W. H. Grice	David Niven
Jack Cartwright	Trevor Howard
"Mrs. Cromwell"	Barbara Kellerman
Maj. Yogi Crossley	Patrick Macnee
Wilton	Kenneth Griffith
Colin MacKenzie	Patrick Allen
Trompeta	Wolf Kahler
U-Boat Captain	Robert Hoffmann
First Officer	Dan Van Husen
Ehrenfels Captain	George Mikell
First Officer	Jurgen Andersen
Underhill	Bernard Archard
Montero	Martin Benson
Mrs. Grice	Faith Brook
Melborne	Allan Cuthbertson
Lumsdaine	Edward Dentith
Sloane	Clifford Earl
Governor	Rusi Ghandhi
Hilliard	Donald Houston
Dennison	Percy Herbert
Barker	Patrick Holt

and Glyn Houston (Peters), Victor Langley (Williamson), Terence Longdon (Malverne), Michael Medwin (Radcliffe), Morgan Sheppard (Lovecroft), John Standing (Finley), Graham Stark (Manners), Keith Stevenson (Manuel), Moray Watson (Mac Lean), Brook Williams (Butterworth), Marc Zuber (Ram Das Gupta), Scot Finch (Croupier), Farid Currim (Waiter), Mohan Agashe (Brothel Keeper), Martin Grace (Kruger)

Top: Roger Moore, Gregory Peck, Marc Zuber
Below: Roger Moore, Gregory Peck Right:
Roger Moore, Barbara Kellerman
© Master Mace Ltd.

Trevor Howard, David Niven, Gregory
Peck, Roger Moore

CLASH OF THE TITANS

(UNITED ARTISTS) Producers, Charles H. Schneer, Ray Harryhausen; Director, Desmond Davis; Screenplay, Beverley Cross; Visual Effects, Ray Harryhausen; Music, Laurence Rosenthal; Photography, Ted Moore; Designer, Frank White; Associate Producer, John Palmer; Editor, Timothy Gee; Costumes, Emma Porteous; Art Directors, Don Picton, Peter Howitt, Giorgio Desideri, Fernando Gonzalez; Assistant Directors, Anthony Waye, Gerry Gavigan, Terry Madden; In Metrocolor and Dolby Stereo; 120 minutes; Rated PG; June release.

CAST

Zeus	Laurence Olivier
Hera	Claire Bloom
Thetis	Maggie Smith
Aphrodite	Ursula Andress
Poseidon	Jack Gwillim
Athena	Susan Fleetwood
Hephaestus	Pat Roach
Perseus	Harry Hamlin
Andromeda	Judi Bowker
Ammon	Burgess Meredith
Cassiopeia	Sian Phillips
Thallo	Tim Piggott-Smith
Calibos	Neil McCarthy
Acrisius	Donald Houston
Danae	Vida Taylor
Huntsman	Harry Jones
Three Blind Witches	Flora Robson, Anna Manahan, Freda Jackson

Left: Susan Fleetwood, Ursula Andress, Pat Roach, Jack Gwillim, Claire Bloom, Maggie Smith, Laurence Olivier Above: Judi Bowker, Harry Hamlin, Burgess Meredith
© Titan Productions

**Laurence Olivier
Above: Donald Houston**

**Harry Hamlin with Bubo
Above: Hamlin, Neil McCarthy**

Harry Hamlin, Judi Bowker Above: Burgess Meredith, Hamlin Top: Ursula Andress, Laurence Olivier (also below)

Harry Hamlin (also above) Top: Judi Bowker

Giancarlo Giannini, Hanna Schygulla
Above and Top: Hanna Schygulla

LILI MARLEEN

(UNITED ARTISTS CLASSICS) Producers, Luggi Waldleitner, Enzo Peri; Director, Rainer Werner Fassbinder; Screenplay, Manfred Purzer, Joshua Sinclair; Based on novel by Lale Andersen; Photography, Eaver Schwarzenberger; Design, Rolf Zehetbauer; Music, Peer Raben; Editors, Franz Walsch, Juliane Lorenz; In color; 120 minutes; Not rated; July release.

CAST

Robert	Giancarlo Giannini
Willie	Hanna Schygulla
David Mendelsson	Mel Ferrer
Henkel	Karl Heinz von Hassel
Von Strehlow	Erik Schwmann
Taschner	Hark Bohm
Aaron	Gottfried John
Anna Lederer	Karin Baal
Miriam	Christine Kaufmann
Drewitz	Udo Kier
Kauffmann	Roger Fritz
Bernt	Rainer Will
Blonsky	Raul Giminez
Ginsberg	Adrian Hoven
Prosel	Willy Harlander
Eva	Barbara Dalentin
Grete	Helen Vita
Marika	Elisabeth Volkman
Tamara	Lilo Pempeit
Polin	Traute Hoss
Neighbor	Brigitte Mira
Reintgen	Herb Andress
Swiss Officer	Michael McLernon
Journalist	Jurgen Drager
Dr. Glaubrecht	Rudolf Lenz
Mrs. Prosel	Toni Netzle

**Top: Hanna Schygulla Below: Giancarlo
Giannini, Christine Kaufmann, Mel
Ferrer, Roger Fritz**
© United Artists Corp.

HEART TO HEART

(NEW YORKER) Producer, Alvina du Boisrouvray; Director, Pascal Thomas; Screenplay, Jacques Lourcelles, Pascal Thomas; Music, Vladimir Cosma; Photography, Renan Polles; Editor, Nathalie Lafaurie; Assistant Directors, Hubert Watrinet, Patrick Cartoux; Costumes, Therese Ripaud; French with English subtitles; In color; 110 minutes; Not rated; July release.

CAST

Emile Roussel	Daniel Ceccaldi
Mme. Roussel	Laurence Ligneres
Brigitte	Anne Caudry
Brigitte as a child	Emilie
Pierrette	Carole Jacquinot
Pierrette as a child	Valerie Jacquinot
Florence	Elisa Servier
Florence as a child	Valerie Pascale
Grandfather Roussel	Henri Cremieux
Grandmother Roussel	Louba Guertchikoff
Cousin Gabriel	Michel Galabru
Francois	Igor Lafaurie
Rodolphe	Jean-Claude Martin
Pierrette's Fiance	Christian Peirera
Paul-Louis	Francois Eric Gendron
Florence's First Fiance	Johnny Pigozzi
Rene	Spillmaecker
Etienne	Bernard Menez
Alain	Alain Bernard
Dora	Ingeborg Prinz
Guimauve	Michele Hermet

Right: Carole Jacquinot, Laurence Ligneres, Anne Caudry, Daniel Ceccaldi, Elisa Servier
Top: Daniel Ceccaldi, Valerie Jacquinot

Valerie Pascale, Christian Peirera, Laurence Ligneres, Daniel Ceccaldi, Valerie Jacquinot

Anne Caudry, Elisa Servier, Carole Jacquinot Above: Igor Lafaurie, Anne Caudry

EYE OF THE NEEDLE

(UNITED ARTISTS) Producer, Stephen Friedman; Director, Richard Marquand; Screenplay, Stanley Mann; Based on novel by Ken Follett; Music, Miklos Rozsa; Editor, Sean Barton; Photography, Alan Hume; Designer, Wilfried Shingleton; Art Directors, Bert Davey, John Hoesli; Assistant Director, Roger Simons; Costumes, John Bloomfield; A Kings Road Production in color; 112 minutes; Rated R; July release.

CAST

Faber	Donald Sutherland
Lieutenant	Stephen MacKenna
Billy Parkin	Philip Martin Brown
Lucy	Kate Nelligan
David	Christopher Cazenove
Lucy's Father	George Belbin
Lucy's Mother	Faith Brook
Constable	Barbara Graley
Peterson	Arthur Lovegrove
Oliphant	Colin Rix
Mrs. Garden	Barbara Ewing
German SS Officer	Chris Jenkinson
German Radio Operator	William Merrow
Inspector Harris	Patrick Connor
Canter	David Hayman
Godliman	Ian Bannen
Muller	Rupert Frazer
Joe	Jonathan Nicholas Haley
Tom	Alex McCrindle
Kleinmann	John Bennett
Colonel Terry	Alan Surtees
Mr. Porter	Bill Fraser

Top: Christopher Cazenove, Kate Nelligan
Below: Donald Sutherland, Nelligan Right:
Sutherland, Cazenove
© United Artists Corp.

Kate Nelligan, Donald Sutherland
Top: David Hayman, Ian Bannen,
Philip Martin Brown

TIM

(SATORI) Producer-Director, Michael Pate; Associate Producer, Geoffrey Gardiner; Photography, Paul Onorato; Screenplay by Michael Pate from novel by Colleen McCullough; Music, Eric Jupp; Art Director, John Carroll; Editor, David Stiven; Assistant Director, Michael Midlan; Costumes, Pat Forster; In color; 90 minutes; Not rated; September release.

CAST

Mary Horton	Piper Laurie
Tim Melville	Mel Gibson
Ron Melville	Alwyn Kurts
Emily Melville	Pat Evison
Tom Ainsley	Peter Gwynne
Dawn Melville	Deborah Kennedy
Mick Harrington	David Foster
Mrs. Harrington	Margo Lee
Mr. Harrington	James Condon
John Martinson	Michael Caulfield
Mrs. Parker	Brenda Senders
Dr. Perkins	Brian Barrie
Curly Campbell	Kevin Leslie
Secretary	Louise Pago
Ambulance Attendant	Arthur Faynes
Minister	Geoff Usher
Marriage Celebrant	Sheila McGuire-Taylor
Storekeeper Thompson	Alan Penny
Mrs. Martinson	Catherine Bray
Barmaid Maudie	Doris Goddard

Top: Piper Laurie, Mel Gibson
© Satori Productions

Mel Gibson, Piper Laurie

GALLIPOLI

(PARAMOUNT) Producers, Robert Stigwood, Patricia Lovell; Director, Peter Weir; Executive Producer, Francis O'Brien; Screenplay, David Williamson; Story, Peter Weir; Photography, Russell Boyd; Assistant Directors, Mark Egerton, Steve Andrews, Marshall Crosby, Robert Pendlebury; Associate Producers, Martin Cooper, Ben Gannon; Design, Wendy Weir: Art Director, Herbert Pinter; Editor, William Anderson; Original Music, Brian May; In Eastmancolor and Panavision; 110 minutes; Rated PG; August release.

CAST

Archy	Mark Lee
Jack	Bill Kerr
Frank Dunne	Mel Gibson
Wallace Hamilton	Ron Graham
Les McCann	Harold Hopkins
Zac	Charles Yunupingu
Stockman	Heath Harris
Rose Hamilton	Gerda Nicolson
Billy	Robert Grubb
Barney	Tim McKenzie
Snowy	David Argue
Officials	Reg Evans, Jack Giddy
Announcer	Dane Peterson
Recruiting Officer	Paul Linkson
Waitress	Jenny Lovell
Billy Snakeskin	Steve Dodd
Stumpy	Harold Baigent
Mary	Robyn Galwey
Lionel	Don Quin
Laura	Phyllis Burford
Gran	Marjorie Irving
Dan Dunne	John Murphy
Major Barton	Bill Hunter
Lt. Gray	Peter Ford
Anne Barton	Diane Chamberlain
Army Doctor	Ian Govett
Sgt. Sayers	Geoff Parry
English Officers	Clive Bennington, Giles Holland-Martin
Egyptian Shopkeeper	Moshe Kedem
Col. Robinson	John Morris
N.C.O. at ball	Don Barker
Soldier on beach	Kiwi White
Sniper	Paul Sonkkila
Observer	Peter Lawless
Sentry	Saltbush Baldock
Artillery Officer	Les Dayman
Sgt. Major	Stan Green
Col. White	Max Wearing
Gen. Gardner	Graham Dow
Radio Officer	Peter R. House

Left: Bill Kerr, Mark Lee
Top: Mel Gibson, Mark Lee
© Associated R & R Films

Mark Lee, Mel Gibson

Mark Lee, Mel Gibson

Mel Gibson, Mark Lee,
David Argue Above: Lee, Gibson
(also at top)

Mel Gibson, Mark Lee
(also above)

THE FRENCH LIEUTENANT'S WOMAN

(UNITED ARTISTS) Producer, Leon Clore; Director, Karel Reisz; Screenplay, Harold Pinter; Based on novel of same title by John Fowles; Photography, Freddie Francis; Editor, John Bloom; Music, Carl Davis; Design, Assheton Gorton; Associate Producers, Tom Maschler, Geoffrey Helman; Costumes, Tom Rand; Art Directors, Norman Dorme, Terry Pritchard, Allan Cameron; Assistant Director, Richard Hoult; In Technicolor; 127 minutes; Rated R; September release.

CAST

Sarah/Anna	Meryl Streep
Charles/Mike	Jeremy Irons
Sam	Hilton McRae
Mary	Emily Morgan
Mrs. Tranter	Charlotte Mitchell
Ernestina	Lynsey Baxter
Cook	Jean Faulds
Mr. Freeman	Peter Vaughan
Vicar	Colin Jeavons
Mrs. Fairley	Liz Smith
Mrs. Poulteney	Patience Collier
Dairyman	John Barrett
Dr. Grogan	Leo McKern
Girl on Undercliff	Arabella Weir
Boy on Undercliff	Ben Forster
Dr. Grogan's Housekeeper	Catherine Willmer

and Anthony Langdon (Asylum Keeper), Edward Duke (Nathaniel), Richard Griffiths (Sir Tom), Graham Fletcher-Cook (Delivery Boy), Richard Hope (3rd Assistant), Michael Elwyn (Montague), Toni Palmer (Mrs. Endicott), Cecily Hobbs (Betty Anne), Doreen Mantle (Lady on train), David Warner (Murphy), Alun Armstrong (Grimes), Gerard Falconetti (Davide), Penelope Wilton (Sonia), Joanna Joseph (Lizzie), Judith Alderson (Red Haired Prostitute), Cora Kinnaird (2nd Prostitute), Orlando Fraser (Tom Elliott), Fredrika Morton (Girl), Alice Maschler (2nd Girl)

Top: (L & R) Meryl Streep,
Jeremy Irons
©United Artists Corp.

Lynsey Baxter, Jeremy Irons
Above: Meryl Streep, Jeremy Irons

Lynsey Baxter, Charlotte Mitchell, Meryl Streep,
Patience Collier, Jeremy Irons Top: Leo McKern,
Jeremy Irons

Emily Morgan, Hilton McRae
Above: Jeremy Irons

Jeremy Irons, Meryl Streep
Above: Hilton McRae, Jeremy Irons

Meryl Streep

BEAU PERE

(NEW LINE CINEMA) Executive Producer, Alain Sarde; Direction and Screenplay, Bertrand Blier; Photography, Sacha Vierny; Art Director, Theobald Meurisse; Costumes, Michele Cerf; Editor, Claudine Merlin; Assistant Director, Denys Granier-Deferre; Music, Philippe Sarde; In color; 120 minutes; Not rated; September release.

CAST

Remi	Patrick Dewaere
Marion	Ariel Besse
Charly	Maurice Ronet
Martine	Nicole Garcia
Charlotte	Nathalie Baye
Nicolas	Maurice Risch
Simone	Genevieve
Birthday Hostess	Macha Meril
Pediatrician	Pierre Lerumeur
Landlord	Yves Gasc
Landlord's Wife	Rose Thierry
Restaurant Manager	Henri-Jacques Huet
Professor	Michel Berto
Emergency Doctor	Catherine Alcover

**Right: Patrick Dewaere, Ariel Besse
(also below)
© New Line Cinema**

Ariel Besse, Patrick Dewaere

Ariel Besse, Patrick Dewaere

THE SHOOTING PARTY

(CORINTH FILMS) Producer, Mosfilm Studios; Direction and Screenplay, Emil Loteanu; Based on novel by Anton Chekhov; Photography, Anatoly Petritsky; Editor, Leonid Knayzevoy; Art Director, Boris Blank; Music, Eugen Doga; Presented by Joseph Papp in association with FDM Foundation for the Arts; Russian with English subtitles; In color; 105 minutes; Not rated; September release.

CAST

Olga Skvortsova	Galya Belyayeva
Sergei Kamysheve	Oleg Yankovsky
Count Alexei Karneyva	Kirill Lavrov
Peter Urbenin	Leonid Markov
Polychrony Kalidis	Grigory Grigoriv
Tina, Gypsy Singer	Svetlana Toma

Right: Oleg Yankovsky, Galya Belyayeva

Galya Belyayeva, Leonid Markov

Oleg Yankovsky, Kirill Lavrov

PIXOTE

(UNIFILM/EMBRAFILM) Executive Producer, Sylvia B. Naves; Director, Hector Babenco; Screenplay, Hector Babenco, Jorge Duran; Based on novel "Infancia Dos Martos" by Jose Louzeiro; Editor, Luiz Elias; Photography, Rodolfo Sanches; Music, John Neschling; Portuguese with English Subtitles; In color; 127 minutes; Not rated; September release.

CAST

Pixote	Fernando Ramos da Silva
Sueli	Marilia Pera
Lilica	Jorge Juliao
Dito	Gilberto Moura
Diego	Jose Nilson dos Santos
Chico	Edilson Lino
Fumaca	Zenildo Oliveira Santos
Garatao	Claudio Bernardo
Cristal	Tony Tornado
Sapatos Brancos	Jardel Filho
Juiz	Rubens de Falco

Left: Fernando Ramos da Silva
© Unifilm/Embrafilm

Fernando Ramos da Silva, Marilia Pera

Marilia Pera, Fernando Ramos da Silva
Top: Jose Nilson dos Santos, Fernando Ramos da Silva

HOME SWEET HOME

(LIBRA) Producer, Jacqueline Pierreux; Director, Benoit Lamy; Screenplay, Rudolph Pauli, Benoit Lamy; Photography, Michel Baudour; Editor, Guido Hendricks; Music, Walter Heynen; In color; 93 minutes; Not rated; September release.

CAST

Nurse	Claude Jade
Jules	Marcel Josz
Police Chief	Jacques Lippe
Flore	Elise Mertens
Social Worker	Jacques Perrin
Directress	Ann Petersen

Top: Jacques Lippe, Ann Petersen
© Libra Films

Jacques Perrin, Claude Jade

PRIEST OF LOVE

(FILMWAYS) Producers, Christopher Miles, Andrew Donally; Director, Christopher Miles; Screenplay, Alan Plater; Based on Harry T. Moore's book and the writings and letters of D. H. Lawrence; Music, Joseph James; Photography, Ted Moore; Designers, Ted Tester, David Brockhurst; Editor, Paul Davies; Costumes, Anthony Powell; Assistant Director, Graham Fowler; A Stanley J. Seeger presentation in color; 125 minutes; Not rated; October release.

CAST

D. H. Lawrence	Ian McKellen
Frieda	Janet Suzman
Mabel Dodge Luhan	Ava Gardner
The Honorable Dorothy Brett	Penelope Keith
Tony Luhan	Jorge Rivero
Angelo Ravagli	Maruizio Merli
Herbert G. Muskett	John Gielgud
Aldous Huxley	James Faulkner
John Middleton Murry	Mike Gwilym
Pini	Massimo Ranieri
Ada Lawrence	Marjorie Yates
Barbara Weekley	Jane Booker
Maria Huxley	Wendy Alnutt
Orioli	Elio Pandolfi

Right: Janet Suzman, Ian McKellen
Left Center: Ian McKellen, Ava Gardner
© Filmways Pictures

Janet Suzman, Ian McKellen

Ian McKellen

CONTRACT

(NEW YORKER) Direction and Screenplay, Krzysztof Zanussi; Photography, Slawomir Idziak; Executive Producer, Tadeusz Drewno; Music, Wojciech Kilar; Editor, Urszula Sliwinska; Costumes, Anna Giedrzycka, Nina Ricci; Polish with English subtitles; In color; 114 minutes; Not rated; October release.

CAST

Dorota	Maja Komorowska
Adam	Tadeusz Lomnicki
Penelope	Leslie Caron
Lilka	Magda Jaroszowna
Piotr	Krzysztof Kolberger
Maria, Adam's first wife	Zofia Mrozowska
Nina, Dorota's sister	Beata Tyszkiewicz
Lilka's Father	Janusz Gajos
Patricia	Christine Paul-Podleski
Sven	Peter Bonke

Left: Tadeusz Lomnicki, Janusz Gajos

Christine Paul-Podleski

TAXI ZUM KLO
(Taxi to the John)

(PROMOVISION INTERNATIONAL) Producers, Frank Rip-ploh, Horst Schier, Laurens Straub; Direction and Screenplay, Frank Ripploh; Assistant Director, Peter Fahrni; Photography, Horst Schier; Music, Hans Wittstadt; Editors, Gela-Marina Runne, Mathias von Gunten; German with English subtitles; In Eastmancolor; 92 minutes; Not rated; October release.

CAST

Frank .... Frank Ripploh
Bernd .... Bernd Broaderup
and Gitte Lederer, Hans-Gerd Mertens, Irmgard Lademacher, Beate Springer, Ulla Topf, Franco Papadou, Hans Jurgen Moller, Tabea Blumenschein, Magdalena Montezuma

Top: Bernd Broaderup, Frank Ripploh

Bernd Broaderup, Frank Ripploh

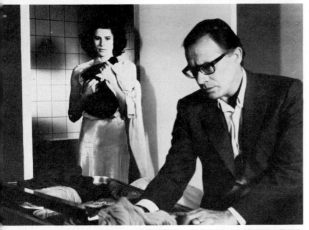

THE WOMAN NEXT DOOR

(UNITED ARTISTS CLASSICS) Director, Francois Truffaut; Screenplay, Francois Truffaut, Suzanne Schiffman, Jean Aurel; Music, Georges Delerue; Photography, William Lubtchansky; Assistant Director, Suzanne Schiffman; Costumes, Michele Cerf; Editor, Martine Barraque; In color; 106 minutes; Not rated; October release.

CAST

Bernard Coudray	Gerard Depardieu
Mathilde Bauchard	Fanny Ardant
Philippe Bauchard	Henri Garcin
Arlette Coudray	Michele Baumgartner
Madame Jouve	Veronique Silver
Roland Duguet	Roger Van Hool
Doctor	Philippe Morier-Genoud

Top: Gerard Depardieu, Michele Baumgartner
Below: Depardieu, Fanny Ardant
© United Artists Corp.

Gerard Depardieu, Fanny Ardant
Above: Ardant, Henri Garcin
Top: Gerard Depardieu

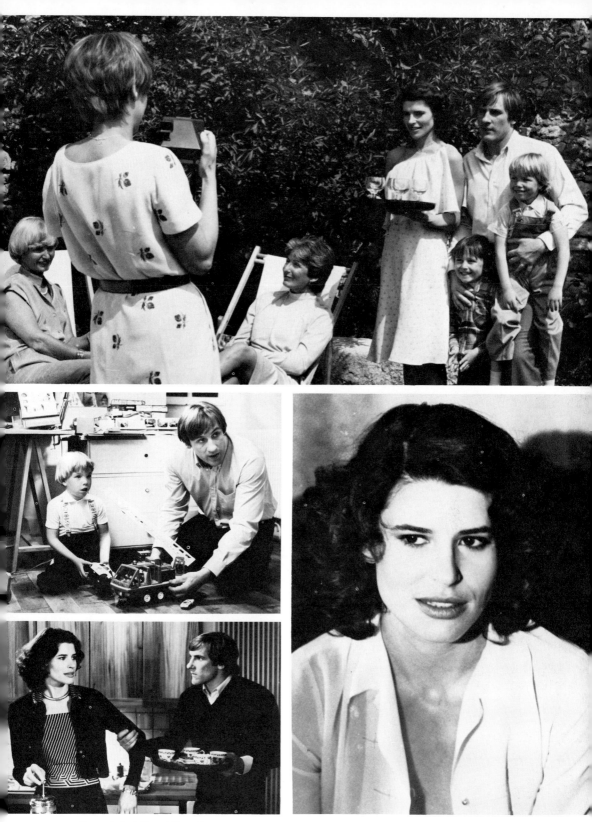

Fanny Ardant, Gerard Depardieu

Fanny Ardant

BLOOD WEDDING

(LIBRA) Producer, Emiliano Piedra; Director, Carlos Saura; Screenplay, Antonio Artero; Based on play by Federico Garcia Lorca; Adapted by Alfredo Manas; Photography, Teo Escamilla; Editor, Pablo del Amo; Spanish with English subtitles; In color; 72 minutes; Not rated; October release.

CAST

Leonardo	Antonio Gades
Bride	Cristina Hoyos
Groom	Juan Antonio Jimenez
Mother	Pilar Cardenas
Wife	Carmen Villena
Wedding Guests	El Guito, Elvira Andres, Marisa Nella, Lario Diaz, Azucena Flores, Antonio Quitana, Candy Roman, Enrique Esteve, Cristina Gombau, Quico Franco

Top: Antonio Gades Right: Juan Antonio, Cristina Hoyos, Antonio Gades
© Libra Films

Carmen Villena, Antonio Gades

THE AVIATOR'S WIFE

(NEW YORKER) Producer, Margaret Menegoz; Direction and Screenplay, Eric Rohmer; Photography, Bernard Lutic, Romain Windig; Editor, Cecile Decugis; In color; French with English subtitles; 104 minutes; Not rated; October release.

CAST

Francois	Philippe Marlaud
Anne	Marie Riviere
Lucie	Anne-Laure Meury
Christian	Matheiu Carriere
Friend	Philippe Caroit
Colleague	Carolie Clement
Girlfriend	Lisa Heredia
Blonde	Haydee Caillot
Tourists	Mary Stephen, Neil Chan
Concierge	Rosette
Mercillat	Fabrice Luchini

Right: Philippe Marlaud

Rosette, Anne-Laure Meury
Above: Anne-Laure Meury

Anne-Laure Meury
Above: Marie Riviere

THE BOAT IS FULL

(QUARTET) Executive Producer, George Reinhart; Direction and Screenplay, Markus Imhoof; Photography, Hans Liechti; Editor, Helena Gerber; Art Director, Max Stubenrauch; A Limbo Film in color; German with English subtitles; 101 minutes; Not rated; October release.

CAST

Judith Kruger	Tina Engel
Olaf Landau, her brother	Martin Walz
Lazar Ostrowskij	Curt Bois
Gitty, his granddaughter	Simone
Maurice	Laurent
Karl Schneider, deserter	Gerd David
Franz Fluckiger, innkeeper	Mathias Gnaedinger
Anna Fluckiger, his wife	Renate Steiger
Peter Bigler, policeman	Michael Gempart
Pastor Hochdorfer	Klaus Steiger
Mrs. Hochdorfer	Alice Bruengger
Hannes Kruger	Hans Diehl
Mrs. Ostrowskuj	Ilse Bahrs
Otti	Otto Dornbierer
Rosemarie, a neighbor	Monika Koch
Dr. Bartschi	Ernst Stiefel

Left: Tina Engel, Gerd David Below: Renate Steiger, Tina Engel (R) Michael Gempart, Engel, Mathias Gnaedinger © Quartet/Films Inc.

Tina Engel, Mathias Gnaedinger

Martin Walz, Laurent, Renate Steiger, Mathias Gnaedinger, Michael Gempart

Top: Martin Walz, Tina Engel, Gerd David, Curt Bois, Simone

Craig Warnock, Sean Connery Above: Ralph
Richardson, David Rappaport

TIME BANDITS

(AVCO EMBASSY) Producer-Director, Terry Gilliam; Screenplay, Michael Palin, Terry Gilliam; Photography, Peter Bizios; Editor, Julian Doyle; Songs, George Harrison; In Dolby Stereo and color; 116 minutes; November release.

CAST

Robin Hood	John Cleese
King Agamemnon	Sean Connery
Pansy	Shelley Duvall
Mrs. Ogre	Katherine Helmond
Napoleon	Ian Holm
Vincent	Michael Palin
Supreme Being	Ralph Richardson
Ogre	Peter Vaughan
Evil Genius	David Warner
Randall	David Rappaport
Fidget	Kenny Baker
Wally	Jack Purvis
Og	Mike Edmonds
Strutter	Malcolm Dixon
Vermin	Tiny Ross
Kevin	Craig Warnock

Top: John Cleese Below: Michael Palin,
Shelley Duvall Top Left: Katherine
Helmond, Peter Vaughan

HUNGARIANS

(IFEX FILMS) Director, Zoltan Fabri; Screenplay, Zoltan Fabri; Based on novel by Jozsef Balazs; Photography, Gyorgy Illes; Music Gyorgy Vukan; In Eastmancolor; Hungarian with English subtitles; 110 minutes; Not rated; November release.

CAST

Andras Fabian	Gabor Koncz
Mrs. Fabian	Eva Pap
Janos Szabo	Bertalan Solti
Mrs. Szabo	Noemi Apor
Elek Tar	Gellert Raksanyi
Mrs. Tar	Erzsi Papai
Daniel Kis	Andras Ambrus
Mrs. Kis	Anna Muszte
Daniel Gaspar	Tibor Molnar
Abris Kondor	Istvan O. Szabo
Brainer	Zoltan Gera
Anton, a driver	Istvan Holl
Farmer	Sandor Szabo
Priest	Janos Koltai

Right: Gabor Koncz, Eva Pap

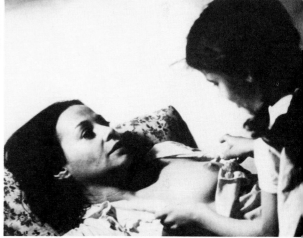

**Gila Almagor, and above with Alex Peleg
Right: Gila Almagor, Liat Pansky**

THE THIN LINE

(NEW YORKER) Producers, Gideon Amir, Avi Kleinberger; Direction and Screenplay, Michal Bat Adam; Photography, Nurith Aviv; Editor, Zion Abrahamiyan; Designer, Gaby Klezmer; Costumes, Tami Mor; Music, Alex Cagan; Hebrew with English subtitles; In color; 90 minutes: Not rated, November release.

CAST

Paula	Gila Almagor
Nadav	Alex Peleg
Nili	Liat Pansky
Maya	Aya Veirov
Dr. Greber	Avner Hizkiya
Dressmaker	S. Mazovetzkaya
Deganit	S. Grinshpan
Bina	Kina L. Hanegbi
Zila	Irit Mohar Alter
Nurse	Miri Fabian
Doctor in hospital	Yitzhak Havis
Woman in shop	Yehudit Koren
Mother in kibbutz	Michal Nedivi
Social Worker	Shlomit Nativ
Hospital Worker	Shmuel Shaked
Children	Ran Levi, Itay Verov
Hospital Patients	Esther Zewko, Bella Ganior, Israela Bashan, Michal Amir, Irit Markowich

MAN OF IRON

(UNITED ARTISTS CLASSICS) Director, Andrzej Wajda; Screenplay, Aleksander Scibor-Rylski, Photography, Edward Klosinki, Janusz Kalicinski; Editor, Halina Prugar; Music, Andrzej Korzynski; Art Director, Allan Starski; Costumes, Wieslawa Starska; Polish with English subtitles; In color; 140 minutes; Rated PG; November release.

CAST

Tomczyk	Jerzy Radziwilowicz
Agnieszka	Krystyna Janda
Winkiel	Marian Opania
Anna Hulewicz' Mother	Irena Byrska
Radio Technician	Boguslaw Linda
Anna	Wieslawa Kosmalska
Captain Wirski	Andrzej Seweryn
Kryszka	Krzysztof Janczar
TV Editor	Boguslaw Sobczuk
Badecki	Franciszek Trzeciak
Szef	Jan Tesarz

and Lech Walesa, Anna Walentynowicz

Left: Jerzy Radziwilowicz
© United Artists Corp.

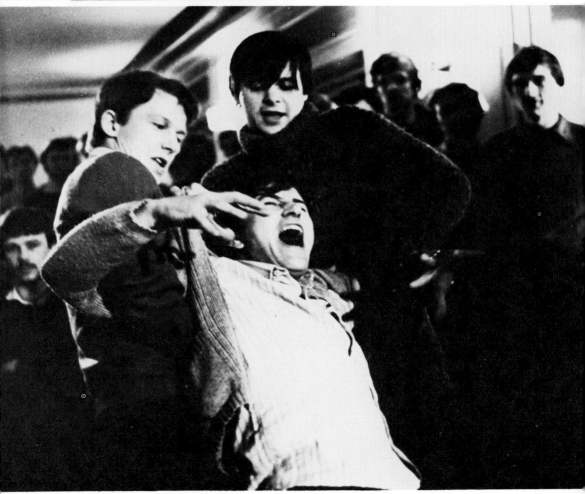

Jerzy Radziwilowicz

Marian Opania (R) Top: Jerzy Radziwilowicz, Krystyna Janda

TALES FROM THE VIENNA WOODS

(CINEMA 5) Producer-Director, Maximilian Schell; Executive Producer, Bernd Eichinger; Photography, Klaus Konig; Editor, Dagmar Hirtz; Screenplay, Christopher Hampton, Maximilian Schell; Based on play by Odon von Horvath; Art Director, Ernst Wurzer; Costumes, Erika Thomasberger; Music, Toni Stricker; Choreography, William Milie; Assistant Directors, Wolfgang Schroter, Marion Craemer; An Austrian-German Co-Production in German with English subtitles; In color; 90 minutes; Not rated; December release.

CAST

Marianne	Birgit Doll
Alfred	Hanno Poschl
Zauberkonig	Helmut Qualtinger
Valerie	Jane Tilden
Alfred's Grandmother	Adrienne Gessner
Oskar	Gotz Kauffmann
Hierlinger	Andre Heller
Captain	Norbert Schiller
American	Eric Pohlmann
Erich	Robert Meyer
Alfred's Mother	Martha Wallner
The Compere	Walter Schmidinger
Baroness	Elisabeth Epp
Helene	Lil Dagover
Confessor	Vadim Glowna
A Lady	Vera Borek
Havlitschek	Gerry Kronberger
Aunt	Maria Englstorfer
A Guest in the Maxim	Henry Gregor
Ida	Manuela Dutter
Mausi	Elisabeth Weiner

Left: Birgit Doll Top: Gotz Kauffmann, Gerry Kronberger, Norbert Schiller

Lil Dagover Above: Hanno Poschl, Adrienne Gessner

Helmut Qualtinger Above: Eric Pohlmann

Belinda Balaski
in "The Howling"

Christopher Stone
in "The Howling"

THE HOWLING (Avco Embassy) Executive Producers, Daniel H. Blatt, Steven A. Lane; Producers, Michael Finnell, Jack Conrad; Director, Joe Dante; Screenplay, John Sayles, Terence H. Winkless; Based on novel by Gary Brandner; Photography, John Hora; Editors, Mark Goldblatt, Joe Dante; Assistant Director, Jack Cummins; Art Director, Robert A. Burns; Set Designer, Steve Legler; Special Effects, Roger George; Music, Pino Donaggio; An International Film Investors presentation in color; 91 minutes; Rated R; January release. CAST: Dee Wallace (Karen), Patrick Macnee (Dr. Waggner), Dennis Dugan (Chris), Christopher Stone (Neill), Belinda Balaski (Terry), Kevin McCarthy (Fred), John Carradine (Kenton), Slim Pickens (Sam), Elisabeth Brooks (Marsha), Robert Picardo (Eddie), Margie Impert (Donna), Noble Willingham, James Murtaugh, Jim McKrell, Kenneth Tobey, Don McLeod, Dick Miller, Steve Nevil, Herb Braha, Joe Bratcher

LONG SHOT (Mithras) Producer-Director, Maurice Hatton; Script, Eoin McCann and The Players from a yarn spun by Maurice Hatton; Editor, Howard Sharp; Photography, Michael Davis, Michael Dobbs, Ivan Strasberg, Maurice Hatton, Teo Davis; Music, Terry Dougherty; In black and white and color; Presented by Joseph Papp in association with FDM Foundation; 85 minutes; Rated PG; January release. CAST: Charles Gormley (Charlie), Neville Smith (Neville), Ann Zelda (Annie), Mary Maddox, Jill Beck, David Stone, Suzanne Danielle, Ron Taylor, Wim Wenders, Stephen Frears, Jim Haines, Jacqui Byford, Maurice Bulbulian, William Forsyth, Richard DeMarco, Alan Bennett, Sarah Boston, Mel Calman, Susannah York, Dennis Sellinger, Sandy Lieberson, John Boorman

LIKE A TURTLE ON ITS BACK (New Line Cinema) Producers, Luc Beraud, Hubert Niogret; Director, Luc Beraud; Screenplay, Luc Beraud, Claude Miller; Photography, Bruno Nuytten; Editor, Joele Van Effenterre; In color; 110 minutes; Not rated; In French with English subtitles; January release. CAST: Bernadette LaFont (Camille), Jean-Francois Stevenin (Paul), Virginie Thevenet (Nathalie), Veronique Silver (Mme. Beuve), Claude Miller (Pierre), Marion Game (Sylvie), Valerie Quenessen (Nietzsche Student), Veronique Dancigers (Arrogant Girl), Jean Daste (Bad-tempered Invalid), Francois LaFarge (Jean-Louis 1), Etienne Chicot (Jean-Louis 2), Michel Blanc (Reveller who read manuscript), Sandy Withelaw (Prokosh), Souare Bhime (Black Man), Jo Perque (Usherette), Florence L. Afuma (Ava)

GULLIVER'S TRAVELS (Sunn Classic Pictures) Executive Producer, Josef Shafter; Producers, Raymond LeBlanc, Derek Horne; Director, Peter Hunt; Photography, Alan Hume; Screenplay and Lyrics, Don Black; Music, Michel LeGrand; Character Design, Denis Rich; Editors, Ron Pope, Robert Richardson; Design, Michael Stringer; Animators, Nic Broca, Marcel Colbrant, Vivian Biessen, Louis-Michel Carpentier, Jose Abel; A Valeness-Belvision Production in Eastman Color; 80 minutes; Rated G; January release. CAST: Richard Harris (Gulliver), Catherine Schell, Norman Shelley, Meredith Edwards, and the animated land of Lilliput.

DYNAMO (World Northal) Producer, Pal Ming; Director, Hwa I. Hung; In color; Rated R; January release. CAST: Bruce Li, Mary Han, James Griffiths, Georges V. Yirikian, Steve Sander, Joseph Soto

SCANNERS (Avco Embassy) Producer, Claude Heroux; Direction and Screenplay, David Cronenberg; Photography, Mark Erwin; Editor, Ron Sanders; In color; 103 minutes; Rated R; January release. CAST: Stephen Lack (Vale), Jennifer O'Neill (Kim), Patrick McGoohan (Dr. Ruth), Lawrence Dane (Keller), Charles Shamata (Gaudi), Adam Ludwig (Crostic), Michael Ironside (Revok), Victor Desy (Dr. Gafineau), Mavor Moore (Trevellyan)

NOTES FOR AN AFRICAN ORESTES (Cinematografica) Direction and Screenplay, Pier Paolo Pasolini; Music, Gato Barbieri; Editor, Cleofe Conversi; In black and white; Not rated; January release.

YOU ARE NOT ALONE (Steen Herdel) Directors, Lasse Nielsen, Ernst Johansen; Screenplay (Danish with English subtitles), Lasse Nielsen, Bent Peterson; Photography, Henrik Herbert; Music, Sebastian; 92 minutes; Not rated; January release. CAST: Anders Agens (Bo), Peter Bier (Kim), Ove Sprog (Headmaster), Ellin Reimer (His Wife), Jan Jorgensen (Carsensen), John Hahn-Peterson (Justesen)

BREAKTHROUGH (Maverick Pictures International) Executive Producers, Wolf C. Hartwig, Ted Richmond; Producers, Achim Sellus, Alex Winitzky; Screenplay, Tony Williamson; Photography, Tony Imi; Music, Peter Thomas; Editor, Raymond Poulton; Assistant Director, Burt Batt; Design, Gerhard Janda; In Eastmancolor; 115 minutes; Rated PG; January release. CAST: Richard Burton (Sgt. Steiner), Rod Steiger (Gen. Webster), Robert Mitchum (Col. Rogers), Curt Jurgens (Gen. Hoffmann), Helmuth Griem (Maj. Stransky), Michael Parks (Sgt. Anderson) Klaus Loewitsch (Cpl. Kreuger), Veronique Vendell (Yvette), Joachim Hansen (Capt. Kirstner)

THIRST (New Line/Marvin) Producer, Antony I. Ginnane; Executive Producer, William Fayman; Director, Rod Hardy; Screenplay, John Pinkney; Photography, Vincent Monton; Art Directors, Jon Dowding, Jill Eden; Assistant Director, Tom Burstall; Music, Brian May; Editor, Phil Reid; In Panavision and Eastmancolor; 98 minutes; Rated R; January release. CAST Chantal Contouri (Kate), David Hemmings (Dr. Fraser), Henry Silva (Dr. Gauss), Max Phipps (Hodge), Shirley Cameron (Mrs. Barker), Rod Mullinar (Derek), Robert Thompson (Sean), Walter Pym (Dichter), Rosie Sturgess (Lori), Lulu Pinkus (Nurse), Amanda Muggleton (Martha)

Bernadette LaFont, Jean-Francois Stevenin
in "Like a Turtle on Its Back"
© New Line Cinema

203

Lori Hallier, Paul Kelman
in "My Bloody Valentine"
© The Secret Film Co.

Stacy Keach, Jamie Lee Curtis
in "Road Games" © AVCO Embassy

MY BLOODY VALENTINE (Paramount) Producers, John Dunning, Andre Link, Stephen Miller; Director, George Mihalka; Screenplay, John Beaird; Story, Stephen Miller; Associate Producer, Lawrence Nesis; Music, Paul Zaza; Photography, Rodney Gibbons; Editor, Jean LaFleur, Art Director, Penny Hadfield; Assistant Directors, Ray Sager, Julian Marks, Anne Murphy, Richard Stanford; Costumes, Susan Hall; In color; 91 minutes; February release. CAST: Paul Kelman (T.J.), Lori Hallier (Sarah), Neil Affleck (Axel), Keith Knight (Hollis), Alf Humphreys (Howard), Cynthia Dale (Patty), Helene Udy (Sylvia), Rob Stein (John), Tom Kovacs (Mike), Terry Waterland (Harriet), Carl Marotte (Dave), Jim Murchison (Tommy), Gina Dick (Gretchen), Peter Cowper (Miner/ Harry Warden), Don Francks (Newby), Patricia Hamilton (Mabel), Larry Reynolds (Mayor), Jack Van Evera (Happy), Jeff Danks (Young Axel), Pat Hemingway (Woman), Graham Whitehead (Mac),- Fred Watters, Jeff Fulton (Supervisors), Pat Walsh (Harvey), Marguerite McNeil (Mrs. Raleigh), Sandy Leim (Ben), John MacDonald (Rescuer)

ONE WILD MOMENT (Quartet) Producer, Pierre Grunstein; Direction and Screenplay, Claude Berri; Photography, Yves Pouffany; Editor, Jacques Witta; Music, Michel Stelio; In color; 88 minutes; Not rated; February release. CAST: Jean-Pierre Marielle (Pierre), Victor Lanoux (Jacques), Agnes Soral (Francoise), Christine DeJoux (Martine), Martine Sarcey (A Woman)

HUNTING FLIES in Polish with English subtitles; Director, Andrzej Wajda; Screenplay, Janusz Glowacki; Photography, Zygmunt Samosiuk; Editor, Halina Prugar; Music, Andrzej Korzynski; 108 minutes; Not rated; February release. CAST: Malgorzata Braunek (Irena), Zygmunt Malanowicz (Wiodek), Ewa Skarzanka (Hanka), Hannah Skarzanka (Mother-in-law), Jozef Pieracki (Father-in-Law), Daniel Oibrychski (Discarded Lover), Irene Laskowska (Editor)

THE BIRCH WOOD directed by Andrzej Wajda; Story and Screenplay, Jaroslaw Isaszkiewica; Photography, Zygmunt Samosluk; Editor, Halina Prugar; Music, Andrzej Korzynski; 99 minutes; Not rated; February release; CAST: Daniel Olbrychski (Boleslaw), Emilia Krakowska (Malina), Olgierd Lukaszewica (Stanislaw), Marek Perepeczko (Michal), Jan Domanski (Janek), Danuta Wodynska (Katarzyna), Elzbieta Zolek (Ola)

SUNDAY LOVERS (United Artists) In color; 127 minutes; Rated R; February release; "An Englishman's Home": Producer, Leo L. Fuchs; Director, Bryan Forbes; Screenplay, Leslie Bricusse; Photography, Claude Lecomte; Editor, Philip Shaw; CAST: Roger Moore (Harry), Denholm Elliot (Parker), Lynn Redgrave (Lady Davina), Priscilla Barnes (Donna) "The French Method": Director, Edouard Molinaro; Screenplay, Francis Veber; Photography, Claude Agostini; Editor, Robert Isnardon; CAST: Lino Ventura (Francois), Robert Webber (Henry), Catherine Salviat (Christine) "Armando's Notebook": Director, Dino Risi; Screenplay, Age and Scarpelli; Photography, Tonino Delli Colli; Editor, Alberto Galitti; CAST: Ugo Tognazzi (Armando), Rosanna Podesta (His Wife), Catherine Spaak (Carletta), Sylva Koscina (Zaira), Beba Loncar (Marisa) "Skippy": Direction and Screenplay, Gene Wilder; Photography, Jerry Hirschfeld; Editor, Chris Greenbury; CAST: Gene Wilder (Skippy), Kathleen Quinlan (Lauri), Dianne Crittenden (Maggie)

ROAD GAMES (Avco Embassy) Producer-Director, Richard Franklin; Executive Producer, Bernard Schwartz; Co-Producer, Barbi Taylor; Screenplay, Everett DeRoche; Photography Vincent Monton; Editor, Edward McQueen-Mason; Design, Jon Dowding; Music, Brian May; Costumes, Aphrodite Kondos; Assistant Director, Tom Burstall; In CFI color; 100 minutes; Rated PG; February release. CAST: Stacy Keach (Pat), Jamie Lee Curtis (Hitch/Pamela), Marion Edward (Frita), Grant Page (Smith or Jones), Bill Stacey (Capt. Careful), Thaddeus Smith (Abbott), Stephen Millichamp (Costello), Alan Hopgood (Lester)

SUPER POWER (Transmedia Distribution Corp.) Producer, Pal Ming; Director, Lin Chan Wai; In color; Rated R; February release. CAST: Billy Chong, Hau Chiu Sing

KARATE WARRIORS (Silverstein Films) Producer, Kenji Takamura; Director, Kazuhiko Yamaguchi; Screenplay, Tatsuhiko Kamoi; Photography, Yoshio Nakajima; In color; Rated R; February release. CAST: Sonny Chiba, Isao Natsuki, Akiko Koyama, Bin Amatsu, Hideo Murota, Tatsuo Umemiya

EDGE OF FURY (Mid-Broadway Releasing) Producer, German Valder; Director, George Ho; In color; Rated R; February release. CAST Bruce Li, Andrew Sage, Michael Danna

Jan Nowicki, Lili Monori
in "Nine Months"

"Image Before My Eyes"

Lucia Bose in "The Lady
without Camelias"

George Kennedy
in "Striking Back"

THE LADY WITHOUT CAMELIAS (Italtoons) Producer, Forges Davanzati; Direction and Story, Michelangelo Antonioni; Screenplay, Suso Cecchi D'Amico, Francesco Maselli, P.M. Pasinetti, Michelangelo Antonioni; Photography, Enzo Serafin; Music, Giovanni Fusco; A 1953 film in black and white; Italian with English subtitles; 106 minutes; March release. CAST: Lucia Bose, Gino Cervi, Andrea Checchi, Anna Carena, Ivan Desny, Enrico Glori, Laura Tiberti, Alain Cuny, Monica Clay, Oscar Andriani

CAFE EXPRESS (Summit Feature Distributors) Producers, Franco Cristaldi, Nicola Carraro; Director, Nanni Loy; Photography, Claudio Cirillo; Music, Giovanna Marini; Editor,Franco Fraticelli; Costumes, Mario Giorsi; Designer, Umberto Turco; Story, Nanni Loy, Elvio Porta; Presented by C. Gregory Earls; In color; Not rated; 105 minutes; March release. CAST: Nino Manfredi (Michele), Adolfo Celi (Train Inspector), Vittorio Mezzogiorno (Amitrano), Luigi Basagaluppi (Vigorito), Silvio Spaccesi (Sanguigno), Gerardo Scala (Scognamiglio), Lina Sastri (Suor Camilia), Vittorio Marsiglia (Picone), Marisa Laurito (Liberata), Ester Carloni (Teresa)

NINE MONTHS (New Yorker) Director, Marta Meszaros; Screenplay, Gyula Hernadi, Ildiko Korody, Marta Meszaros; Photography, Janos Kende; Editor, Mrs. Andras Karmento; Music, Gyorgy Kovacs; Art Director, Tamas Banovich; Assistant Director, Ferenc Jeli; Produced by Hungarofilm in Eastmancolor; 93 minutes; Not rated; March release. CAST: Lili Monori (Juli), Jan Nowicki (Janos), Djoko Rosic (Istvan), Kati Berek (Juli's Mother), Olga Koos (Janos' Mother), Gyongyi Vigh (Juli's Friend)

PICK-UP SUMMER (Film Ventures International) formerly "Pinball Summer" and "Pinball Pickup"; Producer, Jack F. Murphy; Director, George Mihalka; Screenplay, Richard Zelniker; In color; 91 minutes; Rated R; March release. CAST: Michael Zelniker, Carl Marotte, Karen Stephen, Helen Udy

REVENGE OF THE PATRIOTS (World Northal) A First Films Presentation in color; Rated R; March release. CAST: Bruce Li, Bruce Chen, Ka Ling

HOLY TERROR (Dynamite) carried in SCREEN WORLD Volume 30 as "Communion" and "Alice, Sweet Alice"

STRIKING BACK (Film Ventures International) Executive Producer, R. Ben Efraim; Producer, James Margellos; Director, William Fruet; Screenplay, Don Enright; Music, FM; In Panavision and DeLuxe Color; 91 minutes; Rated R; March release. CAST: Perry King (Kip), Tisa Farrow (Kate), Don Stroud (Buddy), George Kenny (Capt. Fusqua), Park Jong Soo (Assassin)

I REMEMBER LOVE (Lone Star Pictures) Producer, Kashen; Direction and Screenplay, Norbert Meisel; Color by CFI; 88 minutes; Rated R; March release. CAST: Matt Greene, Nona Jane Lim, Stephen Nicholoson

SNAKE FIST FIGHTER (21st Century) Director, Chin Hsin; In Eastmancolor; Rated R; March release. CAST: Jackie Chan, Cheng Lung, Yuan Hsiao Hsin

IMAGE BEFORE MY EYES (Cinema 5) Producers, Susan Lazarus, Josh Waletzky; Directed and Edited by Josh Waletzky; Written by Jerome Badanes; Based on the YIVO exhibit and book "Image Before My Eyes" by Dr. Lucjan Dobrszycki and Dr. Barbara Kirshenblatt-Gimlett; Presented by YIVO Institute for Jewish Research; 90 minutes; Not rated; March release. A documentary of life in Poland's Jewish community.

SPOILED CHILDREN (Corinth) Director, Bertrand Tavernier; Screenplay, (French with English subtitles) Charlotte Dubreuil, Christine Pascal, Bertrand Tavernier; Photography, Alain Levent; Editors, Armand Psenny, Arlane Beoglin; Music, Phillippe Sarde; 113 minutes; Not rated; April release. CAST: Michel Piccoli (Bernard), Christine Pascal (Anne), Michel Aumont (Pierre), Gerard Jugnot (Marcel), Arlette Bonnard (Catherine), Georges Riquier (Mouchot), Gerard Zimmerman (Patrice)

JOANNA FRANCESA (Joseph Papp) Producers, Ney Sroulevich, Pierre Cardin; Director, Carlos Diegues; Screenplay, (Portuguese with English subtitles) Mr. Diegues; Photography, Dib Luft; Music, Chico Buarque, Roberto Menescal; In color; 110 minutes; Not rated; April release. CAST: Jeanne Moreau (Joanna), Pierre Cardin (Pierre), Carlos Kroeber (Aurellano), Helber Rangel (Lianinho), Ellezer Gomes (Gismundo), Rodolfo Arena (Padre Seixas), Leina Crespi (Das Dores), Leila Abramo, Tete Maciel, Ney Santana

Michel Piccoli, Christine Pascal
in "Spoiled Children"

Jeanne Moreau
in "Joanna Francesa"

Elise Caron, Philippe Lebas
in "Cocktail Molotov"
© Putnam Square Films

Kees Wientjes
in "Instant Pictures"

THE CON ARTISTS (S.J. International Pictures) Executive Producer, Ted Kneeland; Producer, Mario C. Gori; Director, Serge Corbucci; Presented by Wallace-Kneeland Associates and Capital Films Productions; In color; 93 minutes; Rated PG; April release. CAST: Anthony Quinn (Bang), Adriano Celentano (Felix), Corinne Clery (Charlotte), Capucine (Belle)

COCKTAIL MOLOTOV (Alexandre Filmoso) Direction and Screenplay, Diane Kurys; French with English subtitles; Photography, Philippe Rousellot; Editor, Joelle Van Effenterre; Music, Yves Simon; In color; 100 minutes; Not rated; April release. CAST: Elise Caron (Anne), Philippe Lebas (Frederic), Francois Cluzet (Bruno), Genevieve Fontanei (Anne's Mother), Henri Garcin (Her Step-father), Michel Puterfiam (Her Father), Jenny Cleve (Frederic's Mother), Armando Brancia (His Father), Malene Sveinbjornsson (Little Sister), Stefania Cassini (Anna-Maria), Frederique Meininger (Doctor), Patrick Chesnais (Rucker)

D.O.A. (High Times) Producer-Director, Lech Kowalski; Editor, Val Kuklowsky; Photography, Val Kowalski, Rufus Standfer, Ron Zimmerman, Joe Sutherland, Jared Fitzgedraid, Raffi Ferrucci, Peter Chapman; A Tom Norman presentation in color; 99 minutes; Not rated; April release. CAST: The Sex Pistols, Terry and the Idiots, Iggy Pop, The Clash, The Dead Boys, The Rich Kids, X-Ray Spex, Generation X, Sham 69, Augustus Pablo

TATTOOED DRAGON (World Northal) Producer, Lo Wei; A Golden Harvest Presentation by Raymond Chow; In color; Rated R; April release. CAST: Jimmy Wang Yu

EXCALIBUR (Orion/Warner Bros.) Producer-Director, John Boorman; Screenplay, Rospo Pallenberg, John Boorman; Adapted from Malory's "Le Morte D'Arthur" by Mr. Pallenberg; Photography, Alex Thompson; Editor, John Merritt; Music, Trevor Jones; In color; 140 minutes; Rated R; April release. CAST: Nigel Terry (King Arthur), Helen Mirren (Morgana), Nicholas Clay (Lancelot), Cherie Lunghi (Guenevere), Paul Geoffrey (Perceval), Nicol Williamson (Merlin), Robert Addie (Mordred), Gabriel Byrne (Uther), Keith Buckley (Uryens), Matrine Boorman (Igrayne), Liam Neeson (Gawain), Corin Redgrave (Cronwall)

INSTANT PICTURES (Public Cinema) Producer, Mattijs van Heijningen; Director, George Schouten; Screenplay, George Schouten, Bernard Roeters; Photography, Marc Felperlaan; Art Direction, Apostolos Panagopoulos, Herman Ouwersloot; Editors, George Schouten, Heronimus Wouters; Music, Peter Veenman; In color; Not rated; 79 minutes; April release. CAST: Kees Wientjes (Victor Veri), Shireen Strooker (Cab Driver), Antoinette Polak

WHEN TAEKWONDO STRIKES (World Northal) Presented by Raymond Chow's Golden Harvest; In Color; 93 minutes; Rated R; May release. CAST: Jhoon Rhee, Anne Winton, Angela Mao

AMOR DE PERDICAO (Doomed Love/Ill-Fated Love) Presented by Joseph Papp; Director, Manoel de Oliveira; Screenplay (Portuguese with English subtitles), Manoel de Oliveira; Photography, Manuel Costa e Silva; Editor, Solveig Nordlund; Music, Joao Paes; Producers, Henrique Esperito Santo, Marcilio Krieger, Antonio Lagrifa; Not rated; 270 minutes; May release. CAST: Antonio Sequeira Lopes (Simao), Cristina Hauser (Teresa), Elsa Wallencamp (Mariana), Antonio Costa (Joao de Cruz), Ricardo Pais (Balthasar), Rui Furtado (Domingos), Maria Dulce (Rita), Maria Barroso (Prieure), Henrique Viana (Tadeu), Pedro Pinheiro, Manuela de Melo (Narrators)

BLACK AND WHITE LIKE DAY AND NIGHT (New Yorker) Producer, Georg Althammer; Director, Wolfgang Petersen; Screenplay (German with English subtitles), Jochen Wedgartner, Karl Heinz Willschrei; Photography, Jorg M. Baldenius; Editor, Johannes Nikel, Music, Klaus Doldinger; Art Director, O. Jochen Schmidt; In color; 103 minutes; Not rated; May release. CAST: Bruno Ganz (Thomas) Gila von Weitershausen (Marie), Rene Deltgen (Lindford), Ljuba Tadic (Igor), Joachim Wichmann (Gruenfeld), Annemarie Wendl (Doctor), Alexis von Hagemeister (Wilke), Alexander Hegrath (Thomas' Father), Gudrun Vaupel (Thomas' Mother), Markus Helis (Thomas as a boy), Elke Schuessler (Marie as a girl), Eberhard Stanjek (Moderator)

Nicol Williamson
in "Excalibur"
© Orion Pictures

Gila von Weitershausen, Bruno Ganz
in "Black and White Like Day and Night"

Catherine Retore, Clementine Amouroux
in "Messidor"

Edwige Fenech, Enrico Montesano
in "Il Ladrone"

MESSIDOR (New Yorker) Direction and Screenplay, Alain Tanner; Photography, Renato Berta; Music, Arie Dzierlatka; Editor, Brigitte Sousselier; In French with English subtitles; 120 minutes; Not rated; May release. CAST: Clementine Amouroux (Jeanne), Catherine Retore (Marie)

FIRECRACKER (New World) Director, Cirio Santiago; Producer, Syed Kechiko; Screenplay, Ken Metcalfe, Cirio Santiago; Photography, Don Jones; In color; Not rated; 83 minutes; May release. CAST: Jillian Kesner (Susanne), Darby Hinton (Chuck), Ken Metcalfe (Erik), Chanda Romero (Malow), Tony Ferrar (Tony), Reymond King (Rey), Vic Diaz (Grip), Pete Cooper (Pete)

HAPPY BIRTHDAY TO ME (Columbia) Producers, John Dunning, Andre Link; Line Producer, Stewart Harding; Associate Producer, Lawrence Nesis; Director, J. Lee Thompson; Screenplay, John Saxton, Peter Jobin, Timothy Bond; Story, John Saxton; Photography, Miklos Lente; Music, Bo Harwood, Lance Rubin; Designer, Earl Preston; Editor, Debra Karen; Assistant Directors, Charles Braive, Francois Ouimet, Robert Ditchburn; Costumes, Hugette Gagne; In Metrocolor; 108 minutes; Rated R; May release. CAST: Glenn Ford (Dr. Faraday), Melissa Sue Anderson (Virginia), Lawrence Dane (Hal), Sharon Acker (Estelle), Frances Hyland (Mrs. Patterson), Tracy Bregman (Ann), Jack Blum (Alfred), Matt Craven (Steve), Lenore Zann (Maggie), David Eisner (Rudi), Lisa Langlois (Amelia), Michel Rene LaBelle (Etienne), Richard Rabiere (Greg), Lesleh Donaldson (Bernadette), Earl Pennington (Lt. Tracy), Murray Westgate (Gatekeeper), Jerome Tiberghien (Prof. Heregard), Maurice Pedbrey (Dr. Feinblum), Vlasta Vrana (Bartender), Walter Massey (Conventioneer), Griffith Brewer (Verger), Alan Katz (Ann's Date), Ron Lea (Amelia's Date), Terry Haig (Feinblum's Assistant), Karen Stephen (Ms. Calhoun), Louis Del Grande (Surgeon), Nick Kilbertus (Anesthetist), Damir Andrei (Jr. Surgeon), Gina Dick (Waitress), Stephanie Miller (Nurse), Steven Mayoff (Police), Aram Barkev, Alan Barnett, Paul Board, Marc Degagne, Bruce Gooding, Victor Knight, Rollie Nincheri, Keith Sutherland, Herbert Vool, Len Watt, Joe Wertheimer (Conventioneers), Nancy Allan, Karen Hynes, Tracy-Marie Langdon, Debbie McGellin, Kathy Reid, Lori Timmons, Debbie Tull, Lynn Wilson (Cheerleaders)

IL LADRONE ("The Thief") Director, Pasquale Festa Campanile; Screenplay, Ottavio Jemma, Stefano, Ubezio, Santino Sparta; Costumes, Mario Carlini; Designer, Enzo Fiorentini; Photography, Giancarlo Ferrando; Music, Ennio Morricone; In Telecolor; 108 minutes; Not rated; May release. CAST: Enrico Montesano, Edwige Fenech, Bernadette Lafont, Sara Birgenti Franchetti, Claudio Cassinelli, Susanna Martinkova, Anna Orso, Auretta Gay, Daniele Vargas, Enzo Robutti

L'INGORGO ("The Traffic Jam") Presented by Silvio Clementelli; Director, Luigi Comencini; Photography, Ennio Guarnieri; Screenplay, Luigi Comencini, Ruggero Maccari, Bernardino Zapponi ; Story, Luigi Comencini; Music, Fiorenzo Carpi; In Eastmancolor; 98 minutes; Not rated; May release. CAST: Alberto Sordi, Annie Girardot, Fernando Rey, Patrick Dewaere, Angela Molina, Harry Baer, Marcello Mastroianni, Stefania Sandrelli, Ugo Tognazzi, Miou Miou, Gerard Depardieu, Orazio Orlando, Giovannella Grifeo, Ciccio Ingrassia, Francisco Algora, Jose Prada, Francisco De Zurbano, Jose Vivo, Ferdinando Murolo, Ernst Hannewald, Nando Orfel, Gianni Cavina

THE HAUNTING OF JULIA (Discovery) formerly "Full Circle"; Producers, Peter Fetterman, Alfred Pariser; Director, Richard Loncraine; Executive Producer, Julian Melzack, Music, Colin Towns; Editor, Ron Wisman; Screenplay, Dave Humphries; Based on novel "Julia" by Peter Straub and adaptation by Harry Bromley Davenport; An Anglo-Canadian Co-Production in Panavision and color; 96 minutes; Rated R; May release. CAST: Mia Farrow (Julia), Keir Dullea (Magnus), Tom Conti (Mark), Jill Bennett (Lily), Robin Gammell (Swift), Cathleen Nesbitt (Mrs. Rudge), Anna Wing (Mrs. Flood), Pauline Jameson (Mrs. Branscombe), Peter Sallis (Branscombe), Sophie Ward (Kate), Samantha Gates (Olivia)

THE VALLEY OBSCURED BY CLOUDS (Michael Kaplan/Circle Associates) also released as "The Valley"; Direction and Screenplay, Barbet Schroeder; Adaptation and Dialogue, Paul Gegauff, Mr. Schroeder; French with English subtitles; Photography, Nestor Almendros; Editor, Denise De Casablanca; Music, Pink Floyd; In Techniscope and color; 100 minutes; Not rated; May release. CAST: Bulle Ogier (Viviane), Jean-Pierre Kalfon (Gaetan), Michael Gothard (Colvier), Valerie Lagrange (Hermine), Jerome Beauvarlet (Yann), Monique Giraudy (Monique)

Melissa Sue Anderson, Glenn Ford
in "Happy Birthday to Me"
© Columbia Pictures

Tom Conti, Mia Farrow
in "The Haunting of Julia"

"18 Fatal Strikes"

18 FATAL STRIKES (World Northal) Director, Yang Ching; Presented by First Films; In color; 93 minutes; Rated R; May release. CAST: Tung Wai, Shih Tien, Yang Kuang, Min Chiang Lung

IMPROPER CHANNELS (Crown International) Producers, Alfred Pariser, Morrie Ruvinsky; Director, Eric Till; Screenplay, Morrie Ruvinsky, Ian Sutherland, Adam Arkin; Story, Mr. Ruvinsky; Photography, Anthony Richmond; Editor, Thom Noble; Music, Micky Erbe, Maribeth Solomon; In Panavision and color; 92 minutes; Rated PG; May release. CAST: Alan Arkin (Jeffrey), Mariette Hartley (Diana), Monica Parker (Gloria), Harry Ditson (Harold), Sarah Stevens (Nancy), Danny Higham (Jack), Leslie Yeo (Fred), Richard Farrell (Fraser), Ruth Springford (Mrs. Wharton), Martin Yan (Hu), Tony Rosato (Dr. Arpenthaler), Philip Akin (Cop), Harvey Atkin (Sergeant), Richard Blackburn (Fraser's Assistant)

TOGETHER (Quartet) formerly "I Love You, I Love You Not"; Producers, Valerio DePaolis, Gianni Bozzacchi; Director, Armenia Balducci; Screenplay, Armenia Balducci, Ennio De Concini; Photography, Carlo De Palma; Art Director, Maria Paola Maino; Music, Goblin Bixio-Cemsa; In Technicolor; 100 minutes; Rated R; May release. CAST: Jacqueline Bisset (Louise), Maximilian Schell (John), Terence Stamp (Henry), Monica Guerritore (Giulia), Gian Luca Venantini, Pietro Biondi, Birgitta Hamer, Francesca DeSapio, Carla Tato

THE CHILDREN FROM NUMBER 67 (Road Movies) Producer, Renee Gundelach; Direction and Screenplay, Usch Barthelmess-Weller, Werner Meyer; Photography, Juergen Juerges, Hans-Guenther Buecking; Music, Andi Brauer; In color; 103 minutes; Not rated; May release. CAST: Elfriede Irall, Tilo Brueckner, Bernd Fiedel, Martina Krauel, Peter Franke, Rene Schaaf, Rainer-Goetz Otto

THE GLASS CELL (Roxy/Solaris) Director, Hans C. Geissendoerfer; Screenplay, Mr. Geissendoerfer, Klaus Baedekerl; Based on novel of the same name by Patricia Highsmith; Photography, Robby Mueller; Music, Niels Walen; Editor, Peter Przygodda; In Eastmancolor; 100 minutes; Not rated; May release. CAST: Helmut Griem (Philip), Brigitte Fossey (Lisa), Dieter Laser (David), Walter Kohut (Lasky), Bernhard Wicky (Commissioner), Claudius Kracht, Guenther Stack, Klaus Muenster, Hans Guenther Martens, Christa-Maria Netsch, Gerlinde Egger

Alan Arkin, Mariette Hartley in "Improper Channels"

DIRTY TRICKS (Avco Embassy) Executive Producers, Victor Solnicki, Pierre David, Arnold Kopelson; Producer, Claude Heroux; Director, Alvin Rakoff; Screenplay, William Norton, Sr., Eleanor Elias Norton, Thomas Gifford, Camille Gifford; From a novel by Thomas Gifford; Photography, Richard Ciupka; Editor, Alan Collins; Music, Hagood Hardy; Assistant Director, Jim Kaufman; In color; 91 minutes; May release. CAST: Elliott Gould (Colin), Kate Jackson (Polly), Arthur Hill (Bert), Rich Little (Robert), Nick Campbell (Bill), Angus McInnes (Jones), Michael Kirby (Wicklow), Michael McNamara (Thorn), Martin McNamara (Ozzie), John Juliani (Roselli), Alberta Watson (Tony), Mavor Moore (Underhill), Cindy Girling (Emily)

STREET LAW (S.J. International) Presented by Capitol Film Productions; In color; Rated R; May release. CAST: Franco Nero, Barbara Bach, Reno Palmer

RICHARD'S THINGS (New World) Producer, Mark Shivas, Director, Anthony Harvey; Screenplay, Frederic Raphael; Photography, Freddie Young; Assistant Directors, David Munro, Andrew Warren, Chris Brock; Art Director, Ian Whittaker; Editor, Lesley Walker; Music, Georges Delerue; In color; A Southern Pictures Production presented by Roger Corman; 104 minutes; Not rated; June release. CAST: Liv Ullmann (Kate), Amanda Redman (Josie), Tim Pigot-Smith (Peter), Elizabeth Spriggs (Mrs. Sells), David Markham (Morris), Mark Eden (Richard), Gwen Taylor (Margaret), John Vine (Dr. Mace), Michael Maloney (Bill), Tracy Childs (Joanna), Peter Burton (Colonel), Margaret Lacey (Miss Beale), Ian McDiarmid (Burglar), Lucinda Curtis, Stella Kemball (Receptionists), Athar Malik (Dr. Mustag), Zelah Clarke (Nurse), Dawn Hope (Jamaican Nurse), Amanda Walker (Sister), Willie Holman (Cleaner), Sally Watkins (Brenda), Franco Derosa (Ricci), Alec Linstead (Desk Clerk), Philip York (Man in train), Glyn Grimstead (Boy), Lesley West (Girl Student), Michael Kingsbury (Boy Student), Oscar Narciso (Porter), Rose Power (Mrs. Jenkins), James Galloway (Josh)

A MAN CALLED TIGER (World Northal) Director, Lo Wei; In color; 121 minutes; Rated R; June release, CAST: Jimmy Wang Yu, Okada Kawai, Maria Yi, Tien Chun

NUMERO DEUX (Anne-age-Bela) Directed by Jean-Luc Godard; In color; 88 minutes; Not rated; June release. CAST: Sandrine Barristella (Wife), Pierre Oudry (Husband), Alexandre Rignault (Grandfather)

THE BLOCKHOUSE produced by Anthony Rufus Isaacs, Edgar M. Bronfman, Jr.; Director, Clive Rees; Screenplay, John Gould, Clive Rees; Based on "Le Blockhaus" by Jean Paul Clebert; Photography, Keith Goddard; Editor, Peter Gold; Music, Stanley Myers; 96 minutes; Rated R; June release. CAST: Peter Sellers (Rouquet), Charles Aznavour (Visconti), Per Oscarsson (Lund), Peter Vaughan (Aufret), Jeremy Kemp (Grabinski), Leon Lissek (Kozhek), Nicholas Jones (Kramer), Alfred Lynch (Larshen)

GAIJIN, A BRAZILIAN ODYSSEY (Embrafilme) Executive Producer, Carlos Alberto Diniz; Director, Tizuka Yamasaki; Story and Screenplay, Jorge Duran, Miss Yamasaki; Editors, Lael Alves Rodrigues, Vera Freire; Music, John Neschiling; Japanese and Portugese with English subtitles; In color; 105 minutes; Not rated; June release. CAST: Kyoko Tsukamoto (Tito), Antonio Fagundes (Tonho), Jiro Kawaraski (Yamada), Gianfrancesco Guarnieri (Enrico), Alvaro Freire (Chico), Jose Dumont (Ceara), Carlos Augusto Strazzer (Dr. Heitor)

DEMONOID (American Panorama) Producer-Director, Alfredo Zacharias; Screenplay, David Lee Fein, Alfredo Zacharias, Amos Powell, Music, Richard Gillis; Photography, Alex Phillips, Jr.; Editor, Sandy Nervig; In color; 80 minutes, Rated R; June release. CAST: Samantha Eggar (Jennifer), Stuart Whitman (Cunningham), Roy Cameron Jenson (Mark), Narciso Busquets (Dr. Rivkin), Erika Carlsson (Nurse), Lew Saunders (Sgt. Mason)

KUNG FU EXECUTIONER (Transmedia) Producer, Pal Ming; Director, Lin Chan Wai; In color; Rated R; June release. CAST: Billy Chong, Carl Scott

SCREAMERS (New World) Producer, Lawrence Martin; Director, Dan T. Miller (Sergio Martino); In color; Rated R; June release. CAST: Barbara Bach, Richard Johnson, Charles Cass, Beryl Cunningham, Joseph Cotten, Cameron Mitchell, Mel Ferrer

BEYOND THE FOG (Independent-International) Producer, Richard Gordon; Direction and Screenplay, Jim O'Connolly; Associate Producer, John Pellatt; Story, George Baxt; Assistant Director, Peter Price; Photography, Desmond Dickinson; Art Director, Disley Jones; Music, Ken Jones; Editor, Henry Richardson; In Eastmancolor; 86 minutes; Rated R; June release. CAST: Bryant Haliday (Brent), Jill Haworth (Rose), Anna Palk (Nora), Jack Watson (Hamp), Mark Edwards (Adam), Derek Fowlds (Dan), John Hamill (Gary), Candace Glendenning (Penny), Dennis Price (Bakewell), George Coulouris (Gurney), Robin Askwith (Des), Serretta Wilson (Mae), Fredric Abbott (Saul), Mark McBride (Michael), William Lucas (Det. Hawk), Anthony Valentine (Dr. Simpson), Marianne Stone (Nurse)

**Liv Ullmann
in "Richard's Things"**

**Annie Girardot, Philippe Noiret, Catherine
Alric in "Jupiter's Thigh"**

ILLUSTRIOUS CORPSES ("Cadaveri Eccellenti") Director, Francesco Rosi; Screenplay (Italian with English subtitles), Francesco Rosi, Tonino Guerra, Lino Januzzi; Based on novel "The Context" by Leonardo Sciascia; Executive Producer, Alberto Grimaldi; Photography, Pasquale DeSantis; Editor, Ruggero Mastroianni; Music, Piero Piccioni, Astor Piazzolla; 121 minutes; Not rated; July release. CAST: Lino Ventura (Inspector Rogas), Charles Vanel (Procura), Fernando Rey (Minister of Security), Maz von Sydow (Chief Justice), Tino Carraro (Police Chief), Marcel Bozzuffi (Dr. Maxie), Alain Cuny (Judge Rasto), Maria Carta (Mrs. Cres), Luigi Pistilli (Cusan), Tina Aumont (Prostitute), Renato Salvatori (Commissioner), Pablo Graziosi (Galano)

SOUND OF THE CITY: LONDON 1964-73 (Columbia) Producer-Director, Peter Clifton; Associate Producer, Peter Ryan; Photography, Richard Mordaunt, Peter Whitehead, Graham Lind, Michael Cooper, Peter Neal, Bavin Cook, Ernest Vincze, Ivan Strasburg, Charles Stewart, Bruce Logan; Editor, Thomas Schwain; A World Film Services production in black and white and Technicolor; 104 minutes; Not rated; July release. A documentary featuring the Rolling Stones, Eric Burdon and the Animals, Arthur Brown, Otis Redding, Cream, Blind Faith, Cat Stevens, Jimi Hendrix, Experience, Joe Cocker, Ike and Tina Turner, Pink Floyd, Rod Stewart and Faces

ROCK CITY (Columbia) Producer-Director, Peter Clifton; Photography, Richard Mordaunt, Peter Whitehead, Graham Lind, Michael Cooper, Peter Neal, Bavin Cook, Ernest Vincze, Ivan Strasburg, Charles Stewart, Bruce Logan; Editor, Thomas Schwain; A World Films Services Ltd. production; 104 minutes; Not rated; July release. CAST: The Rolling Stones, Eric Burdon and the Animals, The Crazy World of Arthur Brown, Otis Redding, Peter Townshend, Cream, Steve Winwood, Blind Faith, Cat Stevens, Jimi Hendrix, Experience, Donovan, Joe Cocker, Tina Turner, Ike and Tina Turner Revue, Pink Floyd, Rod Stewart, The Faces

THE LONDON ROCK 'N' ROLL SHOW produced and directed by Peter Clifton; Editor, Thomas Schwalm; 90 minutes; Not rated; July release. CAST: The Houseshakers, Heinz, Lord Sutch, Bo Diddley, Jerry Lee Lewis, Bill Haley and the Comets, Little Richard, Chuck Berry, Mick Jagger

JUPITER'S THIGH (Quartet) Producers, Alexandre Mnouchkine, George Dancigers, Robert Amon; Director, Philippe DeBroca; Screenplay, Philippe DeBroca, Michel Audiard; Photography, Jean-Paul Schwartz; Editor, Henri Lanoe; Music, Georges Hatzinassios; In color; 96 minutes; Rated R; July release. CAST: Annie Girardot (Lise Tanquerelle), Philippe Noiret (Antoine LeMercier), Francis Perrin (Hubert Pochet), Catherine Alric (Agnes Pochet)

GAS (Paramount) Producer, Claude Heroux; Director, Les Rose; Screenplay, Richard Wolf; Story, Richard Wolf, Susan Scranton; Executive Producers, Victor Solnicki, Pierre David; Photography, Rene Verzier; Music, Paul Zaza; Editor, Patrick Dodd; Design, Carol Spier; Assistant Directors, John Fretz, Mac Bradden, Patrick Ferrero; Costumes, Gaudeline Sauriol; A Filmplan International production with the cooperations of Davis-Panzer Productions; In color; 91 minutes; Rated R; July release. CAST: Susan Anspach (Jane), Howie Mandel (Matt), Sterling Hayden (Duke), Helen Shaver (Rhonda), Sandee Currie (Sarah), Peter Aykroyd (Ed), Keith Knight (Ira), Alf Humphries (Lou), Philip Akin (Lincoln), Michael Hogan (Guido), Paul Kelman (Nino), Donald Sutherland (Nick the Noz), Dustin Waln (Earl), Vlasta Vrana (Baron), Harvey Chao (Kwan), Brian Nasimok (Fawsi), Videt Bussy (Mrs. Botts), Vincent Marino (Uncle Lou), Carl Marotte (Bobby), Bob Parson (Ordway), Richard Donat (Fred), Domenico Fiore, Dino Tosques (Hoods), Art Grosser (Lester), Dieto Kretzschmar (Juggler), Gershon Resnik (Yassir), Walter Massey (Major Bright), Jeff Diamond (Bandit), Mac Bradden (Announcer), Terry Haig (Reporter), Ralph Pettofrezzo, Joe Sanza, Joost Davidson, Tony Angelo, Tony Nardi, George Wilson, Barry Edward Blake, Kirsten Bishopric, Rollie Nincheri, Steve Michaels, Michael Mololey, Armand Monroe, Carolyn Maxwell, Caroline Plamondon, Charles Biddles, Jr., Malcolm Nelthorpe, Walker Boone, Sam Montesano, Norris Dominigue, Lawrence Steinberg, Pierre Lemieux, Linda Lonn, Robert Blais

THE PILOT (Summit) Producer, C. Gregory Earls; Director, Cliff Robertson; Screenplay, Robert P. Davis, Cliff Robertson; From novel by Robert P. Davis; Photography, Walter Lassally; Editor, Evan Lottman; In color; Rated PG; 92 minutes; July release. CAST: Cliff Robertson, Frank Converse, Diane Baker, Gordon MacRae, Dana Andrews, Milo O'Shea, Ed Binns

**Jiro Kawarasaki, Kyoko Tsukamoto
in "Gaijin"**

**Cliff Robertson
in "The Pilot"**

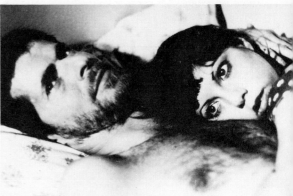

Michael Crawford, Barbara Carrera
in "Condorman"
© Walt Disney Productions

Piotr Garlicki, Christine Paul
in "Camouflage" © Libra Films

BLUE SUEDE SHOES produced by Penny Clark; Director, Curtis Clark; Production Manager, Vivian Pottersman; 95 minutes; Not rated; July release. CAST: Bill Haley, Ray Campi, Crazy Cavan, Freddie (Fingers) Lee

SIXTY SECOND ASSASSIN (East-West Releasing) In color; Rated R; July release; No other credits available. CAST: John Li, Lu Chan, Wang Chang, Sue Chen, Sonny Wan

CONDORMAN (Buena Vista) Executive Producer, Ron Miller; Producer, Jan Williams; Director, Charles Jarrott; Screenplay, Marc Stirdivant; Suggested by "The Game of X" by Robert Sheckley; Photography, Charles F. Wheeler; Music, Henry Mancini; Art Director, Marc Frederix; Design, Albert Witherick; Editor, Gordon D. Brenner; Assistant Directors, Richard Learman, Denys Granier-Deferre, Paul Feyder; Associate Producer, Hugh Attwooll; Special Effects, Colin Chilvers, Art Cruickshank; Costumes, Kent James, Jean Zay; In Technicolor, Panavision, and Dolby Stereo; 90 minutes; Rated PG; August release. CAST: Michael Crawford (Woody), Oliver Reed (Krokov), Barbara Carrera (Natalia), James Hampton (Harry), Jean-Pierre Kalfon (Morovich), Dana Elcar (Russ), Vernon Dobtcheff (Russian Agent), Robert Arden (C.I.A. Chief)

THE UPRISING (King International) Director, Peter Lilienthal; Screenplay (Spanish with English subtitles), Mr. Lilienthal, Antonio Skarmeta; Photography, Michael Balihaus; Editor, Siegrun Jager; 96 minutes; Not rated; August release. CAST: Agustin Pereira (Son), Carlos Catania (Father), Maria Lourdes Centano Zelaya (Mother), Oscar Castillo (Captain), Guido Saenz (Uncle), Vicky Montero (Sister), Saida Mondieta Ruiz (Miriam), Orlando Zelaya Perez (Darwis), Flavio Fernandez (Ignacio), Roger Barrios (Roger), the Lorlo Brothers

I HATE BLONDES (Summit Features) Producers, Silvia and Anna Maria Clementelli; Director, Giorgio Capitani; Screenplay (Italian with English subtitles), Laura Toscano, Franco Marotta; Music, Piero Umiliani; Presented by C. Gregory Earls; In color; 89 minutes; Not rated; August release. CAST: Enrico Montesano (Emilio), Jean Rochefort (Donald), Corinne Clery (Angelica), Marian Langner (Valeria), Paola Tedesco (Teresa), Renato Mori (Agent), Ivan Desny (Mr. Brown), Roberto Della Casa (Serge)

CAMOUFLAGE (Libra) Direction and Screenplay, Krzysztof Zanussi; Polish with English subtitles; Photography, Edward Klosinski; Design, Tadeusz Wybult, Maciej Piotrowski, Ewa Braun, Joanna Lelanow; Music, Wojclech Kilar; In color; Not rated: 106 minutes; August release. CAST: Piotr Garlicki (Jaroslaw), Zbigniew Zapaslewicz (Jakub), Christine Paul (Nelly), Mariusz Drnochowski (Deputy Rector)

AN AMERICAN WEREWOLF IN LONDON (Universal/Polygram) Producer, George Folsey, Jr.; Executive Producers, Peter Guber, Jon Peters; Direction and Screenplay, John Landis; Photography, Robert Paynter; Art Director, Leslie Dilley; Special Makeup Effects, Rick Baker; Music, Elmer Bernstein; Editor, Malcolm Campbell, Assistant Directors, David Tringham, Mike Murray, Russell Lodge; Costumes, Deborah Nadoolman; Associate Editor, Simon Battersby; A Lycanthrope Films Ltd. Production in Technicolor; 97 minutes; Rated R; August release. CAST: David Naughton (David), Jenny Agutter (Alex), Griffin Dunne (Jack), John Woodvine (Dr. Hirsch), Brian Glover (Chess Player), David Schofield (Dart Player), Lila Kaye (Barmaid), Paul Kember (Sgt. McManus), Don McKillop (Ins. Villiers), Frank Oz (Collins), Anne-Marie Davies (Nurse Gallagher), Paula Jacobs (Mrs. Kessler), Gordon Sterne (Mr. Kessler), Mark Fisher (Max), Michele Brisigotti (Rachel), and Joe Belcher, Rik Mayall, Sean Baker, Paddy Ryan, Colin Fernandes, Albert Moses, Claudine Bowyer, Johanna Crayden, Nina Carter, Geoffrey Burridge, Brenda Cavendish, Christopher Scoular, Mary Tempest, Cynthia Powell, Sydney Bromley, Frank Siguineau, Will Leighton, Michael Carter, Elizabeth Bradley, Rufus Deakin, Lesley Ward, George Hilsdon, Gerry Lewis, Dennis Fraser

INDIA SONG (Sunchild) Direction and Screenplay (French with English subtitles), Marguerite Duras; Executive Producer, Stephane Tchaigadileff; Photography, Bruno Nuytten; Editor, Solange Leprince; Music, Carlos d' Alessio; 120 minutes; Not rated; August release. CAST: Delphine Seyrig (Anne-Marie), Michel Lonsdale (Vice Consul), Mathieu Carriere (Attache), Claude Mann (Richardson), Didier Flamand (Stretter's Guest), Vernon Dobchell (Georges)

HOT PURSUIT (New American) Producer-Director, James I. West, Jr.; A Bonnie Blue Films presentation in color; 89 minutes; Rated PG; August release. CAST: Bob Watson, Don Watson, Debbie Washington

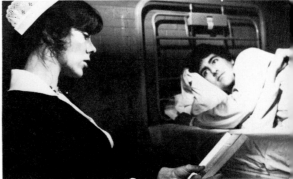

David Naughton, Griffin Dunne
in "An American Werewolf in London"
© Universal City Studios

Jenny Agutter, David Naughton
in "An American Werewolf in London"
© Universal City Studios

"Ten Tigers of Kwangtung"
© World Northal Films

Chuck Norris (L)
in "Slaughter in San Francisco"
© World Northal Films

A WOMAN LIKE EVE (Regency Film Enterprises) Producer, Matthijs van Heyningen; Direction and Screenplay, Nouchka van Brakel; Photography, Nurith Aviv; Editor, Ine Schenkkan; Music, Laurens van Rooyen; Art Director, Inger Kolff; Assistant Director, Hans Kemna; A Sigma Films B.V. production in color; 101 minutes; Dutch with English subtitles; Not rated; August release. CAST: Monique van de Ven (Eve), Maria Schneider (Liliane), Marijke Merckens (Sonja), Peter Faber (Ad)

KILL THE SHOGUN (New American Films) Producer, Young W. Kwak; Director, D. Young Lee; Screenplay, Harim Kim; Photography, Chang An; Music, Hee Kap Kim; In color; 103 minutes; Rated R; August release. CAST: David Kang, Janet Choy, Soo Chun Bae, Moon Kim, Wang Kim, James Nam

SAVAGE MAN, SAVAGE BEAST (Aquarius) A documentary film by Antonio Climati and Mario Morra; A Titanus production in color; 95 minutes; September release.

KUNG FU HALLOWEEN (New American) Producer, Dick Tang; Directors, Lam Chi Kam, Liu Sun; Fighting Instructor, Law Lee; A Henry Park production in color; Presented by Jack H. Harris; 94 minutes; September release. CAST: Law Lee, Ka Ling, Tien I, Chang Wang

SEPTEMBER WHEAT (New Time Films) Written, Photographed and Edited by Peter Krieg; A Teldok Film production In color; 96 minutes; Not rated; September release. A documentary on world hunger.

THE HIGH COUNTRY (Crown International) Producers, Bruce Mallen; Ken Gord; Executive Producer, Gene Slott; Director, Harvey Hart; Screenplay, Bud Townsend; Photography, Robert Ryan; Editor, Ron Wisman; Art Director, Reuben Freed; Costumes, Wendy Partridge; Assistant Director, Jon Anderson; In Panavision and DeLuxe Color; 101 minutes; Rated PG; September release. CAST: Timothy Bottoms (Jim), Linda Purl (Kathy), George Sims (Larry), Jim Lawrence (Casey), Bill Berry (Carter), Walter Mills (Clem), Paul Jolicoeur (Red), Dick Butler (Herbie), Elizabeth Alderton (Maude), Barry Graham (Rancher), John Duthie (Billy), Marsha Stonehouse (Mary)

SLAUGHTER IN SAN FRANCISCO (World Northal) Executive Producer, Leonard K. C. Ho; Direction and Screenplay, William Lowe; Photography, David Bailes; Editor, Fred Cumings; Music, Joe Curtis; A Golden Harvest Production in Widescreen and color; 87 minutes; Rated R; September release. CAST: Chuck Norris, Don Wong, Sylvia Channing, Robert Jones, Dan Ivan, Bob Talbert, Robert J. Herguth, James Economides, Chuck Boyde

TEN TIGERS OF KWANGTUNG (World Northal) A Shaw Brothers Presentation in color; 91 minutes; Rated R; September release. No other credits.

MADE IN U.S.A. (Pathe Contemporary Films) Producer, Georges DeBeauregard; Direction and Screenplay, Jean-Luc Godard; Based on "The Jogger" by Richard Stark; In color; 90 minutes; Not rated; September release. Cast: Anna Karina (Paula), Laszlo Szabo (Richard Widmark), Jean-Pierre Leaud (Donald Siegel), Yves Alfonso (David Goodis), Ernest Manzer (Edgar Typhus)

THE DISAPPEARANCE (World Northal) Executive Producers, James Mitchell, Garth H. Drabinsky; Producers, David Hemmings, Gerry Arbeid; Director, Stuart Copper; Screenplay, Paul Mayersberg; Based on novel by Derek Marlowe; Design, Anne Pritchard; In color; 88 minutes; Rated R; September release. CAST: Donald Sutherland (Jay), Francine Racette (Celandine), Christopher Plummer (Deverell), David Hemmings (Edward), David Warner (Burband), Virginia McKenna (Catherine), and John Hurt, Peter Bowles, Michelle Magny

BRUCE LEE'S DEADLY KUNG FU (21st Century) Producer, Jimmy Shaw; Director, Chin Wah; In Cinemascope and Eastmancolor; Rated R; September release. CAST: Bruce Li

LUCIO FLAVIO (Embrafilme/Unifilm) Producer, H. B. Filmes; Director, Hector Babenco; Screenplay, Jose Louzeiro, Hector Babenco, Jorge Duran; Photography, Lauro Escorel Filho; Editor, Silvio Renoldi; Music, John Neschling; In color; 118 minutes; Not rated; October release. CAST: Reginaldo Farias (Lucio), Ana Maria Magalhaes (Janice), Milton Candido, Ivan Candido, Paulo Cesar Pereio, Lady Francisco, Sergio Otero, Ivan de Almeida, Ivan Setta, Alvaro Freire, Grande Otelo, Stepan Nercessian, Enrico Vidal

Linda Purl, Timothy Bottoms
in "The High Country"

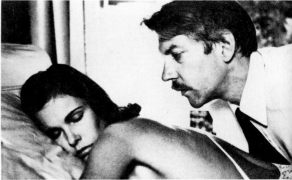

Francine Racette, Donald Sutherland
in "The Disappearance" © World Northal

Gabe Kaplan, Bernadette Peters
in "Tulips" © AVCO Embassy

Michael Murphy
in "Strange Behavior"

THE FLYING GUILLOTINE (World Northal) A Shaw Brothers presentation in color; 111 minutes; Rated R; October release. No other credits.

TULIPS (Avco Embassy) Producer, Don Carmody; Executive Producers, John B. Bennett, Harold Greenberg; Director, Rex Bromfield; Screenplay, Henry Olek, Fred Sappho; Photography, Francois Protat; Art Director, Ted Watkins; Editors, Allan Collins, Yurij Lohovy; Music, Eddie Karam; An Astral Bellevue Pathe/Bennetfilms presentation; In color; 92 minutes; Not rated; October release. CAST: Gabe Kaplan (Leland Irving), Bernadette Peters (Rutanya Wallace), Henry Gibson (Boom Boom), Al Waxman (Bert), David Boxer (Dr. Walburn), Jazzmine Lauzane (Metermaid), Malcolm Nelthorpe (Surgeon), Sean McCann (Roger), Gail Garfinkle (Nurse), Jack Creley (Florist), Cid Darrows (Gunshop Owner)

THE GRIM REAPER (Film Ventures International) Producer, Oscar Santaniello; Director, Joe D'Amato; Screenplay, Aristide Massaccesi, Lewis Montefiore; Photography, Enrico Birbichi; Editor, Ornella Michell; In color; 81 minutes; Rated R; October release. CAST: Tisa Farrow (Julie), Saverio Vallone, Vanessa Steiger, George Eastman, Zora Kerova, Mark Bodin, Bob Larsen, Mark Logan, Rubina Rey

TIEFLAND (Janus Films) Director, Leni Riefenstahl; Based on opera by Eugen d' Albert; German with English subtitles; 98 minutes; Not rated; October release. CAST: Leni Riefenstahl (Marta), Franz Eichberger (Pedro), Bernard Minetti (Don Sebastian), Nando Lusi Rainer (Amelia), Frieda Richard (Josefa), Karl Skraup (Bergermeister), Max Holzboer (Natario)

THE TROUPE (Eastways) Producer, Isaac Kol; Director, Avi Nesher; Screenplay, Sharon Harel, Avi Nesher; Photography, Jacob Kallach; Editor, Isaac Sehiek; Music, Yair Rosenblum; 110 minutes; Not rated; October release. CAST: Gidi Gov (Datner), Meir Swisa (Bazooka), Liron Mirgad (Mickey), Cheli Goldenberg (Orli), Gali Atari (Mali), Gilat Ankori (Sari), Meir Fennigstein (Shuka), Sassi Keshet (Dani), Tuvia Zafir (Aviv), Daphna Aroni (Noa), Toni Chen (Doron), Semedar Brenner (Yaffa), Elle Goremstein (Zami), Dov Clickman (Moti), Uzi Essner (Moni)

STRANGE BEHAVIOR (World Northal) Producers, Anthony I. Ginnane, John Barnett; Director, Michael Laughlin; Screenplay, William Condon, Michael Laughlin; Photography, Louis Horvath; Editor, Petra Von Oelifen; Music, Tangerine Dream; In Widescreen and color; 99 minutes; Rated R; October release. CAST: Michael Murphy (John Brady), Louise Fletcher (Barbara), Dan Shor (Pete), Fiona Lewis (Gwen), Arthur Dignam (Dr. LaSange), Dey Young (Caroline), Marc McClure (Oliver), Scott Brady (Shea), Charles Lane (Donovan), Beryl TeWiata (Mrs. Haskell), Jim Boelsen (Waldo), Elizabeth Cheshire (Lucy), B. Courtenay Leigh (Paula), William Hayward (Robinson), Billy Al Bengston (Felix), William Condon (Bryan), Jack Haines (Randy), Nicole Anderson (Flying Nun)

THE DEVIL'S PLAYGROUND (IFEX-EMC) Direction and Screenplay, Fred Schepisi; Photography, Ian Baker; Music, Bruce Smeaton; In color; 107 minutes; Not rated; October release. CAST: Arthur Dignam (Br. Francine), Nick Tate (Br. Victor), Simon Burke (Tom), Charles McCallum (Br. Sebastian), John Frawley (Br. Celian), Gerry Duggan (Fr. Hanrahan), Peter Cox (Br. James), John Diedrich (Fitz), Thomas Keneally (Fr. Marshall)

QUARTET (New World) Producers, Ismail Merchant, J. P. Mahot de la Querantonials; Director, James Ivory; Screenplay, Ruth Prawer Jhabvala, James Ivory; From novel by Jean Rhys; Photography, Pierre Lhomme; Editor, Humphrey Dixon; Music, Richard Robbins; In color; 101 minutes; Rated R; October release. CAST: Alan Bates (H.J.Heidler), Maggie Smith (Lois), Isabelle Adjani (Marya), Anthony Higgins (Stephen), Armelia McQueen (Nell), Daniel Chatto (Guy), Pierre Clementi (Pornographer), Susanne Flon (Mme. Hautchamp), Sheila Gish (Anna), Daniel Mesguich (Schlamovitz), Virginie Thevenet (Mlle. Chardin), Wiley Wood (Cairn), Bernice Stegers (Miss Nicholson), Pierre Bonnafet (Guard), Romaine Bremond (Adolescent), Isabelle Canto de Maya (Cir-Cri), Jean-Pierre Dravei (Guard), Sebastien Floche (Hatuchmap), Pierre Julien (Impresario), Monique Mauclair (Concierge), Michel Such (Guard)

DIRTY-HO (World Northal) A Shaw Brothers presentation in color; 103 minutes; Rated R; October release. CAST: Gordon Liu

Tisa Farrow in "The Grim Reaper"
© Film Ventures International

Isabelle Adjani, Maggie Smith
in "Quartet" © National Film Trustee

212

"Enter the Ninja"

Susan Anspach in "Montenegro"
© Atlantic Releasing Corp.

ENTER THE NINJA (Cannon/First City) Producers, Judd Bernard, Yoram Globus; Director, Menahem Golan; Screenplay, Dick Desmond, Judd Bernard, Menahem Golan; Photography, David Gurfinkel; Choreography, Mike Stone; Music, W. Michael Lewis, Laurin Rinder; In color; 101 minutes; Rated R; October release. CAST: Franco Nero (Cole), Susan George (Maryann), Sho Kosugi (Hasegawa), Christopher George (Venarius), Alex Courtney (Frank), Will Hare (Dollars), Zachi Noy (The Hook), Constantin DeGoguel (Parker), Dale Ishimoto (Komori), Joonee Gamboa (Mesuda), Leo Martinez (PeeWee), Ken Metcalfe (Elliot), Mike Stone (White Ninja), Alan Amiel, Doug Ivan, Bob Jones, Jack Turner, Derek Webster, Konrad Waalkes, James Gaines, Don Gordon, Isolde Winter, Lucy Bush

ENTER THREE DRAGONS (Cinematic) Producer, Joseph Lai; Directors, Joseph Kong, Godfrey Ho; Action Director, Leung Siu-Chung; Presented by Serafim Karalexis; A Madison World Film; In color; Rated R; October release. CAST: Dragon Lee, Bruce Lea, Yang Tsze, Samuel Walls, Bruce Li, Jackie Chin

BLOOD RELATIVES (Filmcorp/SNC) Director, Claude Chabrol; Screenplay, Claude Chabrol, R. Sydeny from the novel by Ed McBain; Photography, Jean Rabier; Editor, Yves Langlois; Music, Paul Jensen; In Eastmancolor; 100 minutes; not rated; October release. CAST: Donald Sutherland (Carella), Aude Landry (Patricia), Lisa Langlois (Muriel), Laurent Malet (Andrew), Micheline Lanctot (Mrs. Carella), Stephane Audran (Mother), Donald Pleasence (Doniac), David Hemmings (Armstrong)

EYES OF THE DRAGON (Worldwide Entertainment) Producer, Henry Park; Direction and Screenplay, George Vieira; Assistant Producer, T. B. Lime; Executive Producers, John R. K. Tinkle, Edward Borcherdt; Photography, Jack Beckett; Music, Doug Lacky; A United World Picture in color; 83 minutes; Rated PG; October release. CAST: Chris Mitchum, Pu Gill Gwon, Victoria Loveland, Karen Young, Jay Christy, William Zacha, Ill Bong Yoon

THE PLUMBER (Cinema Ventures) Direction and Screenplay by Peter Weir; 76 minutes; Not rated; November release; No other credits available. CAST: Judy Morris, Ivar Kants, Robert Colby, Candy Raymond

ASHRAM (Libra) Produced and Directed by Wolfgang Dobrowolny; A Mu-Film in color; 83 minutes; November release. CAST: Peter Claussen, Friedemann Kliesch, Kirsten Liesenborghs, Wilhelm Schulz, Bhagwan Shree Rajneesh

XXII OLYMPIAD: MOSCOW 1980 (International Film Exchange) Director, Yuri Ozerov; Scenario, Yuri Ozerov, Boris Rytchikov; Text, Nicolai Dobronravov; Music, Aleksandra Pakhmoutove; In color; 120 minutes; Not rated; November release. The officially sanctioned featurelength film of the 1980 summer olympics in Moscow.

MONTENEGRO (Atlantic Releasing Corp.) Producer, Bo Jonsson; Direction and Screenplay, Dusan Makavejev; Photography, Tomislav Pinter; Art Director, Radu Gorusescu; Music, Kornell Kovach; Title song sung by Marianne Faithfull; Associate Producers, Georg Zecevic, Christer Abrahamsen; Editor, Sylvia Ingemarsson; In color; 97 minutes; Not rated; November release. CAST: Susan Anspach (Marilyn Jordan), Erland Josephson (Martin Jordan), Jamie Marsh (Jimmy), Per Oscarsson (Dr. Pazardjian), Bora Todorovic (Alex), Marianne Jacobi (Cookie), John Zacharias (Grandpa), Svetozar Cvetkovic (Montenegro), Patricia Gelin, Lisbeth Zachrisson, Marina Zindahl, Nikola Janic, Lasse Abepg. Dragan Ilic, Milo Petrovic, John Parkinson, Jan Nygren, Kaarina Harvistola, Ewa Gislen, Elsie Holm, Paul Smith, Bo Ivan Peterson

JANE AUSTEN IN MANHATTAN (Putnam Square) Producer, Ismail Merchant; Director, James Ivory; Screenplay, Ruth Prawer Jhabvala; Libretto of "Sir Charles Grandison" by Jane Austen and Samuel Richardson; Photography, Ernst Vincze; Editor, David E. McKenna; Music, Richard Robbins; In color; 108 minutes; Not rated; November release. CAST: Anne Baxter (Lilianna), Robert Powell (Pierre), Michael Wager (George), Tim Choate (Jamie), John Guerrasio (Gregory), Katrina Hodiak (Katya), Kurt Johnson (Victor), Philip Lenkowsky (Fritz), Nancy New (Jenny), Charles McCaughan (Billy), Sean Young (Ariadne), Bernard Barrow (Poison), Lee Doyle (Jarvis), Bella Jarett (Miss Klein), Naomi Riordan (Mrs. Poison)

JADE CLAW (Transmedia) Producer, Pal Ming; Director, Hwa I. Hung; An Eternal Films Co. Ltd. production in color; Rated R; November release. CAST: Billy Chong, Yuen Siu Tin

Isabelle Adjani, Alan Bates
in "Quartet" © National Film Trustee

Anne Baxter, Robert Powell in "Jane
Austen in Manhattan"

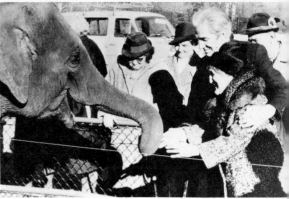

Tatum O'Neal, Richard Burton
in "Circle of Two"

"Land of Silence and Darkness"

CIRCLE OF TWO (World Northal) Producer, Henk Van der Kolk; Executive Producer, William Marshall; Associate Producer, Bob Rodgers; Director, Jules Dassin; Photography, Laszlo George; Screenplay, Thomas Hedley; In color; 99 minutes; Rated R; November release. CAST: Richard Burton, Tatum O'Neal, Kate Reid, Tudi Wiggins, Robin Gammell

MORTAL COMBAT (World Northal) Producer, Runme Shaw; Director, Chang Cheh; A Shaw Brothers presentation in color; 106 minutes; Rated R; November release. CAST: To-Lung (The Tiger of the Southern Sky)

TIBET: A BUDDHIST TRILOGY (Public Cinema) Direction and Screenplay, Graham Coleman; Produced and Photographed by David Lascelles; Editor, Pip Heywood; A Thread Cross Films production in color; Not rated; November release. "A Prophecy" (54 minutes), "The Fields of the Senses" (52 minutes), "Radiating the Fruit of Truth" (125 minutes)

THE PROWLER (UFD) Producers, Joseph Zito, David Streit; Director, Joseph Zito; Screenplay, Glenn Leopold, Neil Barbera; Photography, Raoul Lumas; Design, Lorenzo Man; Music, Richard Einhorn; Editor, Joel Goodman; In color; 88 minutes; Rated R; November release. CAST: Vicki Dawson (Pam), Christopher Goutman (Mark), Cindy Weintraub (Lisa), Farley Granger (Sheriff), John Seitz (Kingsley)

SUPER FUZZ (Avco Embassy) Producer, Transcinema; Director, Sergio Corbucci; Screenplay, Mr. Corbucci, Sabataino Ciuffini; Photography, Silvano Ippoliti; Editor, Eugenio Alabiso; Design, Marco Dentici; Assistant Director, Amanzio Todini; In Technicolor; 97 minutes; Rated PG; November release. CAST: Terence Hill (Dave), Ernest Borgnine (Willy), Joanne Dru (Rosy), Marc Lawrence (Tropedo), Julie Gordon (Evelyn), Lee Sandman (Chief), Herb Goldstein (Silvius), Don Sebastian (Dingo), Sal Borghese (Paradise Alley), Claudio Ruffini (Tragedy Row), Sergio Smacchi (Slot Machine)

CROCODILE (Cobra Media) Producers, Dick Randall, Robert Chan; Director, Sampote Sands; In color; 91 minutes; Rated R; November release. CAST: Nat Puvanai, Tany Tim, Angela Wells, Kirk Warren

LAND OF SILENCE AND DARKNESS) (German with English subtitles) Producer-Director, Werner Herzog; Narrated by Rolf Illig; Photography, Jorg Schmidt-Reitwein; Editor, Beate Mainke-Jellinghaus; 90 minutes; Not rated; December release. A documentary with Fini Straubinger

SPACED OUT (Miramax) Producer, David Speechley; Director, Norman J. Warren; Screenplay, Andrew Payne; Additional Dialogue, Bob Saget, Jeff de Hart; Theme Song performed by The Chance; Editor, Edward Glass; Photography, John Metcalfe, Peter Sinclair; Executive Producers, Peter M. Schlesinger, Alan L. Girney; Assistant Director, Gary White; Music, Alan Brawer, Anna Pepper; In Technicolor; 90 minutes; Rated R; December release. CAST: Barry Stokes (Oliver), Tony Maiden (Willy), Glory Annen (Cosia), Michael Rowlatt (Cliff), Ava Cadell (Partha), Kate Ferguson (Skipper), Lynne Ross (Prudence)

MENSCHENFRAUEN (Top) "Humanwomen" Produced, Directed, Written and Photographed by Valie Export; In color; 120 minutes; Not rated; December release. No other credits available.

COUNTERFEIT COMMANDOS (Aquarius) Executive Producer, Roberto Sbarigia; Director, Enzo G. Castellari; Screenplay, Sergio Grieco; Photography, Gianfranco Bergamini; Editor, Gianfranco Amicucci; Music, Francesci do Masi; In color; Rated R; 99 minutes; December release. CAST: Bo Svenson (Lt. Yeager), Fred Williamson (Fred), Peter Hooten (Tony), Michael Pergolami (Nick), Jackie Basehart (Berle), Raymund Harmstorf (Otto), Michel Constantin (Veronique), Debra Berger (Nicole), Ian Bannen (Col. Buckner)

TRISTAN AND ISOLT (Clar Productions) Producers, Tom Hayes, Claire Labine; Executive Producer, Thomas H. Ryan; Music, Paddy Moloney; Performed by The Chieftans; Photography, Richard H. Kline; In color; Not rated; December release. CAST: Richard Burton (King Mark), Kate Mulgrew (Isolt), Nicholas Clay (Tristan), Cyril Cusack (Gormond), Geraldine Fitzgerald (Bronwyn), Niall Toibin (Andred), Diana van der Vlis (Alix), Niall O'Brien (Gorvenal), Kathryn Dowling (Yseult), John Joe Brooks (Father Colm)

Terence Hill
in "Super Fuzz"

"Mortal Combat"

**Serge Avedikian, Piotr Stanislas
in "We Were One Man"**

SIGNS OF LIFE (New Yorker) Direction and Screenplay, Werner Herzog; Photography, Thomas Mauch; Editors, Beate Mainka-Jellinghaus, Maxi Mainka; Music, Stavros Xarchakos; In German with English subtitles; In black and white; 91 minutes; Not rated; December release. CAST: Peter Brogle (Stroszek), Wolfgang Reichmann (Meinhard), Athina Zacharopoulou (Nora), Wolfgang von Ungern-Sternberg (Becker), Wolfgang Stumpf (Captain), Henry van Lyck (Lieutenant), Julie Pinheiro (Gypsy), Florian Fricke (Pianist), Heinz Usener (Doctor), Achmed Hafiz (Greek)

PRISON FOR WOMEN (Spectrum Films) Produced, Directed and Edited by Holly Dale, Janis Cole; Photography, Nesya Shapiro; Music, Susie and Kas; In color; Not rated; 81 minutes; December release. CAST: Maggie, Debby, Janise, Bev, Susie

WE WERE ONE MAN (Frameline) Direction and Screenplay, Philippe Vallois; Photography, Francois About; Editor, M. Vallois; Music, Jean-Jacques Ruhlmann, Montparnasse 2000; In Eastmancolor; 90 minutes; In German; Not rated; December release. CAST: Serge Avedikian (Guy), Piotr Stanislas (Rolf), Catherine Albin (Janine)

DEAR BOYS (Sigma Films) Producer, Matthijs van Heijningen; Director, Paul de Lussanet; Screenplay, Chiem van Houweninge; Based on novel by Gerard Reve; Photography, Paul van den Bos; Editor, Hans van Dongen; Music, Laurens van Rooyen; In color; Dutch with English subtitles; 90 minutes; Not rated; December release. CAST: Hugo Mesters (Wolf), Hans Dagelet (Beaver), Bill van Dijk (Tiger), Albert Mol (Albert)

CIRCLE BED (Intercontinental) Director, Guy Perol; In color; 90 minutes; Not rated; October release. CAST: Sandra Jullien, Virginie Vignon, Jacques Cornet, Martine Drucker

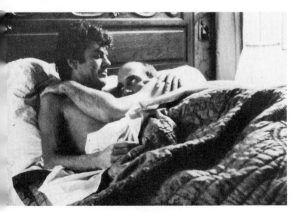

**Hans Dagelet, Hugo Mesters
in "Dear Boys"**

ANGELS BRIGADE (Arista) Producer-Director, Greydon Clark; Screenplay, Greydon Clark, Alvin L. Fast; Executive Producer, Louis George; Photography, Dean Cundy; Music, Gerald Lee; Associate Producer, Don Greer; In color; Rated R; February release. CAST: Sylvia Anderson, Lieu Chinh, Jacqulin Cole, Liza Greer, Robin Greer, Susan Kiger, Noela Velasco, Jack Palance, Peter Lawford, Jim Backus, Neville Brand, Pat Buttram, Arthur Godfrey, Alan Hale

THE MAN WHO LOVED BEARS (Key International) Producer-Director, Marty Stouffer; Narrated by Henry Fonda; In color; 85 minutes; Rated G; February release. A wildlife documentary.

MY MAIN MAN FROM STONEY ISLAND (World Northal) originally "Stoney Island"; Producers, Andrew Davis, Tamar Hoffs; Director, Andrew Davis; Screenplay, Andrew Davis, Tamar Hoffs; Music, David Matthews; Performed by Stoney Island Band; Photography, Tak Fujimoto; Editor, Dov Hoenig; In color; 97 minutes; Rated PG; February release. CAST: Richard Davis, Edward Stoney Robinson, George Englund, Gene Barge, Ronnie Barron, Tennyson Stephens, Larry Ball, Windy Barnes, Rae Dawn Chong, Donnell Hagen, Criss Johnson, Kenneth Brass, Edwin William, Steele L. Seals, Susanna Hoffs, Nathan Davis, Tom Mula, Carmi Simon, Dennis Franz

STONE COLD DEAD (Dimension) Executive Producer, Peter Wilson, Producers, George Mendeluk, John Ryan; Direction and Screenplay, George Mendeluk; Based on novel "The Sin Sniper" by Hugh Garner; Photography, Dennis Miller; Editor, Martin Pepler; Art Director, Ted Watkins; In color; 97 minutes; Rated R; March release. CAST: Richard Crenna, Paul Williams, Linda Sorenson, Belinda J. Montgomery, Charles Shamata, Alberta Watson, Monique Mercure, Andree Cousineau, Frank Moore, George Chuvalo, George Touliatos, Dennis Strong, Jennifer Dale

LEO AND LOREE (United Artists) Producer, Jim Begg; Executive Producer, Ron Howard; Director, Jerry Paris; Screenplay, James Ritz; Photography, Costa Petals; Editor, Ed Cotter; Art Director, Linda Pearl; Assistant Director, Cheryl Downey; Associate Producer, James Ragan; Music, Lance Rubin; In CFI Color; 97 minutes; Rated PG; April release. CAST: Donny Most, Linda Purl, David Huffman, Jerry Paris, Shannon Farnon, Allan Rich, Susan Lawrence

WOLFMAN (Omni) Producer, Earl Owensby; Direction and Screenplay, Worth Keeter; Music, Arthur Smith, David Floyd; Photography, Darrell Cathcart; Editor, Richard Aldridge; In DeLuxe Color; 101 minutes; Rated R; April release. CAST: Earl Owensby, Kristine Reynolds, Richard Dedmon, Ed L. Grady, Maggie Lauterer

GORP (Filmways) Producers, Jeffrey Konvitz, Louis S. Arkoff; Director, Joseph Ruben; Screenplay, Jeffrey Konvitz; In color; 90 minutes; Rated R; May release. CAST: Michael Lembeck, Philip Casnoff, David Huddleston, Dennis Quaid, Fran Drescher

HEADIN' FOR BROADWAY (20th Century-Fox) Producer-Director, Joseph Brooks; Screenplay, Joseph Brooks, Hilary Henkin, Larry Gross; In color; 95 minutes; Rated PG; May release. CAST: Rex Smith, Terri Treas, Vivian Reed, Paul Carafotes, Gene Foote, Gary Gendell

TWICE A WOMAN (The Movie Co.) Producers, William Howerd, Anne Lordon; Director, George Sluizer, Jurrien Rood; Based on novel "Twee Vrouwen" by Harry Mulisch; Photography, Mat van Hensbergen; Music, Willem Breuker; Art Director, Michel Bodt; Assistant Director, Jurrien Rood; In color; 113 minutes; Rated R; Dutch with English soundtrack; May release. CAST: Bibi Andersson (Laura), Anthony Perkins (Alfred), Sandra Dumas (Sylvia), Tilly Perin Bouwmeester, Kitty Courbeois, Astrid Weyman, Georg Frenkel Frank, Charles Gormley, Adrian Brine, Arnold Gelderman

PLANET OF DINOSAURS (Wells Films) Producer-Director, James K. Shea; Screenplay, Ralph Lucas; Associate Producer, James R. Waite; Music, Kelly Lammers, John O'Verlin; In color; Rated PG; August release. CAST: James Whitworth, Pamela Bottaro, Harvey Shain, Charlotte Speer, Chuck Pennington, Derna Wylde, Michael Thayer, Louie Lawless, Mary Appleseth

HOTWIRE (World Premier Pictures) Producer, David L. Ford; Director, Frank Q. Dobbs; Screenplay, Caleb Pirtle III, Frank Q. Dobbs; Executive Producer, Dick Ott; In color; Rated PG; September release. CAST: George Kennedy, Strother Martin, John Terry, Jean Sanders

FIST OF FEAR TOUCH OF DEATH (Aquarius) Producer, Terry Levene; Director, Matthew Mallinson; Screenplay, Ron Harvey; Story, Harvey and Mallinson; Photography, John Hazard; Music, Keith Mansfield; Editors, Mallinson, Jeffrey Brown; In color; 90 minutes; Rated R; September release. CAST: Fred Williamson, Ron Van Clief, Adolph Caesar, Aaron Banks, Bill Louis, Teruyuki Higa, Gail Turner, Richard Barathy, Hollywood Browde, Louis Neglia, Cydra Karlyn, Annett Bronson, Ron Harvey, John Flood, and film clips of Bruce Lee

Maud
Adams

Eddie
Albert

Nancy
Allen

William
Atherton

Eve
Arden

BIOGRAPHICAL DATA

(Name, real name, place and date of birth, school attended)

ABBOTT, DIAHNNE: NYC, 1945.

ABBOTT, JOHN: London, June 5, 1905.

ABEL, WALTER: St. Paul, MN, June 6, 1898. AADA.

ABRAHAM, F. MURRAY: Pittsburgh, PA, Oct. 24, 1939. UTx.

ADAMS, BROOKE: NYC, 1949. Dalton.

ADAMS, DON: NYC, 1927.

ADAMS, EDIE (Elizabeth Edith Enke): Kingston, PA, Apr. 16, 1929. Juilliard, Columbia.

ADAMS, JULIE (Betty May): Waterloo, Iowa, Oct. 17, 1928. Little Rock Jr. College.

ADAMS, MAUD (Maud Wikstrom): Lulea, Sweden.

ADDAMS, DAWN: Felixstowe, Suffolk, Eng., Sept. 21, 1930. RADA.

ADDY, WESLEY: Omaha, NB, Aug. 4, 1913. UCLA.

ADJANI, ISABELLE: Paris, 1955.

ADLER, LUTHER: NYC, May 4, 1903.

ADRIAN, IRIS (Iris Adrian Hostetter): Los Angeles, May 29, 1913.

AGAR, JOHN: Chicago, Jan. 31, 1921.

AGUTTER, JENNY: London, 1953.

AHERNE, BRIAN: Worcestershire, Eng., May 2, 1902. Malvern College, U. of London.

AIELLO, DANNY: June 20, 1935, NYC.

AIMEE, ANOUK: Paris, Apr. 27, 1934. Bauer-Therond.

AKINS, CLAUDE: Nelson, GA, May 25, 1936. Northwestern U.

ALBERGHETTI, ANNA MARIA: Pesaro, Italy, May 15, 1936.

ALBERT, EDDIE (Eddie Albert Heimberger): Rock Island, IL, Apr. 22, 1908. U. of Minn.

ALBERT, EDWARD: Los Angeles, Feb. 20, 1951. UCLA.

ALBRIGHT, LOLA: Akron, OH, July 20, 1925.

ALDA, ALAN: NYC, Jan. 28, 1936. Fordham.

ALDA, ROBERT (Alphonso D'Abruzzo): NYC, Feb. 26, 1914. NYU.

ALDERSON, BROOKE: Dallas, Tx.

ALEJANDRO, MIGUEL: NYC, 1958.

ALEXANDER, JANE (Quigley): Boston, MA, Oct. 28, 1939. Sarah Lawrence.

ALLEN, NANCY: NYC 1950.

ALLEN, REX: Wilcox, AZ, Dec. 31, 1922.

ALLEN, STEVE: New York City, Dec. 26, 1921.

ALLEN, WOODY (Allen Stewart Konigsberg): Brooklyn, Dec. 1, 1935.

ALLYSON, JUNE (Ella Geisman): Westchester, NY, Oct. 7, 1917.

ALVARADO, TRINI: NYC, 1967.

AMECHE, DON (Dominic Amichi): Kenosha, WI, May 31, 1908.

AMES, ED: Boston, July 9, 1929.

AMES, LEON (Leon Wycoff): Portland, IN, Jan. 20, 1903.

AMOS, JOHN: Newark, NJ, Dec. 27, 1940. Colo. U.

ANDERSON, JUDITH: Adelaide, Australia, Feb. 10, 1898.

ANDERSON, MELODY: Canada 1955, Carlton U.

ANDERSON, MICHAEL, JR.: London, Eng., 1943.

ANDERSSON, BIBI: Stockholm, Nov. 11, 1935. Royal Dramatic Sch.

ANDES, KEITH: Ocean City, NJ, July 12, 1920. Temple U., Oxford.

ANDRESS, URSULA: Switz., Mar. 19, 1936.

ANDREWS, DANA: Collins, MS, Jan. 1, 1909. Sam Houston Col.

ANDREWS, EDWARD: Griffin, GA, Oct. 9, 1914. U. VA.

ANDREWS, HARRY: Tonbridge, Kent, Eng., Nov. 10, 1911.

ANDREWS, JULIE (Julia Elizabeth Wells): Surrey, Eng., Oct. 1, 1935.

ANGEL, HEATHER: Oxford, Eng., Feb. 9, 1909. Wycombe Abbey.

ANN-MARGRET (Olsson): Valsjobyn, Sweden, Apr. 28, 1941. Northwestern U.

ANSARA, MICHAEL: Lowell, MA, Apr. 15, 1922. Pasadena Playhouse.

ANTHONY, TONY: Clarksburg, WV, Oct 16, 1937. Carnegie Tech.

ANTON, SUSAN: Yucaipa, CA. 1951. Bernardino Col.

ANTONELLI, LAURA: Pola, Italy.

ARCHER, JOHN (Ralph Bowman): Osceola, NB, May 8, 1915. USC.

ARDEN, EVE (Eunice Quedens): Mill Valley, CA, Apr. 30, 1912.

ARKIN, ALAN: NYC, Mar. 26, 1934. LACC.

ARNAZ, DESI: Santiago, Cuba, Mar. 2, 1915. Colegio de Dolores.

ARNAZ, DESI, JR.: Los Angeles, Jan. 19, 1953.

ARNAZ, LUCIE: Hollywood, July 17, 1951.

ARNESS, JAMES (Aurness): Minneapolis, MN, May 26, 1923. Beloit College.

ARTHUR, BEATRICE: NYC, May 13, 1926. New School.

ARTHUR, JEAN: NYC, Oct. 17, 1905.

ARTHUR, ROBERT (Robert Arthaud): Aberdeen, WA, June 18, 1925. U. Wash.

ASHLEY, ELIZABETH (Elizabeth Ann Cole): Ocala, FL, Aug. 30, 1939.

ASSANTE, ARMAND: NYC, Oct. 4, 1949. AADA.

ASTAIRE, FRED (Fred Austerlitz): Omaha, NB, May 10, 1899.

ASTIN, JOHN: Baltimore, MD, Mar. 30, 1930. U. Minn.

ASTIN, PATTY DUKE (see Patty Duke)

ASTOR, MARY (Lucile V. Langhanke): Quincy, IL, May 3, 1906. Kenwood-Loring School.

ATHERTON, WILLIAM: Orange, CT, July 30, 1947. Carnegie Tech.

ATKINS, CHRISTOPHER: Rye, NY, 1961.

ATTENBOROUGH, RICHARD: Cambridge, Eng., Aug. 29, 1923. RADA.

AUBERJONOIS, RENE: NYC, June 1, 1940. Carnegie Tech.

AUDRAN, STEPHANE: Versailles, Fr., 1933.

AUGER, CLAUDINE: Paris, Apr. 26, 1942. Dramatic Cons.

AULIN, EWA: Stockholm, Sweden, Feb. 14, 1950.

AUMONT, JEAN PIERRE: Paris, Jan. 5, 1909. French Nat'l School of Drama.

AUTRY, GENE: Tioga, TX, Sept. 29, 1907.

AVALON, FRANKIE (Francis Thomas Avallone): Philadelphia, Sept. 18, 1939.

AYRES, LEW: Minneapolis, MN, Dec. 28, 1908.

AZNAVOUR, CHARLES (Varenagh Aznourian): Paris, May 22, 1924.

BACALL, LAUREN (Betty Perske): NYC, Sept. 16, 1924. AADA.

BACKUS, JIM: Cleveland, Ohio, Feb. 25, 1913. AADA.

BADDELEY, HERMIONE: Shropshire, Eng., Nov. 13, 1906. Margaret Morris School.

Martin
Balsam

Anne
Baxter

Robby
Benson

Susan
Blakely

David
Birney

BAILEY, PEARL: Newport News, VA, March 29, 1918.

BAIN, BARBARA: Chicago, Sept. 13, 1934. U. Ill.

BAIO, SCOTT: Brooklyn, 1961.

BAKER, BLANCHE: NYC Dec. 20, 1956.

BAKER, CARROLL: Johnstown, PA, May 28, 1931. St. Petersburg Jr. College.

BAKER, DIANE: Hollywood, CA, Feb. 25, 1938. USC.

BAKER, LENNY: Boston, MA, Jan. 17, 1945. Boston U.

BALABAN, ROBERT: Chicago, Aug. 16, 1945. Colgate.

BALDWIN, ADAM: Chicago, Il. 1962.

BALIN, INA: Brooklyn, Nov. 12, 1937. NYU.

BALL, LUCILLE: Celaron, NY, Aug. 6, 1910. Chatauqua Musical Inst.

BALSAM, MARTIN: NYC, Nov. 4, 1919. Actors Studio.

BANCROFT, ANNE (Anna Maria Italiano): Bronx, NY, Sept. 17, 1931. AADA.

BANNEN, IAN: Airdrie, Scot., June 29, 1928.

BARDOT, BRIGITTE: Paris, Sept. 28, 1934.

BARRAULT, MARIE-CHRISTINE: Paris, 1946.

BARRETT, MAJEL (Hudec): Columbus, OH, Feb. 23. Western Reserve U.

BARRON, KEITH: Mexborough, Eng., Aug. 8, 1936. Sheffield Playhouse.

BARRY, GENE (Eugene Klass): NYC, June 14, 1921.

BARRYMORE, JOHN BLYTH: Beverly Hills, CA, June 4, 1932. St. John's Military Academy.

BARTHOLOMEW, FREDDIE: London, Mar. 28, 1924.

BARYSHNIKOV, MIKHAIL: Riga, Latvia, Jan. 27, 1948.

BASEHART, RICHARD: Zanesville, OH, Aug. 31, 1914.

BATES, ALAN: Allestree, Derbyshire, Eng., Feb. 17, 1934. RADA.

BAXTER, ANNE: Michigan City, IN, May 7, 1923. Ervine School of Drama.

BAXTER, KEITH: South Wales, Apr. 29, 1933. RADA.

BEAL, JOHN (J. Alexander Bliedung): Joplin, MO, Aug. 13, 1909. Pa. U.

BEATTY, ROBERT: Hamilton, Ont., Can., Oct. 19, 1909. U. of Toronto.

BEATTY, WARREN: Richmond, VA, March 30, 1937.

BECK, MICHAEL: Horseshoe Lake, AR, 1948.

BEDELIA, BONNIE: NYC, Mar. 25, 1948. Hunter Col.

BEDI, KABIR: India, 1945.

BEERY, NOAH, JR.: NYC, Aug. 10, 1916. Harvard Military Academy.

BELAFONTE, HARRY: NYC, Mar. 1, 1927.

BELASCO, LEON: Odessa, Russia, Oct. 11, 1902.

BEL GEDDES, BARBARA: NYC, Oct. 31, 1922.

BELL, TOM: Liverpool, Eng., 1932.

BELLAMY, RALPH: Chicago, June 17, 1904.

BELLER, KATHLEEN: NYC, 1957.

BELMONDO, JEAN PAUL: Paris, Apr. 9, 1933.

BENEDICT, DIRK (Niewoehner): White Sulphur Springs, MT. 1945. Whitman Col.

BENJAMIN, RICHARD: NYC, May 22, 1938. Northwestern U.

BENNENT, DAVID: Lausanne, Sept. 9, 1966.

BENNETT, BRUCE (Herman Brix): Tacoma, WA, May 19, 1909. U. Wash.

BENNETT, JILL: Penang, Malay, Dec. 24, 1931.

BENNETT, JOAN: Palisades, NJ, Feb. 27, 1910. St. Margaret's School.

BENSON, ROBBY: Dallas, TX, Jan. 21, 1957.

BERENSON, MARISA: NYC, Feb. 15, 1947.

BERGEN, CANDICE: Los Angeles, May 9, 1946. U. Pa.

BERGEN, POLLY: Knoxville, TN, July 14, 1930. Compton Jr. College.

BERGER, HELMUT: Salzburg, Aus., 1945.

BERGER, SENTA: Vienna, May 13, 1941. Vienna Sch. of Acting.

BERGER, WILLIAM: Austria, Jan. 20, 1928. Columbia.

BERGERAC, JACQUES: Biarritz, France, May 26, 1927. Paris U.

BERGMAN, INGRID: Stockholm, Sweden, Aug. 29, 1915. Royal Dramatic Theatre School.

BERLE, MILTON (Milton Berlinger): NYC, July 12, 1908. Professional Children's School.

BERLIN, JEANNIE: Los Angeles, Nov. 1, 1949.

BERLINGER, WARREN: Brooklyn, Aug. 31, 1937. Columbia.

BERNARDI, HERSCHEL: NYC, 1923.

BERRI, CLAUDE (Langmann): Paris, July 1, 1934.

BERTO, JULIET: Grenoble, France, Jan. 1947.

BEST, JAMES: Corydon, IN, July 26, 1926.

BETTGER, LYLE: Philadelphia, Feb. 13, 1915. AADA.

BEYMER, RICHARD: Avoca, IA, Feb. 21, 1939.

BIEHN, MICHAEL: Ariz. 1957.

BIKEL, THEODORE: Vienna, May 2, 1924. RADA.

BIRNEY, DAVID: Washington, DC, Apr. 23, 1939. Dartmouth, UCLA.

BISHOP, JOEY (Joseph Abraham Gottlieb): Bronx, NY, Feb. 3, 1918.

BISHOP, JULIE (formerly Jacqueline Wells): Denver, CO, Aug. 30, 1917. Westlake School.

BISSET, JACQUELINE: Waybridge, Eng., Sept. 13, 1944.

BIXBY, BILL: San Francisco, Jan. 22, 1934. U. Cal.

BLACK, KAREN (Ziegler): Park Ridge, IL, July 1, 1942. Northwestern.

BLAINE, VIVIAN (Vivian Stapleton): Newark, NJ, Nov. 21, 1923.

BLAIR, BETSY (Betsy Boger): NYC, Dec. 11, 1923.

BLAIR, JANET (Martha Jane Lafferty): Blair, PA, Apr. 23, 1921.

BLAIR, LINDA: Westport, CT, 1959.

BLAKE, AMANDA (Beverly Louise Neill): Buffalo, NY, Feb. 20, 1921.

BLAKE, ROBERT (Michael Gubitosi): Nutley, NJ, Sept. 18, 1933.

BLAKELY, SUSAN: Frankfurt, Germany 1950. U. Tex.

BLAKLEY, RONEE: Stanley, ID, 1946. Stanford U.

BLOOM, CLAIRE: London, Feb. 15, 1931. Badminton School.

BLYTH, ANN: Mt. Kisco, NY, Aug. 16, 1928. New Wayburn Dramatic School.

BOCHNER, HART: Toronto, 1956. U San Diego.

BOGARDE, DIRK: London, Mar. 28, 1918. Glasgow & Univ. College.

BOLGER, RAY: Dorchester, MA, Jan. 10, 1903.

BOLKAN, FLORINDA (Florinda Soares Bulcao): Ceara, Brazil, Feb. 15, 1941.

BOND, DEREK: Glasgow, Scot., Jan. 26, 1920. Askes School.

BOONE, PAT: Jacksonville, FL, June 1, 1934. Columbia U.

BOOTH, SHIRLEY (Thelma Ford): NYC, Aug. 30, 1907.

BORGNINE, ERNEST (Borgnino): Hamden, CT, Jan. 24, 1918. Randall School.

217

Joseph
Bottoms

Genevieve
Bujold

Georg Stanford
Brown

Catherine
Burns

Carleton
Carpenter

BOTTOMS, JOSEPH: Santa Barbara, CA, 1954.

BOTTOMS, TIMOTHY: Santa Barbara, CA, Aug. 30, 1951.

BOULTING, INGRID: Transvaal, So. Africa, 1947.

BOVEE, LESLIE: Bend, OR, 1952.

BOWIE, DAVID: (David Robert Jones) Brixton, South London, Eng. Jan. 8, 1947.

BOWKER, JUDI: Shawford, Eng., Apr. 6, 1954.

BOYLE, PETER: Philadelphia, PA, 1937. LaSalle Col.

BRACKEN, EDDIE: NYC, Feb. 7, 1920. Professional Children's School.

BRADY, SCOTT (Jerry Tierney): Brooklyn, Sept. 13, 1924. Bliss-Hayden Dramatic School.

BRAND, NEVILLE: Kewanee, IL, Aug. 13, 1920.

BRANDO, JOCELYN: San Francisco, Nov. 18, 1919. Lake Forest College, AADA.

BRANDO, MARLON: Omaha, NB, Apr. 3, 1924. New School.

BRANDON, CLARK: NYC 1959.

BRAZZI, ROSSANO: Bologna, Italy, Sept. 18, 1916. U. Florence.

BRIAN, DAVID: NYC, Aug. 5, 1914. CCNY.

BRIDGES, BEAU: Los Angeles, Dec. 9, 1941. UCLA.

BRIDGES, JEFF: Los Angeles, Dec. 4, 1949.

BRIDGES, LLOYD: San Leandro, CA, Jan. 15, 1913.

BRISEBOIS, DANIELLE: Brooklyn, June 28, 1969.

BRITT, MAY (Maybritt Wilkins): Sweden, March 22, 1936.

BRODIE, STEVE (Johnny Stevens): Eldorado, KS, Nov. 25, 1919.

BROLIN, JAMES: Los Angeles, July 18, 1940. UCLA.

BROMFIELD, JOHN (Farron Bromfield): South Bend, IN, June 11, 1922. St. Mary's College.

BRONSON, CHARLES (Buchinsky): Ehrenfield, PA, Nov. 3, 1920.

BROWN, BLAIR: Washington, DC, 1948; Pine Manor

BROWN, BRYAN: Panania, Aust., 1947.

BROWN, GEORG STANFORD: Havana, Cuba, June 24, 1943. AMDA.

BROWN, JAMES: Desdemona, TX, Mar. 22, 1920. Baylor U.

BROWN, JIM: St. Simons Island, NY, Feb. 17, 1935. Syracuse U.

BROWN, TOM: NYC, Jan. 6, 1913. Professional Children's School.

BROWNE, CORAL: Melbourne, Aust., July 23, 1913.

BROWNE, LESLIE: NYC, 1958.

BRUCE, VIRGINIA: Minneapolis, Sept. 29, 1910.

BRYNNER, YUL: Sakhalin Island, Japan, July 11, 1915.

BUCHHOLZ, HORST: Berlin, Ger., Dec. 4, 1933. Ludwig Dramatic School.

BUETEL, JACK: Dallas, TX, Sept. 5, 1917.

BUJOLD, GENEVIEVE: Montreal, Can., July 1, 1942.

BURKE, PAUL: New Orleans, July 21, 1926. Pasadena Playhouse.

BURNETT, CAROL: San Antonio, TX, Apr. 26, 1933. UCLA.

BURNS, CATHERINE: NYC, Sept. 25, 1945. AADA.

BURNS, GEORGE (Nathan Birnbaum): NYC, Jan. 20, 1896.

BURR, RAYMOND: New Westminster, B.C., Can., May 21, 1917. Stanford, U. Cal., Columbia.

BURSTYN, ELLEN (Edna Rae Gillooly): Detroit, MI, Dec. 7, 1932.

BURTON, RICHARD (Richard Jenkins): Pontrhydyfen, S. Wales, Nov. 10, 1925. Oxford.

BUSEY, GARY: Tulsa, OK, 1944.

BUTTONS, RED (Aaron Chwatt): NYC, Feb. 5, 1919.

BUZZI, RUTH: Wequetequock, RI, July 24, 1936. Pasadena Playhouse.

BYGRAVES, MAX: London, Oct. 16, 1922. St. Joseph's School.

BYRNES, EDD: NYC, July 30, 1933. Haaren High.

CAAN, JAMES: Bronx, NY, Mar. 26, 1939.

CABOT, SUSAN: Boston, July 6, 1927.

CAESAR, SID: Yonkers, NY, Sept. 8, 1922.

CAGNEY, JAMES: NYC, July 17, 1899. Columbia.

CAGNEY, JEANNE: NYC, Mar. 25, 1919. Hunter.

CAINE, MICHAEL (Maurice Michelwhite): London, Mar. 14, 1933.

CAINE, SHAKIRA (Baksh): Guyana, Feb. 23, 1947. Indian Trust Col.

CALHOUN, RORY (Francis Timothy Durgin): Los Angeles, Aug. 8, 1922.

CALLAN, MICHAEL (Martin Calinieff): Philadelphia, Nov. 22, 1935.

CALVERT, PHYLLIS: London, Feb. 18, 1917. Margaret Morris School.

CALVET, CORRINE (Corrine Dibos): Paris, Apr. 30, 1929. U. Paris.

CAMERON, ROD (Rod Cox): Calgary, Alberta, Can., Dec. 7, 1912.

CAMP, COLLEEN: San Francisco, 1953.

CAMPBELL, GLEN: Delight, AR, Apr. 22, 1935.

CANALE, GIANNA MARIA: Reggio Calabria, Italy, Sept. 12.

CANNON, DYAN (Samille Diane Friesen): Tacoma, WA, Jan. 4, 1929.

CANOVA, JUDY: Jacksonville, FL, Nov. 20, 1916.

CANTU, DOLORES: 1957, San Antonio, TX.

CAPERS, VIRGINIA: Sumter, SC, 1925. Juilliard.

CAPUCINE (Germaine Lefebvre): Toulon, France, Jan. 6, 1935.

CARA, IRENE: NYC, Mar. 18, 1958.

CARDINALE, CLAUDIA: Tunis, N. Africa, Apr. 15, 1939. College Paul Cambon.

CAREY, HARRY, JR.: Saugus, CA, May 16, 1921. Black Fox Military Academy.

CAREY, MACDONALD: Sioux City, IA, Mar. 15, 1913. U. of Wisc., U. Iowa.

CAREY, PHILIP: Hackensack, NJ, July 15, 1925. U. Miami.

CARMEN, JULIE: Mt. Vernon, NY, Apr. 4, 1954.

CARMICHAEL, IAN: Hull, Eng., June 18, 1920. Scarborough Col.

CARNE, JUDY (Joyce Botterill): Northampton, Eng., 1939. Bush-Davis Theatre School.

CARNEY, ART: Mt. Vernon, NY, Nov. 4, 1918.

CARON, LESLIE: Paris, July 1, 1931. Nat'l Conservatory, Paris.

CARPENTER, CARLETON: Bennington, VT, July 10, 1926. Northwestern.

CARR, VIKKI (Florence Cardona): July 19, 1942. San Fernando Col.

CARRADINE, DAVID: Hollywood, Dec. 8, 1936. San Francisco State.

CARRADINE, JOHN: NYC, Feb. 5, 1906.

CARRADINE, KEITH: San Mateo, CA, Aug. 8, 1951. Colo. State U.

CARRADINE, ROBERT: San Mateo, CA, 1954.

CARREL, DANY: Tourane, Indochina, Sept. 20, 1936. Marseilles Cons.

CARROLL, DIAHANN (Johnson): NYC, July 17, 1935. NYU.

CARROLL, MADELEINE: West Bromwich, Eng., Feb. 26, 1902. Birmingham U.

CARROLL, PAT: Shreveport, LA, May 5, 1927. Catholic U.

CARSON, JOHN DAVID: 1951, Calif. Valley Col.

Peggy Cass	Robert Christian	Joanna Cassidy	Bill Cosby	Gretchen Corbett

CARSON, JOHNNY: Corning, IA, Oct. 23, 1925. U. of Neb.

CARSTEN, PETER (Ransenthaler): Weissenberg, Bavaria, Apr. 30, 1929. Munich Akademie.

CASH, ROSALIND: Atlantic City, NJ, Dec. 31, 1938. CCNY.

CASON, BARBARA: Memphis, TN, Nov. 15, 1933. U. Iowa.

CASS, PEGGY (Mary Margaret): Boston, May 21, 1925.

CASSAVETES, JOHN: NYC, Dec. 9, 1929. Colgate College, AADA.

CASSEL, JEAN-PIERRE: Paris, Oct. 27, 1932.

CASSIDY, DAVID: NYC, Apr. 12, 1950.

CASSIDY, JOANNA: Camden, NJ, 1944. Syracuse U.

CASTELLANO, RICHARD: Bronx, NY, Sept. 3, 1934.

CAULFIELD, JOAN: Orange, NJ, June 1, 1922. Columbia U.

CAVANI, LILIANA: Bologna, Italy, Jan. 12, 1937. U. Bologna.

CELI, ADOLFO: Sicily, July 27, 1922. Rome Academy.

CHAKIRIS, GEORGE: Norwood, OH, Sept. 16, 1933.

CHAMBERLAIN, RICHARD: Beverly Hills, CA, March 31, 1935. Pomona.

CHAMPION, MARGE: Los Angeles, Sept. 2, 1925.

CHANNING, CAROL: Seattle, Jan. 31, 1921. Bennington.

CHANNING, STOCKARD (Susan Stockard): NYC, 1944. Radcliffe.

CHAPIN, MILES: NYC, Dec. 6, 1954. HB Studio.

CHAPLIN, GERALDINE: Santa Monica, CA, July 31, 1944. Royal Ballet.

CHAPLIN, SYDNEY: Los Angeles, Mar. 31, 1926. Lawrenceville.

CHARISSE, CYD (Tula Ellice Finklea): Amarillo, TX, Mar. 3, 1922. Hollywood Professional School.

CHASE, CHEVY (Cornelius Crane Chase): NYC, 1943.

CHER (Cherlin Sarkesian): May 20, 1946, El Centro, CA.

CHIARI, WALTER: Verona, Italy, 1930.

CHRISTIAN, LINDA (Blanca Rosa Welter): Tampico, Mex., Nov. 13, 1923.

CHRISTIAN, ROBERT: Los Angeles, Dec. 27, 1939. UCLA.

CHRISTIE, JULIE: Chukua, Assam, India, Apr. 14, 1941.

CHRISTOPHER, DENNIS (Carrelli): Philadelphia, PA, 1955. Temple U.

CHRISTOPHER, JORDAN: Youngstown, OH, Oct. 23, 1940. Kent State.

CHURCHILL, SARAH: London, Oct. 7, 1916.

CILENTO, DIANE: Queensland, Australia, Oct. 5, 1933. AADA.

CLAPTON, ERIC: London, Mar. 30, 1945.

CLARK, DANE: NYC, Feb. 18, 1915. Cornell, Johns Hopkins U.

CLARK, DICK: Mt. Vernon, NY, Nov. 30, 1929. Syracuse U.

CLARK, MAE: Philadelphia, Aug. 16, 1910.

CLARK, PETULA: Epsom, England, Nov. 15, 1932.

CLARK, SUSAN: Sarnid, Ont., Can., Mar. 8. RADA.

CLAYBURGH, JILL: NYC, Apr. 30, 1944. Sarah Lawrence.

CLERY, CORINNE: Italy, 1950.

CLOONEY, ROSEMARY: Maysville, KY, May 23, 1928.

COBURN, JAMES: Laurel, NB, Aug. 31, 1928. LACC.

COCA, IMOGENE: Philadelphia, Nov. 18, 1908.

COCO, JAMES: NYC, Mar. 21, 1929.

CODY, KATHLEEN: Bronx, NY, Oct. 30, 1953.

COLBERT, CLAUDETTE (Lily Chauchoin): Paris, Sept. 15, 1903. Art Students League.

COLE, GEORGE: London, Apr. 22, 1925.

COLEMAN, GARY: Zion, IL., 1968.

COLLINS, JOAN: London, May 23, 1933. Francis Holland School.

COLLINS, STEPHEN: Des Moines, IA, Oct. 1, 1947. Amherst.

COMER, ANJANETTE: Dawson, TX, Aug. 7, 1942. Baylor, Tex. U.

CONANT, OLIVER: NYC, Nov. 15, 1955. Dalton.

CONAWAY, JEFF: NYC, Oct. 5, 1950. NYC.

CONNERY, SEAN: Edinburgh, Scot., Aug. 25, 1930.

CONNORS, CHUCK (Kevin Joseph Connors): Brooklyn, Apr. 10, 1921. Seton Hall College.

CONNORS, MIKE (Krekor Ohanian): Fresno, CA, Aug. 15, 1925. UCLA.

CONRAD, WILLIAM: Louisville, KY, Sept. 27, 1920.

CONVERSE, FRANK: St. Louis, MO, May 22, 1938. Carnegie Tech.

CONVY, BERT: St. Louis, MO, July 23, 1935. UCLA.

CONWAY, KEVIN: NYC, May 29, 1942.

CONWAY, TIM (Thomas Daniel): Willoughby, OH, Dec. 15, 1933. Bowling Green State.

COOGAN, JACKIE: Los Angeles, Oct. 25, 1914. Villanova College.

COOK, ELISHA, JR.: San Francisco, Dec. 26, 1907. St. Albans.

COOPER, BEN: Hartford, CT, Sept. 30, 1932. Columbia U.

COOPER, JACKIE: Los Angeles, Sept. 15, 1921.

COOTE, ROBERT: London, Feb. 4, 1909. Hurstpierpont College.

CORBETT, GRETCHEN: Portland, OR, Aug. 13, 1947. Carnegie Tech.

CORBY, ELLEN (Hansen): Racine, WI, June 13, 1913.

CORCORAN, DONNA: Quincy, MA, Sept. 29, 1942.

CORD, ALEX (Viespi): Floral Park, NY, Aug. 3, 1931. NYU, Actors Studio.

CORDAY, MARA (Marilyn Watts): Santa Monica, CA, Jan. 3, 1932.

COREY, JEFF: NYC, Aug. 10, 1914. Fagin School.

CORLAN, ANTHONY: Cork City, Ire., May 9, 1947. Birmingham School of Dramatic Arts.

CORLEY, AL: Missouri, 1956. Actors Studio.

CORNTHWAITE, ROBERT: Apr. 28, 1917. USC.

CORRI, ADRIENNE: Glasgow, Scot., Nov. 13, 1933. RADA.

CORTESA, VALENTINA: Milan, Italy, Jan. 1, 1925.

COSBY, BILL: Philadelphia, July 12, 1937. Temple U.

COSTER, NICOLAS: London, Dec. 3, 1934. Neighborhood Playhouse.

COTTEN, JOSEPH: Petersburg, VA, May 13, 1905.

COURTENAY, TOM: Hull, Eng., Feb. 25, 1937. RADA.

COURTLAND, JEROME: Knoxville, TN, Dec. 27, 1926.

CRABBE, BUSTER (LARRY) (Clarence Linden): Oakland, CA, Feb. 7, 1908. USC.

CRAIG, JAMES (James H. Meador): Nashville, TN, Feb. 4, 1912. Rice Inst.

CRAIG, MICHAEL: India, Jan. 27, 1929.

CRAIN, JEANNE: Barstow, CA, May 25, 1925.

CRAWFORD, BRODERICK: Philadelphia, Dec. 9, 1911.

Richard Crenna	Tyne Daly	Brad Davis	Beverly D'Angelo	Bradford Dillman

CRENNA, RICHARD: Los Angeles, Nov. 30, 1926. USC.

CRISTAL, LINDA (Victoria Moya): Buenos Aires, Feb. 25, 1934.

CROSBY, HARRY: Los Angeles, CA, Aug. 8, 1958.

CROSBY, KATHRYN GRANT: (see Kathryn Grant)

CROSBY, MARY FRANCES: Calif., Sept. 14, 1959.

CROSS, MURPHY (Mary Jane): Laurelton, MD, June 22, 1950.

CROUSE, LINDSAY ANN: NYC, May 12, 1948. Radcliffe.

CROWLEY, PAT: Olyphant, PA, Sept. 17, 1932.

CRYSTAL, BILLY: NYC, 1948.

CULLUM, JOHN: Knoxville, TN, Mar. 2, 1930. U. Tenn.

CULP, ROBERT: Oakland, CA., Aug. 16, 1930. U. Wash.

CULVER, CALVIN: Canandaigua, NY, 1943.

CUMMINGS, CONSTANCE: Seattle, WA, May 15, 1910.

CUMMINGS, QUINN: Hollywood, Aug. 13, 1967.

CUMMINGS, ROBERT: Joplin, MO, June 9, 1910. Carnegie Tech.

CUMMINS, PEGGY: Prestatyn, N. Wales, Dec. 18, 1926. Alexandra School.

CURTIS, KEENE: Salt Lake City, UT, Feb. 15, 1925. U. Utah.

CURTIS, TONY (Bernard Schwartz): NYC, June 3, 1924.

CUSACK, CYRIL: Durban, S. Africa, Nov. 26, 1910. Univ. Col.

CUSHING, PETER: Kenley, Surrey, Eng., May 26, 1913.

DAHL, ARLENE: Minneapolis, Aug. 11, 1924. U. Minn.

DALLESANDRO, JOE: Pensacola, FL, Dec. 31, 1948.

DALTON, TIMOTHY: Wales, 1945. RADA.

DALTREY, ROGER: London, Mar. 1, 1945.

DALY, TYNE: NYC, 1947. AMDA.

DAMONE, VIC (Vito Farinola): Brooklyn, June 12, 1928.

D'ANGELO, BEVERLY: Columbus, OH., 1954.

DANIELS, WILLIAM: Bklyn, Mar. 31, 1927. Northwestern.

DANNER, BLYTHE: Philadelphia, PA. Bard Col.

DANO, ROYAL: NYC, Nov. 16, 1922. NYU.

DANTE, MICHAEL (Ralph Vitti): Stamford, CT, 1935. U. Miami.

DANTINE, HELMUT: Vienna, Oct. 7, 1918. U. Calif.

DANTON, RAY: NYC, Sept. 19, 1931. Carnegie Tech.

DARBY, KIM: (Deborah Zerby): North Hollywood, CA, July 8, 1948.

DARCEL, DENISE (Denise Billecard): Paris, Sept. 8, 1925. U. Dijon.

DARREN, JAMES: Philadelphia, June 8, 1936. Stella Adler School.

DARRIEUX, DANIELLE: Bordeaux, France, May 1, 1917. Lycee LaTour.

DA SILVA, HOWARD: Cleveland, OH, May 4, 1909. Carnegie Tech.

DAVIDSON, JOHN: Pittsburgh, Dec. 13, 1941. Denison U.

DAVIES, RUPERT: Liverpool, Eng., 1916.

DAVIS, BETTE: Lowell, MA, Apr. 5, 1908. John Murray Anderson Dramatic School.

DAVIS, BRAD: Fla., 1950. AADA.

DAVIS, MAC: Lubbock, TX, 1942.

DAVIS, NANCY (Anne Frances Robbins): NYC July 8, 1921, Smith Col.

DAVIS, OSSIE: Cogdell, GA, Dec. 18, 1917. Howard U.

DAVIS, SAMMY, JR.: NYC, Dec. 8, 1925.

DAY, DENNIS (Eugene Dennis McNulty): NYC, May 21, 1917. Manhattan College.

DAY, DORIS (Doris Kappelhoff): Cincinnati, Apr. 3, 1924.

DAY, LARAINE (Johnson): Roosevelt, UT, Oct. 13, 1917.

DAYAN, ASSEF: Israel, 1945. U. Jerusalem.

DEAN, JIMMY: Plainview, TX, Aug. 10, 1928.

DeCARLO, YVONNE (Peggy Yvonne Middleton): Vancouver, B.C., Can., Sept. 1, 1922. Vancouver School of Drama.

DEE, FRANCES: Los Angeles, Nov. 26, 1907. Chicago U.

DEE, JOEY (Joseph Di Nicola): Passaic, NJ, June 11, 1940. Patterson State College.

DEE, RUBY: Cleveland, OH, Oct. 27, 1924. Hunter Col.

DEE, SANDRA (Alexandra Zuck): Bayonne, NJ, Apr. 23, 1942.

DeFORE, DON: Cedar Rapids, IA, Aug. 25, 1917. U. Iowa.

DeHAVEN, GLORIA: Los Angeles, July 23, 1923.

DeHAVILLAND, OLIVIA: Tokyo, Japan, July 1, 1916. Notre Dame Convent School.

DELL, GABRIEL: Barbados, BWI, Oct. 7, 1930.

DELON, ALAIN: Sceaux, Fr., Nov. 8, 1935.

DELORME, DANIELE: Paris, Oct. 9, 1927. Sorbonne.

DEL RIO, DOLORES: (Dolores Ansunsolo): Durango, Mex., Aug. 3, 1905. St. Joseph's Convent.

DeLUISE, DOM: Brooklyn, Aug. 1, 1933. Tufts Col.

DEMAREST, WILLIAM: St. Paul, MN, Feb. 27, 1892.

DEMONGEOT, MYLENE: Nice, France, Sept. 29, 1938.

DENEUVE, CATHERINE: Paris, Oct. 22, 1943.

DeNIRO, ROBERT: NYC, Aug. 17, 1943. Stella Adler.

DENISON, MICHAEL: Doncaster, York, Eng., Nov. 1, 1915. Oxford.

DENNER, CHARLES: Tarnow, Poland, May 29, 1926.

DENNIS, SANDY: Hastings, NB, Apr. 27, 1937. Actors Studio.

DEREK, BO (Mary Cathleen Collins): Long Beach, CA, 1957.

DEREK, JOHN: Hollywood, Aug. 12, 1926.

DERN, BRUCE: Chicago, June 4, 1936. U Pa.

DEWAERE, PATRICK: Brittany, FR., 1947.

DEWHURST, COLLEEN: Montreal, June 3, 1926. Lawrence U.

DEXTER, ANTHONY (Walter Reinhold Alfred Fleischmann): Talmadge, NB, Jan. 19, 1919. U. Iowa.

DeYOUNG, CLIFF: Los Angeles, CA, Feb. 12, 1945. Cal State.

DHIEGH, KHIGH: New Jersey, 1910.

DICKINSON, ANGIE: Kulm, ND, Sept. 30, 1932. Glendale College.

DIETRICH, MARLENE (Maria Magdalene von Losch): Berlin, Ger., Dec. 27, 1901. Berlin Music Academy.

DILLER, PHYLLIS: Lima, OH, July 17, 1917. Bluffton College.

DILLMAN, BRADFORD: San Francisco, Apr. 14, 1930. Yale.

DILLON, MATT: Larchmont, NY 1964, AADA.

DILLON, MELINDA: Hope, AR, Oct. 13, 1939. Goodman Theatre School.

DOBSON, TAMARA: Baltimore, MD, 1947. Md. Inst. of Art.

DOMERGUE, FAITH: New Orleans, June 16, 1925.

DONAHUE, TROY (Merle Johnson): NYC, Jan. 27, 1937. Columbia U.

DONAT, PETER: Nova Scotia, Jan. 20, 1928. Yale.

DONNELL, JEFF (Jean Donnell): South Windham, ME, July 10, 1921. Yale Drama School.

| Lesley-Anne Down | Michael Douglas | Sandy Duncan | Sam Elliott | Farrah Fawcett |

DONNELLY, RUTH: Trenton, NJ, May 17, 1896.

DOOHAN, JAMES: Vancouver, BC, Mar. 3. Neighborhood Playhouse.

DOOLEY, PAUL: Parkersburg, WV, Feb. 22, 1928. U WV.

DORS, DIANA (Fluck): Swindon, Wilshire, Eng., Oct. 23, 1931. London Academy of Music.

D'ORSAY, FIFI: Montreal, Can., Apr. 16, 1904.

DOUGLAS, KIRK (Issur Danielovitch): Amsterdam, NY, Dec. 9, 1916. St. Lawrence U.

DOUGLAS, MICHAEL: Hollywood, Sept. 25, 1944. U. Cal.

DOURIF, BRAD: Huntington, WV, Mar. 18, 1950. Marshall U.

DOVE, BILLIE: NYC, May 14, 1904.

DOWN, LESLEY-ANN: London, Mar. 17, 1954.

DRAKE, BETSY: Paris, Sept. 11, 1923.

DRAKE, CHARLES (Charles Rupert): NYC, Oct. 2, 1914. Nichols College.

DREW, ELLEN (formerly Terry Ray): Kansas City, MO, Nov. 23, 1915.

DREYFUSS, RICHARD: Brooklyn, NY, 1947.

DRIVAS, ROBERT: Chicago, Oct. 7, 1938. U. Chi.

DRU, JOANNE (Joanne LaCock): Logan, WV, Jan. 31, 1923. John Robert Powers School.

DUBBINS, DON: Brooklyn, NY, June 28.

DUFF, HOWARD: Bremerton, WA, Nov. 24, 1917.

DUFFY, PATRICK: Montana, 1949. U Wash.

DUKE, PATTY: NYC, Dec. 14, 1946.

DULLEA, KEIR: Cleveland, NJ, May 30, 1936. Neighborhood Playhouse, SF State Col.

DUNAWAY, FAYE: Bascom, FL, Jan, 14, 1941. Fla. U.

DUNCAN, SANDY: Henderson, TX, Feb. 20, 1946. Len Morris Col.

DUNNE, IRENE: Louisville, KY, Dec. 20, 1898. Chicago College of Music.

DUNNOCK, MILDRED: Baltimore, Jan. 25, 1900. Johns Hopkins and Columbia U.

DUPEREY, ANNY: Paris, 1947.

DURBIN, DEANNA (Edna): Winnipeg, Can., Dec. 4, 1921.

DURNING, CHARLES: Highland Falls, NY, Feb. 28, 1933. NYU.

DUSSOLLIER, ANDRE: Annecy, France, Feb. 17, 1946.

DUVALL, ROBERT: San Diego, CA, 1930. Principia Col.

DUVALL, SHELLEY: Houston, TX, 1950.

EASTON, ROBERT: Milwaukee, Nov. 23, 1930. U. Texas.

EASTWOOD, CLINT: San Francisco, May 31, 1930. LACC.

EATON, SHIRLEY: London, 1937. Aida Foster School.

EBSEN, BUDDY (Christian, Jr.): Belleville, IL, Apr. 2, 1910. U. Fla.

ECKEMYR, AGNETA: Karlsborg, Swed., July 2. Actors Studio.

EDEN, BARBARA (Moorhead): Tucson, AZ, 1934.

EDWARDS, VINCE: NYC, July 9, 1928. AADA.

EGAN, RICHARD: San Francisco, July 29, 1923. Stanford U.

EGGAR, SAMANTHA: London, Mar. 5, 1939.

EICHHORN, LISA: Reading, PA, 1952. Queens Ont. U. RADA.

EKBERG, ANITA: Malmo, Sweden, Sept. 29, 1931.

EKLAND, BRITT: Stockholm, Swed., 1942.

ELIZONDO, HECTOR: NYC, Dec. 22, 1936.

ELLIOTT, DENHOLM: London, May 31, 1922. Malvern College.

ELLIOTT, SAM: Sacramento, CA, 1944. U. Ore.

ELY, RON (Ronald Pierce): Hereford, TX, June 21, 1938.

EMERSON, FAYE: Elizabeth, LA, July 8, 1917. San Diego State Col.

ERDMAN, RICHARD: Enid, OK, June 1, 1925.

ERICKSON, LEIF: Alameda, CA, Oct. 27, 1911. U. Calif.

ERICSON, JOHN: Dusseldorf, Ger., Sept. 25, 1926. AADA.

ESMOND, CARL: Vienna, June 14, 1906. U. Vienna.

EVANS, DALE (Francis Smith): Uvalde, TX, Oct. 31, 1912.

EVANS, GENE: Holbrook, AZ, July 11, 1922.

EVANS, MAURICE: Dorchester, Eng., June 3, 1901.

EVERETT, CHAD (Ray Cramton): South Bend, IN, June 11, 1936.

EWELL, TOM (Yewell Tompkins): Owensboro, KY, Apr. 29, 1909. U. Wisc.

FABARES, SHELLEY: Los Angeles, Jan. 19, 1944.

FABIAN (Fabian Forte): Philadelphia, Feb. 6, 1940.

FABRAY, NANETTE (Ruby Nanette Fabares): San Diego, Oct. 27, 1920.

FAIRBANKS, DOUGLAS JR.: NYC, Dec. 9, 1907. Collegiate School.

FAIRCHILD, MORGAN: (Patsy McClenny) Dallas, TX., 1950.

FALK, PETER: NYC, Sept. 16, 1927. New School.

FARENTINO, JAMES: Brooklyn, Feb. 24, 1938. AADA.

FARINA, SANDY (Sandra Feldman): Newark, NJ, 1955.

FARR, DEREK: London, Feb. 7, 1912.

FARR, FELICIA: Westchester, NY, Oct. 4, 1932. Penn State Col.

FARRELL, CHARLES: Onset Bay, MA, Aug. 9, 1901. Boston U.

FARROW, MIA: Los Angeles, Feb. 9, 1945.

FAULKNER, GRAHAM: London, Sept. 26, 1947. Webber-Douglas.

FAWCETT, FARRAH: Texas, Feb. 2, 1947.

FAYE, ALICE (Ann Leppert): NYC, May 5, 1912.

FEINSTEIN, ALAN: NYC, Sept. 8, 1941.

FELDON, BARBARA (Hall): Pittsburgh, Mar. 12, 1941. Carnegie Tech.

FELLOWS, EDITH: Boston, May 20, 1923.

FERRELL, CONCHATA: Charleston, WV, Mar. 28, 1943. Marshall U.

FERRER, JOSE: Santurce, P.R., Jan. 8, 1909. Princeton U.

FERRER, MEL: Elberon, NJ, Aug. 25, 1917. Princeton U.

FERRIS, BARBARA: London, 1943.

FERZETTI, GABRIELE: Italy, 1927. Rome Acad. of Drama.

FIELD, SALLY: Pasadena, CA, Nov. 6, 1946.

FIGUEROA, RUBEN: NYC 1958.

FINNEY, ALBERT: Salford, Lancashire, Eng., May 9, 1936. RADA.

FIRTH, PETER: Bradford, Eng., Oct. 27, 1953.

FISHER, CARRIE: Los Angeles, CA, 1957. London Central School of Drama.

FISHER, EDDIE: Philadelphia, Aug. 10, 1928.

FITZGERALD, GERALDINE: Dublin, Ire., Nov. 24, 1914. Dublin Art School.

FLANNERY, SUSAN: Jersey City, NJ, July 31, 1943.

FLAVIN, JAMES: Portland, ME, May 14, 1906. West Point.

FLEMING, RHONDA (Marilyn Louis): Los Angeles, Aug. 10, 1922.

221

FLEMYNG, ROBERT: Liverpool, Eng., Jan. 3, 1912. Haileybury Col.

FLETCHER, LOUISE: Birmingham, AL, July 1934.

FOCH, NINA: Leyden, Holland, Apr. 20, 1924.

FOLDI, ERZSEBET: Queens, NY, 1967.

FONDA, HENRY: Grand Island, NB, May 16, 1905. Minn. U.

FONDA, JANE: NYC, Dec. 21, 1937. Vassar.

FONDA, PETER: NYC, Feb. 23, 1939. U. Omaha.

FONTAINE, JOAN: Tokyo, Japan, Oct. 22, 1917.

FORD, GLENN (Gwyllyn Samuel Newton Ford): Quebec, Can., May 1, 1916.

FORD, HARRISON: Chicago, IL, July 13, 1942. Ripon Col.

FOREST, MARK (Lou Degni): Brooklyn, Jan. 1933.

FORREST, STEVE: Huntsville, TX, Sept. 29, 1924. UCLA.

FORSLUND, CONNIE: San Diego, CA, June 19, 1950, NYU.

FORSTER, ROBERT (Foster, Jr.): Rochester, NY, July 13, 1941. Rochester U.

FORSYTHE, JOHN: Penn's Grove, NJ, Jan. 29, 1918.

FOSTER, JODIE: Bronx, NY, 1963.

FOX, EDWARD: London, 1937, RADA.

FOX, JAMES: London, 1939.

FOXWORTH, ROBERT: Houston, TX, Nov. 1, 1941. Carnegie Tech.

FOXX, REDD: St. Louis, MO, Dec. 9, 1922.

FRANCIOSA, ANTHONY (Papaleo): NYC, Oct. 25, 1928.

FRANCIS, ANNE: Ossining, NY, Sept. 16, 1932.

FRANCIS, ARLENE (Arlene Kazanjian): Boston, Oct. 20, 1908. Finch School.

FRANCIS, CONNIE (Constance Franconero): Newark, NJ, Dec. 12, 1938.

FRANCISCUS, JAMES: Clayton, MO, Jan. 31, 1934. Yale.

FRANCKS, DON: Vancouver, Can., Feb. 28, 1932.

FRANK, JEFFREY: Jackson Heights, NY, 1965.

FRANKLIN, PAMELA: Tokyo, Feb. 4, 1950.

FRANZ, ARTHUR: Perth Amboy, NJ, Feb. 29, 1920. Blue Ridge College.

FRANZ, EDUARD: Milwaukee, WI, Oct. 31, 1902.

FRAZIER, SHEILA: NYC, 1949.

FREEMAN, AL, JR.: San Antonio, TX, 1934. CCLA.

FREEMAN, MONA: Baltimore, MD, June 9, 1926.

FREY, LEONARD: Brooklyn, Sept. 4, 1938, Neighborhood Playhouse.

FULLER, PENNY: Durham, NC, 1940. Northwestern U.

FURNEAUX, YVONNE: Lille, France, 1928. Oxford U.

GABEL, MARTIN: Philadelphia, June 19, 1912. AADA.

GABOR, EVA: Budapest, Hungary, Feb. 11, 1920.

GABOR, ZSA ZSA (Sari Gabor): Budapest, Hungary, Feb. 6, 1918.

GALLAGHER, PETER: Armonk, NY, 1956, Tufts U.

GAM, RITA: Pittsburgh, PA, Apr. 2, 1928.

GARBER, VICTOR: Montreal, Can., Mar. 16, 1949.

GARBO, GRETA (Greta Gustafson): Stockholm, Sweden, Sept. 18, 1905.

GARDENIA, VINCENT: Naples, Italy, Jan. 7, 1922.

GARDNER, AVA: Smithfield, NC, Dec. 24, 1922. Atlantic Christian College.

GARFIELD, ALLEN: Newark, NJ, Nov. 22, 1939. Actors Studio.

GARLAND, BEVERLY: Santa Cruz, CA, Oct. 17, 1930. Glendale Col.

GARNER, JAMES (James Baumgarner): Norman, OK, Apr. 7, 1928. Okla. U.

GARNER, PEGGY ANN: Canton, OH, Feb. 3, 1932.

GARR, TERI: Lakewood, OH, 1952.

GARRETT, BETTY: St. Joseph, MO, May 23, 1919. Annie Wright Seminary.

GARRISON, SEAN: NYC, Oct. 19, 1937.

GARSON, GREER: Ireland, Sept. 29, 1906.

GASSMAN, VITTORIO: Genoa, Italy, Sept. 1, 1922. Rome Academy of Dramatic Art.

GAVIN, JOHN: Los Angeles, Apr. 8, 1935. Stanford U.

GAYNOR, JANET: Philadelphia, Oct. 6, 1906.

GAYNOR, MITZI (Francesca Marlene Von Gerber): Chicago, Sept. 4, 1930.

GAZZARA, BEN: NYC, Aug. 28, 1930. Actors Studio.

GEESON, JUDY: Arundel, Eng., Sept. 10, 1948. Corona.

GERARD, GIL: Little Rock, AR, 1940.

GERE, RICHARD: Philadelphia, PA, Aug. 29, 1949. U. Mass.

GERROLL, DANIEL: London, Oct. 16, 1951. Central.

GHOLSON, JULIE: Birmingham, AL, June 4, 1958.

GHOSTLEY, ALICE: Eve, MO, Aug. 14, 1926. Okla U.

GIANNINI, GIANCARLO: Spezia, Italy, Aug. 1, 1942. Rome Acad. of Drama.

GIBSON, MEL: Oneonta, NY. NIDA.

GIELGUD, JOHN: London, Apr. 14, 1904. RADA.

GILFORD, JACK: NYC, July 25.

GILLIS, ANNE (Alma O'Connor): Little Rock, AR, Feb. 12, 1927.

GILLMORE, MARGALO: London, May 31, 1897. AADA.

GILMORE, VIRGINIA (Sherman Poole): Del Monte, CA, July 26, 1919. U. Calif.

GINGOLD, HERMIONE: London, Dec. 9, 1897.

GISH, LILLIAN: Springfield, OH, Oct. 14, 1896.

GLASER, PAUL MICHAEL: Boston, MA, 1943. Boston U.

GLASS, RON: Evansville, IN, 1946.

GLEASON, JACKIE: Brooklyn, Feb. 26, 1916.

GLENN, SCOTT: Pittsburgh, PA, Jan. 26, 1942; William and Mary Col.

GODDARD, PAULETTE (Levy): Great Neck, NY, June 3, 1911.

GOLDBLUM, JEFF: Pittsburgh, PA, Oct. 22, 1952. Neighborhood Playhouse.

GOLDEN, ANNIE: NYC, 1952.

GONZALES-GONZALEZ, PEDRO: Aguilares, TX, Dec. 21, 1926.

GOODMAN, DODY: Columbus, OH, Oct. 28, 1915.

GORDON, GALE (Aldrich): NYC, Feb. 2, 1906.

GORDON, KEITH: NYC, Feb. 3, 1961.

GORDON, RUTH (Jones): Wollaston, MA, Oct. 30, 1896. AADA.

GORING, MARIUS: Newport, Isle of Wight, 1912. Cambridge, Old Vic.

GORMAN, CLIFF: Jamaica, NY, Oct. 13, 1936. NYU.

GORTNER, MARJOE: Long Beach, CA, 1944.

GOSSETT, LOUIS: Brooklyn, May 27, 1936. NYU.

GOULD, ELLIOTT (Goldstein): Brooklyn, Aug. 29, 1938. Columbia U.

GOULD, HAROLD: Schenectady, NY, Dec. 10, 1923. Cornell.

GOULET, ROBERT: Lawrence, MA, Nov. 26, 1933. Edmonton.

GRANGER, FARLEY: San Jose, CA, July 1, 1925.

GRANGER, STEWART (James Stewart): London, May 6, 1913. Webber-Douglas School of Acting.

GRANT, CARY (Archibald Alexander Leach): Bristol, Eng., Jan. 18, 1904.

GRANT, DAVID MARSHALL: Westport, CT, 1955. Yale.

GRANT, KATHRYN (Olive Grandstaff): Houston, TX, Nov. 25, 1933. UCLA.

GRANT, LEE: NYC, Oct. 31, 1930. Juilliard.

GRANVILLE, BONITA: NYC, Feb. 2, 1923.

GRAVES, PETER (Aurness): Minneapolis, Mar. 18, 1926. U. Minn.

GRAY, COLEEN (Doris Jensen): Staplehurst, NB, Oct. 23, 1922. Hamline U.

GRAYSON, KATHRYN (Zelma Hedrick): Winston-Salem, NC, Feb. 9, 1922.

GREENE, ELLEN: NYC, Feb. 22. Ryder Col.

GREENE, LORNE: Ottawa, Can., Feb. 12, 1915. Queens U.

GREENE, RICHARD: Plymouth, Eng., Aug. 25, 1914. Cardinal Vaughn School.

GREENWOOD, JOAN: London, Mar. 4, 1919. RADA.

GREER, JANE: Washington, DC, Sept. 9, 1924.

GREER, MICHAEL: Galesburg, IL, Apr. 20, 1943.

GREY, JOEL (Katz): Cleveland, OH, Apr. 11, 1932.

GREY, VIRGINIA: Los Angeles, Mar. 22, 1917.

GRIEM, HELMUT: Hamburg, Ger. U. Hamburg.

GRIFFITH, ANDY: Mt. Airy, NC, June 1, 1926. UNC.

GRIFFITH, MELANIE: NYC, Aug. 9, 1957. Pierce Col.

GRIMES, GARY: San Francisco, June 2, 1955.

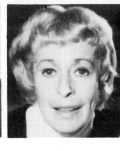

Robert
Forster

Teri
Garr

George
Grizzard

Eileen
Heckart

Dustin
Hoffman

GRIMES, TAMMY: Lynn, MA, Jan. 30, 1934. Stephens Col.

GRIZZARD, GEORGE: Roanoke Rapids, NC, Apr. 1, 1928. UNC.

GRODIN, CHARLES: Pittsburgh, PA, Apr. 21, 1935.

GROH, DAVID: NYC, May 21, 1939. Brown U., LAMDA.

GUARDINO, HARRY: Brooklyn, Dec. 23, 1925. Haaren High.

GUINNESS, ALEC: London, Apr. 2, 1914. Pembroke Lodge School.

GUNN, MOSES: St. Louis, MO, Oct. 2, 1929. Tenn. State U.

GUTTENBERG, STEVEN: Brooklyn, NY, Aug. 1958. UCLA.

GWILLIM, DAVID: Plymouth, Eng., Dec. 15, 1948. RADA.

HACKETT, BUDDY (Leonard Hacker): Brooklyn, Aug. 31, 1924.

HACKETT, JOAN: NYC, May 1, 1939. Actors Studio.

HACKMAN, GENE: San Bernardino, CA, Jan. 30, 1931.

HADDON, DALE: Montreal, Can., May 26, 1949. Neighborhood Playhouse.

HAGMAN, LARRY (Hageman): Texas, 1939. Bard Col.

HALE, BARBARA: DeKalb, IL, Apr. 18, 1922. Chicago Academy of Fine Arts.

HALL, ALBERT: Boothton, AL, Nov. 10, 1937. Columbia.

HAMILL, MARK: Oakland, CA, Sept. 25, 1952. LACC.

HAMILTON, GEORGE: Memphis, TN, Aug. 12, 1939. Hackley.

HAMILTON, MARGARET: Cleveland, OH, Dec. 9, 1902. Hathaway-Brown School.

HAMILTON, NEIL: Lynn, MA, Sept. 9, 1899.

HAMLIN, HARRY: Pasadena, CA, 1952. Yale

HAMPSHIRE, SUSAN: London, May 12, 1941.

HARDIN, TY (Orison Whipple Hungerford II): NYC, June 1, 1930.

HAREWOOD, DORIAN: Dayton, OH, Aug. 6. U Cinn.

HARMON, MARK: Los Angeles, CA, 1951; UCLA.

HARPER, VALERIE: Suffern, NY, Aug. 22, 1940.

HARRINGTON, PAT: NYC, Aug. 13, 1929. Fordham U.

HARRIS, BARBARA (Sandra Markowitz): Evanston, IL, 1937.

HARRIS, JULIE: Grosse Pointe, MI, Dec. 2, 1925. Yale Drama School.

HARRIS, RICHARD: Limerick, Ire., Oct. 1, 1930. London Acad.

HARRIS, ROSEMARY: Ashby, Eng., Sept. 19, 1930. RADA.

HARRISON, GREG: Catalina Island, CA, 1950; Actors Studio.

HARRISON, NOEL: London, Jan. 29, 1936.

HARRISON, REX: Huyton, Cheshire, Eng., Mar. 5, 1908.

HARROLD, KATHRYN: Tazewell, VA. 1950. Mills Col.

HARTMAN, DAVID: Pawtucket, RI, May 19, 1942. Duke U.

HARTMAN, ELIZABETH: Youngstown, OH, Dec. 23, 1941. Carnegie Tech.

HASSETT, MARILYN: Los Angeles, CA, 1949.

HAUER, RUTGER: Amsterdam, Hol. 1944.

HAVER, JUNE: Rock Island, IL, June 10, 1926.

HAVOC, JUNE (June Hovick): Seattle, WA, Nov. 8, 1916.

HAWN, GOLDIE: Washington, DC, Nov. 21, 1945.

HAYDEN, LINDA: Stanmore, Eng. Aida Foster School.

HAYDEN, STERLING (John Hamilton): Montclair, NJ, March 26, 1916.

HAYES, HELEN (Helen Brown): Washington, DC, Oct. 10, 1900. Sacred Heart Convent.

HAYS, ROBERT: San Diego, CA, 1948; SD State Col.

HAYWORTH, RITA (Margarita Cansino): NYC, Oct. 17, 1918.

HEARD, JOHN: Washington, DC, Mar. 7, 1946. Clark U.

HEATHERTON, JOEY: NYC, Sept. 14, 1944.

HECKART, EILEEN: Columbus, OH, Mar. 29, 1919. Ohio State U.

HEDISON, DAVID: Providence, RI, May 20, 1929. Brown U.

HEGYES, ROBERT: NJ, May 7, 1951.

HEMMINGS, DAVID: Guilford, Eng. Nov. 18, 1938.

HENDERSON, MARCIA: Andover, MA, July 22, 1932. AADA.

HENDRY, GLORIA: Jacksonville, FL, 1949.

HENNER, MARILU: NYC, Apr. 4, 1953.

HENREID, PAUL: Trieste, Jan. 10, 1908.

HENRY, BUCK (Zuckerman): NYC, 1931. Dartmouth.

HENRY, JUSTIN: Rye, NY, 1971.

HEPBURN, AUDREY: Brussels, Belgium, May 4, 1929.

HEPBURN, KATHARINE: Hartford, CT, Nov. 8, 1907. Bryn Mawr.

HERRMANN, EDWARD: Washington, DC, July 21, 1943. Bucknell, LAMDA.

HERSHEY, BARBARA: see Seagull, Barbara Hershey.

HESTON, CHARLTON: Evanston, IL, Oct. 4, 1922. Northwestern U.

HEWITT, MARTIN: Claremont, Ca, 1960; AADA.

HEYWOOD, ANNE (Violet Pretty): Birmingham, Eng., Dec. 11, 1932.

HICKMAN, DARRYL: Hollywood, CA, July 28, 1930. Loyola U.

HICKMAN, DWAYNE: Los Angeles, May 18, 1934. Loyola U.

HILL, ARTHUR: Saskatchewan, Can., Aug. 1, 1922. U. Brit. Col.

HILL, STEVEN: Seattle, WA, Feb. 24, 1922. U. Wash.

HILL, TERENCE (Mario Girotti): Venice, Italy, Mar. 29, 1941. U. Rome.

HILLER, WENDY: Bramhall, Cheshire, Eng., Aug. 15, 1912. Winceby House School.

HILLIARD, HARRIET: (see Harriet Hilliard Nelson)

HINGLE, PAT: Denver, CO, July 19, 1923. Tex. U.

HIRSCH, JUDD: NYC, Mar. 15, 1935. AADA.

HOFFMAN, DUSTIN: Los Angeles, Aug. 8, 1937. Pasadena Playhouse.

HOLBROOK, HAL (Harold): Cleveland, OH, Feb. 17, 1925. Denison.

HOLLIMAN, EARL: Tennesas Swamp, Delhi, LA, Sept. 11, 1928. UCLA.

HOLM, CELESTE: NYC, Apr. 29, 1919.

HOMEIER, SKIP (George Vincent Homeier): Chicago, Oct. 5, 1930. UCLA.

HOOKS, ROBERT: Washington, DC, Apr. 18, 1937. Temple.

HOPE, BOB: London, May 26, 1903.

HOPPER, DENNIS: Dodge City, KS, May 17, 1936.

HORNE, LENA: Brooklyn, June 30, 1917.

HORTON, ROBERT: Los Angeles, July 29, 1924. UCLA.

HOUGHTON, KATHARINE: Hartford, CT, Mar. 10, 1945. Sarah Lawrence.

HOUSEMAN, JOHN: Bucharest, Sept. 22, 1902.

HOUSER, JERRY: Los Angeles, July 14, 1952. Valley Jr. Col.

HOUSTON, DONALD: Tonypandy, Wales, 1924.

HOVEY, TIM: Los Angeles, June 19, 1945.

HOWARD, KEN: El Centro, CA, Mar. 28, 1944. Yale.

HOWARD, RON: Duncan, OK, Mar. 1, 1954. USC.

HOWARD, RONALD: Norwood, Eng., Apr. 7, 1918. Jesus College.

HOWARD, TREVOR: Kent, Eng., Sept. 29, 1916. RADA.

HOWELLS, URSULA: London, Sept. 17, 1922.

HOWES, SALLY ANN: London, July 20, 1930.

HUDSON, ROCK (Roy Scherer Fitzgerald): Winnetka, IL, Nov. 17, 1924.

HUFFMAN, DAVID: Berwin, IL, May 10, 1945.

HUGHES, BARNARD: Bedford Hills, NY, July 16, 1915. Manhattan Col.

HUGHES, KATHLEEN (Betty von Gerkan): Hollywood, CA, Nov. 14, 1928. UCLA.

HULCE, THOMAS: Plymouth, MI, Dec. 6, 1953. N.C.Sch. of Arts.

HUNNICUTT, GAYLE: Ft. Worth, TX, Feb. 6, 1943. UCLA.

HUNT, MARSHA: Chicago, Oct. 17, 1917.

HUNTER, KIM (Janet Cole): Detroit, Nov. 12, 1922.

HUNTER, TAB (Arthur Gelien): NYC, July 11, 1931.

HUPPERT, ISABELLE: Paris, Fr., Mar. 16, 1955.

HURT, WILLIAM: Washington, D.C., Mar. 20, 1950. Tufts, Juilliard.

HUSSEY, RUTH: Providence , RI, Oct. 30, 1917. U. Mich.

HUSTON, JOHN: Nevada, MO, Aug. 5, 1906.

HUTTON, BETTY (Betty Thornberg): Battle Creek, MI, Feb. 26, 1921.

HUTTON, LAUREN (Mary): Charleston, SC, Nov. 17, 1943. Newcomb Col.

HUTTON, ROBERT (Winne): Kingston, NY, June 11, 1920. Blair Academy.

HUTTON, TIMOTHY: Malibu, CA, Aug. 16, 1960.

HYDE-WHITE, WILFRID: Gloucestershire, Eng., May 13, 1903. RADA.

HYER, MARTHA: Fort Worth, TX, Aug. 10, 1924. Northwestern U.

INGELS, MARTY: Brooklyn, NY, Mar. 9, 1936.

IRELAND, JOHN: Vancouver, B.C., Can., Jan. 30, 1914.

IVES, BURL: Hunt Township, IL, June 14, 1909. Charleston Ill. Teachers College.

JACKSON, ANNE: Alleghany, PA, Sept. 3, 1926. Neighborhood Playhouse.

JACKSON, GLENDA: Hoylake, Cheshire, Eng., May 9, 1936. RADA.

JACOBI, LOU: Toronto, Can., Dec. 28, 1913.

JACOBS, LAWRENCE-HILTON: Virgin Islands, 1954.

JACOBY, SCOTT: Chicago, Nov. 19, 1956.

JAECKEL, RICHARD: Long Beach, NY, Oct. 10, 1926.

JAFFE, SAM: NYC, Mar. 8, 1892.

JAGGER, DEAN: Lima, OH, Nov. 7, 1903. Wabash College.

JAMES, CLIFTON: NYC, May 29, 1921. Ore. U.

JARMAN, CLAUDE, JR.: Nashville, TN, Sept. 27, 1934.

JASON, RICK: NYC, May 21, 1926. AADA.

JEAN, GLORIA (Gloria Jean Schoonover): Buffalo, NY, Apr. 14, 1927.

JEFFREYS, ANNE (Carmichael): Goldsboro, NC, Jan. 26, 1923. Anderson College.

JEFFRIES, LIONEL: London, 1927, RADA.

JERGENS, ADELE: Brooklyn, Nov. 26, 1922.

JOHN, ELTON: (Reginald Dwight) Middlesex, Eng., Mar. 25, 1947. RAM.

JOHNS, GLYNIS: Durban, S. Africa, Oct. 5, 1923.

JOHNSON, CELIA: Richmond, Surrey, Eng., Dec. 18, 1908. RADA.

JOHNSON, PAGE: Welch, WV, Aug. 25, 1930. Ithaca.

JOHNSON, RAFER: Hillsboro, TX, Aug. 18, 1935. UCLA.

JOHNSON, RICHARD: Essex, Eng., 1927. RADA.

JOHNSON, ROBIN: Brooklyn, NY; May 29, 1964.

JOHNSON, VAN: Newport, RI, Aug. 28, 1916.

JONES, CAROLYN: Amarillo, TX, Apr. 28, 1933.

JONES, CHRISTOPHER: Jackson, TN, Aug. 18, 1941. Actors Studio.

JONES, DEAN: Morgan County, AL, Jan. 25, 1936. Ashburn College.

JONES, JACK: Bel-Air, CA, Jan. 14, 1938.

JONES, JAMES EARL: Arkabutla, MS, Jan 17, 1931. U. Mich.

JONES, JENNIFER (Phyllis Isley): Tulsa, OK, Mar. 2, 1919. AADA.

JONES, SAM J.: Chicago, IL, 1954.

JONES, SHIRLEY: Smithton, PA, March 31, 1934.

JONES, TOM (Thomas Jones Woodward): Pontypridd, Wales, June 7, 1940.

JONES, TOMMY LEE: San Saba, TX, Sept. 15, 1946. Harvard.

JORDAN, RICHARD: NYC, July 19, 1938. Harvard.

JORY, VICTOR: Dawson City, Can., Nov. 28, 1901. Cal. U.

JOURDAN, LOUIS: Marseilles, France, June 18, 1920.

JULIA, RAUL: San Juan, PR, Mar. 9, 1940. U PR.

JURADO, KATY (Maria Christina Jurado Garcia): Guadalajara, Mex., 1927.

KAHN, MADELINE: Boston, MA, Sept. 29, 1942. Hofstra U.

KANE, CAROL: Cleveland, OH, 1952.

KAPLAN, JONATHAN: Paris, Nov. 25, 1947. NYU.

KATT, WILLIAM: Los Angeles, CA, 1955.

KAUFMANN, CHRISTINE: Lansdorf, Graz, Austria, Jan. 11, 1945.

KAYE, DANNY (David Daniel Kominski): Brooklyn, Jan. 18, 1913.

KAYE, STUBBY: NYC, Nov. 11, 1918.

KEACH, STACY: Savannah, GA, June 2, 1941. U. Cal., Yale.

KEATON, DIANE (Hall): Los Angeles, CA, Jan. 5, 1946. Neighborhood Playhouse.

KEATS, STEVEN: Bronx, NY, 1945.

KEDROVA, LILA: Greece, 1918.

KEEL, HOWARD (Harold Keel): Gillespie, IL, Apr. 13, 1919.

KEELER, RUBY (Ethel): Halifax, N.S., Aug. 25, 1909.

KEITH, BRIAN: Bayonne, NJ, Nov. 14, 1921.

KELLER, MARTHE: Basel, Switz., 1945. Munich Stanislavsky Sch.

KELLERMAN, SALLY: Long Beach, CA, June 2, 1938. Actors Studio West.

KELLEY, DeFOREST: Atlanta, GA, Jan. 20, 1920.

KELLY, GENE: Pittsburgh, Aug. 23, 1912. U. Pittsburgh.

KELLY, GRACE: Philadelphia, Nov. 12, 1929. AADA.

KELLY, JACK: Astoria, NY, Sept. 16, 1927. UCLA.

KELLY, NANCY: Lowell, MA, Mar. 25, 1921. Bentley School.

KEMP, JEREMY: Chesterfield, Eng., 1935, Central Sch.

KENNEDY, ARTHUR: Worcester, MA, Feb. 17, 1914. Carnegie Tech.

KENNEDY, GEORGE: NYC, Feb. 18, 1925.

KERR, DEBORAH: Helensburg, Scot., Sept. 30, 1921. Smale Ballet School.

KERR, JOHN: NYC, Nov. 15, 1931. Harvard, Columbia.

KHAMBATTA, PERSIS: Bombay, Oct. 2, 1950.

KIDDER, MARGOT: Yellow Knife, Can., Oct. 17, 1948. UBC.

KIER, UDO: Germany, Oct. 14, 1944.

KILEY, RICHARD: Chicago, Mar. 31, 1922. Loyola.

KINCAID, ARON (Norman Neale Williams III): Los Angeles, June 15, 1943. UCLA.

KING, ALAN: (Irwin Kniberg): Brooklyn, Dec. 26, 1927.

KING, PERRY: Alliance, OH, Apr. 30. Yale.

KINSKI, NASTASSIA: Germany, 1960.

KITT, EARTHA: North, SC, Jan. 26, 1928.

KLEMPERER, WERNER: Cologne, Mar. 22, 1920.

KLUGMAN, JACK: Philadelphia, PA, Apr. 27, 1925. Carnegie Tech.

KNIGHT, ESMOND: East Sheen, Eng., May 4, 1906.

KNIGHT, SHIRLEY: Goessel, KS, July 5, 1937. Wichita U.

KNOWLES, PATRIC (Reginald Lawrence Knowles): Horsforth, Eng., Nov. 11, 1911.

KNOX, ALEXANDER: Strathroy, Ont., Can., Jan. 16, 1907.

KNOX, ELYSE: Hartford, CT, Dec. 14, 1917. Traphagen School.

KOENIG, WALTER: Chicago, IL, Sept. 14. UCLA.

KOHNER, SUSAN: Los Angeles, Nov. 11, 1936. U. Calif.

KORMAN, HARVEY: Chicago, IL, Feb. 15, 1927. Goodman.

KORVIN, CHARLES (Geza Korvin Karpathi): Czechoslovakia, Nov. 21. Sorbonne.

| Lauren Hutton | Page Johnson | Madeline Kahn | Aron Kincaid | Carol Lynley |

KOSLECK, MARTIN: Barkotzen, Ger., Mar. 24, 1907. Max Reinhardt School.

KOTTO, YAPHET: NYC, Nov. 15, 1937.

KREUGER, KURT: St. Moritz, Switz., July 23, 1917. U. London.

KRISTOFFERSON, KRIS: Brownsville, TX, 1936, Pomona Col.

KRUGER, HARDY: Berlin, Ger., April. 12, 1928.

KULP, NANCY: Harrisburg, PA, 1921.

KUNTSMANN, DORIS: Hamburg, 1944.

KWAN, NANCY: Hong Kong, May 19, 1939. Royal Ballet.

LACY, JERRY: Sioux City, IA, Mar. 27, 1936. LACC.

LADD, CHERYL (Stoppelmoor): Huron, SD, 1951.

LADD, DIANE (Ladnier): Meridian, MS, Nov. 29, 1932. Tulane U.

LAHTI, CHRISTINE: Detroit, MI, Apr. 4, 1950; U Mich.

LAMARR, HEDY (Hedwig Kiesler): Vienna, Sept. 11, 1913.

LAMAS, FERNANDO: Buenos Aires, Jan. 9, 1920.

LAMAS, LORENZO: Los Angeles, Jan. 1958.

LAMB, GIL: Minneapolis, June 14, 1906. U. Minn.

LAMOUR, DOROTHY: Dec. 10, 1914. Spence School.

LANCASTER, BURT: NYC, Nov. 2, 1913. NYU.

LANCHESTER, ELSA (Elsa Sullivan): London, Oct. 28, 1902.

LANDAU, MARTIN: Brooklyn, NY, 1931. Actors Studio.

LANDON, MICHAEL (Eugene Orowitz): Collingswood, NJ, Oct. 31, 1936. USC.

LANDRUM, TERI: Enid, OK., 1960.

LANE, ABBE: Brooklyn, Dec. 14, 1935.

LANE, DIANE: NYC, Jan. 1965.

LANGAN, GLENN: Denver, CO, July 8, 1917.

LANGE, HOPE: Redding Ridge, CT, Nov. 28, 1933. Reed Col.

LANGE, JESSICA: Minnesota, 1950. U. Minn.

LANGTON, PAUL: Salt Lake City, Apr. 17, 1913. Travers School of Theatre.

LANSBURY, ANGELA: London, Oct. 16, 1925. London Academy of Music.

LANSING, ROBERT (Brown): San Diego, CA, June 5, 1929.

LAURE, CAROLE: Montreal, Can., 1951.

LAURIE, PIPER (Rosetta Jacobs): Detroit, Jan. 22, 1932.

LAW, JOHN PHILLIP: Hollywood, Sept. 7, 1937. Neighborhood Playhouse, U. Hawaii.

LAWFORD, PETER: London, Sept. 7, 1923.

LAWRENCE, BARBARA: Carnegie, OK, Feb. 24, 1930. UCLA.

LAWRENCE, CAROL (Laraia): Melrose Park, IL, Sept. 5, 1935.

LAWRENCE, VICKI: Inglewood, CA, 1949.

LAWSON, LEIGH: Atherston, Eng., July 21, 1945. RADA.

LEACHMAN, CLORIS: Des Moines, IA, Apr. 30, 1930. Northwestern U.

LEAUD, JEAN-PIERRE: Paris, 1944.

LEDERER, FRANCIS: Karlin, Prague, Czech., Nov. 6, 1906.

LEE, CHRISTOPHER: London, May 27, 1922. Wellington College.

LEE, MARK: Australia, 1958.

LEE, MICHELE (Dusiak): Los Angeles, June 24, 1942. LACC.

LEIBMAN, RON: NYC, Oct. 11, 1937. Ohio Wesleyan.

LEIGH, JANET (Jeanette Helen Morrison): Merced, CA, July 6, 1926. College of Pacific.

LEMMON, JACK: Boston, Feb. 8, 1925. Harvard.

LENZ, RICK: Springfield, IL, Nov. 21, 1939. U. Mich.

LEONARD, SHELDON (Bershad): NYC, Feb. 22, 1907. Syracuse U.

LEROY, PHILIPPE: Paris, Oct. 15, 1930. U. Paris.

LESLIE, BETHEL: NYC, Aug. 3, 1929. Brearley School.

LESLIE, JOAN (Joan Brodell): Detroit, Jan. 26, 1925. St. Benedict's.

LESTER, MARK: Oxford, Eng., July 11, 1958.

LEWIS, JERRY: Newark, NJ, Mar. 16, 1926.

LIGON, TOM: New Orleans, LA, Sept. 10, 1945.

LILLIE, BEATRICE: Toronto, Can., May 29, 1898.

LINCOLN, ABBEY (Anna Marie Woolridge): Chicago, Aug. 6, 1930.

LINDFORS, VIVECA: Uppsala, Sweden, Dec. 29, 1920. Stockholm Royal Dramatic School.

LISI, VIRNA: Rome, 1938.

LITHGOW, JOHN: Rochester, NY, Oct. 19, 1945. Harvard.

LITTLE, CLEAVON: Chickasha, OK, June 1, 1939. San Diego State.

LOCKE, SONDRA: Shelbyville, TN, 1947.

LOCKHART, JUNE: NYC, June 25, 1925. Westlake School.

LOCKWOOD, GARY: Van Nuys, CA, Feb. 21, 1937.

LOCKWOOD, MARGARET: Karachi, Pakistan, Sept. 15, 1916. RADA.

LOLLOBRIGIDA, GINA: Subiaco, Italy, July 4, 1927. Rome Academy of Fine Arts.

LOM, HERBERT: Prague, Czechoslovakia, 1917. Prague U.

LOMEZ, CELINE: Montreal, Can., 1953.

LONDON, JULIE (Julie Peck): Santa Rosa, CA, Sept. 26, 1926.

LONOW, MARK: Brooklyn, N.Y.

LOPEZ, PERRY: NYC, July 22, 1931. NYU.

LORD, JACK (John Joseph Ryan): NYC, Dec. 30, 1928. NYU.

LOREN, SOPHIA: (Sofia Scicolone): Rome, Italy, Sept. 20, 1934.

LOUISE, TINA (Blacker): NYC, Feb. 11, 1934. Miami U.

LOVELACE, LINDA: Bryan, TX, 1952.

LOWITSCH, KLAUS: Berlin, Apr. 8, 1936. Vienna Academy.

LOY, MYRNA (Myrna Williams): Helena, MT, Aug. 2, 1905. Westlake School.

LUCAS, LISA: Arizona, 1961.

LULU: Glasglow, Scot., 1948.

LUND, JOHN: Rochester, NY, Feb. 6, 1913.

LUPINO, IDA: London, Feb. 4, 1916. RADA.

LYDON, JAMES: Harrington Park, NJ, May 30, 1923.

LYNDE, PAUL: Mt. Vernon, OH, June 13, 1926. Northwestern U.

LYNLEY, CAROL (Jones): NYC, Feb. 13, 1942.

LYNN, JEFFREY: Auburn, MA, 1909. Bates College.

LYON, SUE: Davenport, IA, July 10, 1946.

LYONS, ROBERT F.: Albany, NY. AADA.

MacARTHUR, JAMES: Los Angeles, Dec. 8, 1937. Harvard.

MacGINNIS, NIALL: Dublin, Ire., Mar. 29, 1913. Dublin U.

MacGRAW, ALI: NYC, Apr. 1, 1938. Wellesley.

MacLAINE, SHIRLEY (Beatty): Richmond, VA, Apr. 24, 1934.

MacMAHON, ALINE: McKeesport, PA, May 3, 1899. Barnard College.

MacMURRAY, FRED: Kankakee, IL, Aug. 30, 1908. Carroll Col.

MacNEE, PATRICK: London, Feb. 1922.

MacRAE, GORDON: East Orange, NJ, Mar. 12, 1921.

225

MADISON, GUY (Robert Moseley): Bakersfield, CA, Jan. 19, 1922. Bakersfield Jr. College.

MAHARIS, GEORGE: Astoria, NY, Sept. 1, 1928. Actors Studio.

MAHONEY, JOCK (Jacques O'Mahoney): Chicago, Feb. 7, 1919. U. of Iowa.

MAJORS, LEE: Wyandotte, MI, Apr. 23, 1940. E. Ky. State Col.

MAKEPEACE, CHRIS: Toronto, Can., 1964.

MALDEN, KARL (Mladen Sekulovich): Gary, IN, Mar. 22, 1914.

MALONE, DOROTHY: Chicago, Jan. 30, 1925. S. Methodist U.

MANN, KURT: Roslyn, NY, July 18, 1947.

MANZ, LINDA: NYC, 1961.

MARAIS, JEAN: Cherbourg, France, Dec. 11, 1913. St. Germain.

MARGO (Maria Marguerita Guadalupe Boldoay Castilla): Mexico City, May 10, 1917.

MARGOLIN, JANET: NYC, July 25, 1943. Walden School.

MARIN, JACQUES: Paris, Sept. 9, 1919. Conservatoire National.

MARINARO, ED: NYC 1951. Cornell.

MARLOWE, HUGH (Hugh Hipple): Philadelphia, Jan. 30, 1914.

MARSHALL, BRENDA (Ardis Anderson Gaines): Isle of Negros, P.I., Sept. 29, 1915. Texas State College.

MARSHALL, E. G.: Owatonna, MN, June 18, 1910. U. Minn.

MARSHALL, PENNY: Bronx, NY, Oct. 15, 1942. U. N. Mex.

MARSHALL, WILLIAM: Gary, IN, Aug. 19, 1924. NYU.

MARTIN, DEAN (Dino Crocetti): Steubenville, OH, June 17, 1917.

MARTIN, DEAN PAUL: Los Angeles, CA, 1952. UCLA.

MARTIN, MARY: Weatherford, TX, Dec. 1, 1914. Ward-Belmont School.

MARTIN, STEVE: Waco, TX, 1946; UCLA.

MARTIN, TONY (Alfred Norris): Oakland, CA, Dec. 25, 1913. St. Mary's College.

MARVIN, LEE: NYC, Feb. 19, 1924.

MASON, JAMES: Huddersfield, Yorkshire, Eng., May 15, 1909. Cambridge.

MASON, MARSHA: St. Louis, MO, Apr. 3, 1942. Webster Col.

MASON, PAMELA (Pamela Kellino): Westgate, Eng., Mar. 10, 1918.

MASSEN, OSA: Copenhagen, Den., Jan. 13, 1916.

MASSEY, DANIEL: London, Oct. 10, 1933. Eton and King's Col.

MASSEY, RAYMOND: Toronto, Can., Aug. 30, 1896. Oxford.

MASTERSON, PETER: Angleton, TX, June 1, 1934. Rice U.

MASTROIANNI, MARCELLO: Fontana Liri, Italy, Sept. 28, 1924.

MATTHAU, WALTER (Matuschanskayasky): NYC, Oct. 1, 1920.

MATTHEWS, BRIAN: Philadelphia, PA. Jan. 24, 1953. St. Olaf.

MATURE, VICTOR: Louisville, KY, Jan. 29, 1915.

MAY, ELAINE (Berlin): Philadelphia, Apr. 21, 1932.

MAYEHOFF, EDDIE: Baltimore, July 7. Yale.

MAYO, VIRGINIA: (Virginia Clara Jones): St. Louis, Mo; Nov. 30, 1920.

McCALLUM, DAVID: Scotland, Sept. 19, 1933. Chapman Coll.

McCAMBRIDGE, MERCEDES: Jolliet, IL, March 17, 1918. Mundelein College.

McCARTHY, KEVIN: Seattle, WA, Feb. 15, 1914. Minn. U.

McCLORY, SEAN: Dublin, Ire., March 8, 1924. U. Galway.

McCLURE, DOUG: Glendale, CA, May 11, 1935. UCLA.

McCOWEN, ALEC: Tunbridge Wells, Eng., May 26, 1925. RADA.

McCREA, JOEL: Los Angeles, Nov. 5, 1905. Pomona College.

McDERMOTT, HUGH: Edinburgh, Scot., Mar. 20, 1908.

McDOWALL, RODDY: London, Sept. 17, 1928. St. Joseph's.

McDOWELL, MALCOLM (Taylor): Leeds, Eng., June 15, 1943. LAMDA.

McENERY, PETER: Walsall, Eng., Feb. 21, 1940.

McFARLAND, SPANKY: Dallas, TX, 1936.

McGAVIN, DARREN: Spokane, WA, May 7, 1922. College of Pacific.

McGUIRE, BIFF: New Haven, CT, Oct. 25, 1926. Mass. State Col.

McGUIRE, DOROTHY: Omaha, NB, June 14, 1918.

McKAY, GARDNER: NYC, June 10, 1932. Cornell.

McKEE, LONETTE: Detroit, MI, 1954.

McKENNA, VIRGINIA: London, June 7, 1931.

McKEON, DOUG: New Jersey, 1966.

McKUEN, ROD: Oakland, CA, Apr. 29, 1933.

McLERIE, ALLYN ANN: Grand Mere, Can., Dec. 1, 1926.

McNAIR, BARBARA: Chicago, March 4, 1939. UCLA.

McNALLY, STEPHEN (Horace McNally): NYC, July 29, 1913. Fordham U.

McNICHOL, KRISTY: Los Angeles, CA, Sept. 11, 1962.

McQUEEN, BUTTERFLY: Tampa, FL, Jan. 8. 1911. UCLA.

MEADOWS, AUDREY Wuchang, China, 1919. St. Margaret's.

MEADOWS, JAYNE (formerly, Jayne Cotter): Wuchang, China, Sept. 27, 1920. St. Margaret's.

MEDWIN, MICHAEL: London, 1925. Instut Fischer.

MEEKER, RALPH (Ralph Rathgeber): Minneapolis, Nov. 21, 1920. Northwestern U.

MEKKA, EDDIE: Worcester, MA, 1932. Boston Cons.

MELATO, MARIANGELA: Milan, Italy, 1941. Milan Theatre Acad.

MELL, MARISA: Vienna, Austria, Feb. 25, 1939.

MERCADO, HECTOR JAIME: NYC, 1949. HB Studio.

MERCOURI, MELINA: Athens, Greece, Oct. 18, 1915.

MEREDITH, BURGESS: Cleveland, OH, Nov. 16, 1908. Amherst.

MEREDITH, LEE (Judi Lee Sauls): Oct., 1947. AADA.

MERKEL, UNA: Covington, KY, Dec. 10, 1903.

MERMAN, ETHEL (Ethel Zimmerman): Astoria, NY, Jan. 16, 1908.

MERRILL, DINA (Nedinia Hutton): NYC, Dec. 9, 1925. AADA.

MERRILL, GARY: Hartford, CT, Aug. 2, 1915. Bowdoin, Trinity.

MICHELL, KEITH: Adelaide, Aus., Dec. 1, 1926.

MIFUNE, TOSHIRO: Tsingtao, China, Apr. 1, 1920.

MILES, SARAH: Ingatestone, Eng., Dec. 31, 1941. RADA.

MILES, SYLVIA: NYC, Sept. 9, 1932.

MILES, VERA (Ralston): Boise City, OK, Aug. 23, 1929. UCLA.

MILFORD, PENELOPE: Winnetka, IL.

MILLAND, RAY (Reginald Trustcott-Jones): Neath, Wales, Jan. 3, 1908. King's College.

MILLER, ANN (Lucille Ann Collier): Chireno, TX, Apr. 12, 1919. Lawler Professional School.

MILLER, BARRY: NYC 1958.

MILLER, JASON: Long Island City, NY, Apr. 22, 1939. Catholic U.

MILLER, LINDA: NYC, Sept. 16, 1942. Catholic U.

MILLER, MARVIN: St. Louis, July 18, 1913. Washington U.

MILLS, HAYLEY: London, Apr. 18, 1946. Elmhurst School.

MILLS, JOHN: Suffolk, Eng., Feb. 22, 1908.

MILNER, MARTIN: Detroit, MI, Dec. 28, 1931.

MIMIEUX, YVETTE: Los Angeles, Jan. 8, 1941. Hollywood High.

MINNELLI, LIZA: Los Angeles, Mar. 12, 1946.

MIRANDA, ISA (Isabella Sampietro): Milan, Italy, July 5, 1909.

MITCHELL, CAMERON: Dallastown, PA, Nov. 4, 1918. N.Y. Theatre School.

MITCHELL, JAMES: Sacramento, CA, Feb. 29, 1920. LACC.

MITCHUM, JAMES: Los Angeles, CA, May 8, 1941.

MITCHUM, ROBERT: Bridgeport, CT, Aug. 6, 1917.

MONTALBAN, RICARDO: Mexico City, Nov. 25, 1920.

MONTAND, YVES (Yves Montand Livi): Mansummano, Tuscany, Oct. 13, 1921.

MONTGOMERY, BELINDA: Winnipeg, Can., July 23, 1950.

MONTGOMERY, ELIZABETH: Los Angeles, Apr. 15, 1933. AADA.

MONTGOMERY, GEORGE (George Letz): Brady, MT, Aug. 29, 1916. U. Mont.

MOOR, BILL: Toledo, OH, July 13, 1931. Northwestern.

MOORE, CONSTANCE: Sioux City, IA, Jan. 18, 1919.

| Chris
Makepeace | Lonette
McKee | Don
Nute | Olivia
Newton-John | Patrick
O'Neal |

MOORE, DICK: Los Angeles, Sept. 12, 1925.

MOORE, FRANK: Bay-de-Verde, Newfoundland, 1946.

MOORE, KIERON: County Cork, Ire., 1925. St. Mary's College.

MOORE, MARY TYLER: Brooklyn, Dec. 29, 1936.

MOORE, ROGER: London, Oct. 14, 1927. RADA.

MOORE, TERRY (Helen Koford): Los Angeles, Jan. 7, 1929.

MORE, KENNETH: Gerrards Cross, Eng., Sept. 20, 1914.

MOREAU, JEANNE: Paris, Jan. 3, 1928.

MORENO, RITA (Rosita Alverio): Humacao, P.R., Dec. 11, 1931.

MORGAN, DENNIS (Stanley Morner): Prentice, WI, Dec. 10, 1910. Carroll College.

MORGAN, HARRY (HENRY) (Harry Bratsburg): Detroit, Apr. 10, 1915. U. Chicago.

MORGAN, MICHELE (Simone Roussel): Paris, Feb. 29, 1920. Paris Dramatic School.

MORIARTY, CATHY: Bronx, NY, 1961.

MORIARTY, MICHAEL: Detroit, MI, Apr. 5, 1941. Dartmouth.

MORISON, PATRICIA: NYC, 1915.

MORLEY, ROBERT: Wiltshire, Eng., May 26, 1908. RADA.

MORRIS, GREG: Cleveland, OH, 1934. Ohio State.

MORRIS, HOWARD: NYC, Sept. 4, 1919. NYU.

MORROW, VIC: Bronx, NY, Feb. 14, 1932. Fla. Southern College.

MORSE, DAVID: Hamilton, MA, 1953.

MORSE, ROBERT: Newton, MA, May 18, 1931.

MOSS, ARNOLD: NYC, Jan. 28, 1910. CCNY.

MULLIGAN, RICHARD: NYC, Nov. 13, 1932.

MURPHY, GEORGE: New Haven, CT, July 4, 1902. Yale.

MURPHY, MICHAEL: Los Angeles, CA, 1949.

MURRAY, BILL: Evanston, IL, Sept. 21, 1950; Regis Col.

MURRAY, DON: Hollywood, July 31, 1929. AADA.

MURRAY, KEN (Don Court): NYC, July 14, 1903.

MUSANTE, TONY: Bridgeport, CT, June 30, 1936. Oberlin Col.

NADER, GEORGE: Pasadena, CA, Oct. 19, 1921. Occidental College.

NAPIER, ALAN: Birmingham, Eng., Jan. 7, 1903. Birmingham University.

NATWICK, MILDRED: Baltimore, June 19, 1908. Bryn Mawr.

NAUGHTON, JAMES: Middletown, CT, Dec. 6, 1945. Yale.

NEAL, PATRICIA: Packard, KY, Jan. 20, 1926. Northwestern U.

NEFF, HILDEGARDE (Hildegard Knef): Ulm, Ger., Dec. 28, 1925. Berlin Art Academy.

NELL, NATHALIE: Paris, Oct. 1950.

NELSON, BARRY (Robert Nielsen): Oakland, CA, 1920.

NELSON, DAVID: NYC, Oct. 24, 1936. USC.

NELSON, GENE (Gene Berg): Seattle, WA, Mar. 24, 1920.

NELSON, HARRIET HILLIARD (Peggy Lou Snyder): Des Moines, IA, July 18.

NELSON, LORI (Dixie Kay Nelson): Santa Fe, NM, Aug. 15, 1933.

NELSON, RICK (Eric Hilliard Nelson): Teaneck, NJ, May 8, 1940.

NESBITT, CATHLEEN: Cheshire, Eng., Nov. 24, 1889. Victoria College.

NEWHART, BOB: Chicago, IL, Sept. 5, 1929. Loyola U.

NEWLEY, ANTHONY: Hackney, London, Sept. 21, 1931.

NEWMAN, BARRY: Boston, MA, Mar. 26, 1938. Brandeis U.

NEWMAN, PAUL: Cleveland, OH, Jan. 26, 1925. Yale.

NEWMAR, JULIE (Newmeyer): Los Angeles, Aug. 16, 1935.

NEWTON-JOHN, OLIVIA: Cambridge, Eng., 1949.

NICHOLAS, PAUL: London, 1945.

NICHOLS, MIKE (Michael Igor Peschkowsky): Berlin, Nov. 6, 1931. U. Chicago.

NICHOLSON, JACK: Neptune, NJ, Apr. 22, 1937.

NICKERSON, DENISE: NYC, 1959.

NICOL, ALEX: Ossining, NY, Jan. 20, 1919. Actors Studio.

NIELSEN, LESLIE: Regina, Saskatchewan, Can., Feb. 11, 1926. Neighborhood Playhouse.

NIMOY, LEONARD: Boston, MA, Mar. 26, 1931. Boston Col., Antioch Col.

NIVEN, DAVID: Kirriemuir, Scot., Mar. 1, 1909. Sandhurst College.

NOLAN, LLOYD: San Francisco, Aug. 11, 1902. Stanford U.

NOLTE, NICK: Omaha, NB, 1941. Pasadena City Col.

NORRIS, CHRISTOPHER: NYC, Oct. 7, 1943. Lincoln Square Acad.

NORRIS, CHUCK: 1939, California.

NORTH, HEATHER: Pasadena, CA, Dec. 13, 1950. Actors Workshop.

NORTH, SHEREE (Dawn Bethel): Los Angeles, Jan. 17, 1933. Hollywood High.

NORTON, KEN: Aug. 9, 1945.

NOVAK, KIM (Marilyn Novak): Chicago, Feb. 18, 1933. LACC.

NUREYEV, RUDOLF: Russia, Mar. 17, 1938.

NUTE, DON: Connellsville, PA, Mar. 13. Denver U.

NUYEN, FRANCE (Vannga): Marseilles, France, July 31, 1939. Beaux Arts School.

OATES, WARREN: Depoy, KY, July 5, 1928.

O'BRIAN, HUGH (Hugh J. Krampe): Rochester, NY, Apr. 19, 1928. Cincinnati U.

O'BRIEN, CLAY: Ray, AZ, May 6, 1961.

O'BRIEN, EDMOND: NYC, Sept. 10, 1915. Fordham, Neighborhood Playhouse.

O'BRIEN, MARGARET (Angela Maxine O'Brien): Los Angeles, Jan. 15, 1937.

O'BRIEN, PAT: Milwaukee, Nov. 11, 1899. Marquette U.

O'CONNELL, ARTHUR: NYC, Mar. 29, 1908. St. John's.

O'CONNOR, CARROLL: Bronx, NY, Aug. 2, 1925. Dublin National Univ.

O'CONNOR, DONALD: Chicago, Aug. 28, 1925.

O'CONNOR, GLYNNIS: NYC, Nov. 19, 1956. NYSU.

O'CONNOR, KEVIN: Honolulu, HI, May 7. U. Hi.

O'HANLON, GEORGE: Brooklyn, NY, Nov. 23, 1917.

O'HARA, MAUREEN (Maureen FitzSimons): Dublin, Ire., Aug. 17, 1920. Abbey School.

O'HERLIHY, DAN: Wexford, Ire., May 1, 1919. National U.

O'KEEFE, MICHAEL: Paulland, NJ, 1955, NYU, AADA.

OLIVIER, LAURENCE: Dorking, Eng., May 22, 1907. Oxford.

O'LOUGHLIN, GERALD S.: NYC, Dec. 23, 1921. U. Rochester.

OLSON, NANCY: Milwaukee, WI, July 14. UCLA.

O'NEAL, PATRICK: Ocala, FL, Sept. 26, 1927. U. Fla.

O'NEAL, RON: Utica, NY, Sept. 1, 1937. Ohio State.

O'NEAL, RYAN: Los Angeles, Apr. 20, 1941.

O'NEAL, TATUM: Los Angeles, Nov. 5, 1963.

O'NEIL, TRICIA: Shreveport, LA, Mar. 11, 1945. Baylor U.

227

O'NEILL, JENNIFER: Rio de Janeiro, Feb. 20, 1949. Neighborhood Playhouse.

O'SULLIVAN, MAUREEN: Byle, Ire., May 17, 1911. Sacred Heart Convent.

O'TOOLE, ANNETTE: Houston, TX, 1953. UCLA.

O'TOOLE, PETER: Connemara, Ireland, Aug. 2, 1932. RADA.

PACINO, AL: NYC, Apr. 25, 1940.

PAGE, GERALDINE: Kirksville, MO, Nov. 22, 1924. Goodman School.

PAGET, DEBRA (Debralee Griffin): Denver, Aug. 19, 1933.

PAIGE, JANIS (Donna Mae Jaden): Tacoma, WA, Sept. 16, 1922.

PALANCE, JACK (Walter Palanuik): Lattimer, PA, Feb. 18, 1920. UNC.

PALMER, BETSY: East Chicago, IN, Nov. 1, 1929. DePaul U.

PALMER, GREGG (Palmer Lee): San Francisco, Jan. 25, 1927. U. Utah.

PALMER, LILLI: Posen, Austria, May 24, 1914. Ilka Gruning School.

PAMPANINI, SILVANA: Rome, Sept. 25, 1925.

PAPAS, IRENE: Chiliomodion, Greece, Mar. 9, 1929.

PARKER, ELEANOR: Cedarville, OH, June 26, 1922. Pasadena Playhouse.

PARKER, FESS: Fort Worth, TX, Aug. 16, 1927. USC.

PARKER, JAMESON: 1947, Beloit Col.

PARKER, JEAN (Mae Green): Deer Lodge, MT, Aug. 11, 1912.

PARKER, SUZY (Cecelia Parker): San Antonio, TX, Oct. 28, 1933.

PARKER, WILLARD (Worster Van Eps): NYC, Feb. 5, 1912.

PARKINS, BARBARA: Vancouver, Can., May 22, 1943.

PARSONS, ESTELLE: Lynn, MA, Nov. 20, 1927. Boston U.

PARTON, DOLLY: Sevierville, TN, 1946.

PATRICK, DENNIS: Philadelphia, Mar. 14, 1918.

PATTERSON, LEE: Vancouver, Can., Mar. 31, 1929. Ontario Col.

PAVAN, MARISA (Marisa Pierangeli): Cagliari, Sardinia, June 19, 1932. Torquado Tasso College.

PEACH, MARY: Durban, S. Africa, 1934.

PEARSON, BEATRICE: Denison, TX, July 27, 1920.

PECK, GREGORY: La Jolla, CA, Apr. 5, 1916. U. Calif.

PEPPARD, GEORGE: Detroit, Oct. 1, 1928. Carnegie Tech.

PERKINS, ANTHONY: NYC, Apr. 14, 1932. Rollins College.

PERREAU, GIGI (Ghislaine): Los Angeles, Feb. 6, 1941.

PERRINE, VALERIE: Galveston, TX, Sept. 3, 1944. U. Ariz.

PESCOW, DONNA: Brooklyn, NY, 1954.

PETERS, BERNADETTE: Jamaica, NY, Feb. 28, 1948.

PETERS, BROCK: NYC, July 2, 1927. CCNY.

PETERS, JEAN (Elizabeth): Canton, OH, Oct. 15, 1926. Ohio State U.

PETTET, JOANNA: London, Nov. 16, 1944. Neighborhood Playhouse.

PHILLIPS, MacKENZIE: Hollywood, CA, 1960.

PHILLIPS, MICHELLE (Holly Gilliam): NJ, June 4, 1944.

PICERNI, PAUL: NYC, Dec. 1, 1922. Loyola U.

PICKENS, SLIM (Louis Bert Lindley, Jr.): Kingsberg, CA, June 29, 1919.

PIDGEON, WALTER: East St. John, N.B., Can., Sept. 23, 1897.

PINE, PHILLIP: Hanford, CA, July 16, 1925. Actors' Lab.

PISIER, MARIE-FRANCE: Vietnam, May 10, 1944. U. Paris.

PLACE, MARY KAY: Port Arthur, TX, Sept., 1947. U. Tulsa.

PLAYTEN, ALICE: NYC, Aug. 28, 1947. NYU.

PLEASENCE, DONALD: Workshop, Eng, Oct. 5, 1919. Sheffield School.

PLESHETTE, SUZANNE: NYC, Jan. 31, 1937. Syracuse U.

PLUMMER, CHRISTOPHER: Toronto, Can., Dec. 13, 1927.

PODESTA, ROSSANA: Tripoli, June 20, 1934.

POITIER, SIDNEY: Miami, FL, Feb. 27, 1924.

POLITO, LINA: Naples, Italy, Aug. 11, 1954.

POLLARD, MICHAEL J. Pacific, NJ, May 30, 1939.

PORTER, ERIC: London, Apr. 8, 1928, Wimbledon Col.

POWELL, JANE (Suzanne Burce): Portland, OR, Apr. 1, 1928.

POWELL, ROBERT: London, June 1, 1944.

POWELL, WILLIAM: Pittsburgh, July 29, 1892. AADA.

POWER, TARYN: Los Angeles, CA, 1954.

POWERS, MALA (Mary Ellen): San Francisco, Dec. 29, 1921. UCLA.

PRENTISS, PAULA (Paula Ragusa): San Antonio, TX, Mar. 4, 1939. Northwestern U.

PRESLE, MICHELINE (Micheline Chassagne): Paris, Aug. 22, 1922. Rouleau Drama School.

PRESNELL, HARVE: Modesto, CA, Sept. 14, 1933. USC.

PRESTON, ROBERT (Robert Preston Meservey): Newton Highlands, MA, June 8, 1913. Pasadena Playhouse.

PRICE, VINCENT: St. Louis, May 27, 1911. Yale.

PRIMUS, BARRY: NYC, Feb. 16, 1938. CCNY.

PRINCE, WILLIAM: Nicholas, NY, Jan. 26, 1913. Cornell U.

PRINCIPAL, VICTORIA: Tokyo, Jan. 3, 1945. Dade Jr. Col.

PROVAL, DAVID: Brooklyn, NY, 1943.

PROVINE, DOROTHY: Deadwood, SD, Jan. 20, 1937. U. Wash.

PROWSE, JULIET: Bombay, India, Sept. 25, 1936.

PRYOR, RICHARD: Peoria, IL, Dec. 1, 1940.

PURCELL, LEE: Cherry Point, NC, June 15, 1947. Stephens.

PURCELL, NOEL: Dublin, Ire., Dec. 23, 1900. Irish Christian Brothers.

PURDOM, EDMUND: Welwyn Garden City, Eng., Dec. 19, 1924. St. Ignatius College.

PYLE, DENVER: Bethune, CO, 1920.

QUAYLE, ANTHONY: Lancashire, Eng., Sept. 7, 1913. Old Vic School.

QUINE, RICHARD: Detroit, MI, Nov. 12, 1920.

QUINLAN, KATHLEEN: Mill Valley, CA, Nov. 19, 1954.

QUINN, ANTHONY: Chihuahua, Mex., Apr. 21, 1915.

RAFFERTY, FRANCES: Sioux City, IA, June 16, 1922. UCLA.

RAFFIN, DEBORAH: Los Angeles, Mar. 13, 1953. Valley Col.

RAINES, ELLA (Ella Wallace): Snoqualmie Falls, WA, Aug. 6, 1921. U. Wash.

RAMPLING, CHARLOTTE: Surmer, Eng., Feb. 5, 1946. U. Madrid.

RAMSEY, LOGAN: Long Beach, CA, Mar. 21, 1921. St. Joseph.

RANDALL, TONY: Tulsa, OK, Feb. 26, 1920. Northwestern U.

RANDELL, RON: Sydney, Australia, Oct. 8, 1920. St. Mary's Col.

RASULALA, THALMUS (Jack Crowder): Miami, FL, Nov. 15, 1939. U. Redlands.

RAY, ALDO (Aldo DeRe): Pen Argyl, PA, Sept. 25, 1926. UCLA.

RAYE, MARTHA (Margie Yvonne Reed): Butte, MT, Aug. 27, 1916.

RAYMOND, GENE (Raymond Guion): NYC, Aug. 13, 1908.

REAGAN, RONALD: Tampico, IL, Feb. 6, 1911. Eureka College.

REASON, REX: Berlin, Ger., Nov. 30, 1928. Pasadena Playhouse.

REDDY, HELEN: Australia, Oct. 25, 1942.

REDFORD, ROBERT: Santa Monica, CA, Aug. 18, 1937. AADA.

REDGRAVE, CORIN: London, July 16, 1939.

REDGRAVE, LYNN: London, Mar. 8, 1943.

REDGRAVE, MICHAEL: Bristol, Eng., Mar. 20, 1908. Cambridge.

REDGRAVE, VANESSA: London, Jan. 30, 1937.

REDMAN, JOYCE: County Mayo, Ire., 1919. RADA.

REED, DONNA (Donna Mullenger): Denison, IA, Jan. 27, 1921. LACC.

REED, OLIVER: Wimbledon, Eng., Feb. 13, 1938.

REED, REX: Ft. Worth, TX, Oct. 2, 1939. LSU.

REEMS, HARRY (Herbert Streicher): Bronx, NY, 1947. U. Pittsburgh.

REEVE, CHRISTOPHER: NJ, Sept. 25, 1952. Cornell, Juilliard.

REEVES, STEVE: Glasgow, MT, Jan. 21, 1926.

REID, ELLIOTT: NYC, Jan. 16, 1920.

REINER, CARL: NYC, Mar. 20, 1922. Georgetown.

REINER, ROBERT: NYC, 1945. UCLA.

REMICK, LEE: Quincy, MA, Dec. 14, 1935. Barnard College.

RETTIG, TOMMY: Jackson Heights, NY, Dec. 10, 1941.

Mary Kay
Place

Peter
Riegert

Lynn
Redgrave

Roy
Scheider

Diana
Ross

REVILL, CLIVE: Wellington, NZ, Apr. 18, 1930.

REY, FERNANDO: La Coruna, Spain, 1917.

REYNOLDS, BURT: Waycross, GA., Feb. 11, 1935. Fla. State U.

REYNOLDS, DEBBIE (Mary Frances Reynolds): El Paso, TX, Apr. 1, 1932.

REYNOLDS, MARJORIE: Buhl, ID, Aug. 12, 1921.

RHOADES, BARBARA: Poughkeepsie, NY, 1947.

RICH, IRENE: Buffalo, NY, Oct. 13, 1891. St. Margaret's School.

RICHARDS, JEFF (Richard Mansfield Taylor): Portland, OR, Nov. 1. USC.

RICHARDSON, RALPH: Cheltenham, Eng., Dec. 19, 1902.

RICKLES, DON: NYC, May 8, 1926. AADA.

RIEGERT, PETER: NYC Apr. 11, 1947; U Buffalo.

RIGG, DIANA: Doncaster, Eng., July 20, 1938. RADA.

RITTER, JOHN: Burbank, CA, 1949. U. S. Cal.

ROBARDS, JASON: Chicago, July 26, 1922. AADA.

ROBERTS, ERIC: Biloxi, MS, 1956. RADA.

ROBERTS, RALPH: Salisbury, NC, Aug. 17, 1922. UNC.

ROBERTS, TANYA: (Leigh) NYC 1965.

ROBERTS, TONY: NYC, Oct. 22, 1939. Northwestern U.

ROBERTSON, CLIFF: La Jolla, CA, Sept. 9, 1925. Antioch Col.

ROBERTSON, DALE: Oklahoma City, July 14, 1923.

ROBINSON, CHRIS: Nov. 5, 1938, West Palm Beach, FL. LACC.

ROBINSON, JAY: NYC, Apr. 14, 1930.

ROBINSON, ROGER: Seattle, WA, May 2, 1941. USC.

ROBSON, FLORA: South Shields, Eng., Mar. 28, 1902. RADA.

ROCHEFORT, JEAN: Paris, 1930.

ROGERS, CHARLES "BUDDY": Olathe, KS, Aug. 13, 1904. U. Kan.

ROGERS, GINGER (Virginia Katherine McMath): Independence, MO, July 16, 1911.

ROGERS, ROY (Leonard Slye): Cincinnati, Nov. 5, 1912.

ROGERS, WAYNE: Birmingham, AL, Apr. 7, 1933. Princeton.

ROLAND, GILBERT (Luis Antonio Damaso De Alonso): Juarez, Mex., Dec. 11, 1905.

ROLLINS, HOWARD E., Jr.: 1951, Baltimore, MD.

ROMAN, RUTH: Boston, Dec. 23, 1922. Bishop Lee Dramatic School.

ROME, SIDNE: Akron, OH. Carnegie-Mellon.

ROMERO, CESAR: NYC, Feb. 15, 1907. Collegiate School.

ROONEY, MICKEY (Joe Yule, Jr.): Brooklyn, Sept. 23, 1920.

ROSS, DIANA: Detroit, MI, Mar. 26, 1945.

ROSS, KATHARINE: Hollywood, Jan. 29, 1943. Santa Rosa Col.

ROSSITER, LEONARD: Liverpool, Eng., Oct. 21, 1926.

ROUNDS, DAVID: Bronxville, NY, Oct. 9, 1938. Denison U.

ROUNDTREE, RICHARD: New Rochelle, NY, Sept. 7, 1942. Southern Ill.

ROWLANDS, GENA: Cambria, WI, June 19, 1936.

RUBIN, ANDREW: New Bedford, MA, June 22, 1946. AADA.

RUDD, PAUL: Boston, MA, May 15, 1940.

RULE, JANICE: Cincinnati, OH, Aug. 15, 1931.

RUPERT, MICHAEL: Denver, CO, Oct. 23, 1951. Pasadena Playhouse.

RUSH, BARBARA: Denver, CO, Jan. 4. 1929. U. Calif.

RUSSELL, JANE: Bemidji, MI, June 21, 1921. Max Reinhardt School.

RUSSELL, JOHN: Los Angeles, Jan. 3, 1921. U. Calif.

RUSSELL, KURT: Springfield, MA, March 17, 1951.

RUTHERFORD, ANN: Toronto, Can., Nov. 2, 1917.

RUYMEN, AYN: Brooklyn, July 18, 1947. HB Studio.

SACCHI, ROBERT: Bronx, NY, 1941; NYU.

SAINT, EVA MARIE: Newark, NJ, July 4, 1924. Bowling Green State U.

ST. JACQUES, RAYMOND (James Arthur Johnson): CT.

ST. JAMES, SUSAN: Los Angeles, Aug. 14. Conn. Col.

ST. JOHN, BETTA: Hawthorne, CA, Nov. 26, 1929.

ST. JOHN, JILL (Jill Oppenheim): Los Angeles, Aug. 19, 1940.

SALMI, ALBERT: Coney Island, NY, 1925. Actors Studio.

SALT, JENNIFER: Los Angeles, Sept. 4, 1944. Sarah Lawrence Col.

SANDS, TOMMY: Chicago, Aug. 27, 1937.

SAN JUAN, OLGA: NYC, Mar. 16, 1927.

SARANDON, CHRIS: Beckley, WV, July 24, 1942. U. WVa., Catholic U.

SARANDON, SUSAN (Tomaling): NYC, Oct. 4, 1946. Catholic U.

SARGENT, RICHARD (Richard Cox): Carmel, CA, 1933. Stanford.

SARRAZIN, MICHAEL: Quebec City, Can., May 22, 1940.

SAVAGE, JOHN (Youngs): Long Island, NY, Aug. 25, 1949. AADA.

SAVALAS, TELLY (Aristotle): Garden City, NY, Jan. 21, 1925. Columbia.

SAVOY, TERESA ANN: London, July 18, 1955.

SAXON, JOHN (Carmen Orrico): Brooklyn, Aug. 5, 1935.

SCARWID, DIANA: Savannah, GA; AADA, Pace U.

SCHEIDER, ROY: Orange, NJ, Nov. 10, 1935. Franklin-Marshall.

SCHELL, MARIA: Vienna, Jan. 15, 1926.

SCHELL, MAXIMILIAN: Vienna, Dec. 8, 1930.

SCHNEIDER, MARIA: Paris, Mar. 27, 1952.

SCHNEIDER, ROMY: Vienna, Sept. 23, 1938.

SCHRODER, RICKY: Staten Island, NY, Apr. 13, 1970.

SCHWARZENEGGER, ARNOLD: Austria, 1947.

SCOFIELD, PAUL: Hurstpierpoint, Eng., Jan. 21, 1922. London Mask Theatre School.

SCOTT, DEBRALEE: Elizabeth, NJ, Apr. 2.

SCOTT, GEORGE C.: Wise, VA, Oct. 18, 1927. U. Mo.

SCOTT, GORDON (Gordon M. Werschkul): Portland, OR, Aug. 3, 1927. Oregon U.

SCOTT, MARTHA: Jamesport, MO, Sept. 22, 1914. U. Mich.

SCOTT, RANDOLPH: Orange County, VA, Jan. 23, 1903. UNC.

SCOTT-TAYLOR, JONATHAN: Brazil, 1962.

SEAGULL, BARBARA HERSHEY (Herzstein): Hollywood, Feb. 5, 1948.

SEARS, HEATHER: London, 1935.

SECOMBE, HARRY: Swansea, Wales, Sept. 8, 1921.

SEGAL, GEORGE: NYC, Feb. 13, 1934. Columbia.

SELLARS, ELIZABETH: Glasgow, Scot., May 6, 1923.

SELWART, TONIO: Watenberg, Ger., June 9, 1906. Munich U.

SERNAS, JACQUES: Lithuania, July 30, 1925.

SEYLER, ATHENE (Athene Hannen): London, May 31, 1889.

SEYMOUR, ANNE: NYC, Sept. 11, 1909. American Laboratory Theatre.

SEYMOUR, JANE (Joyce Frankenberg): Hillingdon, Eng., Feb. 15, 1951.

SHARIF, OMAR (Michel Shalboub): Alexandria, Egypt, Apr. 10, 1932. Victoria Col.

SHARKEY, RAY: Brooklyn, NY, 1952; HB Studio.

SHATNER, WILLIAM: Montreal, Can., Mar. 22, 1931. McGill U.

SHAW, SEBASTIAN: Holt, Eng., May 29, 1905. Gresham School.

SHAW, STAN: Chicago, IL, 1952.

SHAWLEE, JOAN: Forest Hills, NY, Mar. 5, 1929.

SHAWN, DICK (Richard Shulefand): Buffalo, NY, Dec. 1, 1929. U. Miami.

SHEARER, MOIRA: Dunfermline, Scot., Jan. 17, 1926. London Theatre School.

SHEARER, NORMA: Montreal, Can., Aug. 10, 1900.

SHEEN, MARTIN (Ramon Estevez): Dayton, OH, Aug. 3, 1940.

SHEFFIELD, JOHN: Pasadena, CA, Apr. 11, 1931. UCLA.

SHEPARD, SAM (Rogers): Ft. Sheridan, IL, Nov. 5, 1943.

SHEPHERD, CYBIL: Memphis, TN, Feb. 18, 1950. Hunter, NYU.

SHIELDS, BROOKE: NYC, May 31, 1965.

SHIRE, TALIA: Lake Success, NY. Yale.

SHORE, DINAH (Frances Rose Shore): Winchester, TN, Mar. 1, 1917. Vanderbilt U.

SHOWALTER, MAX (formerly Casey Adams): Caldwell, KS, June 2, 1917. Pasadena Playhouse.

SIDNEY, SYLVIA: NYC, Aug. 8, 1910. Theatre Guild School.

SIGNORET, SIMONE (Simone Kaminker): Wiesbaden, Ger., Mar. 25, 1921. Solange Sicard School.

SILVERS, PHIL (Philip Silversmith): Brooklyn, May 11, 1911.

SIMMONS, JEAN: London, Jan. 31, 1929. Aida Foster School.

SIMON, SIMONE: Marseilles, France, Apr. 23, 1910.

SIMPSON, O. J. (Orenthal James): San Francisco, CA, July 9, 1947. UCLA.

SINATRA, FRANK: Hoboken, NJ, Dec. 12, 1915.

SINDEN, DONALD: Plymouth, Eng., Oct. 9, 1923. Webber-Douglas.

SKALA, LILIA: Vienna; U. Dresden.

SKELTON, RED (Richard): Vincennes, IN, July 18, 1910.

SKERRITT, TOM: Detroit, MI, 1935. Wayne State U.

SLEZAK, WALTER: Vienna, Austria, May 3, 1902.

SMITH, ALEXIS: Penticton, Can., June 8, 1921. LACC.

SMITH, CHARLES MARTIN: Los Angeles, CA, 1954. CalState U.

SMITH, JOHN (Robert E. Van Orden): Los Angeles, Mar. 6, 1931. UCLA.

SMITH, KATE (Kathryn Elizabeth): Greenville, VA, May 1, 1909.

SMITH, KENT: NYC, Mar. 19, 1907. Harvard U.

SMITH, LOIS: Topeka, KS, Nov. 3, 1930. U. Wash.

SMITH, MAGGIE: Ilford, Eng., Dec. 28, 1934.

SMITH, ROGER: South Gate, CA, Dec. 18, 1932. U. Ariz.

SMITHERS, WILLIAM: Richmond, VA, July 10, 1927. Catholic U.

SNODGRESS, CARRIE: Chicago, Oct. 27, 1946. UNI.

SNOWDEN, LEIGH: Memphis, TN, June 28, 1932. Lambeth Col.

SOLOMON, BRUCE: NYC, 1944. U. Miami, Wayne State U.

SOMERS, SUZANNE (Mahoney): San Bruno, CA, Oct. 16, 1946. Lone Mt. Col.

SOMMER, ELKE (Schletz): Berlin, Nov. 5, 1940.

SONNY (Salvatore Bono): 1935.

SORDI, ALBERTO: Rome, Italy, 1919.

SORVINO, PAUL: NYC, 1939. AMDA.

SOTHERN, ANN (Harriet Lake): Valley City, ND, Jan. 22, 1907. Washington U.

SPACEK, SISSY: Quitman, TX, Dec. 25, 1949. Actors Studio.

SPENSER, JEREMY: Ceylon, 1937.

SPRINGER, GARY: NYC, July 29, 1954. Hunter Col.

STACK, ROBERT: Los Angeles, Jan. 13, 1919. USC.

STADLEN, LEWIS J.: Brooklyn, Mar. 7, 1947. Neighborhood Playhouse.

STAFFORD, NANCY: Ft. Lauderdale, FL.

STALLONE, SYLVESTER: NYC, 1946. U. Miami.

STAMP, TERENCE: London, 1940.

STANDER, LIONEL: NYC, Jan. 11, 1908. UNC.

STANG, ARNOLD: Chelsea, MA, Sept. 28, 1925.

STANLEY, KIM (Patricia Reid): Tularosa, NM, Feb. 11, 1925. U. Tex.

STANWYCK, BARBARA (Ruby Stevens): Brooklyn, July 16, 1907.

STAPLETON, JEAN: NYC, Jan. 19, 1923.

STAPLETON, MAUREEN: Troy, NY, June 21, 1925.

STEEL, ANTHONY: London, May 21, 1920. Cambridge.

STEELE, TOMMY: London, Dec. 17, 1936.

STEENBURGEN, MARY: Newport, AR, 1953. Neighborhood Playhouse.

STEIGER, ROD: Westhampton, NY, Apr. 14, 1925.

STERLING, JAN (Jane Sterling Adriance): NYC, Apr. 3, 1923. Fay Compton School.

STERLING, ROBERT (William Sterling Hart): Newcastle, PA, Nov. 13, 1917. U. Pittsburgh.

STERN, DANIEL: Bethesda, MD, 1957.

STEVENS, ANDREW: Memphis, TN, June, 1955.

STEVENS, CONNIE (Concetta Ann Ingolia): Brooklyn, Aug. 8, 1938. Hollywood Professional School.

STEVENS, KAYE (Catherine): Pittsburgh, July 21, 1933.

STEVENS, MARK (Richard): Cleveland, OH, Dec. 13, 1920.

STEVENS, STELLA (Estelle Eggleston): Hot Coffee, MS, Oct. 1, 1936.

STEVENSON, PARKER: CT, 1953.

STEWART, ALEXANDRA: Montreal, Can., June 10, 1939. Louvre.

STEWART, ELAINE: Montclair, NJ, May 31, 1929.

STEWART, JAMES: Indiana, PA, May 20, 1908. Princeton.

STEWART, MARTHA (Martha Haworth): Bardwell, KY, Oct. 7, 1922.

STIMSON, SARA: Helotes, TX, 1973.

STOCKWELL, DEAN: Hollywood, March 5, 1936.

STORM, GALE (Josephine Cottle): Bloomington, TX, Apr. 5, 1922.

STRAIGHT, BEATRICE: Old Westbury, NY, Aug. 2, 1916. Dartington Hall.

STRASBERG, SUSAN: NYC, May 22, 1938.

STRAUD, DON: Hawaii, 1943.

STRAUSS, PETER: NY, 1947.

STREEP, MERYL (Mary Louise): Basking Ridge, NJ, Sept. 22, 1950. Vassar, Yale.

STREISAND, BARBRA: Brooklyn, Apr. 24, 1942.

STRITCH, ELAINE: Detroit, MI, Feb. 2, 1925. Drama Workshop.

STRODE, WOODY: Los Angeles, 1914.

STRUDWICK, SHEPPERD: Hillsboro, NC, Sept. 22, 1907. UNC.

STRUTHERS, SALLY: Portland, OR, July 28, 1948. Pasadena Playhouse.

SULLIVAN, BARRY (Patrick Barry): NYC, Aug. 29, 1912. NYU.

SUTHERLAND, DONALD: St. John, New Brunswick, Can., July 17, 1934. U. Toronto.

SVENSON, BO: Goteborg, Swed., Feb. 13, 1941. UCLA.

SWANSON, GLORIA (Josephine May Swenson): Chicago, Mar. 27, 1899. Chicago Art Inst.

SWEET, BLANCHE: Chicago, 1896.

SWINBURNE, NORA: Bath, Eng., July 24, 1902. RADA.

SWIT, LORETTA: Passaic, NJ, Nov. 4, AADA.

SYLVESTER, WILLIAM: Oakland, CA, Jan. 31, 1922. RADA.

SYMS, SYLVIA: London, June 1, 1934. Convent School.

TABORI, KRISTOFFER (Siegel): Los Angeles, Aug. 4, 1952.

TAKEI, GEORGE: Los Angeles, CA, Apr. 20. UCLA.

TALBOT, LYLE (Lysle Hollywood): Pittsburgh, Feb. 8, 1904.

TALBOT, NITA: NYC, Aug. 8, 1930. Irvine Studio School.

TAMBLYN, RUSS: Los Angeles, Dec. 30, 1934.

TANDY, JESSICA: London, June 7, 1909. Dame Owens' School.

TAYLOR, DON: Freeport, PA, Dec. 13, 1920. Penn State U.

TAYLOR, ELIZABETH: London, Feb. 27, 1932. Byron House School.

TAYLOR, KENT (Louis Weiss): Nashua, IA, May 11, 1906.

TAYLOR, ROD (Robert): Sydney, Aust., Jan. 11, 1929.

| Martin Sheen | Barbara Stanwyck | Joey Travolta | Cicely Tyson | Jon Voight |

TAYLOR-YOUNG, LEIGH: Wash., DC, Jan. 25, 1945. Northwestern.

TEAGUE, ANTHONY SKOOTER: Jacksboro, TX, Jan. 4, 1940.

TEEFY, MAUREEN: Minneapolis, MN, 1954; Julliard.

TEMPLE, SHIRLEY: Santa Monica, CA, Apr. 23, 1927.

TERRY-THOMAS (Thomas Terry Hoar Stevens): Finchley, London, July 14, 1911. Ardingly College.

TERZIEFF, LAURENT: Paris, June 25, 1935.

THACKER, RUSS: Washington, DC, June 23, 1946. Montgomery Col.

THAXTER, PHYLLIS: Portland, ME, Nov. 20, 1921. St. Genevieve.

THOMAS, DANNY (Amos Jacobs): Deerfield, MI, Jan. 6, 1914.

THOMAS, MARLO (Margaret): Detroit, Nov. 21, 1938. USC.

THOMAS, PHILIP: Columbus, OH, May 26, 1949. Oakwood Col.

THOMAS, RICHARD: NYC, June 13, 1951. Columbia.

THOMPSON, JACK (John Payne): Sydney, Aus., 1940. U. Brisbane.

THOMPSON, MARSHALL: Peoria, IL, Nov. 27, 1925. Occidental.

THOMPSON, REX: NYC, Dec. 14, 1942.

THOMPSON, SADA: Des Moines, IA, Sept. 27, 1929. Carnegie Tech.

THULIN, INGRID: Solleftea, Sweden, Jan. 27, 1929. Royal Drama Theatre.

TICOTIN, RACHEL: Bronx, NY, 1958.

TIERNEY, GENE: Brooklyn, Nov. 20, 1920. Miss Farmer's School.

TIERNEY, LAWRENCE: Brooklyn, Mar. 15, 1919. Manhattan College.

TIFFIN, PAMELA (Wonso): Oklahoma City, Oct. 13, 1942.

TODD, RICHARD: Dublin, Ire., June 11, 1919. Shrewsbury School.

TOLO, MARILU: Rome, Italy, 1944.

TOMLIN, LILY: Detroit, MI, Sept. 1, 1939. Wayne State U.

TOPOL (Chaim Topol): Tel-Aviv, Israel, Sept. 9, 1935.

TORN, RIP: Temple, TX, Feb. 6, 1931. U. Tex.

TORRES, LIZ: NYC, 1947. NYU.

TOTTER, AUDREY: Joliet, IL, Dec. 20, 1918.

TRAVERS, BILL: Newcastle-on-Tyne, Eng., Jan. 3, 1922.

TRAVIS, RICHARD (William Justice): Carlsbad, NM, Apr. 17, 1913.

TRAVOLTA, JOEY: Englewood, NJ, 1952.

TRAVOLTA, JOHN: Englewood, NJ, Feb. 18, 1954.

TREMAYNE, LES: London, Apr. 16, 1913. Northwestern, Columbia, UCLA.

TREVOR, CLAIRE (Wemlinger): NYC, March 8, 1909.

TRINTIGNANT, JEAN-LOUIS: Pont-St. Esprit, France, Dec. 11, 1930. Dullin-Balachova Drama School.

TRYON, TOM: Hartford, CT, Jan. 14, 1926. Yale.

TSOPEI, CORINNA: Athens, Greece, June 21, 1944.

TUCKER, FORREST: Plainfield, IN, Feb. 12, 1919. George Washington U.

TURNER, KATHLEEN: Springfield, MO., June 19, 1954. UMd.

TURNER, LANA (Julia Jean Mildred Frances Turner): Wallace, ID, Feb. 8, 1921.

TUSHINGHAM, RITA: Liverpool, Eng., 1940.

TUTIN, DOROTHY: London, Apr. 8, 1930.

TUTTLE, LURENE: Pleasant Lake, IN, Aug. 20, 1906. USC.

TWIGGY (Lesley Hornby): London, Sept. 19, 1949.

TYLER, BEVERLY (Beverly Jean Saul): Scranton, PA, July 5, 1928.

TYRRELL, SUSAN: San Francisco, 1946.

TYSON, CICELY: NYC, Dec. 19.

UGGAMS, LESLIE: NYC, May 25, 1943.

ULLMANN, LIV: Tokyo, Dec. 10, 1938. Webber-Douglas Acad.

USTINOV, PETER: London, Apr. 16, 1921. Westminster School.

VACCARO, BRENDA: Brooklyn, Nov. 18, 1939. Neighborhood Playhouse.

VALLEE, RUDY (Hubert): Island Pond, VT, July 28, 1901. Yale.

VALLI, ALIDA: Pola, Italy, May 31, 1921. Rome Academy of Drama.

VALLONE, RAF: Riogio, Italy, Feb. 17, 1916. Turin U.

VAN CLEEF, LEE: Somerville, NJ, Jan. 9, 1925.

VAN DE VEN, MONIQUE: Holland, 1957.

VAN DEVERE, TRISH (Patricia Dressel): Englewood Cliffs, NJ, Mar. 9, 1945. Ohio Wesleyan.

VAN DOREN, MAMIE (Joan Lucile Olander): Rowena, SD, Feb. 6, 1933.

VAN DYKE, DICK: West Plains, MO, Dec. 13, 1925.

VAN FLEET, JO: Oakland, CA, 1922.

VAN PATTEN, DICK: NYC, Dec. 9, 1928.

VAN PATTEN, JOYCE: NYC, Mar. 9, 1934.

VAUGHN, ROBERT: NYC, Nov. 22, 1932. USC.

VEGA, ISELA: Mexico, 1940.

VENNERA, CHICK: Herkimer, NY, Mar. 27, 1952. Pasadena Playhouse.

VENTURA, LINO: Parma, Italy, July 14, 1919.

VENUTA, BENAY: San Francisco, Jan. 27, 1911.

VERDON, GWEN: Culver City, CA, Jan. 13, 1925.

VEREEN, BEN: Miami, FL, Oct. 10, 1946.

VICTOR, JAMES: (Lincoln Rafael Peralta Diaz) Santiago, D.R., July 27, 1939. Haaren HS/NYC.

VILLECHAIZE, HERVE: Paris, Apr. 23, 1943.

VINCENT, JAN-MICHAEL: Denver, CO, July 15, 1944. Ventura.

VIOLET, ULTRA (Isabelle Collin-Dufresne): Grenoble, France.

VITALE, MILLY: Rome, Italy, July 16, 1938. Lycee Chateaubriand.

VOHS, JOAN: St. Albans, NY, July 30, 1931.

VOIGHT, JON: Yonkers, NY, Dec. 29, 1938. Catholic U.

VOLONTE, GIAN MARIA: Milan, Italy, Apr. 9, 1933.

VON SYDOW, MAX: Lund, Swed., July 10, 1929. Royal Drama Theatre.

WAGNER, LINDSAY: Los Angeles, 1949.

WAGNER, ROBERT: Detroit, Feb. 10, 1930.

WAHL, KEN: Chicago, IL, 1957.

WAITE, GENEVIEVE: South Africa, 1949.

WALKEN, CHRISTOPHER: Astoria, NY, Mar. 31, 1943. Hofstra.

WALKER, CLINT: Hartfold, IL, May 30, 1927. USC.

WALKER, NANCY (Ann Myrtle Swoyer): Philadelphia, May 10, 1921.

WALLACH, ELI: Brooklyn, Dec. 7, 1915. CCNY, U. Tex.

WALLACH, ROBERTA: NYC, Aug. 2, 1955.

WALLIS, SHANI: London, Apr. 5, 1941.

WALSTON, RAY: New Orleans, Nov. 22, 1917. Cleveland Playhouse.

WALTER, JESSICA: Brooklyn, NY, Jan. 31, 1940. Neighborhood Playhouse.

WANAMAKER, SAM: Chicago, June 14, 1919. Drake.

WARD, BURT (Gervis): Los Angeles, July 6, 1945.

| Jennifer Warren | Billy Dee Williams | Raquel Welch | Paul Winfield | Ann Zacharias |

WARD, RACHEL: London, 1957.

WARD, SIMON: London, 1941.

WARDEN, JACK: Newark, NJ, Sept. 18, 1920.

WARNER, DAVID: Manchester, Eng., 1941. RADA.

WARREN, JENNIFER: NYC, Aug. 12, 1941. U. Wisc.

WARREN, LESLEY ANN: NYC, Aug. 16, 1946.

WARRICK, RUTH: St. Joseph, MO, June 29, 1915. U. Mo.

WASHBOURNE, MONA: Birmingham, Eng., Nov. 27, 1903.

WASHINGTON, DENZEL: Mt. Vernon, NY. Dec. 28, 1954. Fordham.

WASSON, CRAIG: Ontario, Or., Mar. 15, 1954. UOre.

WATERSTON, SAM: Cambridge, MA, Nov. 15, 1940. Yale.

WATLING, JACK: London, Jan. 13, 1923. Italia Conti School.

WATSON, DOUGLASS: Jackson, GA, Feb. 24, 1921. UNC.

WAYNE, DAVID (Wayne McKeehan): Travers City, MI, Jan. 30, 1914. Western Michigan State U.

WAYNE, PATRICK: Los Angeles, July 15, 1939. Loyola.

WEAVER, DENNIS: Joplin, MO, June 4, 1924. U. Okla.

WEAVER, MARJORIE: Crossville, TN, Mar. 2, 1913. Indiana U.

WEAVER, SIGOURNEY: NYC, 1949. Stanford, Yale.

WEBB, ALAN: York, Eng., July 2, 1906. Dartmouth.

WEBB, JACK: Santa Monica, CA, Apr. 2, 1920.

WEBBER, ROBERT: Santa Ana, CA, Sept. 14, 1925. Compton Jr. Col.

WEDGEWORTH, ANN: Abilene, TX, Jan. 21. U. Tex.

WEISSMULLER, JOHNNY: Chicago, June 2, 1904. Chicago U.

WELCH, RAQUEL (Tejada): Chicago, Sept. 5, 1940.

WELD, TUESDAY (Susan): NYC, Aug. 27, 1943. Hollywood Professional School.

WELDON, JOAN: San Francisco, Aug. 5, 1933. San Francisco Conservatory.

WELLES, GWEN: NYC, Mar. 4.

WELLES, ORSON: Kenosha, WI, May 6, 1915. Todd School.

WERNER, OSKAR: Vienna, Nov. 13, 1922.

WESTON, JACK (Morris Weinstein): Cleveland, OH, Aug. 21, 1915.

WHITAKER, JOHNNY: Van Nuys, CA, Dec. 13. 1959.

WHITE, CAROL: London, Apr. 1, 1944.

WHITE, CHARLES: Perth Amboy, NJ, Aug. 29, 1920. Rutgers U.

WHITE, JESSE: Buffalo, NY, Jan. 3, 1919.

WHITMAN, STUART: San Francisco, Feb. 1, 1929. CCLA.

WHITMORE, JAMES: White Plains, NY, Oct. 1, 1921. Yale.

WHITNEY, GRACE LEE: Detroit, MI, Apr. 1, 1930.

WIDDOES, KATHLEEN: Wilmington, DE, Mar. 21, 1939.

WIDMARK, RICHARD: Sunrise, MN, Dec. 26, 1914. Lake Forest.

WILCOX-HORNE, COLIN: Highlands NC, Feb. 4, 1937. U. Tenn.

WILCOXON, HENRY: British West Indies, Sept. 8, 1905.

WILDE, CORNEL: NYC, Oct. 13, 1915. CCNY, Columbia.

WILDER, GENE (Jerome Silberman): Milwaukee, WI, June 11, 1935. U. Iowa.

WILLIAMS, BILLY DEE: NYC, Apr. 6, 1937.

WILLIAMS, CINDY: Van Nuys, CA, Aug. 22, 1947. LACC.

WILLIAMS, DICK A.: Chicago, IL, Aug. 9, 1938.

WILLIAMS, EMLYN: Mostyn, Wales, Nov. 26, 1905. Oxford.

WILLIAMS, ESTHER: Los Angeles, Aug. 8, 1921.

WILLIAMS, GRANT: NYC, Aug. 18, 1930. Queens College.

WILLIAMS, JOHN: Chalfont, Eng., Apr. 15, 1903. Lancing College.

WILLIAMS, TREAT (Richard): Rowayton, CT. 1952.

WILLIAMSON, FRED: Gary, IN, Mar. 5, 1938. Northwestern.

WILSON, DEMOND: NYC, Oct. 13, 1946. Hunter Col.

WILSON, FLIP (Clerow Wilson): Jersey City, NJ, Dec. 8, 1933.

WILSON, NANCY: Chillicothe, OH, Feb. 20, 1937.

WILSON, SCOTT: Atlanta, GA, 1942.

WINDE, BEATRICE: Chicago, Jan. 6.

WINDOM, WILLIAM: NYC, Sept. 28, 1923. Williams Col.

WINDSOR, MARIE (Emily Marie Bertelson): Marysvale, UT, Dec. 11, 1924. Brigham Young U.

WINFIELD, PAUL: Los Angeles, 1940. UCLA.

WINKLER, HENRY: NYC, Oct. 30, 1945. Yale.

WINN, KITTY: Wash., D.C., 1944. Boston U.

WINTERS, JONATHAN: Dayton, OH, Nov. 11, 1925. Kenyon Col.

WINTERS, ROLAND: Boston, Nov. 22, 1904.

WINTERS, SHELLEY (Shirley Schrift): St. Louis, Aug. 18, 1922. Wayne U.

WINWOOD, ESTELLE: Kent, Eng., Jan. 24, 1883. Lyric Stage Academy.

WITHERS, GOOGIE: Karachi, India, Mar. 12, 1917. Italia Conti.

WITHERS, JANE: Atlanta, GA, 1926.

WOODLAWN, HOLLY (Harold Ajzenberg): Juana Diaz, PR, 1947.

WOODS, JAMES: Vernal, UT, Apr. 18, 1947. MIT.

WOODWARD, JOANNE: Thomasville, GA, Feb. 27, 1930. Neighborhood Playhouse.

WOOLAND, NORMAN: Dusseldorf, Ger., Mar. 16, 1910. Edward VI School.

WOPAT, TOM: Lodi, WI, 1950.

WORONOV, MARY: Brooklyn, Dec. 8, 1946. Cornell.

WRAY, FAY: Alberta, Can., Sept. 15, 1907.

WRIGHT, TERESA: NYC, Oct. 27, 1918.

WYATT, JANE: Campgaw, NJ, Aug. 10, 1911. Barnard College.

WYMAN, JANE (Sarah Jane Fulks): St. Joseph, MO, Jan. 4, 1914.

WYMORE, PATRICE: Miltonvale, KS, Dec. 17, 1926.

WYNN, KEENAN: NYC, July 27, 1916. St. John's.

WYNN, MAY (Donna Lee Hickey): NYC, Jan. 8, 1930.

WYNTER, DANA (Dagmar): London, June 8, 1927. Rhodes U.

YORK, DICK: Fort Wayne, IN, Sept. 4, 1928. De Paul U.

YORK, MICHAEL: Fulmer, Eng., Mar. 27, 1942. Oxford.

YORK, SUSANNAH: London, Jan. 9, 1941. RADA.

YOUNG, ALAN (Angus): North Shield, Eng., Nov. 19, 1919.

YOUNG, LORETTA (Gretchen): Salt Lake City, Jan. 6, 1912. Immaculate Heart College.

YOUNG, ROBERT: Chicago, Feb. 22, 1907.

ZACHARIAS, ANN: Stockholm, Sw., 1956.

ZADORA, PIA: Forest Hills, NY. 1954.

ZETTERLING, MAI: Sweden, May 27, 1925. Ordtuery Theatre School.

ZIMBALIST, EFREM, JR.: NYC, Nov. 30, 1918. Yale.

OBITUARIES

JACK ALBERTSON, 74, born in Malden, MA, veteran actor on stage, film, tv and in vaudeville, died of cancer Nov. 25, 1981 in his home in Hollywood Hills, CA. His first film was in 1937 in "Rebecca of Sunnybrook Farm," followed by "Top Banana," "The Harder They Fall," "Monkey on My Back," "Man of a Thousand Faces." "Don't Go Near the Water," "Teacher's Pet," "Never Steal Anything Small," "Lover Come Back," "Convicts 4," "Period of Adjustment," "Kissin' Cousins," "A Tiger Walks," "How to Murder Your Wife," "The Flim Flam Man," "How to Save a Marriage," "The Subject Was Roses" for which he received an Oscar (also a Tony for the original Broadway play), "The Poseidon Adventure" "Changes," "Justine," "Rabbit Run," "Willy Wonka and the Chocolate Factory," and "Dead and Buried." In tv he had continuing roles in "The Thin Man," "Ensign O'Toole," "Room for One More," and "Chico and the Man." Survivors include his wife, and a daughter Maura Dhu who is a singer-actress.

MATTHEW "STYMIE" BEARD, 57, one of the "Our Gang" comedy actors, died Jan. 8, 1981 after a stroke in Los Angeles, CA. As "The Little Rascals" the "Our Gang" comedies appeared on TV and Stymie was the baldheaded boy with the derby. He later appeared in "Kid Millions," "Rainbow on the River," "Jezebel," "Beloved Brat," "Way Down South" and "The Return of Jesse James." His sister and five brothers survive.

BEULAH BONDI, 92, Chicago-born character actress of stage, film and television, died in Woodland Hills, CA., Jan. 11, 1981 of pulmonary complications following a fall that fractured several ribs. She went to Hollywood in 1931 to re-create her role from the Broadway play "Street Scene," and remained to appear in over 50 films, including "Arrowsmith," "Rain," "Painted Veil," "Trail of the Lonesome Pine," "The Gorgeous Hussy," "Make Way for Tomorrow," "The Buccaneer," "Of Human Hearts," "On Borrowed Time" "Mr. Smith Goes to Washington," "Our Town," "Shepherd of the Hills," "Penny Serenade," "One Foot in Heaven," "Watch on the Rhine," "And Now Tomorrow," "Our Hearts Were Young and Gay," "The Southerner," "Back to Bataan," "Breakfast in Hollywood," "Sister Kenny," "So Dear to My Heart," "The Snake Pit," "Life of Riley," "The Furies," "Lone Star," "Back from Eternity," "A Summer Place," "Tammy Tell Me True," and "Track of the Cat." In 1977 she received an Emmy for her appearance in a segment of "The Waltons." She was never married and left no immediate survivors.

RICHARD BOONE, 63, Los Angeles-born character actor of stage, film and tv, died Jan. 10, 1981 of throat cancer in his home in St. Augustine, FL. He appeared in 65 movies and 11 plays, but was best known for his role of Paladin in the tv series "Have Gun Will Travel" from 1957 to 1963. His film credits include "The Halls of Montezuma," "Call Me Mister," "The Desert Fox," "Way of a Gaucho," "Man on a Tightrope," "Vickie," "The Robe," "Dragnet," "Away All Boats," "The Garment Jungle," "The Alamo," "A Thunder of Drums," "Rio Conchos," "The War Lord," "Hombre," "Big Jake," "Night of the Following Day," "The Kremlin Letter," "Little Big Man," "The Devil's Backbone," and "The Shootist." In 1972 he retired to Florida to paint, and was later appointed Florida's cultural ambassador. Surviving are his widow, and a son Peter.

KEEFE BRASSELLE, 58, Ohio-born singer, drummer, comedian and film actor, died July 7, 1981 of cirrhosis of the liver in Downey, CA. After appearing with bands, he made his film debut in 1944 in "Janie," subsequently appearing in "River Gang," "Not Wanted," "Dial 1119," "A Place in the Sun," "The Unknown Man," "It's a Big Country," "Skirts Ahoy!," "The Eddie Cantor Story," "Three Young Texans," "Mad at the World," "Bring Your Smile Along," "Battle Stations," "The Fighting Wildcats." He also wrote a novel "The Cannibals," and produced 3 films for tv. A daughter survives.

HOAGY CARMICHAEL, 82, composer, singer and character actor, died Dec. 27, 1981 of cardiac problems in Rancho Mirage, CA. He wrote more than 50 hit songs, including "Stardust," "Old Buttermilk Sky," "Skylark," "Lazy Bones," "Blue Orchids,"

"Small Fry," "I Get Along without You Very Well," "Two Sleepy People," and "In the Cool, Cool, Cool of the Evening" for which he received a 1951 "Oscar." His film roles were in "Topper," "To Have and Have Not,", "Johnny Angel," "The Best Years of Our Lives," "Night Song," "Young Man with a Horn," "Johnny Holiday," "Las Vegas Story," "Belles on Their Toes" and "Timberjack." Surviving are his second wife, actress Wanda McKay, and two sons by his first wife. He was buried in his native Bloomington, Indiana.

PADDY CHAYEFSKY, 58, nee Sidney Q. Chayefsky in The Bronx, award-winning playwright and screenwriter, died Aug. 1, 1981 of cancer NYC. His credits include "Marty" for which he received a 1955 Oscar, "As Young as You Feel," "The Catered Affair," "The Bachelor Party," "The Goddess," "Middle of the Night," "The Americanization of Emily," "The Hospital" (1971 Academy Award), "Network" (his third Oscar in 1976), and "Altered States." He is survived by his widow, and a son Daniel.

RENE CLAIR, 82, nee Chomette, one of the great directors of the French cinema, screenwriter and novelist, died Mar. 15, 1981 in his home in Neuilly, France. He was the first person elected to the French Academy solely for film work, and for many years headed the jury at the Cannes Film Festival. As director and writer his 28 films (between 1923 and 1965) include "Under the Roofs of Paris," "The Million," "The Horse Ate the Hat," "A Nous, La Liberte," "The Ghost Goes West," "Break the News," "Flame of New Orleans," "I Married a Witch," "Forever and a Day," "It Happened Tomorrow," "And Then There Were None," "Man about Town," "Beauty and the Devil," "Beauties of the Night," "The Grand Maneuver," "Gates of Paris," "Love and the Frenchwoman," "Three Fables of Love," "Le Silence Est d'Or," "Les Fetes Galantes." Surviving are his widow and their son Jean-Francois Clair.

STANLEY CLEMENTS, 55, NY-born actor, who began his career as a child, died Oct. 16, 1981 of emphysema in Los Angeles, CA. His movies include "Accent on Love," "Down in San Diego," "On the Sunny Side," "Smart Alecks," "Neath the Brooklyn Bridge," "The More the Merrier," "Sweet Rosie O'Grady," "Going My Way," "See My Lawyer," "Salty O'Rourke," "Babe Ruth Story," "Winner Take All," "Bad Boy," "Johnny Holiday," "10th Avenue Gang," "Destination Murder," "Pride of Maryland," "Boots Malone," "Army Bound," "Off Limits," "Canon City," "Rocket Man," "Looking for Danger," "In the Money," "Saintly Sinners," "Tammy and the Doctor," "That Darn Cat." He is survived by his second wife and her orphaned nephew whom he adopted. His first wife was actress Gloria Grahame.

MORGAN CONWAY, 81, retired film and stage actor, died Nov. 16, 1981 in Livingston, NJ. He was a founding member of the Screen Actors Guild. His picture credits include "Looking for Trouble," "Nurse from Brooklyn," "Crime Ring," "Blackwell's Island," "Charlie Chan in Reno," "The Saint Takes Over," "Brother Orchid," "Jack London," "Badman's Territory," "The Truth About Murder," "Dick Tracy" and "Dick Tracy vs Cueball." He retired in 1949. His widow and son survive.

JIM DAVIS, 65, Missouri-born film and tv actor, died Apr. 26, 1981 in his sleep at his home in Northridge, CA. where he was recovering from abdominal surgery. He had appeared in over 150 films and 300 tv episodes, but his greatest success came with the character Jock Ewing in the tv series "Dallas" from which he was on hiatus. His picture credits include "Gallant Bess," "White Cargo," "What Next, Corporal Hargrove?," "Romance of Rosie Ridge," "Louisiana," "Winter Meeting," "Hellfire," "California Passage," "The Showdown," "Little Big Horn," "Three Desperate Men," "The Outcast," "Oh! Susanna," "The Big Sky," "Woman of the North Country," "Timberjack," "Bottom of the Bottle," "The Maverick Queen," "Alias Jesse James," "Fort Utah," "The Blood Seekers," "Monte Walsh," "Rio Lobo," "One Little Indian," "Dracula vs. Frankenstein" and "The Choirboys." He is survived by his wife of 36 years.

| Jack Albertson | Beulah Bondi | Richard Boone | Hoagy Carmichael | Melvyn Douglas | Madge Evans |

BRENDA de BANZIE, 65, British character actress on stage, film and tv, died Mar. 5, 1981 following surgery in Maywards Heath, Sussex, Eng. Among her film credits are "The Long Dark Hall," "Hobson's Choice," "Doctor at Sea," "A Kid for Two Farthings," "The Man Who Knew Too Much," "Too Many Crooks," "The Entertainer," "The 39 Steps," "Come September," "The Mark," "Flame in the Streets," "A Pair of Briefs," "The Pink Panther," "A Matter of Innocence." Surviving are her husband, Rupert Marsh, their son, and a niece, actress Lois de Banzie.

FRANK DeKOVA, 71, film, tv and stage character actor, was found dead Oct. 19, 1981 in his home in Sepulveda, CA. His movies include "The Mob," "Viva Zapata!," "Pony Soldier," "The Big Sky," "Desert Song," "Arrowhead," "The Robe," "King of the Khyber Rifles," "Drum Beat," "Passion," "Man from Laramie," "Hold Back Tomorrow," "The Ten Commandments," "Cowboy," "Brothers Karamazov," "Apache Territory," "The Rise and Fall of Legs Diamond," "Atlantis," "The Greatest Story Ever Told" and "The Mechanic." He was probably best known for his continuing role of Chief White Eagle on the "F-Troop" tv series. His widow and daughter survive.

JEAN DIXON, 85, Connecticut-born screen and stage actress, died Feb. 12, 1981 after a long illness in NYC. After establishing herself on Broadway, she went to Hollywood for such films as "The Lady Lies," "The Kiss before the Mirror," "Sadie McKee," "I'll Love You Always," "Mr. Dynamite," "She Married Her Boss," "To Mary with Love," "My Man Godfrey," "The Magnificent Brute," "You Only Live Once," "Swing High, Swing Low," "Joy of Living," "Holiday." Her husband of 40 years predeceased her by a year. No immediate survivors.

MELVYN DOUGLAS, 80, né Hesselberg, Atlanta-born award-winning screen, stage and tv actor, died in NYC Aug. 4, 1981 of pneumonia complicated by a heart ailment. After achieving success on Broadway, he made his film debut in 1931 in "Tonight or Never," followed by "The Wiser Sex," "As You Desire Me," "The Old Dark House," "Nagana," "Counsellor-at-Law," "She Married Her Boss," "Mary Burns, Fugitive," "Annie Oakley," "The Gorgeous Hussy," "Theodora Goes Wild," "Captains Courageous," "Angel," "I'll Take Romance," "Arsene Lupin Returns," "There's Always a Woman," "Fast Company," "That Certain Age," "The Shining Hour," "Good Girls Go to Paris," "Ninotchka," "Too Many Husbands," "This Thing Called Love," "A Woman's Face," "Two Faced Woman," "We Were Dancing," "They All Kissed the Bride," "Sea Grass," "Mr Blanding Builds His Dream House," "Billy Budd," "Hud" for which he received an Oscar (Best Supporting Actor), "The Americanization of Emily," "Rapture," "Hotel," "I Never Sang for My Father," "One Is a Lonely Number," "The Candidate," "The Tenant," "Twilight's Last Gleaming," "Being There" for which he received his second Oscar in 1979 and "Ghost Story," his last film. He was married for 49 years to actress Helen Gahagan who also served three terms as U.S. Representative from California, and died in 1980. Survivors include a daughter and two sons.

ALLAN DWAN, 96, Canadian-born pioneer film director, died of heart failure Dec. 21, 1981 in Woodland Hills, CA. Before he retired in 1961 he estimated that he had directed 1850 films, many of them one-reelers, from the time he became a director in 1909. Among his credits are "Robin Hood," "Zaza," "Manhandled," "Wages of Virtue," "Night Life of New York," "Heidi," "Rebecca of Sunnybrook Farm," "Suez," "Sands of Iwo Jima," "The Iron Mask," "Belle Le Grand," "The Three Musketeers" with the Ritz Brothers, "Up in Mabel's Room," "Friendly Enemies," "Abroad with Two Yanks," "Brewster's Millions," "The Wild Blue Yonder," "I Dream of Jeanie," "Passion," "Tennessee's Partner," "Slightly Scarlet," "River's Edge," and his last "Most Dangerous Man Alive." No reported survivors.

ISOBEL ELSOM, 87, British-born screen and stage actress, died Jan. 12, 1981 of heart failure in Woodland Hills, CA. Her film credits include "Monsieur Verdoux," "Stranglehold," "Illegal," "Ladies in Retirement," "Eagle Squadron," "Seven Sweethearts," "War against Mrs. Hadley," "You Were Never Lovelier," "Between Two Worlds," "Casanova Brown," "The Unseen," "Two Sisters from Boston," "Of Human Bondage," "The Two Mrs. Carrolls," "Ivy," "The Ghost and Mrs. Muir," "Escape Me Never," "Love from a Stranger," "The Paradine Case," "The Philadelphians," "Deep in My Heart," "The Bellboy," "Desiree," "Love Is a Many Splendored Thing," "Lust for Life," "The Miracle," "My Fair Lady" and "The Pleasure Seekers." She retired in 1964. Her third husband, actor Carl Harbord, died in 1958.

MADGE EVANS, 71, NYC-born actress on screen and stage, died of cancer Apr. 26, 1981 at her home in Oakland, NJ. She began her career as a child model for Fairy Soap and made her film debut at 5 in "The Sign of the Cross," followed by such silent pictures as "Zaza," "Seventeen," "Husband and Wife," "Sudden Riches," "Beloved Adventures," "Little Duchess," "The Burglar," "The Volunteer," "Web of Desire," "Corner Grocer," "Maternity," "Gates of Gladness," "Golden Wall," "Power and the Glory," "Stolen Orders," "Neighbor," "Wanted—A Mother," "The Love Nest," "Home Wanted," "On the Banks of the Wabash," "Classmates," Her talking films include "Son of India," "Sporting Blood," "Guilty Hands," "Heartbreak," "Lovers Courageous," "Huddle," "Fast Life," "Hallelujah I'm a Bum," "Hell Below," "Made on Broadway," "Dinner at 8," "Broadway to Hollywood," "Day of Reckoning," "The Show-Off," "Stand Up and Cheer," "Paris Interlude," "What Every Woman Knows," "David Copperfield," "Age of Indiscretion," "Men without Names," "Transatlantic Tunnel," "Exclusive Story," "Moonlight Murder," "Piccadilly Jim," "Pennies from Heaven," "Espionage," "The Thirteenth Chair," "Sinners in Paradise," and her last in 1938 "Army Girl!" She is survived by her husband, playwright Sidney Kingsley.

HUGO FRIEDHOFER, 80, San Francisco-born composer and orchestrator, died May 17, 1981 after a fall in his home in Hollywood, CA. He was nominated six times for Academy Awards, and won an Oscar for "The Best Years of Our Lives" in 1947. His other scores include "Sunny Side Up," "The Sea Hawk," "The Sea Wolf," "Anthony Adverse," "Marco Polo" (1937), "The Young Lions," "One-Eyed Jacks, "Valley of the Giants" and "Joan of Arc." A daughter survives.

CHIEF DAN GEORGE, 82, Canadian-born American Indian film and tv actor, died Sept. 23, 1981 in his sleep in Vancouver, Canada. After becoming an actor at age of 62, his films include "The Ecstasy of Rita Joe," "The Bears and I," "Spirit of the Wind," "Americathon," "The Outlaw Josey Wales," "Shadow of the Hawk," "Smith," and "Little Big Man" for which he received an Academy nomination. In addition to being chief of his tribe, he was also an eloquent spokesman for native rights and the environment. Six children survive.

GLORIA GRAHAME, 55, screen, stage and tv actress, died of cancer Oct. 5, 1981 in NYC. She was born in Pasadena, CA., but began her career on stage in Chicago and NYC. She moved to Hollywood in 1944 where she appeared in such films as "Cry Havoc," "Blonde Fever," "Without Love," "It's a Wonderful Life," "It Happened in Brooklyn," "Crossfire," "Merton of the Movies," "Song of the Thin Man," "Roughshod," "In a Lonely Place," "The Greatest Show on Earth," "Macao," "Sudden Fear," "Man on a Tightrope," "The Big Heat," "Naked Alibi," "Not as a Stranger," "The Cobweb," "Oklahoma!," "Odds against Tomorrow," "Head over Heels," "Melvin and Howard," and in 1952 she won an Oscar for her supporting role in "The Bad and the Beautiful." She was married and divorced four times, and leaves four children. Interment was in California.

| Chief Dan George | Gloria Grahame | Sara Haden | Ann Harding | Wanda Hendrix | William Holden |

MICHAEL GRANGER, 58, film, stage and tv actor, died of a heart attack Oct. 22, 1981 in NYC. After his film debut in 1952, he appeared in over 35 pictures, including "Hiawatha," "Salome," "White Witch Doctor" and "The Big Heat." No reported survivors.

SARA HADEN, 82, Texas-born character actress, died Sept. 15, 1981 in Woodland Hills, CA. After launching her career in 1934 in "Spitfire," she appeared in over 70 films, including Aunt Milly in the Andy Hardy series, "Finishing School," "The Fountain," "Music in the Air," "Anne of Green Gables," "Black Fury," "Way Down East," "Magnificent Obsession," "Captain January," "Half Angel," "Little Miss Marker," "Poor Little Rich Girl," "Reunion," "The Last of Mrs. Cheyney," "A Family Affair," "First Lady," "You're Only Young Once," "Four Girls in White," "The Secret of Dr. Kildare," "The Shop Around the Corner," "Boom Town," "The Trial of Mary Dugan," "Barnacle Bill," "H. M. Pulham, Esq.," "Woman of the Year," "Best Foot Forward," "Above Suspicion," "Thousands Cheer," "Our Vines Have Tender Grapes," "Our Hearts Were Growing Up," "Mr. Ace," "Roughshod," "The Big Cat," "A Lion Is in the Streets," "Betrayed Woman," and her last in 1958 "Andy Hardy Comes Home." She was married to actor Richard Abbott 1921-48. A cousin survives.

ANN HARDING, 79, stage, screen and tv actress for over 30 years, died after a long illness on Sept. 1, 1981 in her home in Sherman Oaks, CA. Born in San Antonio, TX., she began her career on Broadway in 1921, and her first Hollywood film, "Paris Bound," in 1929. She subsequently appeared in over 40 films, including "Condemned," "Holiday," "Girl of the Golden West," "East Lynne," "Devotion," "Westward Passage," "Animal Kingdom," "When Ladies Meet," "Gallant Lady," "The Fountain," "The Flame Within," "Enchanted April," "Peter Ibbetson," "Love from a Stranger," "Stella Dallas," "Biography of a Bachelor Girl," "The Male Animal," "Mission to Moscow," "North Star," "Nine Girls," "Janie," "Those Endearing Young Charms," "Magnificent Yankee," "Man in the Gray Flannel Suit" and "Strange Intruder." She married and divorced actor Harry Banister and conductor Werner Janssen. A daughter survives.

ROBERT HARRIS, 70, stage, screen and tv character actor, died Nov. 30, 1981 in Los Angeles, CA. He was probably best known for his character Jake on the tv series "The Goldbergs." His films include "The Big Caper," "Abandon Ship," "No Down Payment," "Peyton Place," "Oscar Wilde," "Convicts 4," "America America," "The Model Murder Case," "Reprieve," "Mirage" and "Valley of the Dolls." No reported survivors.

RUSSELL "LUCKY" HAYDEN, 70, romantic film cowboy, died of viral pneumonia June 9, 1981 in Palm Springs, CA. He began his film career in 1937 with "Hills of Old Wyoming" and in 1943-44 was voted one of the top ten western stars. He was Lucky in the Hopalong Cassidy movies, and appeared in the tv series "Cowboy G-Men," "26 Men" and "Judge Roy Bean." Among his many pictures are "Texas Trail," "Pride of the West," "In Old Mexico," "The Mysterious Rider," "Sunset Trail," "Law of the Pampas," "In Old Colorado," "Two in a Taxi," "West of Tombstone," "Minesweeper," "Albuquerque," "Apache Chief," "Outlaw Fury," "Texans Never Cry," and "Valley of Flame." Surviving is his widow, former actress Lillian Porter.

EDITH HEAD, 82, celebrated costume designer, died of a rare disease of the bone marrow in Los Angeles on Oct. 24, 1981. In a career that spanned more than 50 years, she received 8 Academy Awards and was nominated for 34 during her career. She began her career in 1923 at Paramount and was working on a new film at the time of her death. She was born in San Bernardino, Ca., and after graduation from college, taught French until she decided to submit sketches to Paramount. She received Oscars for "The Heiress," "All about Eve," "A Place in the Sun," "Roman Holiday," "Sabrina," "The Facts of Life," "Samson and Delilah" and

"The Sting." She was married for 30 years to Oscar-winning art director Wiard (Bill) Ihnen who died in 1979. There are no survivors.

WANDA HENDRIX, 52, diminutive Florida-born actress, died of pneumonia Feb. 1, 1981 in Burbank, CA. She began her career at 15 and it spanned 20 years. Her first film, "Confidential Agent," was followed by "Nora Prentiss," "Welcome Stranger," "Ride the Pink Horse," "Miss Tatlock's Millions," "My Own True Love," "Prince of Foxes," "Capt. Carey, U.S.A.," "Sierra," "The Admiral Was a Lady," "Saddle Tramp," "My Outlaw Brother," "Highway Dragnet," "The Golden Mask," "Black Dakotas," "Johnny Cool," and "Stage to Thunder Rock." She was married to and divorced from actor Audie Murphy, and socialite James Stack. No reported survivors.

WILLIAM HOLDEN, 63, nee William Franklin Beedle, Jr., in O'Fallon, Il., Oscar-winning actor, was found dead Oct. 16, 1981 in his apartment in Santa Monica, CA. The autopsy indicated his death was accidental, from excessive bleeding caused by tripping on a rug and falling into an end table. He made his film debut in 1939 in "Million Dollar Legs" and changed his name. Among his more than 50 subsequent films are "Golden Boy," "Those Were the Days," "Our Town," "Arizona," "I Wanted Wings," "The Fleet's In!," "Dear Ruth," "Rachel and the Stranger," "Apartment for Peggy," "Man from Colorado," "Dear Wife," "Miss Grant Takes Richmond," "Father Is a Bachelor," "Sunset Boulevard," "Born Yesterday," "Union Station," "Submarine Command," "The Turning Point," "Stalag 17" for which he won an Oscar, "The Moon Is Blue," "Executive Suite," "Sabrina," "Bridges of Toko-Ri," "The Country Girl," "Love Is a Many-Splendored Thing," "Picnic," "The Proud and the Profane," "Bridge on the River Kwai," "The Key," "World of Suzie Wong," "The Lion," "Paris When it Sizzles," "Seventh Dawn," "The Wild Bunch," "Network" and "S.O.B." He was divorced from former actress Brenda Marshall. Their two sons, Peter and Scott, survive. After cremation, his ashes were scattered over the Southern California desert.

GEORGE JESSEL, 83, NYC-born actor, producer, comedian, and "Toastmaster General of the U.S.," died May 24, 1981 of a heart attack in Los Angeles, CA. He began his career at age of 9, working his way up to vaudeville headliner, Broadway performer and star of "The Jazz Singer" that was responsible for his film career. His pictures include "The Other Man's Wife," "Vitaphone," "Pvt. Izzy Murphy," "Lucky Boy," "Love, Live and Laugh," "Stage Door Canteen," "Four Jills in a Jeep," "The Busy Body," "Valley of the Dolls," "Can Hieronymus Merkin Ever Find True Happiness?," and "The Phynx." He produced over 15 films, including "I Wonder Who's Kissing Her Now," "Nightmare Alley," "Wait Till the Sun Shines, Nellie," and "Tonight We Sing." During his later years he toured the world raising money for charitable organizations. He was married and divorced four times. Two daughters survive.

ALLYN JOSLYN, 79, Pennsylvania-born versatile actor on stage, screen, radio and tv, died of cardiac failure Jan. 21, 1981 in Woodland Hills, CA. His film debut in the 1937 "They Won't Forget," was followed by, among others, "Expensive Husbands," "Hollywood Hotel," "The Shining Hour," "Sweethearts," "Only Angels Have Wings," "Cafe Society," "The Great McGinty," "No Time for Comedy," "This Thing Called Love," "Bedtime Story," "My Sister Eileen," "The Immortal Sergeant," "Heaven Can Wait," "Bride by Mistake," "The Horn Blows at Midnight," "Junior Miss," "The Shocking Miss Pilgrim," "If You Knew Susie," "Harriet Craig," "The Jazz Singer," "Titanic," "The Fastest Gun Alive," and "The Brothers O'Toole." He had continuing parts in the tv series "The Addams Family," "Don't Call Me Charlie," "The Eve Arden Show." No reported survivors.

| Robert H. Harris | George Jessel | Patsy Kelly | Lola Lane | Lotte Lenya | Margaret Lindsay |

ROBERT EMMETT KEANE, 96, character actor, died July 2, 1981 in his Hollywood, CA., home. After a successful vaudeville career, he made his first film in 1931, "Laugh and Get Rich," followed by over 70 pictures, including "Captain Thunder," "Men Call It Love," "The Big Noise," "Hot Money," "Jailbreak," "Under Suspicion," "Boys Town," "Confessions of a Nazi Spy," "Spellbinder," "Double Alibi," "Lillian Russell," "The Saint Takes Over," "Tin Pan Alley," "The Devil and Miss Jones," "Men of Boys Town," "The Cowboy and the Blonde," "Hello Sucker," "Remember Pearl Harbor," "Crazy House," "The Whistler," "Scared Stiff," "Fear in the Night," "I Wonder Who's Kissing Her Now," "When My Baby Smiles at Me," "Trouble Investigator," "Jolson Sings Again," "Everybody Does It," "Blondie's Hero," "The Atomic Kid," "When Gangland Strikes." No reported survivors.

PATSY KELLY, 71, Brooklyn-born stage and screen comedienne, died Sept. 24, 1981 in Woodland Hills, CA., following a long illness and a stroke. As a teenager, she began performing in vaudeville, and in 1930 was taken to Hollywood where she made over 50 short comedies with Thelma Todd. Her first feature film was "Going Hollywood" in 1933, followed by "Girl from Missouri," "Go into Your Dance," "Page Miss Glory," "Every Night at 8," "Sing, Baby, Sing," "Pigskin Parade," "Nobody's Baby," "Wake Up and Live," "Ever Since Eve," "Merrily We Live," "There Goes My Heart," "The Cowboy and the Lady," "Hit Parade of 1941," "Topper Returns," "Broadway Limited," "Danger! Women at Work!," "Ladies' Day," "Please Don't Eat the Daisies," "The Naked Kiss," "Come On, Let's Live a Little," "Rosemary's Baby," "Freaky Friday," and "The North Avenue Irregulars." She was never married and is survived by several nephews and nieces.

LOLA LANE, 75, nee Dorothy Mulligan in Indiana, died in her Santa Barbara, CA., home on June 22, 1981 after a long illness with inflammation of the arteries. She and her sisters Rosemary and Priscilla were popular stars of the 1930's and 1940's. After being discovered playing piano and singing, she got her first film role in 1929 in "Speakeasy," followed by 38 pictures, including "Follies of 1929," "Girl from Havana," "Let's Go Places," "Good News," "Women Who Dared," "Alias Mary Dow," "His Night Out," "Hollywood Hotel," "Four Daughters," "Four Wives," "Four Mothers," "Why Girls Leave Home," and "Deadline at Dawn" in 1946, after which she retired. Her first husband was Lew Ayres. She is survived by her second husband, Robert Hanlon, and her sister Priscilla Howard.

BERNARD LEE, 73, British character actor, died of cancer Jan. 16, 1981 in London. He had appeared in over 100 films, but was probably best known as the spy chief "M" in all 12 James Bond movies from "Dr. No" through "Moonraker." His other roles were in "Let George Do It," "Quartet," "Fallen Idol," "The Third Man," "The Blue Lamp," "Odette," "Beat the Devil," "Cage of Gold," "The Detective," "Ring of Treason," "Trouble in the Sky," "The Purple Plain," "The Key," "Dunkirk," "The L-Shaped Room," and "The Spy Who Loved Me." He is survived by his widow.

LOTTE LENYA, 83, nee Karoline Blamauer in Austria, star of stage and screen, died of cancer Nov. 27, 1981 in NYC. With her first husband, composer Kurt Weill, she settled in NYC in 1935. After his death in 1950, she spent most of her time keeping Weill's work before the public. Her films include "The Threepenny Opera," "The Roman Spring of Mrs. Stone" for which she received an Oscar nomination, "From Russia with Love," "What?" and "Semi-Tough." She was predeceased by her second and third husbands. No immediate survivors.

MARGARET LINDSAY, 70, nee Margaret Kies in Iowa, screen and stage actress, died of emphysema May 8, 1981 in Hollywood, CA. Among the 88 films in which she appeared during her 30 year career are "Cavalcade," "Baby Face," "Voltaire," "The House on 56th Street," "Lady Killer," "Fog over Frisco," "Bordertown," "Frisco Kid," "Dangerous," "The Lady Consents," "G-Men," "Green Lights," "Song of the City," "Jezebel," "Three Girls on Broadway," "Hell's Kitchen," "Honeymoon Deferred," "House of Seven Gables," "Ellery Queen, Master Detective," "The Spoilers," "Tragedy at Midnight," "Crime Doctor," "Scarlet Street," "Cass Timberlane," "Please Don't Eat the Daisies" and "Tammy and the Doctor." Surviving are four sisters and a brother.

ANITA LOOS, 88, screenwriter, playwright and novelist, died Aug. 18, 1981 in NYC. Born in California, she got her first break with the Biograph Studio and in 1912 D. W. Griffith directed her first screenplay, "The New York Hat." Subsequently she wrote "Temperamental Wife," "Virtuous Vamp," "In Search of a Sinner," "Let's Get a Divorce," "Come On In," "Isle of Conquest," "Red Hot Romance," "Learning to Love," "Biography of a Bachelor Girl," "Riffraff," "San Francisco," "Saratoga," "The Women," "Susan and God," "Blossoms in the Dust," "They Met in Bombay," "When Ladies Meet," "I Married an Angel," and her most successful "Gentlemen Prefer Blondes." A niece survives.

LOUISE LORRAINE, retired actress in her 80's, died Feb. 2, 1981 in Sacramento, CA. She started in silent films in 1910 as a comedienne, became a "Baby Wampus Star," the second Jane to Elmo Lincoln's Tarzan, and was in such serials as "The Jade Box," "The Great Circus Mystery" and "Fighting Blood." Other films include "Rookies," "Legionnaires in Paris," "Baby Mine" and "Circus Rookies." She retired after divorcing her first husband, cowboy actor Art Acord in 1935, and later married businessman Chester J. Hubbard who died in 1963. Surviving are her daughter, two granddaughters and a sister.

ENID MARKEY, 91, Colorado-born screen, stage, tv and radio actress, died Nov. 15, 1981 of a heart attack while visiting a friend in Bay Shore, NY. Her film career began at 15 in silent pictures. She was the first Jane to Elmo Lincoln's Tarzan, wore the first Hollywood sarong in "Aloha Oe," and was the first actress to ride bareback and use a six-shooter in "The Darkening Trail." Her later pictures include "Snafu," "The Naked City" and "The Boston Strangler." She was the widow of executive George W. Cobb of the American Can Co. There are no survivors.

ROSS MARTIN, 61, Polish-born stage, film and tv actor, died of a heart seizure while playing tennis in Ramona, CA., on July 3, 1981. He made his film debut in 1954 in "Conquest of Space," followed by "Underwater Warrior," "The Colossus of New York," "Geronimo," "Experiment in Terror," "The Ceremony" and "The Great Race." He was probably best known for his tv appearances in the series "The Wild Wild West," "Mr. Lucky" and "Stump the Stars." His widow survives.

JESSIE MATTHEWS, 74, British musical star of stage and screen, died of cancer Aug. 20, 1981 in London. She began her career at 12 dancing in vaudeville, and rose to stardom on stage. Her films include "There Goes the Bride," "Good Companions," "Friday the 13th," "Evergreen," "Strauss's Great Waltz," "First a Girl," "It's Love Again," "Head over Heels in Love," "Gangway," "Sailing Along," "Climbing High," "Forever and a Day," "Tom Thumb." She was married and divorced three times. An adopted daughter survives.

PHILO McCULLOUGH, 87, veteran character actor, died June 5, 1981 at his home in Burbank, CA. He began his picture career in 1912 in Fatty Arbuckle comedies, Selig's Shorts, and the Rin Tin Tin Series. Among his many credits are "Soldiers of Fortune," "Trilby," "Daughters of Today," "Wife of the Centaur," "Dick Turpin," "Boomerang," "Everybody's Acting," "Ladies at Play," "Easy Pickings," "Night Flyer," "Lost in the Arctic," "Leatherneck," "Buccaneer," "The Great Race," and "They Shoot Horses, Don't They?" His widow survives.

FRANK McHUGH, 83, Pennsylvania-born character actor on stage and screen, died Sept. 11, 1981 in Greenwich, CT. He was one of Hollywood's most active supporting actors, and among his many credits are "Dawn Patrol," "Kiss Me Again," "Going Wild," "The Front Page," " Corsair," "The Crowd Roars," "One Way Passage," "Private Jones," "Blessed Event," "Elmer the Great," "Lilly Turner," "42nd Street," "Footlight Parade," "Heat Lightning," "Here Comes the Navy," "Gold Diggers of 1935," "Page Miss Glory," "A Midsummer Night's Dream," "Stars over Broadway," "Stage Struck," "Three Men on a Horse," "Ever Since Eve," "Swing Your Lady," "Four Daughters," "Boy Meets Girl," "Valley of the Giants," "Dodge City," "Dust Be My Destiny," "On Your Toes," "The Roaring 20's," "The Fighting 69th," "Four Mothers," "Back Street," "Manpower," "Going My Way," "State Fair," "The Hoodlum Saint," "Carnegie Hall," "Mighty Joe Young," "A Lion Is in the Streets," "The Last Hurrah," "Easy Come, Easy Go." Surviving are his wife, former actress Dorothy Spencer, a son and a daughter.

ROBERT MONTGOMERY, 77, NY-born actor-producer-director on stage, radio, screen and tv, died of cancer Sept. 27, 1981 in NYC. After some Broadway success, he made his film debut in 1926 in "College Days," subsequently appearing in, among others, "Untamed," "The Divorcee," "The Big House," "Our Blushing Brides," "War Nurse," "Private Lives," "Letty Lynton," "Blondie of the Follies," "Hell Below," "When Ladies Meet," "Another Language," "Night Flight," "Riptide," "Forsaking All Others," "Biography of a Bachelor Girl," "Vanessa," "No More Ladies," "Petticoat Fever," "The Last of Mrs. Cheyney," "Night Must Fall," "Yellow Jack," "Earl of Chicago," "Mr. & Mrs. Smith," "Rage in Heaven," "Here Comes Mr. Jordan," "Lady in the Lake," "Ride a Pink Horse," " Once More, My Darling," and "Eye Witness." He was the first president of the Screen Actors Guild and was television adviser to President Eisenhower. His tv series, "Robert Montgomery Presents," a popular dramatic tv show, lasted for 7 years. His first marriage to actress Elizabeth Allen ended in divorce. He is survived by his second wife, and two children by his first, a son and a daughter, actress Elizabeth Montgomery.

ARTHUR O'CONNELL, 73, NY-born character actor, died of Altzheimer's disease on May 18, 1981 in Hollywood, CA. After a successful Broadway career, he devoted his time to films, and was nominated twice for an Oscar ("Picnic" and "Anatomy of a Murder"). Other pictures include "Open Secret," "The Whistle at Eaton Falls," "Man in the Gray Flannel Suit," "Bus Stop," "Solid Gold Cadillac," "April Love," "Man of the West," "Gidget," "Operation Petticoat," "Cimarron," "The Great Impostor," "Misty," "A Pocketful of Miracles," "Nightmare," "The Silencers," "Fantastic Voyage," "What a Wonderful Life," "The Poseidon Adventure," He was divorced, and left no immediate survivors.

MARIA PALMER, 57, Vienna-born stage, film and tv actress, died of cancer Sept. 6, 1981 in Los Angeles, CA. She moved to NYC in 1938 and appeared in several Broadway productions. Her screen credits include "Mission to Moscow," "Days of Glory," "Lady on a Train," "The Other Love," "The Web," "Surrender," "Strictly Dishonorable," "By the Light of the Silvery Moon," "Three for Jamie Dawn," "Flight Nurse," "City of Women," "The Evil of Frankenstein," and "Nostradamus and the Queen." She is survived by her mother.

NIGEL PATRICK, 68, versatile British actor of stage and screen, died of cancer Sept. 21, 1981 in London. After his film debut in 1939, he appeared in over 30 pictures, including "Mrs. Pym of Scotland Yard," "Spring in Park Lane," "Silent Dust," "Trio," "The Noose," "The Perfect Women," "The Browning Version," "The Sound Barrier," "Encore," "Pickwick Papers," "Pandora and the Flying Dutchman," "Young Wives' Tale," "Tonight at 8:30," "Raintree County, "The Man Inside," "Sapphire," "Johnny Nobody," "The Trials of Oscar Wilde," and "The Mackintosh Man." A son and daughter survive.

ELEANOR PERRY, 66, screenwriter, died of cancer Mar. 14, 1981 in her NYC home. Her credits include "David and Lisa" for which she received an Oscar nomination, "Ladybug Ladybug," "Trilogy," "The Swimmer," "Last Summer," "Diary of a Mad Housewife," and "The Man Who Loved Cat Dancing." She was divorced from her second husband, director, Frank Perry, and is survived by a son and a daughter from her first marriage.

HAZEL SCOTT, 74, jazz pianist and singer, who appeared on stage and screen, died of cancer Oct. 2, 1981 in NYC. Born in Trinidad, she moved to NYC in 1924 and at 18 made her Broadway debut. Her film appearances include "Something to Shout About," "I Dood It," "The Heat's On," "Broadway Rhythm," "Rhapsody in Blue" and "Night Affair". She is survived by her son, Adam Clayton Powell III.

YUKI SHIMODA, 59, character actor on stage, screen and tv, died of cancer May 21, 1981 in Los Angeles, CA. After appearing on Broadway he went to Hollywood where he had roles in over 25 pictures, including "Auntie Mame," "A Majority of One," "Horizontal Lieutenant," "Once a Thief," "MacArthur," "Midway" and "The Last Flight of Noah's Ark." On tv he was seen in "Kung Fu," "Ironside" and "Hawaii Five-O." No reported survivors.

RICHARD TALMADGE, 88, nee Sylvester Metzetti in Switzerland, silent screen star, died of cancer Jan. 25, 1981 in his home in Carmel, CA. He began his career as a stuntman, doubling for Douglas Fairbanks, but subsequently became a star in his own right. His many credits include "American Manner," "The Cavalier," "Poor Millionaire," "Bachelor's Club," "Dancing Dynamite," "Yankee Don," "Speed Madness," "Get That Girl," "The Speed Reporter," and the "Pirate Treasure" series. His widow survives.

NORMAN TAUROG, 82, Chicago-born actor who became a director, died Apr. 8, 1981 in Rancho Mirage, CA. During his last 17 years, after he became blind, he was a director of the Braille Institute. His long list of directing credits include his Oscar-winning "Skippy," and "Huckleberry Finn," "Sooky," "If I had a Million," "Bedtime Story," "Mrs. Wiggs of the Cabbage Patch," "College Rhythm," "Big Broadcast of 1936," "Rhythm on the Range," "Adventures of Tom Sawyer," "Boys Town," "Young Tom Edison," "Broadway Melody of 1940," "Little Nelly Kelly," "A Yank at Eton," "Presenting Lilly Mars," "Girl Crazy," "Toast of New Orleans," "The Stooge," "You're Never Too Young," "Room for One More," "Blue Hawaii," "G. I. Blues," "The Caddy," "We're Not Dressing," "Mad about Music," and "Speedway." Surviving are his widow, a son and two daughters.

Torin
Thatcher

Vera-Ellen

George
Voskovec

Natalie
Wood

William
Wyler

TORIN THATCHER, 76, British-born stage, screen and tv actor, died of cancer Mar, 4, 1981 at his home in Newberry Park, CA. Included among his more than 70 films are "Gen. John Regan," "U-Boat 29," "Major Barbara," "Great Expectations," "The Smugglers," "Fallen Idol," "Affair in Trinidad," "Snows of Kilimanjaro," "Blackbeard the Pirate," "Desert Rats," "Houdini," "The Robe," "Love Is a Many-Splendored Thing," "Lady Godiva," "Helen of Troy," "Witness for the Prosecution," "Seventh Voyage of Sinbad," "The Miracle," "Mutiny on the Bounty," "The Sandpiper," "Hawaii," "The Crimson Pirate." He is survived by his widow and a son.

VERA-ELLEN, 55 or 61, nee Vera-Ellen Rohe in Cincinnati, singer-dancer-actress on stage and screen, died of cancer Aug. 30, 1981 in Los Angeles, CA. She began her career in her teens and appeared on Broadway before going to Hollywood in 1945 for "Wonder Man" with Danny Kaye. She subsequently performed in "The Kid from Brooklyn," "Three Little Girls in Blue," "Carnival in Costa Rica," "Words and Music," "On the Town," "Love Happy," "Three Little Words," "Happy Go Lovely," "Belle of New York," "Call Me Madam," "White Christmas," "Let's Be Happy," and "Web of Evidence." She was divorced from oilman Victor Rothschild in 1966 and lived in seclusion until her death. No reported survivors.

HARRY VON ZELL, 75, Indianapolis-born radio announcer, and actor on screen and tv, died of cancer Nov. 21, 1981 in Calabas, CA. Before becoming a screen actor, he was an announcer for Paul Whiteman's radio show, The March of Time, Fred Allen, Phil Baker, Eddie Cantor, and Burns and Allen. His films include "Uncle Harry," "Till the End of Time," "How Do You Do?," "The Guilt of Janet Ames," "Where There's Life," "Saxon Charm," "Dear Wife," "Two Flags West," "For Heaven's Sake," "Call Me Mister," "I Can Get It For You Wholesale," "Son of Paleface," "You're in the Navy Now" and "Boy, Did I Get a Wrong Number!" Surviving are his widow, a son and a daughter.

GEORGE VOSKOVEC, 76, character actor on stage, screen and tv, died July 1, 1981 in his home in Pearblossom, CA. Born in Czechoslovakia, he came to the U. S. in 1939. His films include "Powder and Gas," "Your Money or Your Life," "The Golem," "The World Is Ours," "Anthing Can Happen," "Affair in Trinidad," "Iron Mistress," "12 Angry Men," "The 27th Day," "Uncle Vanya," "The Bravados," "Wind across the Everglades," "Butterfield 8," "Hamlet," "The Spy Who Came in from the Cold," "Mr. Buddwing," "Beyond the Mountains," "The Desperate Ones," "The Boston Strangler." He is survived by his widow and two daughters.

GEORGE WALSH, 92, former screen actor, died of pneumonia June 13, 1981 in Pomona, CA. He was the younger brother of the late director Raoul Walsh. He began his film career in 1914 and appeared in such pictures as "Vanity Fair," "Rosita," "Slave of Desire," "Reno," "Me and My Gal," "Black Beauty," "The Bowery," "Belle of the '90's," "Under Pressure," "Klondike Annie," "Rio Grande Romance" and "Put on the Spot." He retired from films in 1936. Surviving are a daughter by his first wife, actress Seena Owen, and two sons by his second wife who died in 1971.

JOHN WARBURTON, 78, Irish-born stage and screen actor, died of cancer Oct. 27, 1981 in his home in Sherman Oaks, CA. After Broadway success in the 1920's, he went to Hollywood in 1932 for "The Silver Lining." Other film credits include "Cavalcade," "A Study in Scarlet," "Charlie Chan's Greatest Case," "Love Is Dangerous," "Love Is Like That," "Let's Talk It Over," "Becky Sharp," "The Sisters," "Captain Fury," "Marriage Is a Private Affair," "The White Cliffs of Dover," "Confidential Agent," "Saratoga Trunk," "Tarzan and the Huntress," "Living in a Big Way," "City Beneath the Sea," "East of Sumatra," "King Rat," "Funny Girl." He is survived by his widow, a son and a daughter.

HARRY WARREN, 87, nee Salvatore Guaragna in Brooklyn, one of the most successful composers of popular songs, and three-time Academy Award winner, died of kidney failure Sept. 22, 1981 in Los Angeles, CA. In his career of 59 years, he composed over 300 songs for more than 50 films, his most popular "42nd Street" is in the current Broadway production of the same title. He won Oscars for "Lullaby of Broadway" 1935, "You'll Never Know" 1940 and "On the Atchison, Topeka and the Santa Fe" 1946. Among the other films for which he composed are "Gold Diggers of 1933," "Footlight Parade," "Roman Scandals," "Moulin Rouge," "Wonder Bar," "20 Million Sweethearts," "Dames," "Go into Your Dance," "Shipmates Forever," "Stars over Broadway," "Colleen," "Gold Diggers in Paris," "Cowboy from Brooklyn," "Honolulu," "Down Argentine Way," "Tin Pan Alley," "Sun Valley Serenade," "Springtime in the Rockies," "The Harvey Girls," "Ziegfeld Follies," "Pagan Love Song," "The Barkleys of Broadway," and "Summer Stock." In addition to his widow, a daughter survives.

NATALIE WOOD, 43, beautiful screen and television actress, was found dead Nov. 29, 1981 off Santa Catalina Island, CA., a victim of accidental drowning after falling from her yacht. Born Natasha Gurdin in San Francisco, at 8 she began her film career in 1946 in "Tomorrow Is Forever," and changed her name to Wood. She subsequently appeared in "The Bride Wore Boots," "Miracle on 34th Street," "The Ghost and Mrs. Muir," "Chicken Every Sunday," "No Sad Songs for Me," "Never a Dull Moment," "Dear Brat," "The Star," "The Silver Chalice," "Rebel without a Cause," "The Searchers," "A Cry in the Night," "The Searchers," "The Girl He Left Behind," "Marjorie Morningstar," "Kings Go Forth," "Cash McCall," "All the Fine Young Cannibals," "Splendor in the Grass," "West Side Story," "Gypsy," "Love with the Proper Stranger," "Sex and the Single Girl," "Inside Daisy Clover," "This Property Is Condemned," "Bob and Carol and Ted and Alice," "Penelope," "Peeper," "Meteor," "The Candidate," and "The Last Married Couple in America." She had only five days to complete on her last picture "Brainstorm." After a brief marriage to director Richard Gregson, she re-married her first husband, Robert Wagner, who survives. She also leaves two daughters, her mother and two sisters, one, actress Lana Wood.

WILLIAM WYLER, 79, German-born director, died of a massive heart attack July 27, 1981 in his home in Beverly Hills, CA. He had directed more Oscar-winning (14) and Oscar-nominated (20) performances than any other director. He received Oscars for his direction of "Mrs. Miniver" 1942, "The Best Years of Our Lives" 1946 and "Ben Hur" 1959 that received ten other Oscars, an all-time record for a film. His other credits include "The Shakedown," "Hell's Heroes," "The Storm," "A House Divided," "Tom Brown of Culver," "Counsellor-at-Law," "Glamour," "The Good Fairy," "These Three," "Dodsworth," "Dead End," "Jezebel,""Wuthering Heights," "The Westerner," "The Letter," "The Little Foxes," "Detective Story," "Carrie," "Roman Holiday," "The Desperate Hours," "Friendly Persuasion," "The Big Country," "The Children's Hour," "The Collector," "How to Steal a Million," "Funny Girl" and "The Liberation of L. B. Jones." He was married briefly to actress Margaret Sullivan. Surviving are his second wife, former actress Margaret Tallichet, a son, and three daughters.

239

241

247

249

250

252

253